John Nelson Darby
(1800-1882)

Cyrus Ingerson Scofield
(1843-1921)

THE ORIGINS OF DISPENSATIONALISM

The Darby Factor

LARRY V. CRUTCHFIELD

With a Forward by John A. Witmer
and Illustrations by Ron Crutchfield

UNIVERSITY
PRESS OF
AMERICA

Lanham • New York • London

Copyright © 1992 by
University Press of America®, Inc.
4720 Boston Way
Lanham, Maryland 20706

3 Henrietta Street
London WC2E 8LU England

Library of Congress Cataloging-in-Publication Data
Crutchfield, Larry V.
The Origins of Dispensationalism : The Darby factor / by
Larry V. Crutchfield ; with a forward [sic] by John A.
Witmer and illustrations by Ron Crutchfield.
p. cm.
Originally presented as the author's thesis (Ph.D.)
—Drew University, 1985.
Includes bibliographical references and index.
1. Dispensationalism—History.
2. Darby, J. N. (John Nelson), 1800-1882. I. Title.
BT157.C78 1991
230' .046—dc20 91-32857 CIP

ISBN 0-8191-8467-5 (cloth : alk. paper)
ISBN 0-8191-8468-3 (pbk. : alk. paper)

#24380389

The paper used in this publication meets the minimum requirements of
American National Standard for Information Sciences—Permanence
of Paper for Printed Library Materials, ANSI Z39.48–1984.

To my wife

RUTH

who proves the proverb that
*"An excellent wife is the
crown of her husband"*
(Proverbs 12:4)

TABLE OF CONTENTS

CHAPTER 4-PART 2: DARBY'S SYSTEM OF DISPENSATIONS (CHURCH AGE TO ETERNAL STATE)

CHAPTER 5. DARBY'S VIEW OF PROPHECY

CHAPTER 6. DARBY'S ESSENTIAL ESCHATOLOGY

CHAPTER 7. DARBY'S LASTING LEGACY

APPENDICES

FOREWARD

Although he was not, as many assumed, the founder of the movement popularly known as Plymouth Brethrenism, John Nelson Darby (1800-1882) was the man largely responsible for its solid establishment in Great Britain as well as its extension to Europe. He ministered as well in North America and New Zealand.

Darby is also considered by many to be the father of modern Dispensationalism, popularized in large part among theological conservatives by C. I. Scofield and his *Scofield Reference Bible*. This judgment likewise is subject to review as a result of Dr. Crutchfield's work, which shows that Scofield's system of dispensations differs widely from Darby's system of ages and dispensations. Darby's system is important and influential nonetheless.

Darby was a prolific writer with more than fifty volumes published and still in print, including his personal translation of the Bible and his five-volumed *Synopsis of the Books of the Bible* (reprint ed., Sunbury, PA: Believers Bookshelf, n.d.). Because of his abstruse and convoluted style of writing, however, friends as well as foes seldom read his works extensively and become intimately acquainted with his thought. Dr. Crutchfield has made a substantial contribution to contemporary theological study, as a result, by examining, analyzing and organizing Darby's teaching in this crucial area of biblical doctrine.

The outstanding research performed by Dr. Crutchfield, as well as the clarity of his organization and written presentation of the material secured the designation of his dissertation at Drew University as "distinguished" by the Graduate Faculty on recommendation of his dissertation committee. As the extramuro member of that committee, I concur in that judgment and commend University Press of America for publishing the work.

JOHN A. WITMER
Archivist and formerly Director
of Mosher Library and Associate
Professor of Systematic Theology,
Dallas Theological Seminary,
Dallas, Texas

PREFACE

John Nelson Darby is called by many the father of modern dispensational theology, a theology made popular first by the *Scofield Reference Bible* and more recently by the *Ryrie Study Bible*. It is a theology that has gained wide influence through the publications and educational efforts of institutions like Dallas Theological Seminary and Moody Bible Institute. Yet while Darby is the center of almost every controversy over the origin of this theological system, his works are little known and seldom read. This is true among the critics and champions of dispensational theology alike.

This neglect is unfortunate, for Darby is credited with much of the theological content of the Fundamentalist movement. There is little doubt too, that Darby has had a tremendous part in the systematization and promotion of dispensational theology. In addition to this, his dispensational approach to Scripture is cited as most influential in the lives of such men as James H. Brookes and A. C. Gaebelein, who in turn exerted great influence upon the doctrinal position of C. I. Scofield. The latter's work, the *Scofield Reference Bible*, is called by many the most effective tool for the dissemination of dispensationalism in America.

In piecing together Darby's doctrine of dispensations, we have attempted to answer the following questions: What constitutes normative dispensationalism today? What is Darby's philosophy of dispensations? What is his system of dispensations? What is his view of prophecy? What are Darby's essential eschatological features? What are the important areas of comparison and contrast between the dispensational concepts of Darby and Scofield? The last question constitutes a secondary objective of this study.

If one is to assert with any degree of confidence that Darby is the "father of modern dispensationalism," it is essential to first determine the content of his dispensational theology. The purpose of this study, therefore, is to facilitate a greater understanding of Darby's dispensational doctrine and its link with contemporary dispensational concepts. Whether one views Darby's teachings as good or evil, or whether one canonizes or anathematizes him, the fact remains that he has had a solid impact upon contemporary theological options.

LARRY V. CRUTCHFIELD

Fort Dix, New Jersey

CHAPTER 1

DARBY'S LIFE AND INFLUENCE

The Scope of the Study

THE PURPOSE

A comprehensive study of John Nelson Darby's concept of ages and dispensations has long been overdue. In the past, the very most that one could expect to find regarding his teaching on the subject were bare-bones outlines of his dispensational scheme, and even these as we shall see, are usually lacking in agreement. While it is readily admitted that Darby is not always easy to follow and his position therefore sometimes difficult to arrived at, we must nevertheless agree with Clarence Mason's evaluation of the matter. "As one reads some of Darby's critics," he says, "one sometimes wonders if the writer has ever read Darby carefully, or anything more than snatches."[1] The same could be said of some of Darby's admirers as well.

This deficiency is especially noticeable when contemporary dispensationalism enters the discussion. Opponents of dispensational theology routinely assert "that the teaching of Chafer came from Scofield, who in turn got it through the writings of Darby and the Plymouth Brethren."[2] Proponents of dispensationalism insist, however, that "Dispensationalists differ from Darby in many particulars and rest their faith not in what Darby held or did, but in what they believe the Scriptures to teach."[3] So what exactly are the facts of the matter?

No dispensationalist who is aware of the facts can deny that Darby played a key role in the systematization and promotion of dispensational concepts. Neither can the impact of the *Scofield Reference Bible* be minimized as a tool in the spread of dispensational theology. It may even be granted as true, as Cox has said, that "The Father of dispensationalism, Darby, as well as his teachings, probably would be unheard of today were it not for...Scofield....Darby's books are gathering dust on the shelves of the comparatively few libraries stocking them. Information concerning him is scarce indeed."[4] It seems curious to us that even among dispensationalists, Darby's name appears not very prominently in bibliographies if at all.

While it is true that there are similarities and a definite connection between the teachings of Darby and Scofield, it is also true that there are marked dissimilarities between them. One has only to compare the two men's patterns of ages and dispensations to see that they are not the same. Charles C. Ryrie maintains that, "If Scofield parroted anybody's scheme it was Watts', not Darby's."[5] The great hymn writer, Isaac Watts (1674-1748), was also a theologian. His collected works are contained in six volumes and his concept of dispensations is outlined in a forty-page essay entitled, "The Harmony of all the Religions Which God ever Prescribed to Men, and all His Dispensations towards them."[6]

Mason, on the other hand, draws a different conclusion. He believes that "There is really more similarity between Poiret and Scofield than between Darby and Scofield."[7] Pierre Poiret (1646-1719), was a French mystic and philosopher who set forth a dispensational system in his six volume work, *L' OEconomie Divine.*[8] The differences between Darby and Scofield, as we shall show, do not merely involve questions of nomenclature, but revolve around basic theological assumptions (e.g., Darby's views on God's government of the earth).

To add to the confusion, dispensationalists do not agree among themselves about the outline of Darby's dispensational scheme. While Ryrie names the "Paradisaical state to the flood" and "the Millennium" as Darby's first and seventh dispensations respectively,[9] Arnold D. Ehlert also lists them (in brackets), but points out that they, along with "the Church" age, are not properly identified as dispensations by Darby.[10] In actuality, while Darby clearly states that the paradisaical state is not a dispensation,[11] and does not include the millennium as a dispensation in categorical discussions of the subject, he nevertheless suggests that the latter is to be so designated.[12]

Our purpose in this study is to set forth a systematic statement of Darby's dispensational theology. It is hoped that by so doing, some of the aforementioned confusion may be eliminated. One can only assume that in the absence of such a statement, misunderstanding will persist.

<u>THE PROCEDURE</u>

Darby's teachings concerning dispensational concepts are scattered throughout the whole of his works. Some of the more important discussions of the subject are found in volume 1 of his *Collected Works*, in an article entitled, "The Apostasy of the Successive Dispensations" (pp. 124-30); volume 2, "The Hopes of the Church of God" (pp. 374-84); and volume 5, "The Principles Displayed in the Ways of God, Compared with His Ultimate Dealings" (pp. 383-91). This study, however, will cover the complete library of Darby's theological and exegetical works.

In piecing together Darby's doctrine of dispensations, we will attempt to answer the following questions:

1. <u>What constitutes normative dispensationalism today</u>? In order to fully appreciate the impact of Darby's dispensational theology upon contemporary dispensationalism and to keep it in proper perspective, it is necessary to set forth, as nearly as possible, the main features of what might pass as the current norm for dispensational theology. This will include:
   a. The meaning and origin of the term *dispensation.*
   b. The characteristics of dispensations in general.

       1). Primary characteristics.
       2). Secondary characteristics.
  c. The essential factors of dispensationalism.
       1). Distinction between Israel and the church.
       2). Hermeneutical principle of literal interpretation.
       3). Unifying principle of glory of God.
  d. The number, names, and characteristics of the individual
     dispensations.
  e. The eschatology of dispensationalism.

    2. <u>What is Darby's philosophy of dispensations?</u> Of importance here are the theological assumptions upon which Darby's dispensational system is based, such as:
  a. The meaning and origin of the term *dispensation.*
  b. The nature of the dispensations.
  c. The characteristics of dispensations.
  d. The intentions versus the counsels of God and dispensations.
  e. The purpose of dispensations.
  f. The end of all dispensations.

    3. <u>What is Darby's system of dispensations?</u> The structure of Darby's ages and dispensations is most difficult to get at. However, with some effort it is possible to forge an outline, the main divisions of which are:
  a. (Paradisaical State - not a dispensation).
  b. (Conscience - not a dispensation).
  c. Noah.
  d. Abraham.
  e. Israel under the Law.
  f. Israel under the Priesthood.
  g. Israel under the Kings.
  h. Gentiles.
  i. Spirit (also called Church/Christian/Present/Gentile dispensation).
  j. Millennium.
  k. (Eternal State - not a dispensation).
The essential features and characteristics of each of the dispensations will be discussed in turn.

    4. <u>What is Darby's view of prophecy?</u> Some of Darby's most important theological assumptions are embedded in his view of prophecy. It is at this point that one sees the clear expression of his hermeneutical principle of literal interpretation and sharp distinction between Israel and the church. The chief elements of Darby's view of prophecy include:
  a. Interest in prophecy.
  b. Nature of prophecy.
  c. Purpose of prophecy.
  d. Approach to prophecy
  e. Interpretation of prophecy.
  f. Subjects of prophecy.
       1). The hopes of the church.
       2). The hopes of Israel.

5. What are Darby's essential eschatological features? Inherent in Darby's dispensational system, are a number of important end-time events which have become regular features of contemporary dispensational, premillennial eschatology. The most important of these are:

    a. The rapture.
    b. The millennium.

6. What are the important areas of comparison and contrast between the dispensational concepts of Darby and Scofield? In regard to this last question it is often asked if Scofield was "the disciple if not the apostle of Darby."[13] Scofield's teachings, asserts Cox, "were taken almost *in toto* from John Nelson Darby."[14] Such testimony from opponents of dispensationalism, those who see Darby as Scofield's Gamaliel, could be produced seemingly without end. They would quote approvingly, "I am a dispensationalist...educated under Darby, strictly according to the law of the Brethren..." (liberal paraphrase of Acts 22:3, NASB).[15] That Scofield owed a great debt to Darby and the Brethren is beyond question, but that the debt was as complete or direct as some have assumed, is indeed open to challenge. Throughout the course of this study, an attempt will be made to show the important areas of contrast and comparison between the two men's positions. Each made his own unique contributions to dispensational thought.

There can be no question that Darby, a champion of orthodoxy in the last century, has had a solid impact upon contemporary theological options. Ernest R. Sandeen, a non-dispensationalist, has well said that "John Nelson Darby deserves better treatment from historians than he has received either from those who have praised him or those who have reviled him. The assessment of his career has not been objectively written or the scope of his influence adequately appreciated."[16] In some small measure, perhaps this study will help to rectify the situation.

The Focus of the Study

<u>DARBY'S LIFE</u>[17]

John Nelson Darby (1800-1882), one of the leading forces behind the Plymouth Brethren movement in England--styled by one "the Tertullian of these last days"[18]--and "credited with the great revival and a substantial advance of the whole subject of ages and dispensations,"[19] was born in London of Irish parents on November 18, 1800. Ireland furnished the backdrop for Darby's earliest years of development and education. In 1819 at the age of eighteen, he graduated from Trinity College Dublin as a Classical Medalist.[20]

While Darby had trained for a career in law, a deep spiritual struggle between the years 1818 and 1825, culminating in his conversion, caused him to abandon that profession after only one year of practice from 1822, and to receive ordination as deacon in the Church of England in 1825. The ordination was performed by Archbishop Magee as was that the following year when Darby was elevated to the priesthood in the Church of England. During this time, Darby served in a curacy in County Wicklow,[21] apparently with such great success that "Roman Catholics were passing over to Protestantism many hundreds in the week."[22]

After only twenty-seven months and thoroughly dissatisfied with what he viewed as rampant Erastianism and clericalism, Darby sought fellowship and ministry outside the established church. He writes:

> I find no such thing as a National Church in Scripture. Is the Church of England--was it ever--God's assembly in England? ... It was that I was looking for the body of CHRIST (which was not there, but perhaps in all the parish not one converted person); and collaterally, because I believed in a divinely-appointed ministry. If Paul had come, he could not have preached (he had never been ordained); if a wicked ordained man, he had his title *and must be recognised as a minister; the truest minister of Christ unordained could not.* It was a system contrary to what I found in Scripture.[23]

It was while Darby served as a priest in Dublin that the event which ultimately led him from the Church of England occurred. Neatby describes it in these terms:

> The archbishop [Magee] delivered a charge, and the clergy published a declaration addressed to Parliament denouncing the Roman Catholic Church, and claiming special favour and protection for themselves on avowedly Erastian principles. They based their demands simply on the ground that Romanism was opposed to the State, while their own system was allied with, if not even subservient to, it. Darby's mind revolted against such a miserably low, unspiritual view of the Church. He drew up, therefore, and circulated privately a very vigorous protest against the action of the clergy...Darby's protest was unavailing. The Establishment was everything to Churchmen of that time, the Church of God was nothing regarded, and Darby's soul was vexed thereat.[24]

Darby's response to this declaration is in a tract entitled, "Considerations Addressed to the Archbishop of Dublin and the Clergy who Signed the Petition to the House of Commons for Protection."[25]

It is important to observe here that Darby's disaffection for the Church of England was not precipitated by prophetic teachings. What passes as perhaps the first Brethren tract is that written by Darby in 1828 and bearing the title "Considerations on the Nature and Unity of the Church of Christ."[26] His first published work on prophecy, "Reflections upon the Prophetic Inquiry and the Views Advanced in It," is dated 1829.[27] It isn't until 1836 that we have Darby's first published statement on a dispensational theme. It appeared in a small paper called *The Christian Witness,* started by Darby and others in 1834, and proclaimed "The Apostasy of the Successive Dispensations."[28]

Eventually, Darby made the acquaintance of a group of like-minded believers, members of the Church of England in Dublin, and met with them for prayer and Bible study during the winter of 1827-28.[29] It was this group which would later become known as the Plymouth Brethren. The two guiding principles of the movement were to be the breaking of bread every Lord's Day, and ministry based upon the call of Christ rather than the ordination of man.[30] It should be noted that Darby was not the founder of this group, which existed some time before his arrival, and that the meetings were not intended to be a protest, as witnessed by the fact that most of the men in the group continued in their association with the church. Concerning the origin of the Brethren and Darby's part in it, Bass maintains that:

> Whatever else may be said of the origin of the Plymouth Brethren movement, it cannot be stated that it started at a specific place or time. Attempts to trace its history can only begin with a series of independent groups meeting at various locations....We do know, however, that the movement gained impetus through the amalgamation of several of these small meetings, and that after these common meetings its growth was furthered by several early leaders: A. N. Groves, B. W. Newton, W. H. Dorman, E. Cronin, J. G. Bellett, S. P. Tregelles, and J. N. Darby.
>
> The founder of Brethrenism as a system, however, was undeniably J. N. Darby, who became its energizing and guiding spirit throughout.[31]

Darby, writes Bass elsewhere, "has been universally acknowledged as the synthesizer" of the Plymouth Brethren movement.[32]

By 1840, the Plymouth movement had grown to 800 strong and would reach more than 1200 within the next five years.[33] While Darby disliked any denominational label, it was inevitable that these "Brethren at Plymouth" should become known as the "Plymouth Brethren."[34] Many other Brethren groups formed in Britain and subsequently in other parts of the world. As a result of his extensive travels, Darby himself was responsible for the spread of Brethren doctrine to other countries. Of these travels, John Goddard relates that,

> He made frequent visits to the continent, preaching in Germany, Switzerland, Italy, France, and Holland....He made six trips to the United States and Canada (1859, 1864-65, 1866-68, 1870, 1872-73, and 1874) and labored in all the principal cities as well as in many outlying districts. He also visited the West Indies and made one trip to New Zealand. Everywhere he went his ministry was a combination of gospel preaching and instruction of believers in his system of ecclesiology. He preached frequently on prophetic subjects....It is sufficient to state that until his death in 1882 he continued to expound the views he had first embraced in 1827 and to which he clung more firmly as time went on.[35]

When one considers the extent of Darby's travels and the volume of his literary output, it is no overstatement to say that this Brethren cleric was an indefatigable worker.

DARBY'S WORKS

Three things may be said about Darby as a writer without fear of contradiction. He was a prolific writer. He was a singularly abstruse writer. And owing to the last point as much as anything else, in modern times he has been a much neglected writer. This is true even among those who are most indebted to him for a significant portion of the theological foundation upon which they stand.

A Prolific Writer

Darby's literary legacy includes in excess of fifty-three volumes, each averaging some four hundred pages. These works show evidence of a knowledge of biblical languages, church history and philosophy. Whatever else may be said of his writings, they are not deficient in scholarship.

Among Darby's most important works are the *Collected Writings of J.N. Darby* (34 vols. plus an index), *Synopsis of the Books of the Bible* (5 vols.), *The Holy Scriptures: A New Translation from the Original Languages*, the *Letters of J.N.D.* (3 vols.), *Notes and Comments on Scripture* (7 vols.), *Miscellaneous Writings* (2 vols., which actually constitute vols. 35-36 of the *Collected Writings*), *Miscellaneous Writings* (2 vols), and *Notes and Jottings* (1 vol.). In addition to these works, Darby produced a number of pamphlets and magazine articles, as well as a volume of verse entitled *Spiritual Songs*.

Darby's writings are of uneven value. While the *Collected Works* and the *Synopsis* provide the primary source for his theology, it is the latter plus his translation of the Bible which usually come in for the highest praise. The *Synopsis*, we are told, "recommended by Bishop Ellicott to the Gloucester theological students, acquired amongst J.N.D.'s adherents authority like that commanded by Wesley's 'Notes' amongst Methodists. Professor Stokes has described it as 'the standard of appeal. Every departure from that model is bitterly resented' ('Expositor's Bible,' Acts 1, page 382)."[36] Oswald T. Allis calls this expository work a "great treasure-house of Dispensational teaching" and asserts that it was "highly commended by Scofield" who held the "*Synopsis*, which is the standard commentary among the Brethren, in high esteem."[37] Allis gives no documentation for this assertion concerning Scofield.

Rated next to the *Synopsis* in value is Darby's translation of the Bible. Turner calls it the "Foremost amongst his works..." and says that it is "an entirely free and independent rendering of the whole original text, using all known helps."[38] Others, as Ehlert points out, are not so kind. He says that "There is an extensive criticism of the Darby New Testament in Spurgeon's *Sword and Trowel* for November and December, 1872. The articles are unsigned, but designated as 'communicated.' Here the Darby New Testament is called 'a faulty and pitiable translation of the sacred Book' (p. 514)."[39]

A prominent feature of the translation is the notes, the volume of which varies with the edition used. The introductory notice to the 1961 edition in our possession, says that while references to the original Greek and Hebrew manuscripts have been omitted, further notes from Darby's French and German Bibles, as well as from the *Collected Writings*, have been added.[40] Our edition, it would seem then, contains one of the fuller complements of notes.

Of interest regarding the notes and the general pattern of the Darby translation, is a statement made by Bass. He maintains that "The pattern of the Scofield Bible is set by Darby's translation of the Bible, in which there are copious notes of 'explanation' of the correct meaning of the passages. While Darby's is not organized as the Scofield Bible was later, the pattern is undoubtedly there."[41]

This seems to us a gratuitous attempt to make a comparison between the two men where there is little or none. The text of both Bibles is set in parallel columns and both have notes at the bottom of the page, but there the comparison ends. Darby's translation has no testament or book introductions, cross references, or chapter headings. In the notes, almost total attention is given to the task of strict translation with only rare forays into the field of commentary. The notes contain practically nothing of a distinctly dispensational nature. The sum total of his dispensational expression is found in a note on Colossians 1:25, part of which Darby translates "…I became a minister, according to the dispensation1 of God which [is] given me…" Here, in dealing with the translation of *oikonomia*, Darby suggests, "Or, 'economy,' as 'administration' in 1 Cor. 9. 17; Eph. 1. 10; 3. 2, 9; 'dispensation,' 1 Tim. 1. 4; and 'stewardship,' Luke 16. 2, 3, 4 "[42] Certainly if Darby had been inclined to offer unbridled commentary on his dispensational system, this would have been the place to do it. It is our conclusion that the two translations share as much in common as an eagle and a jet aircraft. While both have wings and can fly and both employ some of the same principles of aerodynamics, the essential character and inner workings of the two are quite dissimilar.

An Abstruse Writer

Only the most intrepid of scholars deliberately choose to tackle Darby's works, which are labeled with terms ranging from merely unpleasant to downright repugnant.[43] Even Darby's closest friend and perhaps greatest admirer, the editor of his *Collected Works*, William Kelly, was painfully aware of this defect in his friend. Says he,

> Mr. Darby was deliberate and prayerful in weighing a scripture; but he wrote rapidly, as thoughts arose in his spirit, and often with scarcely a word changed. He delighted in a concatenated sentence, sometimes with parenthesis within parenthesis, to express the truth fully, and with guards against misconception. An early riser and indefatigable worker, he yet had not time to express his mind as briefly and clearly as he could wish. "You write to be read and understood," he once said playfully to me; "I only think on paper." This made his writings, to the uninitiated, anything but pleasant reading, and to a hasty glance almost unintelligible; so that many, even among highly educated believers, turned away, because of their inability to penetrate sentences so involved.[44]

Kelly goes on to say that Darby fancied himself but a miner who "left it to others to melt the ore."

To this may be added the testimony of another of Darby's supporters. Neatby writes:

> …reference should be made to another peculiarity that must have had a great deal to do with making or marring his influence. He carried his neglect of appearance into his written and spoken composition; and that to such an extent that the style of his writings to the readers of to-day seems half ludicrous, half disgusting. This peculiarity is almost necessarily fatal to abiding influence; but there may well be something singularly impres-

sive in it at the time. All misgiving as to the teacher's sincerity--even as to his absorbing earnestness of aim--disappears before it. Darby's own account of the matter was that he could have equalled the rhetorical flights of great masters, but that he never thought it worth while....indeed it is hard to read Darby's better works without fancying that a noble eloquence was really at his command, if only he had chosen to cultivate it. Bad as his style is, it is the badness of an almost incredible carelessness rather than a defective power.[45]

All of this leads us to conclude that this shortcoming in Darby was caused first of all by his passion to expound the cause of Christ and secondly by a careless disregard for literary form. We can only agree with Sandeen's assessment that "most unfortunately for his historical reputation, the clarity with which he perceived the will of God was never matched by his ability to write it down."[46]

That Darby was not unaware of this problem has already been hinted at in Kelly's remarks, and is further evident in Darby's own writings. He feels compelled to say in one place,

> I might, I dare say, have made some passages clearer...It seems to me that, as it stands, it is quite sufficiently clear to any upright mind. I am not so foolish as to think that all the expressions in it are the best, or absolutely exact or just, as if I were inspired; but what is taught (taught I think sufficiently clearly for any one willing to learn) I believe to be the truth...To the humblest and weakest of God's saints I should gladly explain my meaning, and should be bound to do so.[47]

With regard to that last offer to "gladly explain [his] meaning," this writer has wished more than once that as He did with the departed Samuel in the Witch of Endor episode, God might see fit to send forth Darby's spirit to clarify a point or two.

Although Darby's style leaves much to be desired, it is generally agreed that his words are not lacking in a certain kind of force and power. An unidentified "heterodox teacher" with whom Darby is said to have disputed, remarked that Darby "writes with a pen in one hand and a thunderbolt in the other," and this was twenty-five years after the encounter had taken place![48] Indeed, one reads Darby in polemical pursuit of an enemy to the faint sounds of Zeus' rumblings on Mt. Olympus.

In stark contrast to Darby's literary liabilities is the characterization of Scofield's style by James M. Gray, who became president of Moody Bible Institute in 1925. One of Scofield's richest gifts, writes Gray, is his ability to read God's Word, "give the sense, and cause the people to understand the reading." "He never writes or speaks in a haze," he continues, and "His insight pierces the intricacies."[49] Trumbull adds that,

> ...satisfied as to the conclusions of truth, [Scofield] asked God that he might be simple, like the Bible itself, and make no display of what he calls "even the poor learning" that he himself might have. As a successful

lawyer, he had been trained, especially in jury practice, to be simple and clear. He has never had any ambition to be impressive; he has had a great longing to help God's people and feed Christ's sheep. The result was the Scofield Reference Bible as it is to-day.[50]

Darby's neglect of literary form is unfortunate for he can be read with great profit indeed. While it is true that between Darby and Scofield, the thought of the latter is more easily understood, it is also true that the thought of the former is more original. Any legitimate understanding and evaluation of dispensationalism's development requires that both men be read with care to ascertain the many contributions of each.

A Neglected Writer

It is probably this perception that the works of Darby are almost uniformly unintelligible and perhaps the belief among some that even "If the author would write in plain English his readers would probably discover that there is nothing very valuable in his remarks,"[51] that has led to the great and unfortunate neglect of his literary legacy and that of the Brethren in general. While Darby's works are certainly well worth the reading, it is true that they will likely remain unread. This state of affairs is true among the critics and champions of dispensational theology alike.

H. A. Ironside chides A. H. Strong, for example, for not familiarizing himself with the teachings of the Brethren before attempting "to expose them as unscriptural and heretical." Ironside suspected that Strong had based his charges upon statements made by others and attributed to the Brethren in lieu of a firsthand examination of the teachings in question. This, says Ironside, is "an unwise course for any one to take in determining the exact views of any people..."[52]

Even among those who have inherited a great deal from the Brethren, there are many who have neglected this body of literature. Lewis Sperry Chafer, founder of Dallas Theological Seminary and author of a distinctly dispensational systematic theology has observed that men like Darby, Charles H. Mackintosh, William Kelly and F. W. Grant, among others in the Brethren movement, "created an extended literature of surpassing value which is strictly Biblical and dispensational, which literature, however, has been strangely neglected by many conservative theologians."[53] E. Schuyler English expresses the sentiments of a number of people when he says that, "the work of Darby, humanly speaking would have been lost or forgotten had it not been for a lawyer-turned-preacher, C. I. Scofield."[54]

DARBY AND THE BRETHREN'S INFLUENCE

Upon Dispensationalism

There can be little question that Darby and the Plymouth Brethren as a whole had a tremendous part in the systematization and promotion of dispensational theology. English, a leading dispensationalist and chairman of the editorial committee of *The New Scofield Reference Bible* says that while some trace the roots of dispensational concepts to the patristic period, "most theologians credit J. N. Darby, a Plymouth Brethren scholar, with first systematizing dispensational theology in the middle of the 19th century."[55] The operative words here are "systematizing" and "promoting," but not "originating." Ryrie asserts that, "There is no question that the Plymouth Brethren, of which John Nelson Darby (1800-1882) was a leader, had much to do with the systematizing and promoting of dispensationalism. But neither Darby nor the Brethren originated the concepts involved in the system..."[56] Regardless of how one states it, Darby's contribution to dispensationalism is of the most substantial sort. His concept of the church, a concept which sharply distinguishes the church from Israel, is one of the main tributaries of the dispensational stream.

Upon Fundamentalism

Few today who would identify themselves as fundamentalist or evangelical Christians have ever heard of Darby or the Plymouth Brethren and are consequently unaware of the impact which they have had upon their theological beliefs. But according to Sandeen, Darby is to be credited with much of the theological content of the fundamentalist movement. He says that,

> ...the form of futurism taught by John Nelson Darby and known since then as dispensationalism began to outdistance other varieties in both Britain and America. The millenarian movement was strongly marked by this British tradition, and much of the thought and attitudes of those who are known as Fundamentalists can be mirrored in the teachings of this man.[57]

Sandeen maintains further that the editorial committee of _The Fundamentals_, a twelve-volumed series published between 1910 and 1915, the purpose of which was to defend fundamental Christian truths against the inroads of liberalism, was composed of millenarians who were "quite probably" dispensationalists as well.[58]

This truth has not gone unnoticed by some of the leading dispensationalists of the past and present. John F. Walvoord, chancellor of Dallas Theological Seminary, maintains that "Much of the Truth promulgated by fundamental Christians to-day had its rebirth in the movement known as the 'Plymouth Brethren.'" Walvoord credits the Brethren with the restoration of two doctrines--the body of Christ concept of the church and the imminent return of the Lord as the blessed hope of the church--which he says "form the heart of the whole premillennial system."[59]

Ironside, "the prince of dispensational preachers,"[60] is no less aware of the Brethren's contribution to fundamentalism. In an appendix entitled "The Doctrines of Early Brethren" in _A Historical Sketch of the Brethren Movement_, he appends a note to inform the reader that this letter written by Darby is "In answer to an inquiry from the Editor of a Catholic paper, _The Francais_, as to 'The Brethren, their Doctrines, etc.'" It is, says Ironside, "A useful statement for all Fundamentalists."[61] Indeed, "The Brethren as a whole," states Ehlert, "are fundamentalists."[62] Neatby describes the theology of the Brethren as that "of Evangelicals of a firmly but moderately Calvinistic type..."[63]

Upon Individuals

Between 1870 and 1874, Darby made three trips to the United States to teach his views in any church that was open to him. He and other Brethren preachers found a hearing in New York, Chicago, Detroit, St. Louis, Boston, and Philadelphia.[64] In Chicago, one of those who heard Darby was Dwight L Moody (1837-1899), founder of the Chicago Evangelization Society (later to become known as Moody Bible Institute) and one of the early leaders in the Bible Conference movement begun at Northfield in 1880. These conferences were practically dominated by men with a dispensationalist outlook.

While Moody's relationship with Darby was stormy,[65] the impact of C. H. Mackintosh (1820-1896) upon him--the man most responsible for popularizing Darby's works--was considerable. Of Mackintosh's writings, Moody said,

> Some time since I had my attention called to C. H. M.'s Notes, and was so much pleased and at the same time profited by the way they opened up Scripture truths, that I secured at once all the writings of the same author, and if they could not be replaced, would rather part with my entire library, excepting my Bible, than with these writings. They have been to me a very key to the Scriptures.[66]

During the Opera House meetings in London, we are told, "scarcely a day passed that Mr. Moody did not spend an hour with Mr. F. C. Bland over the Bible."[67] Mr. Bland was a prominent Brethren teacher of his day.

Whether and to what extent Moody's theology influenced Scofield in turn is difficult to say, but that Scofield greatly admired Moody is attested by his own words. He writes:

> Moody was one of the greatest men of his generation. I have sometimes thought that Dwight L. Moody and General Grant were, in any true definition of greatness, the greatest men I have ever met. Moody had the strength of his Yankee birth and ancestry; he was a man also of great kindness of heart, with a zeal for souls, and absolutely loyal to the Word of God.[68]

When it came to prophecy at least, according to Gaebelein, it was Moody who needed "a better knowledge ... and Scofield was the man to lead him into it."[69]

Henry Allen Ironside (1878-1951), one of the most popular dispensational teachers of all time and visiting professor at Dallas Theological Seminary from 1925 to 1943 - to 1951, joined the Plymouth Brethren in 1896. He writes:

> During the past twelve years I have been pastor of the Moody Memorial Church of Chicago, an independent church standing very largely upon the very truths which the brethren love and from which Dwight L. Moody profited so definitely. This has, in measure, cut me off from that full communion with assemblies of brethren which I enjoyed for years, but has in no sense lessened my love and respect for them.[70]

Arno Clemens Gaebelein (1861-1945), regarded by many as the best scholar among the early dispensational teachers, did as much as anyone to disseminate dispensational concepts. Says he of Darby, "I found in his writings, in the works of William Kelly, McIntosh [Mackintosh], F. W. Grant, Bellett, and others the soul food I needed. I esteem these men next to the Apostles in their sound and spiritual teachings."[71] In another place he speaks of four saints named John who will be present at that great celestial meeting when Christ returns--Calvin, Knox, Wesley and Darby.[72]

Gaebelein, who served as one of the consulting editors for the *Scofield Reference Bible*, seems to have been for many years one of Scofield's closest friends and confidants. It was to Gaebelein in the week of July 23-29, 1901, that Scofield laid out most fully for the first time his plans for a reference Bible. While he had mentioned the idea to others in a tentative way, it was Gaebelein's positive support and encouragement that seems to have given the project wings.[73]

James Hall Brookes (1830-1897), was an outstanding Bible teacher of his day and without doubt the most prominent leader in the Bible conference movement for twenty two years from 1875 until his death in 1897. His association with Darby and the Brethren is of special interest to us as he became Scofield's tutor immediately after the latter's conversion in 1879. Scofield said of Brookes, he "was the greatest Bible student I have ever known."[74] On another occasion he wrote, "During the last twenty years of his life Dr. Brookes was perhaps my most intimate friend, and *to him I am indebted more than to all other men in the world for the establishment of my faith.*"[75] The question before us at this point is, what influence did the Brethren, particularly Darby, have upon the theology of Brookes?

That Brookes admired the Brethren is clear, for he said that they were "a people who are on the whole the soundest in faith, and most intelligent in the knowledge of our Lord Jesus Christ."[76] The only testimony we have forging a direct link between Brookes and Darby, however, is an undocumented statement by Ironside that Darby preached in Brookes' Walnut Street Presbyterian Church (later called the Washington and Compton Avenues Presbyterian Church), in St. Louis. He maintains that "Dr. Brookes knew and loved many of them [the Brethren]. His pulpit had often been opened to them. J. N. Darby, Malachi Taylor, Paul J. Loizeaux and others had preached in his church at various times."[77] Darby's own account of his visits to America are not very complete and therefore of less assistance than they might be. He says of his work in a letter written from St. Louis in 1872, that he has "had good opportunities here" and that he is "in pretty full intercourse with those exercised, among whom are more than one official minister."[78] One of these "official ministers" was very likely Brookes.

When one examines Brookes' works, particularly *Maranatha*, it becomes apparent that he owed a great debt to the Brethren. That he failed to give credit to Darby or the Brethren may have been due to certain negative attachments to Darby's name which caused the omission to be viewed as an expediency of the time.[79] Whatever the reason for the practice, it was not confined to Brookes.

Darby makes one intriguing remark concerning progress in the States, in a letter dated September, 1872. He reports that,

> They are going on happily enough in the east, some added, but no great progress in numbers; in the west a good many Presbyterians, several ministers among them, teach the Lord's coming, the presence of the Holy Ghost, that all sects are wrong, but as yet few move from their place.[80]

Apparently, Darby found an interest in the Lord's coming and some other subjects of special concern to him already in place in the churches in which he ministered. But it must have caused him a great deal of distress to find that few were willing to exchange what he considered an apostate Christendom for his proposed polity. Instead, most remained solidly within their denominations.

We have established that Moody, Gaebelein, and Brookes were all influenced by the Brethren and Darby (by the latter at least indirectly) and that they each in turn to a greater or lesser degree had an impact upon Scofield's life and doctrine. The question remaining is: What evidence do we have of the direct influence of the Brethren and Darby upon Scofield? The importance of the question is obvious when we realize that it was the *Scofield Reference Bible* that provided the most effective tool for the dissemination of dispensationalism in America. Sandeen writes that it is,

> ...perhaps the most influential single publication in millenarian and Fundamentalist historiography. The *Scofield Reference Bible* combined an attractive format of typography, paragraphing, notes, and cross references with the theology of Darbyite dispensationalism. The book has thus been subtly but powerfully influential in spreading those views among hundreds of thousands who have regularly read that Bible and who often have been unaware of the distinction between the ancient text and the Scofield interpretation.[81]

Boettner calls Scofield's notes, "The nearest thing approaching a [dispensationalist] creed,"[82] while Kraus terms the *Reference Bible* "the classic expression of the mainstream of the movement in America."[83]

Of course dispensationalists themselves are quick to add their own testimony to the great impact of this Bible. English asserts that "It would be difficult to measure the multitudes to whom the English Bible has become a new and living book through dispensational theology as exemplified in the notes of the *Scofield Reference Bible*."[84] Chafer, for ten years Scofield's song leader and soloist, challenges the "Objector" to "produce something better than the Scofield Bible" and hales it as "'one of God's greatest gifts to the church in these last days.' It goes on the record," he continues, "That the Dallas Theological Seminary uses, recommends, and defends the Scofield Bible."[85]

It is beyond question that Scofield had not only casual contact but close fellowship with the Plymouth Brethren. Francis Emory Fitch, head of the printing firm which printed and published The Scofield Bible Correspondence Course, according to Gaebelein, "was a member of the so-called Plymouth Brethren, a body of believers who probably have had as large a share in bearing testimony for the faith delivered unto the saints and also prophecy as any body during the nineteenth century." Fitch's company became the printer also for Gaebelein's periodical, *Our Hope*, in the fall of 1898.[86]

Again, after the plan was conceived to produce the *Reference Bible*, it was Brethren who were approached to garner financial backing. In addition to Fitch, Alwyn Ball, Jr., a young real estate broker who was a member of a large and successful firm and John T. Pirie, the owner and New York representative of a Chicago department store called, Carson, Pirie, Scott and Company, made the project financially feasible. So enthusiastic was Ball about the concept, reports Gaebelein, that "He fairly bubbled over with joy, and fully endorsed the plan..."[87]

Scofield's association with the Brethren was not confined to business however. During trips to England, between 1902 and 1909, while working on the *Reference Bible* in Oxford, England, he and Mrs. Scofield found fellowship in a small group of Plymouth Brethren who gathered for worship there.[88] It is interesting to note that when this fact was made known, the question was raised as to how far the Scofields shared "the peculiar beliefs of these people?" Scofield's reply was to the effect that he was a Presbyterian minister of firm persuasion, but that for "certain personal reasons," he had found it convenient to worship with "a sect...of the so-called 'Open Brethren'" just as he had worshipped with almost all other sects in his wide-ranging ministry. With respect to Brethren doctrine, Scofield offers only one disclaimer. "I gathered," he says, "that 'Brethren' are emphatic for separatism--with their idea of which Mrs. Scofield and I are not in accord."[89]

It is clear from the foregoing that Scofield was subject to Darby's influence, at least in a predigested form as a result of his tutelage by Brookes and close friendship with Gaebelein, as well as any others in the Bible conference movement who might have assimilated Darby's teachings. It is evident also that he was exposed to these teachings in the casual contacts and close fellowship he had with the Brethren in England. It seems improbable that through all of these contacts and associations that Scofield would not have also had opportunity and occasion to examine Darby's works firsthand.

What is not clear and lacks documentation, however, at least as far as we have been able to determine the matter, is the assertion routinely made by antidispensationalists that Scofield was a "devoted disciple of John Darby,"[90] who "copiously borrowed ideas, words, and phrases" from him.[91] Typical of those who make such unsubstantiated claims is Kraus and his *Dispensationalism in America*. Here, rather than offering any direct proof for the assumption, he quotes Reese's undocumented statement that "Scofield was for a generation an assiduous and admiring student of Darby's writings."[92]

The above quotation immediately follows one from Gaebelein in which he maintains that in the writings of Darby and other leading Brethren he found the "soul food" he needed and esteemed "these men next to the Apostles in their sound and spiritual teaching."[93] "Scofield," says Kraus, "might have given the same type of testimony."[94] He might have, but in point of fact, he did not. We realize that to say that Scofield was a devoted disciple of Brookes who was apparently influenced greatly by Darby, does not carry as much polemical punch as saying he learned his "'rediscovered truths'... at the feet" of a "separatist" like Darby, but to say otherwise is to exceed the bounds of the available evidence. It is hoped that the comparisons and contrasts made between the two men's dispensational doctrines in this study will result in a fairer evaluation of the matter.[95]

DARBY'S SOURCES

While it is not a specific goal of this study to reconstruct the sources from which Darby derived his ideas, in so far as that is possible, it is of value to make some observations in this regard. The task of arriving at Darby's sources is extremely difficult if not impossible for a number of reasons. Of first importance is the fact that Darby himself gives almost no credit at all--save to the Holy Spirit for the illumination of Scripture--for his theological concepts. This practice is traceable, perhaps, to two basic assumptions. The first was the belief that all past scholarship was nearly worthless because too far removed from the control of Scripture. And the corollary to this was Darby's belief that all spiritual truth is generated from a study of the Bible itself as the Holy Spirit reveals the meaning. Robert H. Gundry touches upon the heart of this issue when he says, "Brilliant but eccentric, Darby is usually considered a poor witness in his own behalf, for he did not like to acknowledge the priority of another in putting forward his teachings."[96]

This, as we have said, was due in part to Darby's disdain for past scholarship. In speaking of the "doctors" of the early church, he maintains that "None are more untrustworthy on every fundamental subject than the mass of primitive Fathers."[97] The truth of the matter, Darby says elsewhere, is that "the Fathers were men, and reasoned as it suited them," but "scriptures are the word of God, and speak plainly."[98]

The Reformation receives somewhat better treatment by Darby. While it may be praised for emphasizing the authority of the word and reaffirming justification by faith, he says, it was nevertheless "much and manifestly mixed with human agency."[99] According to Darby, among the several truths which the Reformation overlooked "and even let fall into the hands of fanatics, into the hands of the enemy" was the return of the Lord.[100]

It was the "Millenarian" writers of the past and of his day that received some of Darby's most strenuous denunciation. "For my own part," he says, "if I were bound to receive all that has been said by the Millenarians, I would reject the whole system; but their views and statements weigh with me not one feather."[101] The problem as Darby saw it, was that these Millenarians were too far removed from the control of Scripture. He says,

> This is what I would press and urge upon every one: to apply themselves, for themselves, to the testimony of Scripture, to draw ideas simply and directly from this (and I can assure them, they will ever find them sanctify-

ing ideas) but trust no man's mind, whether millenarian or antimillenarian; to use the scriptural rule--"to prove all things, and hold fast that which is good"; to adopt nothing unexamined, and to reject nothing unexamined, however weak it may be in its positions. If taken in itself, it may distract; if it lead to the examination of Scripture, it may prove the indirect source of abundant knowledge and grace.[102]

In a letter dated March 25, 1850, Darby sets forth the same position in the form of advice to a "brother." He agrees that,

> ...as you say, you have studied too much, and read the Bible too little. I always find that I have to be on my guard on this point. It is the teaching of God and not the labour of man that makes us enter into the thoughts and the purpose of God in the Bible. We search it without doubt, but the cream is not found through much labour of the mind of man....The word of God is the communication of divine things to the understanding (rendered capable by the Spirit) of man...[103]

In the same letter, we find what seems to be the core of Darby's thinking on this subject. After stating that it is his habit to proceed very slowly in the study of the Bible in order to ascertain the mind of God, a practice which causes him to "seldom have to retrace [his] steps," Darby says the "few details that I have adopted from others" affect "but rarely, the thoughts that I have received." Then he adds, "I often find brethren who have received *ideas* from the Spirit of God, and *I profit by these*; the conclusion which they draw from them, what they like as the *system* which they have formed from them, *I totally reject*; this is by no means an unusual case."[104]

That Darby borrowed ideas and profited from them, but rejected many systems based upon them is undoubtedly true. That he also examined these ideas under the light of Scripture is also sure. That we will probably never know for certain where Darby received many of his ideas, if not in fact from his own personal study of Scripture, seems also fairly certain. This brings us to a second reason for the difficulty in arriving at Darby's sources.

Among the early Brethren, the sharing of new ideas occurred primarily in their informal meetings by word of mouth. When literature was published, it appeared anonymously or the author was identified by initials only. "For that reason," says Ehlert, "we have many title-as-main-entry items, some of which will probably never be identified."[105] This practice was common even among the Brethren's opponents.

With this understanding of the difficulty involved in identifying the source(s) of Darby's inspiration, we will attempt where appropriate and possible to make them known. We readily admit that, while the task of determining Darby's influence upon others has its own peculiar problems, that of uncovering the extra-biblical influences upon Darby may very well be past finding out. In the final analysis, as to the origin of Darby's ideas, we may have to echo Origen's words in his assessment of the authorship of the epistle to the Hebrews, "The truth God alone knows."

The Need for the Study

The need for a study of this kind is, we feel, fairly self-evident from what has been said above. Darby has had a permanent impact upon contemporary theological options, yet few who have either benefited from his ideas or who have attacked him can claim a firsthand acquaintance with his works. Those who can, often come away bewildered at the convoluted manner in which he writes and the endless repetition. It is said of William Kelly--who highly valued and circulated Darby's works--that to the last he used to say, "Read Darby!"[106] Yet even Turner, who believes that Darby's works "are well worth reading," maintains that they are "little likely to be read."[107]

Is John Nelson Darby the "father of modern dispensationalism"? To answer this important question, it is essential that his teaching on ages and dispensations be clearly expounded. Until this task is completed, the link between Darby's dispensational theology and contemporary dispensational concepts will not be fully understood and appreciated.

Endnotes

[1]Clarence E. Mason, "A Review of 'Dispensationalism' by John Wick Bowman," *Bibliotheca Sacra* 114 (January 1957):18.

[2]Daniel P. Fuller, "The Hermeneutics of Dispensationalism" (Ph.D. dissertation, Northern Baptist Theological Seminary, 1957), p. 136.

A number of dispensationalists like Charles Ryrie and Arnold Ehlert, maintain that the basic features of dispensationalism are evident in the teachings of the early church Fathers. For a summary of the dispensational views of the Fathers see Larry V. Crutchfield, "Israel and the Church in the Ante-Nicene Fathers: Part 1 of Rudiments of Dispensationalism in the Ante-Nicene Period," *Bibliotheca Sacra* 144 (July-September, 1987):272-276.

[3]John F. Walvoord, review of *Backgrounds to Dispensationalism*, by Clarence B. Bass, in *Bibliotheca Sacra*, January 1961, p. 70.

[4]William E. Cox, *An Examination of Dispensationalism* (Phillipsburg, N.J.: Presbyterian and Reformed Publishing Co., 1963), p. 13.

[5]Charles Caldwell Ryrie, *Dispensationalism Today* (Chicago: Moody Press, 1965), p. 76.

[6]Isaac Watts, *The Works of the Reverend and Learned Isaac Watts, D.D.*, 6 vols., comp. Rev. George Burder (London: J. Barfield, 1810), 4:1-40. See Arnold Ehlert's, *A Bibliographic History of Dispensationalism*, pp. 39-40.

[7]Mason, p. 19.

[8]Pierre Poiret, *The Divine Oeconomy; or, An Universal System of the Works and Purposes of God Toward's Men, Demonstrated*, 6 vols. (London: 1713). See Arnold Ehlert's, *A Bibliographic History of Dispensationalism*, pp. 34-6. **Appendix A** contains a comparative chart of the dispensational schemes of Poiret, Watts, Darby and Scofield. As one examines the systems of the four men side by side, it becomes apparent at once that Watts' and Scofield's divisions of the ages have by far the most in common.

[9]Ryrie, p. 75.

[10]Arnold D. Ehlert, *A Bibliographic History of Dispensationalism* (Grand Rapids: Baker Book House, 1965), p. 50.

[11]John Nelson Darby, *The Collected Writings of J. N. Darby*, 34 vols., ed. William Kelly, vol. 1: *Ecclesiastical No. 1* (Sunbury, Pa.: Believers Bookshelf, n.d.), p. 125.

[12]Ibid., vol. 2: *Prophetic No. 1*, pp. 92, 98.

[13]Mason, p. 18.

[14]Cox, p. 56.

[15]All Biblical quotations in this study are from the *New American Standard Bible* unless otherwise stated.

[16]Ernest R. Sandeen, *The Roots of Fundamentalism* (Chicago: University of Chicago Press, 1970; reprint ed., Grand Rapids: Baker Book House, 1978), p. 31.

[17]For the most complete accounts of Darby's life see: Clarence B. Bass, *Backgrounds to Dispensationalism* (Grand Rapids: Wm. B. Eerdmans Publishing Co., 1960), pp. 48-99; Howard E. Sturgeon, "The Life of John Nelson Darby" (Th.M. thesis, Southern Baptist Theological Seminary, 1957), 66pp; W. G. Turner, *John Nelson Darby* (London: C. A. Hammond, 1944), 88pp.

[18]Hy. Pickering, *Chief Men among the Brethren*, 2nd ed. (London: Pickering and Inglis, 1931), p. 11.

[19]Ehlert, p. 48.

[20]Pickering, p. 12.

[21]W. G. Turner, *John Nelson Darby* (London: C. A. Hammond, 1944), pp. 13-15.

[22]Darby, vol. 20: *Ecclesiastical No. 4*, p. 288.

[23]Turner, p. 18.

[24]W. Blair Neatby, *The History of the Plymouth Brethren*, 2nd ed. (London: Hodder and Stoughton, 1902), p. 15.

[25]Darby, vol. 1: *Ecclesiastical No. 1*, pp. 1 19.

[26]Neatby, p. 18.

[27]Darby, vol. 2: *Prophetic No. 1*, p. 1.

[28]Ehlert, p. 49.

[29]Clarence B. Bass, *Backgrounds to Dispensationalism* (Grand Rapids: Baker Book House, 1960), p. 51.

[30]Ibid., p. 67.

[31]Ibid., p. 64.

[32]Ibid., p. 7.

[33]Turner, p. 47.

[34]Bass, p. 72.

[35]John Howard Goddard, "The Contribution of John Nelson Darby to Soteriology, Ecclesiology, and Eschatology" (Th.D. dissertation, Dallas Theological Seminary, 1948), pp. 23-4.

[36]Pickering, p. 14.

[37]Oswald T. Allis, *Prophecy and the Church* (Phillipsburg, N.J.: Presbyterian and Reformed Publishing Co., 1947), pp. 13, 14, 288.

[38]Turner, p. 53.

[39]Arnold D. Ehlert, "The Darby Translation," *The Bible Collector* (April-June, 1967):7.

[40]John Nelson Darby, *The Holy Scriptures: A New Translation from the Original Languages* (Addison, Ill.: Bible Truth Publishers, 1975), p. iii.

[41]Bass, p. 18, note 13.

[42]Darby, *Translation*, p. 1423.

[43]Pickering, p. 14.

[44]Turner, pp. 72-3.

[45]Neatby, pp.49-50.

[46]Sandeen, p. 31.

[47]Darby, *Writings*, vol. 7: *Doctrinal No. 2*, p. 139.

[48]Turner, p. 31.

[49]Charles Gallaudet Trumbull, *The Life Story of C. I. Scofield* (New York: Oxford University Press, 1920), p. 85.

[50]Ibid., p. 106.

[51]C. H. Spurgeon, *Commenting and Commentaries* (London: Passmore and Alabaster, 1887),

p. 84.

[52]H. A. Ironside, *A Historical Sketch of the Brethren Movement* (Grand Rapids: Zondervan Publishing Co., 1942; reprint ed., Neptune, N.J.: Loizeaux Brothers, 1985), p. 205.

[53]Lewis Sperry Chafer, "Dispensationalism," *Bibliotheca Sacra* 93 (October 1936):392.

[54]E. Schuyler English, "E. Schuyler English Looks at Dispensationalism," *Christian Life* 17 (September 1956):24.

[55]Ibid.

[56]Ryrie, p. 74.

[57]Sandeen, p. xix.

[58]Ibid., p. 197.

[59]John F. Walvoord, review of *An Historical Sketch of the Brethren Movement*, by H. A. Ironside, in *Bibliotheca Sacra*, 1942, p. 378.

[60]Ryrie, p. 31.

[61]Ironside, p. 188. This is a useful summary of Brethren doctrine; see also, *Letters of J.N. Darby*, vol. 2, pp. 431-440.

[62]Arnold D. Ehlert, *Brethren Writers: A Checklist with an Introductory Essay and Additional Lists* (Grand Rapids: Baker Book House, 1969), p. 36.

[63]Neatby, p. 230.

[64]Turner, p. 19.

[65]Ibid., pp. 21-22. The conflict was over the question of freedom of the will. Moody considered Darby to be an extreme Calvinist on this point. So heated did the controversy become, that the two men parted company on the unfriendliest of terms.

[66]Sandeen, p. 173.

[67]Pickering, p. 91. See pp. 89-93 for a brief account of Bland's significance in the Brethren movement.

[68]Trumbull, p. 52.

[69]Arno C. Gaebelein, "The Story of the Scofield Reference Bible: Part II-A Brief Biographical Sketch," *Moody Monthly* 43 (November 1942):129.

[70]Ironside, p. 4.

[71]A. C. Gaebelein, *Half a Century* (New York: *Our Hope* Publication Office, 1930), p. 85.

[72]Ibid., p. 243.

[73]Arno C. Gaebelein, "The Story of the Scofield Reference Bible: Part IV-Remarkable Providential Leadings and the Beginning of a New Testimony," *Moody Monthly* 43 (January 1943):279.

[74]Trumbull, p. 35. For a brief biographical sketch and appraisal of Scofield's life and work see Larry V. Crutchfield, "C. I. Scofield," in *Twentieth-Century Shapers of American Popular Religion*, ed. Charles H. Lippy (New York: Greenwood Press, 1989), pp. 371-381.

[75]Sandeen, p. 223 (italics added; quoted by Lyman Stewart in a letter to George S. Fisher, 5 May, 1911, Stewart Papers).

[76]C. Norman Kraus, *Dispensationalism in America* (Richmond: John Knox Press, 1958), p. 47.

[77]Ironside, p. 196.

[78]John Nelson Darby, *Letters of J. N. Darby*, 3 vols., reprint ed. (Sunbury, Pa.: Believers Bookshelf, 1971), 2:180.

[79]Ironside, p. 196ff. These negative attachments to Darby's name had to do mostly with the divisions among the Brethren.

[80]Darby, *Letters*, vol. 2, p. 182.

[81]Sandeen, p. 222.

[82]Loraine Boettner, *The Millennium* (Philadelphia: The Presbyterian and Reformed Publishing Co., 1957), p. 140.

[83]Kraus, p. 19.

[84]English, p. 27.

[85]Lewis Sperry Chafer, "The Scofield Bible," *Bibliotheca Sacra* 109 (April-June 1952):98-9.

[86]Gaebelein, "The Story of the Scofield Reference Bible," part IV, p. 277.

[87]Ibid., pp. 277, 279.

[88]Trumbull, pp. 115, 116.

[89]Ibid., pp.115-17.

[90]Cox, p. 51.

[91]Bass, p. 18.

[92]Kraus, p. 113; cf. Alexander Reese, *The Approaching Advent of Christ* (London: Marshall, Morgan, and Scott Co., 1937; reprint ed., Grand Rapids: Grand Rapids International Publications, 1975), p. 19.

[93]Gaebelein, *Half a Century*, p. 85.

[94]Kraus, p. 113.

[95]For a graphic presentation of the relationships among the Brethren, Darby, Brookes, Gaebelein, and Scofield, see **Appendix B**.

[96]Robert H. Gundry, *The Church and the Tribulation* (Grand Rapids: Zondervan Publishing House, 1973), pp. 186-7.

[97]Darby, *Writings*, vol. 14: *Ecclesiastical No. 3*, p. 68.

[98]Ibid., vol. 18: *Doctrinal No 5*, p. 86.

[99]Ibid., vol. 1: *Ecclesiastical No. 1*, pp. 24 and 21.

[100]Ibid., vol. 4: *Ecclesiastical No. 2*, p. 120.

[101]Ibid., vol. 2: *Prophetic No. 1*, p. 4.

[102]Ibid., p. 10.

[103]Darby, *Letters*, 3:256-7.

[104]Ibid., 3:259 (italics added).

[105]Ehlert, *Brethren*, p. 19.

[106]Napoleon Noel, *The History of the Brethren* (Denver: W. F. Knapp, 1936), p. 64.

[107]Turner, p. 53.

CHAPTER 2

NORMATIVE DISPENSATIONAL THEOLOGY

In order to gain a better understanding of Darby's influence upon dispensational theology, we feel it necessary to set forth the main features of normative dispensationalism as it is presented today. In order to accomplish this, we shall first determine the meaning and origin of the term *dispensation*. Next, we shall examine the characteristics, names and number of dispensations, and conclude with a look at the main elements of dispensational eschatology. Let us first consider the origin of the word *dispensation*.

Meaning and Origin of Term Dispensation

ETYMOLOGY OF THE WORD

oikonomia

Etymologically, the English word *dispensation* is the anglicized form of the Latin *dispensatio*, the Vulgate rendering of the Greek word *oikonomia*.[1] The meaning of the feminine Latin noun is "weighing out; management, administration; the office of a treasurer."[2] The Greek feminine noun *oikonomia* means: "1. management of a household; 2. arrangement, order, plan," while the masculine noun *oikonomos* refers to the one who acts as the "manager" or serves as the "steward" of the household.[3] The word *oikonomia* itself is a compound of *oikos*, which means "house," and *nemo*, meaning "to dispense, manage or hold sway."[4] The primary idea in the word *dispensation* then, is the administration or management of a household's affairs by a steward or manager (e.g., Luke 16, "parable of rich man and steward"). It "relates primarily to household administration."[5] Our English word *economy* is derived from the Greek *oikonomia*.

William Graham Scroggie points out that,

> The word *oikonomia* bears one significance, and means "an administration," whether of a house, of property, of a state, or a nation, or as in the present study, *the administration of the human race or any part of it*, at any given time. Just as a parent would govern his household in different ways, according to varying necessity, yet every one for one good end, so God has at different times dealt with men in different ways, according to the necessity of the case, but throughout for one great, grand end.[6]

The different forms of the word *dispensation* are used some twenty times in

23

the New Testament. The masculine noun form *oikonomos* occurs ten times (Luke 12:42; 16:1, 3, 8; Rom. 16:23; I Cor. 4:1, 2; Gal. 4:2; Titus 1:7; and I Pet. 4:10) where it is translated "steward" except in Romans 16:23 where it is "city treasurer" (as in the New American Standard Bible). The feminine noun form *oikonomia* appears nine times (Luke 16:2, 3, 4; 1 Cor. 9:17; Eph. 1:10; 3:2, 9; Col. 1:25; and 1 Tim. 1:4) and is usually translated either "stewardship" or "administration" (NASB). In Luke 16:2, the verb *oikonomeo* occurs and is rendered "to be a steward" (NASB).

aion

One other word warrants consideration in connection with dispensational concepts. The word *aion* or "age" is important to the discussion as it is often given undue prominence in definitions of dispensations. In the New Testament, *aion* "age" as a "segment of time,"[7] is often used with reference to the "present" age and to the age "to come." In Matthew 28:20, for example, Christ says, "...and lo, I am with you always, even to the end of the age" (cf. Matt. 13:40). In Matthew 12:32, we are told that blasphemy against the Holy Spirit shall not be forgiven "...either in this age, or in the age to come" (cf. Heb. 6:5).

Dispensationalists frequently declare, as does Aldrich, that "a dispensation includes the two factors of a religious order and the age during which the order is in effect."[8] Ehlert says the same thing in a slightly different way when he contends that "A dispensation has two major aspects: a time-period aspect, and a redemptive-program aspect." He affirms that either one alone does not constitute dispensationalism.[9]

In this regard, Ryrie correctly points out that primarily, a dispensation is a stewardship arrangement and not a period of time. Consequently, age and dispensation are not exactly synonymous terms, although it is obvious that a dispensational arrangement takes place within a period of time and that a particular arrangement and historical period of time may actually coincide.[10] This emphasis upon the stewardship arrangement rather than the time period is in perfect keeping with the meaning of *oikonomia*.

DEFINITIONS OF THE WORD

One of the chief problems in dispensationalism is that of definition. While there is no lack of definitions, there is lack of agreement upon those proposed. We suspect that the primary reason for this is the desire to formulate a simple, succinct definition for a complex theological system that refuses to be so reduced. Men of few words may be the best men as Shakespeare suggests,[11] but if they happen to be dispensational scholars these few words in the form of a definition may be a few words too little. Almost any brief definition is in for a certain amount of criticism.

A perfect example of this is found in the definition probably most quoted. Scofield affirms that "A dispensation is a period of time during which man is tested in respect of obedience to some *specific* revelation of the will of God."[12]

The principal objection here is the emphasis placed upon the time-period aspect of the dispensations. John Wick Bowman goes to the extreme, however, when he excludes the time element totally from the meaning of *oikonomia*. He maintains that it "never means nor does it ever have reference to a period of time as such, as Scofield's definition demands."[13]

While it is admitted that Scofield's definition might better have been cast in different terms emphasizing the time element less, Bowman's criticism goes too far. The Bible itself connects the ideas of administration and ages in Ephesians 1:10 and 3:9 and beyond that, it is impossible to divorce the two concepts in actual practice. Clarence E. Mason is correct in saying that,

> <u>Dispensation</u> may technically not be a time word, but its inevitable relation to time, and usually a specific period of time, has brought it into usage as a time word, as is confirmed by the dictionary definition and its use in theological writings. There is no such thing as a dispensation unrelated to time.[14]

The English Oxford Dictionary definition is one such as that referred to by Bowman. It gives as the theological definition of dispensation:

> A religious order or system, conceived as divinely instituted, or as a stage in a progressive revelation expressly adapted to the needs of a particular nation or period of time, as the patriarchal, Mosaic (or Jewish) dispensation, the Christian dispensation; also the age or period during which such system has prevailed.[15]

Lewis Sperry Chafer sets forth both aspects of dispensations, but gives prominence to the stewardship arrangement. He says that "A dispensation can be defined as a stage in the progressive revelation of God constituting a distinctive stewardship or rule of life. Although the concept of a dispensation and an age in the Bible is not precisely the same, it is obvious that each age has its dispensation."[16]

Two of the most complete definitions of the concept of dispensations that we have found are those set forth by John F. Walvoord and Charles C. Ryrie. Both definitions focus upon the stewardship arrangement of God and are based upon the resultant meaning of *oikonomia* as used in the New Testament. Walvoord says that,

> A dispensation is considered a divinely-given stewardship based on a particular rule of life revealed in the progressive unfolding of divine truth in Scripture. Each new major deposit of truth had its own demand for faith and obedience. Generally speaking, a dispensation is created by the revelation of a major system of truth sufficient to constitute a new rule of life and is often marked off from the preceding period by some spiritual crisis in the history of God's people.[17]

In his definition, Ryrie adheres even more closely to the basic meaning of *oikonomia*. Here the world is pictured as a household that functions under the direction of God, who acts as the *oikonomos* or steward. Ryrie maintains that,

> In this household-world God is dispensing or administering its affairs according to His own will and in various stages of revelation in the process of time. These various stages mark off the distinguishably different economies in the outworking of His total purpose, and these economies are the dispensations. The understanding of God's differing economies is essential to a proper interpretation of His revelation within those various economies.[18]

While definitions have their value, the true nature of the dispensations is best arrived at through an examination of their common characteristics.

Characteristics of Dispensations

PRIMARY CHARACTERISTICS[19]

A Distinct Administration

There are three essential characteristics which together set each dispensation off as distinct from all other dispensations. First of all, each dispensation must have its own particular manifestation of God's administrative rule. Every dispensation is characterized by a unique governing relationship between God and the world. Adam and Eve, for example, experienced God's direct rule. They enjoyed direct fellowship with God in a way produced only rarely since. In the Mosaic dispensation for instance, while God communicated face to face with Moses, the principal form of administration or government was the Law given in all its forms through Moses. This Law was a new thing unknown to Adam and Eve.

A Distinct Responsibility

The second primary characteristic of each dispensation, is the establishment of a new responsibility placed upon humankind as a result of the new governmental relationship. The Edenic responsibility was to fellowship with God and exhibit obedience in abstaining from eating the fruit of the tree of the knowledge of good and evil. In the Mosaic period, obviously humankind no longer had access to this tree and was responsible rather to be in perfect conformity to all the requirements of the Law.

A Distinct Revelation

The final essential characteristic of each dispensation is a new, unique revelation to implement the new governmental relationship with its resultant responsibility. In the case of the Mosaic dispensation, it is obvious that prior to that time humankind was not accountable for something that did not exist. The Law was a new revelation of God which established a new administrative rule with a correspondingly new responsibility. It should be borne in mind that while each dispensation has a unique principle of government and responsibility introduced, their introduction does not necessarily abrogate those of preceding dispensations. As we shall see, there is usually a certain amount of overlapping involved.

In addition to the three primary characteristics enumerated above, there are three secondary elements present in every dispensation. It is these three characteristics which usually receive the bulk of attention from those who oppose dispensational theology. Each new dispensation is characterized by a test, followed by failure and judgment.

The Test

The test in each dispensation is essentially the same as the responsibility. "Obviously, whenever God gives revelation concerning His method of running the affairs of the world," says Ryrie, "there is also given a corresponding responsibility or test to man as to whether or not he will align himself with God's economy and the revelation of it."[20] In essence, the test in every dispensation is the same: Will the individual live up to the responsibility under which God has placed him; will he be obedient? Would Adam and Eve refrain from eating the fruit of the tree of the knowledge of good and evil? Would those in the Mosaic economy keep all the commands of the Law?

The Failure

It is a fact of history that every governmental system under which God has placed humankind with its corresponding responsibility/test has ended in failure. Adam and Eve ate the fruit and the Israelites broke the Law at every turn. As Ryrie points out,

> Each dispensation is filled with failures simply because history is. The failures are in at least two realms--the realm of governmental economy and the realm of salvation. In both areas not all men have failed, but in both realms most men have. Sin often seems to come to a climax at certain points in human history, and such climaxes mark the end of the various dispensations.[21]

The Judgment

Just as in every dispensation one or more failures occur--the Israelites broke the Law of Moses repeatedly--so also every dispensation may experience one or more judgments of God. The flood and the tribulation are examples of climactic judgments which follow climactic failures. The Mosaic dispensation, on the other hand, was judged in stages. As a result of their failure to obey God's Law and in their rejection of the Messiah, the Jews were dispersed throughout the world. This was accomplished beginning with the Assyrian exile (734 B.C.) and ending with Hadrian in 135 A.D.

One final word is required with respect to the importance of these three secondary characteristics of which so much is made. Ryrie says of them:

> While the matters of testing, failure, and judgment are not the basics that mark off the dispensations, they seem to be part and parcel of them. If,

however, there were no decisive test there still could be a dispensational arrangement. If there were no climactic failure and judgment, there still could be a change in the dispensational arrangement. The presence of a test, failure, and judgment is not the *sine qua non* of a dispensational government of the world.[22]

More will be said about these characteristics of dispensationalism in connection with Darby's dispensational concepts.

Essential Factors of Dispensationalism

At this point it may be fairly asked: What is it exactly that makes a person a dispensationalist? What are the indispensable ingredients of dispensational theology? As Ryrie puts it, "What is the *sine qua non* of the system?"[23]

NON-ESSENTIAL FACTORS

It is not the issue of distinguishably different economies in God's governance of world affairs, for nondispensationalists frequently employ the term "dispensation" in the development of their own dispensational schemes. Augustine, for example, often called the "father of modern amillennialism," held that there were various dispensations in the outworking of God's plan and speaks of "the completed course of time, the component parts of which are the dispensations adapted to each successive age…"[24] Covenant theologian, Charles Hodge, outlines four dispensations in a section in his *Systematic Theology* entitled, "Different Dispensations."[25]

The number of dispensations to which one holds and the question of premillennialism--belief in Christ's return to reign over a literal thousand year earthly kingdom--are not the deciding factors either. Most dispensationalists hold to at least three dispensations but some see as many as seven or eight. And while being a dispensationalist necessarily makes one a premillennialist, the reverse is not true (e.g., George Eldon Ladd's "historic premillennialism").[26]

Neither are the doctrines of the pretribulation rapture of the saints and the parenthetical nature of the church the essential ingredients of dispensational theology as Sandeen suggests. These two doctrines introduced by Darby, says Sandeen, "constituted the basic tenets of the system of theology since referred to as dispensationalism."[27] While the rapture or catching up of believers to meet Christ in the air prior to the Tribulation period and the view of the church as parenthetical, that is as a mystery unknown in Old Testament times but revealed in the New--an intercalation in God's program--so to speak, have become an integral part of dispensational theology, they are not that which reduces it to its lowest common denominator. They are not the heart of the system.

ESSENTIAL FACTORS

Ryrie suggests that there are three essential factors--the *sine qua non* of the system--in determining who is and is not a dispensationalist.[28]

Distinction Between Israel and the Church

First, a dispensationalist makes a sharp distinction between Israel and the church. It is the dispensationalist's belief that throughout history, God has pursued two distinct purposes. One program involves the earthly people--Israel (Judaism), while the other involves a heavenly people--the church (Christianity). According to Ryrie, this distinction between Israel and the church "is probably the most basic theological test of whether or not a man is a dispensationalist, and it is undoubtedly the most practical and conclusive." He says that the person who holds to this distinction will inevitably be a dispensationalist and the one who doesn't, won't.[29] "Indeed, ecclesiology, or the doctrine of the Church," says Ryrie, "is the touchstone of dispensationalism."[30]

John Walvoord attaches no less importance to this concept. He maintains that,

> As related to premillennial interpretation, normative dispensationalism tends to emphasize certain important distinctives. One of the most significant is the contrast provided between God's program for Israel and God's present program for the Church. The Church composed of Jew and Gentile is considered a separate program of God which does not advance nor fulfill any of the promises given to Israel. The present age is regarded as a period in which Israel is temporarily set aside as to its national program. When the Church is translated however, Israel's program will then proceed to its consummation.[31]

A generation ago, Walvoord's predecessor at Dallas Theological Seminary, Lewis Sperry Chafer, suggested that this is one of the basic premises upon which dispensationalism stands. He writes:

> The dispensationalist believes that throughout the ages God is pursuing two distinct purposes: one related to the earth with earthly people and earthly objectives involved, while the other is related to heaven with heavenly people and heavenly people involved....Over against this, the partial dispensationalist, though dimly observing a few obvious distinctions, bases his interpretation on the supposition that God is doing but one thing, namely, the general separation of the good from the bad, and, in spite of all the confusion this limited theory creates, contends that the earthly people merge into the heavenly people; that the earthly program must be given a spiritual interpretation or disregarded altogether; and that there is nothing in eternity but heaven and hell.[32]

Clarence Bass is correct in saying that "Whatever evaluation history may make of this movement, it will attest that dispensationalism is rooted in Darby's concept of the church--a concept that sharply distinguishes the church from Israel..."[33] This whole distinction between Israel and the church is based upon the unique character of the church. The church is unique as to its nature, its time and its relation to Israel.

1. The church is distinct in nature.[34] Many passages of Scripture speak of the

church's unique relationship to Christ (I Cor. 12:27; Eph. 1:22-23, 5:23; Col. 1:18). Paul clearly teaches that the church as a living organism is the Body of which Christ is the Head. This Body is composed of both Jews and Gentiles (Eph. 2:16), and indwelt by the living Christ (Col. 1:27). This, says Paul, was a mystery unknown to past generations but "...has now been revealed to His holy apostles and prophets in the Spirit;" (Eph. 3:5, 6; Col. 1:27). This unique relationship of Jews and Gentiles together as the Body indwelt by Christ as the Head constitutes a mystery, a relationship unknown in Old Testament times but now revealed and made possible by the cross of Christ (Eph. 2:15).

2. The church is distinct in time. If the foregoing is true, it is obvious that the church is limited to a specific time period. If the unique relationship of Jews and Gentiles together as the Body indwelt by Christ was a mystery, unknown in Old Testament times but revealed in the New and made possible only by the cross, then the church could not have existed in the Old Testament period.

This is further substantiated by what the Bible has to say about the beginning and end of the church age. Christ says, in an obvious reference to Pentecost, "...'for John baptized with water, but you shall be baptized with the Holy Spirit not many days from now'" (Acts 1:5). Paul explains the significance of this event in I Corinthians 12:13. At Pentecost, Jew and Greek were placed into one Body by the baptizing work of the Holy Spirit and thus the church began.

With regard to the completion of the church age when the saints will be resurrected and raptured, Paul specifically refers to those who shall rise first as the "dead in Christ" (I Thess. 4:16). "This clearly distinguishes those who have died in this age from believers who died before Christ's first advent," says Ryrie, "thus marking the Church off as distinct to this age and a mystery hidden in Old Testament times but now revealed."[35]

3. The church is distinct from Israel. In his *Systematic Theology,* Chafer lists twenty-four contrasts between Israel and the church[36] "which show us conclusively that these two groups cannot be united into one, but that they must be distinguished as two separate entities with whom God is dealing in a special program."[37] While it is lengthy, due to its centrality in dispensational theology, we feel it useful to reproduce Pentecost's summary of Chafer's twenty-four contrasts between Israel and the church. He says,

> These contrasts may be outlined as follows: (1) The extent of Biblical revelation: Israel--nearly four-fifths of the Bible; Church--about one-fifth. (2) The Divine purpose: Israel--the earthly promises in the covenants; Church--the heavenly promises in the gospel. (3) The seed of Abraham: Israel--the physical seed, of whom some become a spiritual seed; Church--a spiritual seed. (4) Birth: Israel--physical birth that produces a relationship; Church--spiritual birth that brings relationship. (5) Headship: Israel--Abraham; Church--Christ. (6) Covenants: Israel--Abrahamic and all the following covenants; Church--indirectly related to the Abrahamic and new covenants. (7) Nationality: Israel--one nation; Church--from all nations. (8) Divine dealing: Israel--national and individual; Church--individual only. (9) Dispensations: Israel--seen in all ages from Abraham; Church--

seen only in this present age. (10) Ministry: Israel--no missionary activity and no gospel to preach; Church--a commission to fulfill. (11) The death of Christ: Israel--guilty nationally, to be saved by it; Church--perfectly saved by it now. (12) The Father: Israel--by a peculiar relationship God was Father to the nation; Church--we are related individually to God as Father. (13) Christ: Israel--Messiah, Immanuel, King; Church--Saviour, Lord, Bridegroom, Head. (14) The Holy Spirit: Israel--came upon some temporarily; Church--indwells all. (15) Governing principle: Israel--Mosaic Law system; Church--grace system. (16) Divine enablement: Israel--none; Church--the indwelling Holy Spirit. (17) Two farewell discourses: Israel--Olivet discourse; Church--upper room discourse. (18) The promise of Christ's return: Israel--in power and glory for judgment; Church--to receive us to Himself. (19) Position: Israel--a servant; Church--members of the family. (20) Christ's earthly reign: Israel--subjects; Church--co-reigners. (21) Priesthood: Israel--had a priesthood; Church--is a priesthood. (22) Marriage: Israel--unfaithful wife; Church--bride. (23) Judgments: Israel--must face judgment; Church--delivered from all judgments. (24) Positions in eternity: Israel--spirits of just men made perfect in the new earth; Church--church of the firstborn in the new heavens.[38]

One point of clarification is necessary with respect to the twenty-fourth point. Because of the distinction in God's purposes for Israel and the church, it is often assumed that dispensationalism teaches that there is no heavenly hope for Israel, only an earthly one. This impression is given by Darby,[39] Scofield[40] and Chafer.[41] In actuality, the earthly hope of Israel applies to the promises made to national Israel in the form of the Abrahamic and Davidic covenants to be fulfilled in the millennial kingdom, but Israel's hope is by no means confined to the earth. Pentecost summarizes the matter well when he says that,

> The conclusion to this question would be that the Old Testament held forth a national hope, which will be realized fully in the millennial age. The individual Old Testament saint's hope of an eternal city will be realized through resurrection in the heavenly Jerusalem, where, without losing distinction or identity, Israel will join with the resurrected and translated of the church age to share in the glory of His reign forever. The nature of the millennium, as the period of the test of fallen humanity under the righteous reign of the King, precludes the participation by resurrected individuals in that testing. Thus the millennial age will be concerned only with men who...are living in their natural bodies.[42]

Hermeneutical Principle of Literal Interpretation

The second essential factor in dispensationalism concerns its hermeneutical principles. The above mentioned distinction between Israel and the church is derived from a system of hermeneutics called literal interpretation. This is a principle of interpretation which does not spiritualize or allegorize as nondispensational theologies do at various points, but interprets all Scripture, including prophecy, in its plain, normal, literal sense. "Consistently literal or plain interpretation," says Ryrie, "is indicative of a dispensational approach to the interpretation of the Scriptures."[43]

Bernard Ramm quotes the *Webster's New International Dictionary* meaning of the word "literal" as "...the natural or usual construction and implication of a writing or expression; following the ordinary and apparent sense of words; not allegorical or metaphorical."[44] The dispensationalist would concur with this definition. He would also give hearty approval to Horne's definition of "literal" as it applies to literal interpretation. He writes:

> Further, in common life, no prudent and *conscientious* person, who either commits his sentiments to writing or utters anything, intends that a diversity of meanings should be attached to what he writes or says; and, consequently, neither his readers, nor those who hear him, affix to it any other than the true and obvious sense....*The Literal Sense* of any place of Scripture is that which the words signify, or require, in their natural and proper acceptation, without any trope [figure of speech], metaphor, or figure, and abstracted from mystic meaning.[45]

In order to get at the exact meaning of the word "literal," other words like "normal," "plain," "natural," are used to emphasize the fact that it is the meaning conveyed by the ordinary, everyday usage of words that is intended. This is not to imply that the dispensationalist discounts the use of figures of speech. What he insists on is that there is a literal meaning conveyed by the figure and thus it is to be interpreted in accordance with the normal usage of words.

A. Berkeley Mickelsen gives an excellent example of this procedure in terms of an animal "devouring" a meal and a fire "devouring" a building. He explains that, while a dog devours a meal (a literal statement) by chewing, swallowing, and digesting it, a fire devours a building (a figurative statement) through the process of combustion. A fire does not masticate buildings the way a dog eats food, nevertheless, it removes what lies before it by consuming it as the dog removes the food by consumption. In either case, says Mickelsen, "both realities are removed from the scene. One is not imaginary and the other real. Both occurrences are actual experiences."[46]

It is this principle of interpretation which constitutes, according to Chafer, "The outstanding characteristic of the dispensationalist...the fact that he *believes* every statement of the Bible and gives to it the plain, natural meaning its words imply."[47] It is, says Walvoord, "the guiding principle of dispensational premillennialism."[48] Ryrie sums up the position by affirming that,

> It is only by adjusting or adding to the principle of literal interpretation that dispensationalism is avoided. Face-value understanding incorporates distinctions; distinctions lead to dispensations. Normal interpretation leads to the clear distinction between words, concepts, peoples and economies. This consistent hermeneutical principle is the basis of dispensationalism.[49]

Unifying Principle of the Glory of God

The third and final essential factor in dispensationalism has to do with the overarching purpose of God in human history.[50] "All the events of the created world," says Walvoord, "are designed to manifest the glory of God."[51] Thus based on Ephesians 1:6, 12, and 14, the dispensationalist maintains that God's underlying purpose in the world is His own glory, not salvation as the covenant theologian suggests.[52]

With respect to the glory of God, Ryrie associates it with the goal of history, namely the millennial kingdom. He asserts that a "requirement of a philosophy of history is a proper unifying principle." He says,

> In dispensationalism the principle is theological or perhaps better eschatological, for the differing dispensations reveal the glory of God as he manifests His character in the differing stewardships culminating in history with the millennial glory....If the goal of history is the earthly millennium, and if the glory of God will be manifest at that time in the personal presence of Christ in a way hitherto unknown, then the unifying principle of dispensationalism may be said to be eschatological (if viewed from the goal toward which we are moving) or theological (if viewed from the self-revelation of God in every dispensation.[53]

It is obvious then that dispensationalism is closely associated with and intimately involved in the study of eschatology. Dispensationalists are quick to point out, however, that their theology does not merely revolve around the twentieth chapter of Revelation, but that "it involves a system of interpretation of the entire Scripture from Genesis to Revelation."[54] This system of interpretation known as dispensational premillennialism, "not only includes a description of the future," says Ryrie, "but also involves the meaning and significance of the entire Bible."[55] Before we examine dispensational eschatology more closely, a look at the dispensations themselves is in order.

Number, Names and Characteristics of the Dispensations

Normative dispensationalism at this point is usually identified with the sevenfold dispensational arrangement of Scofield:[56] 1. Innocency, 2. Conscience, 3. Human Government, 4. Promise, 5. Law, 6. Grace, and 7. Kingdom. In each of these dispensations humankind is placed under a new responsibility (test) of obedience in accordance with the governmental arrangement established by the introduction of new revelation. In each dispensation there is failure followed by divine judgment and salvation only through divine grace.

IMPORTANCE OF NUMBER AND NAMES OF DISPENSATIONS

There is no slavish insistence among dispensationalists upon seven as the number of the dispensations or upon the names applied to them by Scofield. The number of dispensations may range from as few as four to as many as eight, but seven is the number most generally held to even if at times throughout history they have not been the same seven. Roy L. Aldrich's position is typical. While there may be disagreement as to the titles and number of dispensations, it is nevertheless "believed that a system of dispensationalism, such as Dr. Scofield uses, is absolutely necessary for a correct understanding of the Word of God."[57]

The cause of this disagreement, as Ryrie correctly observes, is a lack of information or revelation concerning the earliest Biblical periods. There are fewer than twelve chapters covering the first three dispensations (dispensation of Promise begins with Abraham in Gen. 11:27). It's interesting to note that one of the criticisms aimed at dispensationalists in general and Chafer and Darby in particular by Daniel P. Fuller, is that one would expect the beginning point for analysis of the system to "be the early dispensations in the first few chapters of Genesis." Yet, he goes on to say, "J. N. Darby scarcely has more than a dozen lines in his entire writings about God's dispensational dealings with man before Abraham."[58]

Fuller clearly shows a lack of familiarity with Darby's writings. In the first place, as will be shown later, Darby did not consider the pre-Noahic periods to be dispensations. Nevertheless, he devotes a considerable amount of space to God's dealings with humankind prior to Abraham.[59]

While dispensationalism does not stand or fall on the basis of the question of the number of dispensations involved, it is not an unimportant one. Obviously it is an integral part of the dispensational system. In the final analysis, we must agree with Ryrie that "if one has a consistently workable definition and if one applies it throughout all history, then it seems hard not to arrive at seven."[60]

<u>NAMES AND CHARACTERISTICS OF THE DISPENSATIONS</u>

The Dispensation of Innocency (Genesis 1:26-3:24)

1. <u>The Governing Principle</u>. While few like this designation for the first dispensation, which extends from humanity's creation to its fall, it is generally agreed nevertheless, that it is probably the best single word and therefore it persists. The objection arises because dispensations are normally named on the basis of the main governmental principle introduced in them. In this instance, it is not that Adam was created innocent that forms the basis for his responsibility before God, but that he was created in a state of unconfirmed holiness.

It was this state of holiness which allowed Adam to have direct communication with God. This state of holiness was "unconfirmed," however, meaning that it was not permanent. Humankind was originally created with a favorable disposition toward God, but it is clear that faced with an alternative choice, it was in its power to forfeit this state and standing.

2. <u>The New Revelation</u>. The revelation given to Adam and Eve setting forth their responsibility in obedience and forming the basis for the governmental relationship is stated in Genesis 1:28-29; 2:15-17, 24. It was revealed that they were to engage in continued maintenance of the garden and to abstain from eating the fruit of the tree of the knowledge of good and evil.

3. <u>The Responsibility</u>. In this economy, the responsibility placed upon humankind was to obey God's commands about maintaining (the garden) and ab-

staining (from eating the fruit of the tree of the knowledge of good and evil) on the basis of an unconfirmed holiness.

a. The Test. As stated previously, the test is essentially the same as the responsibility. In this instance, the test concerned the question of whether or not humankind would obey God by not eating the fruit of the forbidden tree.

b. The Failure. Satan, we are told, enters the garden in the form of a Serpent and offers an alternative to obedience to the commands of God. Rather than continue in obedience under the governmental relationship of holiness or freedom established by God, humankind disobeys by eating the fruit.

c. The Judgment. The judgments were multiple. Humankind experienced spiritual death in that it was separated from God as its favorable disposition toward Him was replaced with enmity (Gen. 2:16-17: Rom. 8:7). In addition to spiritual death, humankind was now subject to disease and physical death (Gen. 3:19). The ground was cursed so that humankind would forever toil to sustain his existence (Gen. 3:17-19). The woman was told that she would bear children in pain and be ruled by her husband (Gen. 3:16). It was here, however, that the first indication was given of a coming Redeemer (Gen. 3:15).

The Dispensation of Conscience (Genesis 4:1-7:24)

1. The Governing Principle. The principal way in which God governed in the period between the fall of humanity and Noah, was through the dictates of the conscience. It is evident from Paul's epistle to the Romans (2:14-15) that even the Gentiles could know instinctively the things of the Law and have an awareness of good and evil through the promptings of the conscience.

2. The New Revelation. The new revelation given in this period appears to be that humankind was to approach God on the basis of blood sacrifice (Gen. 3:21; 4:4; Heb. 11:4). This is the implication of Genesis 4:3-7.

3. The Responsibility. It was the responsibility of humankind during this dispensation to respond to God on the basis of the dictates of conscience. The manifestation of this was apparently to be in the bringing of the blood sacrifice as prescribed by God.

a. The Test. The test, as always, involved obedience. Would humankind obey God by living up to the dictates of conscience exemplified by offering the blood sacrifice?

b. The Failure. Cain refused to offer the appropriate sacrifice and when God rejected it, Cain murdered his brother Abel. Failure to yield to God's governmental authority progressed to the point that the wickedness of the race was so great upon the earth that "...every intent of the thoughts of his heart was only evil continually" (Gen. 6:5).

c. The Judgment. The judgment came in the form of a worldwide flood. All living things, save Noah and his family, were destroyed. It should be noted that in addition to Noah, Abel and Enoch may be cited as those who pleased God by living in accord with His governmental arrangement. One of Darby's recurring themes is the existence in every dispensation of a faithful remnant.

The Dispensation of Human Government (Genesis 8:1-11:26)

1. The Governing Principle. In this dispensation, extending from the flood to the call of Abraham, a new principle of government is introduced *in addition to,* but not to replace, the principle of conscience. After Noah and his family left the ark, God instituted capital punishment for those who committed murder (Gen. 9:5-7). In the nature·of it, capital punishment presupposes a human governmental authority to carry it out (cf. Romans 13:1-7). This human government with its authority to administer capital punishment, then, constituted the new governing principle in the third dispensation.

2. The New Revelation. In Genesis 9:1-17, God instructed humankind to multiply and populate the earth. Animals, Adam and Eve are told, will now fear them and serve as a source of food. The rainbow is placed in the sky as a sign that the earth will never again be destroyed by flood, and the execution of murderers is required.

3. The Responsibility. Humankind was still under obligation to obey the dictates of conscience in addition to obeying God on the basis of human government. In essence, the distinctive element in this dispensation was the responsibility of individuals to govern effectively on the basis of God's revelation to them.

a. The Test. Would people obey God by following the dictates of conscience and would they govern on the basis of divinely revealed principles?

b. The Failure. At the outset, Noah became drunk and incapable of ruling effectively. And in disobedience to God's command to populate the earth, people clung together and conceived the plan to build a city with a tower reaching into the heavens (Gen. 11:1-6).

c. The Judgment. At this time, all the inhabitants of earth spoke the same language. This enabled those who worked on the city and tower to work together in harmony. In order to frustrate this plan which was in obvious disregard of God's command to scatter and populate the earth, He brought confusion of languages upon the people. This resulted in the accomplishment of God's plan to fill the earth. Unfortunately, because of humankind's sin, it also resulted in the establishment of nations with an enmity among many which persists to the present.

The Dispensation of Promise (Genesis 11:27-Exodus 18)

1. The Governing Principle. In the fourth dispensation extending from the call of Abraham to the giving of the Law at Sinai, the governing principles of conscience and human government were still operative. But due to humankind's failure, to these was added the new governing factor of promise (see Hebrews 6:15; 11:8-30). Whereas in the past, all people had been related directly to the rule of God, now a single man to head a single family or nation, was called out with promise to represent all humankind.

2. The New Revelation. The new revelation given to Abraham and his descendants is recorded in Genesis 12:2-3; 13:14-17; 15; 17:1-22 and 22:16-18. Here God promises to bless Abraham by making his name great and by giving him innumerable descendants. He promises also to make Abraham the father of many nations and to give him as his everlasting possession, the land of Canaan. There are blessings also for those who bless Abraham's descendants and curses for those who curse his descendants.

3. The Responsibility. In this dispensation, in addition to living up to the dictates of conscience, and obeying God on the basis of human government, Abraham and his descendants were to believe God on the basis of His promises to them and to serve Him. The promised land and blessings were theirs as long as they abided in the land.

a. The Test. The test of obedience, was of course, would they abide in the land and would they believe and serve God?

b. The Failure. Failure was manifested in the fact that Abraham refused to believe God's promises of innumerable descendants and fathered a son by Hagar, his wife's servant. The failures to believe, trust, and serve God were frequent. The greatest failure, however, came when Jacob deserted the land of promise for Egypt, the land of grain, and failed to leave that land after the famine had ended.

c. The Judgment. The Israelites' sojourn in Egypt ended in slavery. And to this very day there is enmity between the sons of Ishmael (the Arabs) and the sons of Isaac (the Israelites).

The Dispensation of Law (Exodus 19:1-Acts 1:26)

1. The Governing Principle. A distinctively new principle of God's government was introduced during this dispensation which extended from Moses to the death of Christ. In addition to conscience, human government and promise, the children of Israel received the Law of Moses. This Law was to serve as God's means of administering His rule over Israel during this dispensation.

2. The New Revelation. This great code of some 613 commands (including the decalogue), revealed the will of God in all areas of life. Recorded in Exodus 20 through the end of Deuteronomy, this Mosaic legislation was unknown prior to the time of Moses.

3. The Responsibility. Put simply, Israel's responsibility was, in addition to obeying God on the basis of conscience, human government, and promise, to do all that the Law required (James 2:10).

a. The Test. Would Israel obey God on this basis? Would she keep all the commands of the Law?

b. The Failure. Israel failed throughout her history (Jer. 31:32; Ezek. 16). Her failure culminated in the rejection and crucifixion of the promised Messiah.

c. The Judgment. There were many judgments upon Israel as a result of these failures. The ten northern tribes of Israel were taken captive by the Assyrians, while the two southern tribes were held captive by the Babylonians. As a result of their rejection of Christ, the Israelites experienced worldwide dispersion (Matt. 23:37-39).

The Dispensation of Grace (Acts 2:1-Revelation 19:21)

1. The Governing Principle. The distinctive ruling principle of God during the sixth dispensation is the grace of God. This is in addition to the governing principles of conscience, human government, and promise (the nations of the earth are promised blessing if they bless Abraham's descendants). Paul makes it clear, however, that the governing principle of Law has ended (Rom. 6:14). It was through the incarnation of Christ that grace was brought to humankind in a way heretofore unknown. To be sure, the grace of God was operative in all of the previous dispensations, but these manifestations of grace pale by comparison to that displayed by the coming of Christ.

2. The New Revelation. This dispensation is the recipient of all that is said about the gospel of Christ in Acts and the Epistles. The church is revealed as the Body of which Christ is the Head. Jews and Gentiles alike are on an equal footing as they exercise faith in Christ to form this living organism which in turn is indwelt by the living Christ. The church is to carry out the Great Commission as well as the various commands to maintain moral and doctrinal purity within.

3. The Responsibility. Humankind is responsible in this dispensation to obey God on the basis of conscience, human government, promise and the gracious offer of the gift of righteousness made available through faith in Christ.

a. The Test. Will humankind obey God on the basis of conscience, human government, promise and grace? Will people exercise faith in Christ in the dispensation of grace?

b. The Failure. Unbelief will be widespread for the vast majority of Jews and Gentiles refuse the offer of the gift of righteousness. At the end of the present dispensation organized Christendom will have totally apostatized (Rev. 17). This last point bears a closer look as it is one of the dominant themes in Darby's writings and one for which he receives a great deal of criticism.[61]

Religious apostasy is mentioned five times in the New Testament. Two times the noun *apostasia* is used (Acts 21:21; II Thess. 2:3) and the verb *aphistemi* occurs three times (Luke 8:13; I Tim. 4:1; Heb. 3:12). In Acts 21:21 it is said of Paul that he is teaching the Jews to "abandon" Moses (for Christ). And Paul speaks in II Thessalonians 2:3 of *the* apostasy or "rebellion"[62] which is to come at a later time (inspired by Antichrist), before the day of the Lord. The three references in which the verb is used teach that there are (Luke 8:13) or will be (I Tim. 4:1) those who "become apostate" or "fall away"[63] from the living God (Heb. 3:12). Apostasy (compound of *apo*, "away," and *histemi*, "to stand") may be defined then as "The deliberate repudiation of belief once formerly held. An apostate is one who thus abandons Christianity."[64]

Of special interest in the II Thessalonians 2:3 passage is the use of the definite article with the noun *apostasia*. The articular construction serves to emphasize the noun by giving it particularity.[65] This distinguishes a certain period of apostasy as future and indicates that it is of such a distinctive nature that it can be designated *the* apostasy.

c. <u>The Judgment</u>. The second coming of Christ marks the end of this dispensation and is preceded by the seven year period of judgment--the Tribulation--upon the Christ rejectors who are still living at the end of this age. During this period of judgment, apostate Christendom will be destroyed (Rev. 17:16), divine judgment will be poured out upon the world (Rev. 6-19), and the final rebellion of the unsaved will be crushed (Rev. 19:17-21).

In general, dispensationalists outline end-time events as follows:

1). The rapture - At the end of the church age, just prior to commencement of the Tribulation period, Christ will return *for* the saints--His church. Believers who have died will rise first (this is the first resurrection or resurrection of the just), and those who are still alive will be changed in the twinkling of an eye. The church, the Bride of Christ, will meet Christ in the air and return with Him to heaven where the saints will appear before the judgment seat of Christ and the marriage supper of the Lamb will take place.

2). The Tribulation - Following the rapture or translation of the saints, the seven-year period[66] (Dan. 9:24-27) of judgment upon the nations (Rev. 6:15-16; 11:18) and persecution of Israel (Matt. 24:9, 22; Rev. 12:17) known as the Tribulation begins.

3). The Second Coming - At the conclusion of the Tribulation, Christ will return *with* His saints and fight the war to end all wars, the battle of Armageddon. At that time, Satan will be bound and consigned to the bottomless pit for the duration of the millennium, while the beast and false prophet will be cast into the lake of fire.

4). The Millennium - After Satan's forces have been neutralized, Israel will be regathered, judged, and restored to the land promised to Abraham, Isaac, and Jacob. Those whose faith cost them their lives during the Tribulation are raised to share in the millennium. The millennium consists of a thousand years of peace and righteousness on earth during which time the promises to Israel find their fulfillment.

5). The Postmillennial Events - At the conclusion of the thousand years, Satan is released from the pit, tries one last revolt in company with his followers, but is quickly defeated and cast into the lake of fire. The unbelieving dead are then raised (this is the second resurrection or resurrection of the unjust) to face the great white throne judgment. Finally, the new heaven and earth are created and the eternal state begins (Rev. 21).

The Dispensation of the Kingdom (Revelation 20:1-6)

1. <u>The Governing Principle</u>. The seventh and final dispensation will begin

after Christ's Second Coming, and end prior to Satan's release and final revolt. Since the promises to Israel will be fulfilled during this time, and Christ will reign personally, we may assume that only conscience as a governing principle from the past still applies. The primary principle of rule, however, will be the personal, righteous reign of Christ Himself from the throne of David.

2. The New Revelation. In many passages of both the Old and New Testaments, we are told that Christ the Messiah will restore the direct theocratic rule of God forfeited by humanity's fall. An ideal world order will emerge, in which peace and righteousness abound. There will be unprecedented harmony and fertility upon the earth.

3. The Responsibility. Simply put, humankind's responsibility will be to obey the King and His laws on the basis of conscience and His righteous rule.

a. The Test. The question as always is, will humankind conform to the will of God? Will humankind obey the King on the basis of conscience and His righteous rule?

b. The Failure. During the millennium, there will be those who will openly rebel against the King (Isa. 11:3-4; 29:20-21; Jer. 31:19-30). At the end of the millennium, a released Satan will be able to muster a fighting force of considerable size to attack the seat of government (Rev. 20:7-9).

c. The Judgment. Those who rebel during the millennium will be executed (Isa. 11:3-4; 29:20-21; Jer. 31:29-30). Those who join Satan in his rebellion at the close of the millennium will be destroyed by fire while the leader himself will be cast into the lake of fire (Rev. 20:9-10).

Eschatology of Dispensationalism

Ryrie identifies five of what he calls the salient features of dispensational eschatology: 1. The Hermeneutical principle of literal interpretation; 2. Fulfillment of Old Testament prophecies; 3. Distinction between Israel and the church; 4. Pretribulation rapture; and 5. The millennial kingdom.

THE HERMENEUTICAL PRINCIPLE OF LITERAL INTERPRETATION

The hermeneutical principle of literal interpretation is fundamental in dispensational theology including the doctrine of last things. Ryrie maintains that this principle, consistently applied, "is at the heart of dispensational eschatology." In proof of this position, Ryrie points to the covenant (also termed "historic") premillennialism of Ladd, in which literalism is abandoned at points throughout the Gospels with the result that no earthly kingdom is in view for Israel in this portion of Scripture.[67]

THE LITERAL FULFILLMENT OF OLD TESTAMENT PROPHECIES

This principle of literal interpretation, according to Ryrie, leads to the second feature of dispensational premillennialism--a literal fulfillment of the prophecies of the Old Testament. This he identifies as the "basic tenet of premillennial eschatology." If these Old Testament prophecies concerning Israel are to be fulfilled literally, says Ryrie, then the only time remaining for their fulfillment is in the future millennial kingdom. It is a basic point of dispensational eschatology that the church in no way participates in the fulfillment of the promises to Israel, but rather that the time of fulfillment is during the earthly reign of Christ and constitutes one of the chief features of His kingdom.[68]

THE DISTINCTION BETWEEN ISRAEL AND THE CHURCH

The understanding of the how and when of the fulfillment of Old Testament prophecies leads naturally to a third feature, the recognition of a distinction between Israel and the church, which as we saw above is a vital part of the dispensational scheme. Dispensationalism, says Ryrie, is the only theological system which completely excludes the church from the fulfillment of prophecies concerning Israel. "The understanding of the how and when of the fulfillment of Israel's prophecies," he concludes, "is in direct proportion to one's clarity of distinction between Israel and the Church."[69]

THE DOCTRINE OF THE RAPTURE

A fourth feature of dispensational eschatology, which grows out of the distinction between Israel and the church, is the belief that the church will be raptured, or caught up out of the world to meet Christ in the air.[70] The word "rapture" is the English translation of the Latin word *rapio*, meaning to "seize" or to "snatch."[71] The corresponding Greek verb *harpadzo* in I Thessalonians 4:17, is translated to "snatch" or to "take away."[72] The time of this event is believed by most, but not all dispensationalists, to occur just prior to that period known as the Tribulation.

The issue here is the relation of the rapture to the Tribulation. As indicated above, most dispensationalists place the rapture before the Tribulation and are thus called pre-tribulationists. It is this pretribulationism that is identified by Ryrie as the fourth salient feature of dispensational eschatology. Among earlier writers, this doctrine was related to the emphasis on the imminency of the return of the Lord, more recently, however, it's connection has been with the concept of the church's distinctive nature.[73] While Ryrie contends that pretribulationism has become a regular feature of dispensational eschatology, he is quick to point out that one's tribulational views do not determine whether premillennialism stands or falls.[74]

THE MILLENNIAL KINGDOM

The fifth and final feature of dispensational eschatology, is the millennial reign of Christ on earth. Concerning the meaning of the term and the various interpretations of the millennial concept, Henry C. Thiessen says,

The word comes from the Latin *mille* and *annus*, meaning a thousand years. The doctrine of the Millennium is often spoken of as "Chiliasm" (fr. *chilioi*, a thousand). It holds that Christ will reign over an earthly kingdom for a thousand years. It implies that Christ will come back before the Millennium. This is known as the doctrine of Premillennialism. Those who hold that Christ will come back "after" a period of universal peace and righteousness, hold the doctrine of Postmillennialism. Those who deny that there will be a Millennium [actually they teach that Christ returns after a spiritual or heavenly rather than literal millennium] hold what is known as the doctrine of Amillennialism. The word "millennium" does not occur in the Bible, but the thousand years are mentioned six times in Rev. 20:2-7.[75]

Ryrie explains further that,

The millennium is the period of a thousand years of the visible, earthly reign of the Lord Jesus Christ, who, after His return from heaven, will fulfill during that period the promises contained in the Abrahamic, Davidic, and new covenants to Israel, will bring the whole world to a knowledge of God, and will lift the curse from the whole creation.[76]

This doctrine of the earthly, millennial kingdom of Christ is an integral part of the dispensationalist's entire theological system. It is not merely an addendum, says Ryrie, as is the case in nondispensational systems.[77] These then are the salient features or chief characteristics of dispensational eschatology. With this look at normative dispensationalism in mind, we now pass on to an examination of Darby's dispensational concepts.

Endnotes

[1]W. W. Skeat, *An Etymological Dictionary of the English Language* (Oxford: Clarendon Press, 1946), p. 174.

[2]D. P. Simpson, compiler, *Cassell's New Compact Latin Dictionary* (New York: Dell Publishing Co., 1963), p. 70.

[3]William F. Arndt and F. Wilbur Gingrich, *A Greek-English Lexicon of the New Testament* (Chicago: The University of Chicago Press, 1957), p. 562.

[4]Henry George Liddell, and Robert Scott, *An Intermediate Greek-English Lexicon*, new ed., revised by Henry Stuart Jones (Oxford: The Clarendon Press, 1966), p. 528.

[5]Otto Michel, *"Oikonomia,"* *Theological Dictionary of the New Testament*, Vol. V, ed. by Gerhard Friedrich, trans. and ed. by Geoffrey W. Bromiley (Grand Rapids: Wm. B. Eerdmans Publishing Co., 1967), p. 151.

[6]William Graham Scroggie, *Ruling Lines of Progressive Revelation* (London: Marshall, Morgan and Scott, n.d.), p.p. 62-3.

[7]Arndt and Gingrich, p. 26-7.

[8]Roy L. Aldrich, "A New Look at Dispensationalism," *Bibliotheca Sacra* 120 (1963):42.

[9]Arnold D. Ehlert, *A Bibliographic History of Dispensationalism* (Grand Rapids: Baker Book House, 1965), p. 33.

[10]Charles Caldwell Ryrie, *Dispensationalism Today* (Chicago: Moody Press, 1965), p. 29.

[11]William Shakespeare, *Henry V*, III, ii, 40.

[12]C. I. Scofield, *The Scofield Reference Bible* (New York: Oxford University Press, 1945), p. 5.

[13]John Wick Bowman, "The Bible and Modern Religions: II. Dispensationalism," *Interpretation* 10 (April 1956), p. 174.

[14]Clarence E. Mason, "A Review of 'Dispensationalism' by John Wick Bowman," *Bibliotheca Sacra* 114 (April 1957):103.

[15]*The Oxford English Dictionary* (Oxford University Press, 1933), 3:481.

[16]Lewis Sperry Chafer, *Major Bible Themes*, rev. by John F. Walvoord (Grand Rapids: Zondervan Publishing House, 1974), p. 126.

[17]John F. Walvoord, "Dispensational Premillennialism," *Christianity Today* 15 (September 1958):12.

[18]Ryrie, p. 31. For one of the best recent definitions of the term "dispensationalism," one that attempts to encompass the essential factors of this system of theology, see note 53 following.

[19]For this and the following section see Ryrie, *Dispensationalism Today*, pp. 36-39; and Renald E. Showers, "A Presentation of Dispensational Theology," *Israel My Glory* 42 (April/May 1984):28-9.

[20]Ryrie, p. 38.

[21]Ibid, p. 39.

[22]Ibid.

[23]Ibid., p. 43.

[24]Augustine, *Letter CXXXVIII* (To Marcellinus), para. 5.

[25]Charles Hodge, *Systematic Theology*, 3 vols. (Grand Rapids. Wm. B. Eerdmans Publishing Co., 1946), 2:373-77.

[26]See the introduction to Ladd's, *The Blessed Hope* (Grand Rapids: Wm. B. Eerdmans Publishing Co., 1956), pp. 5-14.

[27]Ernest R. Sandeen, *The Roots of Fundamentalism* (Chicago: University of Chicago Press, 1970; reprint ed., Grand Rapids: Baker Book House, 1978), p. 38.

[28]Ryrie, pp. 43-47; see also Robert P. Lightner, "Theonomy and Dispensationalism: Part 1 of Theological Perspectives on Theonomy," *Bibliotheca Sacra* 143 (January-March 1986):34, and Renald E. Showers, *There Really Is a Difference: A Comparison of Covenant and Dispensational Theology* (Bellmawr, N.J.: The Friends of Israel Gospel Ministry, 1990), pp. 52-53. For dissenting opinions see Robert L. Saucy, "The Critical Issue between Dispensational and Non-Dispensational Systems," *Criswell Theological Review* 1 (Fall 1986):149-65, and Craig A. Blaising, "Development of Dispensationalism by Contemporary Dispensationalists: Part 2 of Developing Dispensationalism," *Bibliotheca Sacra* 145 (July-September 1988):254-80.

[29]Ryrie, pp. 44-5.

[30]Ibid., p. 132.

[31]Walvoord, p. 13.

[32]Lewis Sperry Chafer, "Dispensationalism," *Bibliotheca Sacra* 93 (October 1936):448.

[33]Clarence B. Bass, *Backgrounds to Dispensationalism* (Grand Rapids: Baker Book House, 1977), p. 127.

[34]For this and the following two sections, see Ryrie, pp. 133-40.

[35]Ibid., p. 136.

[36]Lewis Sperry Chafer, *Systematic Theology*, 8 vols. (Dallas: Dallas Seminary Press, 1975), 4:47-53.

[37]J. Dwight Pentecost, *Things to Come* (Grand Rapids: Zondervan Publishing House, 1958), p. 201. Pentecost summarizes Chafer's twenty-four contrasts on pp. 201-2.

[38]Ibid.

[39]John Nelson Darby, *Collected Writings of J. N. Darby*, 34 vols., ed. William Kelly, vol. 2: *Prophetic No. 1* (Sunbury, Pa.: Believers Bookshelf, n.d.), pp. 372-3.

[40]C. I. Scofield, *Rightly Dividing the Word of Truth* (Fincastle, Va.: Scripture Truth Book Co., 1896), pp. 5-6.

[41]Chafer, "Dispensationalism," p. 448.

[42]Pentecost, p. 546.

[43]Ryrie, pp. 45-6.

[44]Bernard Ramm, *Protestant Biblical Interpretation*, 3rd rev. ed. (Grand Rapids: Baker Book House, 1970), p. 119.

[45]Quoted by Ramm, p. 121.

[46]A. Berkeley Mickelsen, *Interpreting the Bible* (Grand Rapids: Wm. B. Eerdmans Publishing Co., 1963), p. 307.

[47]Chafer, "Dispensationalism," p. 446.

[48]Walvoord, "Dispensational Premillennialism," p. 12.

[49]Ryrie, pp. 97-8.

[50]Ibid., pp. 46-7.

[51]John F. Walvoord, *The Millennial Kingdom* (Grand Rapids: Zondervan Publishing House, 1959), p. 92.

[52]Ryrie, p. 46.

[53]Ibid., pp. 18-19. Lightner has come closest perhaps to formulating a definition of dispensationalism that incorporates all of the systems essential features. He says, "dispensationalism may be defined as that system of theology which interprets the Bible literally--according to normal usage--and places primary emphasis on the major biblical covenants--Abrahamic, Palestinian, Davidic, New--and sees the Bible as the unfolding of distinguishable economies in the outworking of God's major purpose to bring glory to Himself" (Robert P. Lightner, "Theological Perspectives on Theonomy," 143:33).

[54]Walvoord, *The Millennial Kingdom*, p. vii.

[55]Ryrie, p. 157.

[56]C. I. Scofield, *Rightly Dividing the Word of Truth*, pp. 12-16.

[57]Roy L. Aldrich, "An Apologetic for Dispensationalism," *Bibliotheca Sacra* 112 (1955):47.

[58]Daniel P. Fuller, *Gospel and Law: Contrast or Continuum?* (Grand Rapids: William B. Eerdmans Publishing Co., 1980), p. 121.

[59]Darby, vol. 22: *Doctrinal No. 6*, pp. 365-8. In this one reference alone, and there are many others like it, Darby devotes three and one half pages to the innocence of Adam, the period of conscience following, and the Noahic dispensation. Fuller's "dozen lines" charge is hardly accurate.

[60]Ryrie, p. 52.

[61]See Bass, p.127.

[62]Arndt and Gingrich, p. 97.

[63]Ibid., p. 126.

[64]Colin Brown, ed., *The New International Dictionary of New Testament Theology*, 3 vols. (Grand Rapids: Zondervan Publishing House, 1975), 1:51.

[65]H. E. Dana and Julius R. Mantey, *A Manual Grammar of the Greek New Testament* (Toronto, Ontario: The Macmillan Co., 1955), p. 141.

[66]In Darby's reckoning, it is only three and a half years (see p. 169).

[67]Ryrie, p. 158.

[68]Ibid., pp. 158-9.

[69]Ibid., p. 159.

[70]Ibid.

[71]Colin Brown, vol. 3, p. 601.

[72]Arndt and Gingrich, p. 108.

[73]Ryrie, pp. 159-60.

[74]Charles Caldwell Ryrie, *The Basis of the Premillennial Faith* (Neptune, N.J.: Loizeaux Brothers, 1953), p. 139.

[75]Henry C. Thiessen, *Introductory Lectures in Systematic Theology* (Grand Rapids: Wm. B. Eerdmans Publishing Co., 1949), p. 506.

[76]Ryrie, *Basis*, pp. 145-6.

[77]Ryrie, *Dispensationalism*, p. 160.

CHAPTER 3

DARBY'S PHILOSOPHY OF DISPENSATIONS

As with the discussion of normative dispensationalism in its present form in the previous chapter, we begin here with the meaning of the term *dispensation* as it is used in Darby's doctrine of dispensations. This is followed by discussions of Darby's view of the nature and character of dispensations--including the government of God as it relates to them--the intentions versus the counsels of God, and the purpose and end of all dispensations. Where appropriate, Scofield's concepts are compared and contrasted with Darby's.

Meaning and Origin of Term Dispensation[1]

ETYMOLOGY OF THE WORD

oikonomia

The word "economy," says Darby, "signifies the administration of a house; and, taken in an extended sense, it means any order of things that God has arranged, as when one says, animal economy, vegetable economy."[2] Here Darby uses the English word "economy" derived from the Greek noun *oikonomia,* rather than the Greek word itself. But it is clear elsewhere that it is *oikonomia* itself which is intended.[3]

Darby appears to reject the idea that *oikonomia* is derived from a combination of *oikos,* "house" and *nomos,* "rule, management, etc." He seems to prefer, rather, a combination of *oikos* and *nemo,* the latter having a classical rather than Biblical usage. His position here is that of Liddell and Scott.[4] "*Nemo,*" says Darby, "means to distribute, divide, feed, etc.; and thus in a house there was steward, and an economy--a man who arranged, distributed, provided for the family; and all the order which resulted from this was the *economy,* the *administration,* of the house." Thus for Darby, "when God had established a certain order of things upon the earth" (e.g., Eph. 1:10), it is correctly called an economy.[5]

Darby suggests a possible distinction between what he calls the "scriptural" and the "conventional" use of the word economy. Scripturally, he says, the word adheres closely to its original meaning of an "active administration." At this point he associates the word "dispensation" with the word "economy." The former, he says, is often used in the same way that the latter is (e.g., "God *dispenses* His favours") and has "the same etymological meaning." In its conventional usage, according to Darby, economy means "an order of things established by God: the

45

Jewish economy, the *present economy*, etc."[6] While this distinction with its resultant twofold definition is never clearly developed by Darby, it is nevertheless implemented by him and provides an important key to an understanding of his dispensational divisions, as will be shown.

As stated previously, the different forms of the word "dispensation" are used some twenty times in the New Testament. The masculine noun form *oikonomos* occurs ten times (Luke 12:42; 16:1, 3, 8; Rom. 16:23; I Cor. 4:1, 2; Gal. 4:2; Titus 1:7; and I Pet. 4:10). In his translation, Darby renders it consistently as "steward," even Romans 16:23 which is usually given a somewhat different meaning (e.g., "city treasurer," NASB). The feminine noun form *oikonomia* appears nine times (Luke 16:2, 3, 4; I Cor. 9:17; Eph. 1:10; 3:2, 9; Col. 1:25; and I Tim. 1:4) and is usually translated either "stewardship" or "administration." Darby translates it "stewardship" for all of the occurrences in Luke 16, and as "administration" in Ephesians 1:10 and 3:9. In all of these instances, the New American Standard Bible translates as Darby does. In I Corinthians 9:17 and Ephesians 3:2, however, the NASB substitutes "stewardship" for "administration." While the NASB renders *oikonomia* "stewardship" in Colossians 1:25 and "administration" in I Timothy 1:4, Darby translates both "dispensation." The verb *oikonomeo* in Luke 16:2, he translates in the sense "to be a steward" as does the NASB.[7]

aion

While affirming that the Adamic state was not a "dispensation, or *oikonomia*, or anything like it,"[8] Darby also insists that *oikonomia* nowhere signified period.[9] There is a word in Scripture, says Darby, which does signify distinct or divisional periods, "which Christians in general call dispensations, as when the principles on which they are carried on are distinct; namely, the word *aion* and *aiones*."[10] Darby cites Matthew 13 [vv. 39 and 49], "the end of *this* age" and Hebrews 9 [v.26] "at the consummation of the ages He has been manifested" as examples of passages in which *aion* "clearly signified…a period or course of time in which certain principles have sway on God's part." These "periods," he continues, are "very justly, in substance, translated dispensations…"[11] It is interesting to note that Scofield also gives "dispensation" as a viable translation of *aion* or "age" in Matthew 13.[12]

It is difficult to sort out the ways in which the words *oikonomia* and *aion* relate to each other and are yet different in Darby's assessment of them. It is clear that both can and do mean "dispensation." The word *oikonomia* can signify a dispensation, for example, as an earthly order of things established by God which He actively administers (usually through another party as Noah, Abraham, etc.). The word *aion*, on the other hand, can signify a dispensation when it relates to a divisional period of time during which distinct principles of God are in effect. The key for Darby in determining which word does or does not apply to any given period appears to be whether it is either the concept of an administration or God's governing principles that are in view. The one obvious difference for Darby is the fact that *oikonomia* has no divisional period or time aspect, while *aion* does.

It is apparent from what has been said before concerning contemporary dispensationalism, that Darby's distinctions in terms pose certain difficulties. While he is correct in emphasizing the stewardship and administrative aspect of *oikonomia* and the time-period element of *aion,* his limited application of the former and excessive application of the latter to what are called "dispensations" is not in keeping with the concept of dispensations as derived from the Biblical meaning of *oikonomia.* At the same time, his idea of a dispensation as that which arises from certain "principles" which hold sway in a particular period based on the word *aion,* seems contrived and unconvincing. That there are certain "principles" which govern and distinguish each dispensation, such as the ruling principle, the elements of responsibility, etc., is certainly true, but these grow out of the concept of *oikonomia* as a stewardship arrangement established by God and not from the meaning of *aion.* It bears repeating also, that while "age" (*aion*) and "dispensation" or "economy" (*oikonomia*) are not synonymous terms, it is obvious that a dispensation takes place within a period of time and that a particular economy and historical period of time may coincide.

<u>DEFINITIONS OF THE WORD</u>

Darby gives a number of what may be termed short definitions of the word "dispensation," none of which alone is adequate. However, if they are combined, perhaps an eclectic definition can be forged. As generally used, says Darby, the word dispensation "specif[ies] a certain state of things, established by the authority of God, during a given period."[13] It is according to this state or "order of things" established or arranged by God that "He governs individuals who are in a relationship with Himself."[14] This relationship with God, Darby defines in terms of responsibility. The importance of the word dispensation, he writes, is in the fact that "it is only a question of man and his position when God has placed him under responsibility."[15] Darby seems to equate in a number of places, "dispensations," "the ways of God," and "God's government of the world."[16]

We may formulate Darby's definition in its simplest form, then, in the following way: A dispensation, age, or economy, is any order, state or arrangement of things established by the authority of God, whereby He governs or administers the affairs of humankind during a given period of time on the basis of distinct principles which place humankind in a specific relation of responsibility to Him. These dispensations, also called the ways of God and His government of the world, are marked off and distinguished by the declaration of some new principle,[17] with an attendant new responsibility, which is distinctive to each.

It becomes apparent as one studies Darby's dispensations that his definition is not applied consistently. He has in effect, two classes of dispensations--a <u>general</u> and a <u>particular</u> classification. Darby clearly omits all that preceded Noah from his categorical discussions of dispensations. He explains that with Noah, "dispensations, properly speaking, begin," for prior to this time, there was no government of God upon the earth.[18] Yet Darby calls the period from Adam to Abraham the "patriarchal dispensation."[19] This seems to fit the general definition of a dispensation as "any order of things that God has arranged."[20]

Darby also makes a distinction between the Old and New Testament dispensations, suggesting that the twenty-four elders ("twice twelve") of Revelation 4:4, perhaps represent both the twelve patriarchs of the old dispensation and the twelve apostles of the new.[21] These are examples of what might be called Darby's general dispensations. They seem to fit what he terms the "conventional sense" of the word *economy* discussed above. These are states or orders of things established by God without specific reference to His government. It is this latter fact, the government of God, which sets an order of things apart as a particular or proper dispensation (e.g., Noah, Abraham, etc.) and it is these which usually appear in Darby's categorical discussions of dispensations.[22]

Scofield defines a dispensation in the *Reference Bible* as "a period of time during which man is tested in respect of obedience to some *specific* revelation of the will of God."[23] In another place, he defines it as "a period of time during which God deals in a particular way with man in respect to sin, and to man's responsibility."[24] While Darby and Scofield both emphasize the period of time and responsibility aspects in their definitions, Scofield places a greater emphasis upon the concept of obedience and the revelation of God's will. The greatest difference, however, concerns the concept of God's government of the earth so central to Darby's dispensational distinctions--a distinction which causes him to exclude certain periods of God's dealings with humankind in history from his dispensational system, and to vacillate on the dispensational status of the church. Scofield's definition of dispensation is consistently applied to all of Biblical history from the creation of Adam to the end of human history just prior to the new heaven and new earth.

Nature of Dispensations[25]

God's desire for humankind, says Darby, is that all should be in communion with Him in a new nature. The apostles teach us that as we become partakers of the divine nature, we tap into the source of eternal blessedness and all true knowledge. It is through this means that God both finds delight in us and brings us to a knowledge of Himself.[26]

The provisional basis upon which the partaking of the divine nature and consequently God's communication with us rests, Darby explains, is the incarnation of Christ. Good and evil alike play an important part in the believer's instruction in grace, an instruction which causes the believer to apprehend and adequately esteem, in principle and desire if in no other way, the value and excellence of the divine provision made possible in Christ. And how is it that we learn the value, excellence, and divine provision of the incarnate Lord? Darby writes:

> This...we have to learn in its details, in the various dispensations which led to or have followed the revelation of the incarnate Son in whom all the fulness was pleased to dwell....The detail of the history connected with these dispensations brings out many most interesting displays, both of the principles and patience of God's dealing with the evil and failure of man; and of the workings by which He formed faith on His own thus developed perfections. But the dispensations themselves all declare some leading *principle* or interference of God [*new revelation*], some *condition* in which He has placed man [*governing principle*] principles which in themselves are everlastingly sanctioned of God, but in the course of those dispensa-

tions placed *responsibility* in the hands of man for the display and discovery of what he was [*test*], and the bringing in their infallible establishment in Him to whom the *glory* of them all rightly belonged... in every instance, there was total and immediate *failure* as regarded man, however the patience of God might tolerate and carry on by grace the dispensation in which man has thus failed in the outset; and further, that there is no instance of the restoration of a dispensation afforded us, though there might be partial revivals of it through faith.[27]

In order for the character of God, what He is in essence, to find its unfolding in humankind's state and a knowledge of it to become known in the heart, says Darby, it is necessary for the individual to "pass through the different phases which furnish occasion for God to unfold Himself thus in grace."[28]

In another place, Darby outlines "the uniform method of God's dealings" as follows: First there is a "strong *manifestation of divine glory.*" Next comes "a *declension* from the practical faith of that glory" (disobedience in the face of certain responsibility is inferred). This is followed by a *testimony* so that those who will pay heed (a faithful remnant) may escape the *judgment* pronounced upon humanity's failure.[29]

Scofield says of the nature of dispensations, whoever reads the Bible with attentiveness, realizes that in it one may trace the "gradual unfolding of Divine truth and purpose." This understanding leads to the conclusion that there is "a beautiful system" involved in this gradual unfolding. "The past," he says, "is seen to fall into periods marked off by distinct limits, and distinguishable period from period by something peculiar to each. Thus it comes to be understood that there is the **Doctrine of the Ages**, of Dispensations, in the Bible."[30]

The nature and substance of this system, Scofield sets forth as follows:

> The Scriptures divide time (by which is meant the entire period from the creation of Adam to the "new heaven and a new earth" of Rev. 21:1) into seven unequal periods, usually called "Dispensations" (Eph. 3:2), although these periods are also called "ages" (Eph. 2:7) and "days"--as, "day of the Lord," etc.
> These periods are marked off in Scripture by some change in God's method of dealing with mankind, or a portion of mankind, in respect of the two questions of sin, and of man's responsibility. Each of the dispensations may be regarded as a new test of the natural man, and each ends in judgment--marking his utter failure in every dispensation.[31]

It is clear that Darby and Scofield share a number of points in common. Both men see the dispensations as a system which serves as a vehicle for the revelation of divine truth and God's purpose for humankind. They both view a dispensation as a period of time during which God institutes some specific method of dealing with humankind. They both see humankind as placed under certain responsibility in each dispensation based upon this governing relationship of God with them. In every instance, humankind fails the test, fails to live up to this responsibility and therefore is judged by God. As we shall see, however, major points of difference between Darby and Scofield become evident when these dispensational elements are applied to the various dispensations.

Characteristics of Dispensations

PRIMARY CHARACTERISTICS

By far the most important characteristic of the dispensations in Darby's system is the government of God or ruling principle in each. In the absence of government, there is no dispensational arrangement in the particular sense. The responsibility of humankind also plays a major role in each of the successive dispensations. While it may be inferred that a distinct revelation is necessary to implement the new governing relationship and to set forth the resultant responsibility, Darby nevertheless says little about it. Scofield, on the other hand, includes it in his definition of dispensations.[32]

The Government of God

Due to its importance, a rather full treatment of God's governmental relationship with humankind as set forth by Darby is in order here. It will be amplified further throughout our examination of Darby's dispensational theology and particularly in the discussions of the individual dispensations.

1. Pre-Noahic State. Prior to the flood, says Darby, though not left without witness or testimony (e.g., Abel, Enoch, et al.), humankind was otherwise left to itself--a fallen creature before God. Before the flood, there were no "dispensational dealings," or "institutions," or "special ways," or "public dealings" of God with His creatures. After the flood, a new world cleansed of its pollution through the judgment of God began. God commenced to deal with humanity in this new world--the world that exists now--by the establishment of government upon the earth, first under Noah's leadership.[33]

2. Noah. In this new world, says Darby, there are two great principles: *rule* placed in humankind's hands and *separation from the world by God's call*.[34] The first of these principles, rule in humankind's hands, he explains, is easily corrupted, "and men may shew themselves in this, and in everything else, unfaithful in maintaining the glory of God..." It was this principle which was first established with Noah. On the basis of Genesis 9:6, "Whoever sheds man's blood, by man his blood shall be shed...," human or self-government was placed in the hands of humankind by virtue of the fact that God's authority over life had been entrusted to it. Failure soon came, however, when Noah got drunk and proved himself incapable of governing.[35]

3. Abraham. After Noah's failure, the principle of human government was replaced by the principle of "*separation from the world* by the call of God," or the principle of calling and election. Abraham was called out by God and placed in a new relationship with Him on the basis of promise. Because this dispensation was placed beyond the effects of human responsibility, God could institute unconditional promises. Thus God reveals Himself to Abraham, the father of the

faithful, as the God of promise who calls him out to separate a people to Himself.[36]

Concerning the continuation and future implications of these principles of government and calling, Darby writes:

> The existence of this principle of the call of God has been developed, since the time of Abraham, under various forms; but God has constantly maintained the principle. In the history of the government of the world from that time there have been many changes of the greatest importance, in which the government of God has been displayed; and the truth of it will yet be honoured by the results which shall spring from them in the latter day. These are the subjects of the Old Testament prophecies; as the precious subjects of the New are the faithfulness of God to His call, as respects His ancient people, and the manifestation of this call in a new form, which leads the church into the knowledge and enjoyment of heavenly things--things plainly revealed by the holy Spirit which has been given to it.[37]

The principle of government can also be seen as the "principle of judgment and daily retribution" as it forms a constituent part of the new world under Noah, while the "principle of grace, holiness, and the supremacy of God" may be identified with the new order of things under Abraham termed the principle of calling.[38]

4. Israel. On the same basis of election, Abraham's descendants--the nation Israel--become the objects of God's earthly care. Not only are they the recipients of the promises made to Abraham, but the two principles of government and calling are united in them. "Israel was the called, separated people--separated indeed only to earthly blessings, and to enjoy the promise;" explains Darby, "but, at the same time, to be subject to the exercise of the government of God according to the law."[39]

Successively, under the Law, under the priesthood and under the kings, Israel failed, says Darby. As a consequence of her failure, he continues,

> ...Israel...ceased thenceforward to be capable of manifesting the principle of the government of God, because God in Israel acted in righteousness; and unrighteous Israel could no longer be the depository of the power of God. God, then, quitted His terrestrial throne in Israel. Notwithstanding this, as to the earthly calling, Israel continued to be the called people: "for the gifts and calling of God are without repentance." As to government, God transports it where He will; and it went to the Gentiles. There are, indeed, the called from among the nations (namely, the church), but it is for the heavens they are called. The calling of God for the earth is never transferred to the nations; it remains with the Jews.[40]

5. Gentiles. Upon the failure of Israel and the transfer of the government of God to the Gentiles, with Nebuchadnezzar as their head, a new order of things began. Responsibility for the government of the world was placed in the hands of the Babylonian king and as in all other dispensations was met with failure. Neb-

uchadnezzar set up a golden image, persecuted those faithful to God and was made like a beast as judgment for his pride.[41]

Darby's concept of government or God's rule becomes somewhat difficult to decipher after Nebuchadnezzar, but in general he speaks of the continuation of what he calls the "general government of God," until the millennial kingdom begins. This is in contrast to the "earthly," "direct," or "manifested" government of God which Israel was under and which the millennial period will experience at the close of the present dispensation.[42] The next point for consideration is a closer look at the relationship between these two types of government and the relationship of the present dispensation to them.[43]

6. Spirit/Christian. In his synopsis of I Peter 2, Darby discusses the relationship of the individual Christian in this present age or dispensation to the government of God. The believers to whom Peter wrote were suffering and these sufferings, we are told by Darby, are explained by Peter on the basis of the principles of the divine government. This suffering, whether for righteousness' sake or for Christ's name, is permitted by God in the Christian's walk in this world.[44] In the one suffering, it is a glory which allows him to share in the sufferings of Christ.[45]

The course, then, of the Christian's walk in this world, Darby asserts, is marked out. For the sake of the Lord, he is subject to human ordinances and institutions. In order to avoid all reproach, he gives honor to all individuals, whether good or bad. He is to be submissive to his masters, and if he must suffer, he suffers patiently as Christ did at the hands of evil people for our sakes. Likewise wives are to be subject to their husbands, husbands are to exhibit an affection for their wives, and both relationships are to be governed by faithfulness to God and Christian knowledge. Finally, all are to follow that which is good "by having the tongue governed by the fear of the Lord, by avoiding evil and seeking peace" that they might quietly "enjoy the present life under the eye of God."[46]

This, says Darby, "is the government of God, the principle on which He superintends the course of this world."[47] It is not, however, the "direct and immediate government" in which all wrong is prevented. Evil's power is still active in the world, as is indicated by the hostility of those under its influence toward believers. But when will the direct and immediate government of God be established? At Christ's appearing, when He returns in judgment. Then will come the time of the manifestation of the principles of God's government.[48] "It is at that period," explains Darby, "that the ways of God in government--of which the Jews were the earthly centre--shall be fully manifested." It is also at that time that the crown of glory will be presented to the faithful.[49]

It becomes evident in Darby's concept of government, that there is a distinction between the "direct," or "immediate," or "manifested" government of God and His "general" government of the world. Israel had experienced and the millennium will yet come under the former, while we are now living under the latter. Sin, says Darby, brought everything into disorder so that "we are not under the *manifested* government of God as Israel was..."[50] This form of government was set aside in the days of Nebuchadnezzar (and those of Saul to some extent), but all traces of it were eliminated when its sovereign the Messiah was rejected, and its seat Jerusalem was destroyed.[51] The consequence of this for Israel was great. Darby believes that,

> The relations of an earthly people with God, on the ground of man's responsibility, were ended. The general government of God took the place of the former; a government always the same in principle...And, until the time of judgment, the wicked will persecute the righteous, and the righteous must have patience. With regard to the nation, those relations only subsisted till the destruction of Jerusalem; the unbelieving hopes of the Jews, as a nation, were judicially overthrown.[52]

In Darby's elaborate outline of God's governmental affairs, it is never quite clear how the present dispensation, what he elsewhere calls the dispensation of the Spirit,[53] is related to that government. This is due no doubt to the fact that he views the present church age as entirely parenthetical in God's earthly dealings. According to Darby, the church is based upon the failure of all that went before-- culminating in the rejection of Christ by the Jews and Gentiles alike--and thus it only "fills up the gap during the power of the Gentiles" and the setting aside of Israel.[54] Darby admits only with reservation that a dispensation, as the word is defined in the particular sense, exists at this time (all of which will be discussed in greater detail in the following chapter). The basis for the idea that the present dispensation is both parenthetical and thus above all dispensations and yet somehow constitutes a dispensation, is Darby's concept of the twofold nature of the church.

The true church, composed of all believers from Pentecost to the rapture, is heavenly in character, according to Darby, and has nothing to do with the dispensations. The professing church, organized Christendom, on the other hand, may be viewed as a dispensation because it is earthly in character and has indeed failed in its responsibilities. As we have seen, the former is related to God's general government of the world in the sense that it is subjected to suffering at the hands of evil men for righteousness' sake. At the same time, to a certain extent the church is under the principle of the calling of God for He is calling out a people from among the nations for His own name (this, in Darby's estimation, is a *heavenly* calling whereas Israel is always and only the object of God's *earthly* call).

How that which is the dispensation itself, the professing church, is related to God's government is not stated. Since the general government of God extends from Nebuchadnezzar to Christ's return, it is obvious that it at least falls under this form of God's rule. Beyond that, however, we can only infer from Darby's teachings that God's intention for the church as first established was that it should be governed under the presidency of the Holy Spirit. Darby believes that in this it has failed, for it preferred a manmade clerical system to the direct governing influence of the Holy Spirit.[55]

Darby does tell us that the Jews and Gentiles are subjects of God's earthly government "in different degrees."[56] However, the one who becomes a believer, is not governed when he is introduced into the church. Darby says rather that,

> He is taken as a rebellious lost sinner, a hater of God, a child of wrath, be he Jew or Gentile, and set in the same place as Christ. This is not gov-

ernment, it is grace. The Jews are the centre of God's immediate government, morally displayed according to His revealed will. The Gentiles are brought to recognize His power and sovereignty displayed in His dealings with them.[57]

Darby goes on to explain that the *object* of government is different for the Christian and the Jew. By it, the former is prepared for heaven, while for the latter, "it is to display God's righteousness on the earth..." The Christian, Darby explains, suffers for righteousness and reigns, but the Jew suffers for sin.[58]

7. Millennium. It is not until Christ returns and executes judgment, Darby maintains, that the direct government of God will be reestablished. The millennial kingdom, with Satan imprisoned and Christ enthroned, will bring a certain moral restitution of things to the heavens and earth. A rebuilt Jerusalem will serve as the capital of God's government of the earth.[59] And in those days under Christ's reign, says Darby, the principles of government and calling will once again be united.[60]

8. Eternal State. Following the millennium, righteousness will reign in the new heavens and new earth. It is with the commencement of the eternal state, according to Darby, that the government of God will end. The government "that has brought all things into order, will terminate, and unhindered blessing will flow from God, the kingdom being given up to God the Father."[61]

It is very clear that Scofield knows practically nothing of this elaborate governmental and ruling scheme of God as set forth by Darby. There is no period of human history, including that before the flood and the present age, in Scofield's system, which does not fall under God's dispensational dealings with humankind. Each new dispensation, according to Scofield, is marked at its beginning "by some new probation of man, as ...The age of innocency, for example, began with man under the probation of abstinence from the fruit of one tree..."[62] God's governmental relationship in each dispensation, in other words, is based on the institution of some new probationary arrangement which includes a test of obedience for those subject to it. Scofield's system is marked by a consistency, simplicity and clarity, regrettably absent from Darby's. This will become more apparent in our discussion of the individual dispensations in the chapter to follow.

The Responsibility of Humanity

The second primary characteristic of the dispensations, is Darby's concept of humankind's responsibility. It is a concept closely related to God's government of the earth. In the "dispensational display," according to Darby, individuals are placed under responsibility in their relationship with God. Concerning "the field of responsibility," Darby explains that,

> ...if God reveals Himself to Abraham as Almighty, Abraham is to live and walk in the power of that name. And so of the promises given to him. Israel is to dwell in the land as the redeemed people of the Lord--their affections, ways, responsibility, and happiness flowing from what God was to them as having placed them there. So to us--the presence of the Holy

Ghost Himself being the great distinguishing fact, with the knowledge He affords. Because all this is what faith ought to act upon, and the life which we live in the flesh we live by faith, for the just shall live by faith.[63]

Darby points out that this responsibility is cumulative in nature, and that we actually inherit the sin of those in previous dispensations who depart from God "when it is a question of His government with respect to a dispensation."[64]

The question of humankind's sin in its departure from the prescribed responsibility in any given dispensation, says Darby, relates directly to certain consequences under God's government--namely, judgment.[65] The existence or duration of an economy, in other words, is directly dependent upon humankind's faithfulness in observing the conditions of the covenant governing that dispensation.[66] God's government, then, is clearly not exercised independently of humankind's responsibility.[67]

In his concept of responsibility, again Darby's analysis takes a strange turn when he reaches the present dispensation. In his view, the phrase "the ends of the ages have come" in I Corinthians 10:11 (NASB and Darby's translation), signifies that "the world now is not under any dispensation but the whole course of God's dealings with it are over until He comes to judgment."[68] Thus, from Adam to Christ, humankind was under responsibility, but that responsibility ended with the cross. He gives the following as the outline of history as he sees it:

> ...up to the flood no dealings [no dispensations] of God, but a testimony in Enoch. We see a man turned out of paradise, and presently God comes in by a solemn act, and puts that world all aside. Then after the flood we see various ways [dispensations] of God with the world. He begins by putting it under Noah. He gave promises to Abraham, then law raising the question of righteousness, which promise did not. Law was brought in to test flesh, and see whether righteousness could be got from man for God. Then God sent prophets...then...[His] Son [who was killed]...and then, so far as responsibility went, God was turned out of the world. Then comes the cross, and atonement for sin, and a foundation for a new state of things altogether, and that was the completion of the ages. God is not now dealing with man to try if he is lost or not.[69]

In every possible way, affirms Darby, humankind from creation to the cross had been put to the test. But now as far as individuals are concerned (not as far as God's government is concerned), all this progress of development is finished, for there has been nothing but failure, culminating in the rejection of Christ. God is now dealing with humankind on the basis of grace.[70] "Christ rejected," says Darby, "the history of responsibility is over and we come in in grace as already lost."[71] This state of affairs without the intervention of Christ, goes on "from the sowing of the seed until the harvest [the return of Christ]."[72]

Darby maintains that the consequence of this termination of the first Adam's history with the rejection of Christ, is that morally, the world came to an end and was judged.[73] The cross proves not only that humankind is a sinner, he says, for this is manifested with the fall, but that in itself, it is irreclaimable. This Darby gets from Hebrews 9:26, "'Now once in the end of the world' (literally 'in the end [or consummation] of the ages,' those ages in which God was testing man in responsibility as a reclaimable sinner)..." As Darby explains it, Christ came looking for fruit, but humankind had none to give Him. He offered a feast as an expression of God's grace to humankind, but it would not dine. Consequently, humankind's responsibility is over; its state of probation is finished.[74]

As is often the case with Darby, after he has signed the death certificate and delivered the eulogy, it becomes apparent that the cadaverous concept under discussion may yet rise from the ashes like the Phoenix. With respect to human responsibility, for example, Darby writes:

> Now, although the ground of man's responsibility is over in the sense of having wholly failed under it, when proved in every possible way, yet as to moral dealing with each individual, the responsibility is there to the full; and as an individual under moral dealing, a man has to go through the history of the process of responsibility and its failure; but he goes through it to bring out this, that he is lost already. He has to prove the truth of God's verdict that in man there is no good thing; and so the result of the principle of responsibility is for him to find out that he is lost, that the responsibility is over;...It is all over with the first man, and no mending him will do: he is lost and ruined; but Christ came to save the lost.[75]

Now Christ comes in as the second Man or second Adam to replace the first. On the cross, affirms Darby, Christ met responsibility completely. He met all the failure of humankind's eating the fruit of the tree of responsibility (i.e., tree of knowledge of good and evil). In fact, in Christ, both trees of Paradise are united and fulfilled, for He bore our sins and put sins away by His sacrifice and by becoming life in righteousness. In the atonement, responsibility is met and both the trees of Paradise find reconciliation.[76]

In the sense of responsibility as a characteristic of the dispensations, it is clear that Darby assigns a specific responsibility (actually he frequently names more than one) to the present dispensation--the church as earthly, organized Christendom--and thus the concept seems very much alive. Here below, this dispensation has a destiny as did the Jewish economy, he says, and from the standpoint of responsibility, "it is the purity and the faithfulness of the church, which are the basis on which this destiny rests." The church was to display unity and the glory of Christ in the Holy Spirit's power. In this it has totally failed, says Darby, having become corrupted and disorganized.[77]

In keeping with his concept of the dual nature of the church, Darby assigns a different responsibility to the church as heavenly, the Body of Christ composed of all true believers. Since righteousness has been established in Christ, he points out, the Christian's standing is not based upon responsibility as a child of the first Adam, but upon redemption as a child of God. As Darby explains, there are two trees in grace--one of life and one of responsibility. Under the Law, it was responsibility first, then life. Under grace, it is life first, then responsibility. Our responsibility individually now, which flows from our position as heirs of God and joint heirs with Christ, is to display this character before the world as Christ's epistles.[78]

With respect to the last dispensation, the millennium, Darby says almost nothing about responsibility. In Darby's view, in the absence of Satanic influence, temptation is eliminated (contra Isa. 11:3-4; 29:20-21; Jer. 31:29-30). Obedience to the King may be inferred as the responsibility, for Darby says, "It would be extraordinary in a dispensation for man not to be subject to trial and temptation in the ways of God. Those of the millennium are to be tempted like others. The consequence of it is the same--man falls."[79] According to Darby, however, this temptation and trial does not occur throughout the course of the thousand years, only at its conclusion when Satan is released.[80]

Again it is evident (and will become even more so in the next chapter) that Scofield makes few of the distinctions in the concept of responsibility that Darby does. Each of Scofield's seven dispensations--from Adam to the millennium--has its unique responsibility. And that responsibility is not merely appended as it is in Darby's Paradisaical state and the millennial dispensation, nor is it practically denied as it is under Abraham[81] in Darby's system. Neither does it live on a split level as in Darby's view of the present dispensation. The whole idea of responsibility somehow ending with the cross is completely foreign to Scofield. Here as with the concept of God's governmental dealings with humankind, Scofield applies the principle of dispensational characteristics more consistently and uniformly throughout his system.

One other point, the relationship between responsibility and salvation, warrants discussion before we leave this topic. Darby makes it clear that humankind's responsibility under any dispensation is distinct from its salvation under that dispensation. If the two are confounded, he says, the understanding of God's dealings with humankind becomes impossible, for either the security of the Lord's faithfulness, or humankind's responsibility in an economy is lost. By way of example, Darby explains that,

> Noah was responsible for the ordering of his house and family (we may say, then, the world) in holy government. The failure of this, though producing most important results, has nothing to do with Noah's salvation. In a word, if God deals in a process of government *here* for the manifestation of His character, this and the salvation of individuals, while that process is going on, are quite distinct; though the conduct of the saved may be guided and formed by the dispensation here below.[82]

It is the dispensation itself which is judged on the basis of responsibility, says Darby, while individuals are saved by grace.[83] If there is one thing that Darby makes perfectly clear, it is that salvation is always by grace in every dispensation, from beginning to end. "Grace from the beginning was, through the introduction of sin," he says, "the only means of remedy, and shall be to the end..."[84]

While Scofield, according to Ryrie, left himself open for some criticism in this latter respect, he is sure that were Scofield alive today he would probably phrase things differently.[85] At any rate, later dispensationalists like Chafer, are absolutely clear that salvation is always by grace.[86] Ryrie's position is concise and to the point. "The *basis* of salvation in every age," he says, "is the death of Christ; the *requirement* for salvation in every age is faith; the *object* of faith in every age is God; the *content* of faith changes in the various dispensations."[87]

The Revelation of God

Darby does not lay a great deal of emphasis upon the revelation necessary in each dispensation to effect the change in government with the resultant new responsibility under which humankind is placed. That he nevertheless recognizes the fact that it occurs and that it is important in the dispensational dealings of God with humankind, is evident. Darby affirms that,

> Every dispensation has its character, from the manner in which Christ is manifested and introduced in it; and its order from Him under whom it takes its rise as to ministration. God not yet known to the church in covenant, but the same God revealed as Almighty, was the dispensation to Abraham called out to trust in Him, and gave its character to the path in which he had to walk in hope.[88]

As stated previously, Scofield's definition of the word dispensation itself emphasizes that the dispensations are periods of time during which humankind faces testing in obedience on the basis of "some specific revelation of the will of God."[89]

SECONDARY CHARACTERISTICS

The Test

As is the case in contemporary dispensational theology, what might pass as the test in each dispensation in Darby's system, is essentially the same as the responsibility under which humankind is placed. "Every dispensation," says Darby, "has some special deposit, so to speak, entrusted to it, by which its fidelity is tried."[90] He maintains further that it would be an extraordinary thing, if in a dispensation, individuals were not subject to trial and temptation in God's ways.[91] That Darby would agree that the test in each dispensation is essentially a question of humankind's obedience in its responsibility under God's ruling principles is evident from the following:

> In different dispensations, God puts Himself in relation with men, on certain principles; He judges them according to those principles. If those who are found in this outward relationship are unfaithful to the principles of the dispensation, although God may long forbear, He puts an end to it, while at the same time preserving the faithful for Himself; this is what He has done as to the Jewish dispensation.[92]

The Failure

Every dispensation, Darby laments, has failed and will fail under Satan's power and unsustained by God's direct power.[93] This, he says, is the uniform account of Scriptures with regard to God's "public dealings, and man's conduct when God had instituted anything on earth--man's history."[94] And what is the cause of humankind's failure? It is part of the government of God to have us tested in responsibility. If under this responsibility we forget our dependence and weakness, we also forget that it is God's grace which strengthens and perfects us even in weakness. Inevitably individuals do forget and therefore they fall.[95]

After humankind has failed in each dispensation to fulfill his duty, God is long-suffering in that He does not immediately end the dispensation upon the first failure, but employs a multitude of means to call humanity back to its duty. An example of God's patience, says Darby, is seen in the non-covenanted Amorites, whose iniquity it is said, "*was not yet full*" (Gen. 15:13-16) and therefore Abraham's seed could not yet possess the promised land.[96] God's patience notwithstanding, failure is immediate in every instance upon the establishment of responsibility, says Darby, and always progresses until "there is no remedy."[97]

Darby maintains that once the dispensation has failed there is no restoration ever recorded in Scripture. As a result of grace and faith during God's long-suffering, revivals may occur, but never restorations. Any attempt to restore a fallen dispensation, he continues, not only shows ignorance of the principles of God's dealings,[98] but is actually sin.[99] In any case, when Satan's activity in a dispensation results in its destruction, it also results in its replacement with a better one.[100]

While humankind's failure is consistent throughout the successive dispensations, Darby is just as sure that these ways of God will all be made good in Christ. In Christ, God will be glorified even on the proven failure of humankind in each economy.[101] As the head and center of the glories which are His as man, the second Adam, Christ unites all the various ways and dispensations of God in Himself.[102] When these glories were initially tried in the first Adam's hands, his failure was proved. And in what way will all the dispensations be made good in Christ? Darby catalogs Christ's accomplishments on behalf of the dispensations as follows:

Adam as man, failed: the last Adam is true Head over all things. God is glorified in Him victorious over Satan in trial, as the first succumbed. Man in *Israel* is tried by the law given as a proving rule of life; hereafter the law will be written in their hearts, and the statutes of God kept by them. Priesthood was set up in man, and failed: Christ will present all saved to the end by His. Royalty in David's son failed, and the kingdom was broken up. It will be set up, never to fail, in Christ. Sovereign power in rule over the *Gentiles* and the world failed in Nebuchadnezzar who set idolatry up for unity of religion's sake, and consequently persecuted God's saints. It will be set up in Christ in perfectness, and in Him shall the Gentiles trust. The *assembly* [present dispensation] has been set up in its responsibility, that God might be glorified in it, and a glorious Christ fully known. It has failed in this; but when Christ comes, He will be glorified in His saints, and admired in all them that believe....But it is not the less true that the assembly has been set to glorify God and the Lord Jesus by the present power of the Holy Ghost, and that it has failed in its responsible place here below, and has taken a place in flesh, out of which it has been called; but the sure counsels of God will be accomplished in the assembly united to Christ in glory.[103]

The Judgment

The result of humankind's failure, according to Darby, is that "the professing mass (the body at large or their leaders)" experience God's judgment. The believers in each dispensation, however, remain secure and untouched. Furthermore, the saints are always adequately forewarned of impending judgments in order that they might "flee from the wrath to come."[104]

Darby and Scofield agree that humankind in each dispensation is tested and fails and therefore experiences the judgment of God. They differ, however, as we shall see, in their understanding of many of the details and content of these characteristics as they apply to the various dispensational arrangements. The question of consistency and clarity in the two men's systems has as great a bearing here as it does with regard to the principal characteristics of government, responsibility, and revelation.

Intentions Versus Counsels of God
in Dispensations

There is an important distinction which Darby makes in the outworking and success of God's purposes among humankind in the dispensations. A knowledge of this distinction enables the reader to understand what otherwise seems like double talk in many instances in Darby's writings. That distinction is between the intentions of God on the one hand, and the counsels of God on the other.[105] The former relates to the responsibility of humankind and the latter to the purposes of God.[106]

Darby explains that the confounding of God's intentions for a dispensation with His counsels with respect to the faithful in it, leads to serious error and misunderstanding. "These counsels can never fail in their effect," says Darby, "but the dispensation itself may pass away and come to an end..." We know for example, Darby continues, that the Levitical dispensation has ceased to exist, but the faithful of that dispensation have been saved according to God's counsels.[107]

Darby gives a full statement of the distinction between the intentions and counsels of God as they relate to the present church age which goes a long way to explain how it can be a dispensation on the one hand, but above all dispensations on the other; how it can be heavenly and succeed and yet earthly and fail, both at the same time. The intentions of God for this dispensation, Darby explains, were for the church to be a manifestation of the union of the Body of Christ on earth. The church, however, failed in this when it substituted a manmade clerical system for the priesthood of all believers under the presidency of the Holy Spirit. Thus with respect to the intentions of God, this dispensation of the church as an earthly thing (and dispensations relate only to the earthly realm) has failed and is in a state of ruin. The counsels of God on the other hand, can never fail and therefore the union of the Body of Christ--composed of all true believers who come out of apostate Christendom--with Himself, will take place in heaven, above all dispensations.[108]

Israel furnishes another example of this principle. God intended for Israel to manifest the principle of His government on the earth as He acted in righteousness in her. An unrighteous Israel failed, however, and could no longer serve as the depository of God's power. Consequently, the reins of government passed to the Gentile nations.[109] But has God rejected His people for good? On the basis of His counsels, says Darby, He cannot. He explains, "For that which God has once chosen and called He never casts off. He does not repent of His counsels, nor of the call which gives them effect."[110]

Scofield makes no such distinction between the intentions and the counsels of God in the various economies. In Scofield's system, God gives a specific revelation of His will in each dispensation which sets forth the governing relationship in it. In every case, except the millennium (where it may be a rebellion of the minority), the majority fail the test of responsibility and obedience. Nevertheless, there are the few faithful in every dispensation who find grace in the eyes of the Lord and therefore fulfill His purposes. Up to this point, Scofield and Darby are in essential agreement, but hereafter they take somewhat different paths.

In the case of the church age or dispensation of grace, for example, Scofield sees the faithful and unfaithful alike as constituting the participants in this economy. That the unfaithful Gentiles and apostate church or Christendom will experience the judgment of God while the faithful among the Jews and Gentiles together enter into a unique relationship with Christ, is certainly Scofield's position.[111] But the view that the faithful (the church as the Body of Christ composed of true believers) are somehow lifted above this dispensation and reckoned as the end result of His counsels while the unfaithful are the end result of failed intentions, is not part of Scofield's philosophy of dispensations.

Purpose of Dispensations

Darby seems to assign a twofold purpose for the dispensational display of God. In the first place, the dispensations themselves all serve to unfold the character of God so that the conscience of humankind may take knowledge of that which God is. In order for this to be accomplished, says Darby, "man must pass through the different phases which furnish occasion for God to unfold Himself in grace."[112] Unfortunately, a residual effect of this process is the manifestation of the failure and fall of humankind.[113] Humanity's sad character as responsible beings under the divine governorship of God is fully brought out as is the gracious character of God in His dealings with humanity's failure.

The second principal purpose of the dispensations, as set forth by Darby, follows naturally from the first. The display of what God is and of His gracious character to fallen humankind during the course of the successive dispensations results in the manifestation of His divine glory. Darby explains that,

These differences of dispensation are the displays of God's glory; and therefore of all importance, and most essential, because a positive part of His glory. The law maintained His majesty, and title to claim obedience, as the gospel displayed His grace, and gave the obedience of a child....Let us only remember that dispensations are the necessary displays of God's glory...[114]

Darby indicates that the principal way in which God is glorified is through His Son. "The divine glory is ever the end of all things;" he writes, "but I speak now of the effect of divine counsels in which God glorifies Himself. Now this is altogether in Christ, known in the various glories in which He is revealed."[115] Darby insists that everything in the ways of God and His Word are directed toward the end of glorifying Christ as the object of God's counsels and he warns that failure to understand this will result in an inability to "get the intelligence of the word."[116] The dispensations, he explains elsewhere, are "the manifestations of the ways of God for the final bringing out the full glory of Christ."[117] The three great spheres in which the glory of Christ is brought out, says Darby, are the church, Jews, and Gentiles.[118]

It is of interest to note here, that Darby is in essential agreement with the contemporary dispensational position that the ultimate purpose of God in history is to bring glory to Himself, and not with the Covenant view that it is to effect the salvation of the elect.[119] Those who attach the greater importance to the final salvation of the elect, says Darby, "do not know anything about dispensations..." He explains further that,

> ...the salvation of the elect is not the great end of any Christian's thoughts, but the divine glory; and that God has been pleased to glorify Himself and display His character in these dispensations for the instruction of the church; and that if the church casts it aside, they are casting aside the instruction which God has afforded of His ways. They are making themselves wise without God, and wiser than He, for He has thought fit for His glory to instruct us in these things.[120]

It is clear from the foregoing that Darby would have no problem with Ryrie's statement that, "The unifying principle of dispensationalism is doxological, or the glory of God, and the dispensations reveal the glory of God as He manifests His character in the differing stewardships given to man."[121]

In his evaluation of the purpose of the dispensations, Scofield fails to lay the same stress upon the glory of God. His emphasis rather, is upon the dispensations as an orderly means for the unfolding of divine truth and their purpose for humankind. He says, "The Dispensations are distinguished, exhibiting the majestic, progressive order of the divine dealings of God with humanity, 'the increasing purpose' which runs through and links together the ages, from the beginning of the life of man to the end of eternity."[122] Without a clear understanding of dispensational divisions, writes Scofield, "the majestic and beautiful synthesis of truth is inevitably lost." "For this unfolding of truth and purpose by distinct stages, and according to a necessary order of progress," he continues, "is one of the seals of God upon the whole Book, marking it as His own."[123]

End of All Dispensations

Both Darby and Scofield conclude all dispensational arrangements with the final judgment upon Satan and his rebel army at the close of the millennial reign of Christ. Satan, who had been bound for the duration of the thousand-year earthly reign of Christ, is loosed at its close. In one final attempt to usurp the power of God, he leads an army of those who had refused to accept the authority of Christ during the millennial monarchy. The final battle ends quickly, whereupon the eternal state begins. With Satan's final defeat, according to Darby, "the close of all dispensation, and the end of all question and title of authority shall come, and, all being finished, God shall be all in all without question and without failure."[124]

Endnotes

[1]John Nelson Darby, *The Collected Writings of J. N. Darby*, 34 vols., ed. William Kelly, vol. 1: *Ecclesiastical No. 1* (Sunbury, Pa.: Believers Bookshelf, n.d.), pp. 288-9. This is one of the few places where Darby discusses the origin and meaning of the word dispensation.

[2]Ibid., pp. 288-9.

[3]Ibid., vol. 13: *Critical No. 1*, p. 155. Here Darby clearly says that *oikonomia* itself means "administration."

[4]Henry George Liddell, and Robert Scott, *An Intermediate Greek-English Lexicon*, new ed., revised by Henry Stuart Jones (Oxford: The Clarendon Press, 1966), p. 528.

[5]Darby, vol. 1: *Ecclesiastical No. 1*, p. 289.

[6]Ibid.

[7]John Nelson Darby, *The Holy Scriptures: A New Translation from the Original Languages* (Addison, Ill.: Bible Truth Publishers, 1975), p. 1423 (note 1 to Col. 1:25).

[8]Darby, *Writings*, vol. 13: *Critical No. 1*, p. 153.

[9]Ibid., p. 161.

[10]Ibid., pp. 153-4.

[11]Ibid., p. 155.

[12]C. I. Scofield, *Prophecy Made Plain* (Glasgow: Pickering and Inglis; London: Alfred Holness, n.d.), p. 23; *The Scofield Reference Bible* (New York: Oxford University Press, 1945), p. 32 (note 1 to Genesis 21:33).

[13]Darby, *Writings*, vol. 1: *Ecclesiastical No. 1*, p. 169.

[14]Ibid., vol. 4: *Ecclesiastical No. 2*, p. 272.

[15]Ibid., vol. 1: *Ecclesiastical No 1*, p. 287.

[16]John Nelson Darby, *Synopsis of the Books of the Bible*, 5 vols., reprint ed. (Sunbury, Pa.: Believers Bookshelf, 1971), 3:386.

[17]Darby, *Writings*, vol. I: *Ecclesiastical No. 1*, pp. 124-5; cf. John Nelson Darby, *Letters of J.N. Darby*, 3 vols., reprint ed. (Sunbury, Pa.: Believers Bookshelf, 1971), 3:256.

[18]Ibid., *Writings*, vol. I: *Ecclesiastical No. 1*, p. 125.

[19]Ibid., vol. 2: *Prophetic No. 1*, pp. 95-6.

[20]See **Appendix C** for an overview of Darby's "general" dispensations contrasted with his "particular" ones.

[21]Ibid., vol. 5: *Prophetic No. 5*, p. 14; cf. vol. 4: *Ecclesiastical No. 2*, p. 329 and vol. 11: *Prophetic No. 4*, p. 347.

[22]Ibid., vol. 1: *Ecclesiastical No. 1*, p. 124f; vol. 2: *Prophetic No. 1*, p. 374f; vol. 5: *Prophetic No. 2*, p. 384f, et al.

[23]Scofield, *Reference Bible*, p. 5.

[24]C. I Scofield, *Scofield Bible Correspondence Course* (Chicago: Moody Bible Institute, 1934), 1:17.

[25]For some of the more important discussions of Darby's dispensational concepts see his *Writings*, vol. 1: *Ecclesiastical No. 1*, "The Apostasy of the Successive Dispensations," pp. 124-30; vol. 2: *Prophetic No. 2*, "Evidence from Scripture of the Passing Away of the Present Dispensation," pp. 89-121, "The Hopes of the Church of God," pp. 374-84; and vol. 5: *Prophetic No. 2*, "The Principles Displayed in the Ways of God Compared with His Ultimate Dealings," pp. 383-91.

[26]Darby, *Writings*, vol. 1: *Ecclesiastical No. 1*, p. 124.

[27]Ibid., pp. 124-5 (italics added).

[28]Ibid., vol. 22: *Doctrinal No. 6*, p. 337.

[29]Ibid., vol. 2: *Prophetic No. 1*, pp. 95, 97.

[30]Scofield, *Prophecy Made Plain*, p. 21 (boldface Scofield's).

[31]C. I. Scofield, *Rightly Dividing the Word of Truth* (Fincastle, Va.: Scripture Truth Book Co., n.d.), p. 12.

[32]Scofield, *Reference Bible*, p. 5.

[33]Darby, *Synopsis*,1:30-1, 3:31-2, 4:19-20; *Writings*, vol. 13: *Critical No. 1*, pp. 160-1.

[34]Darby, *Writings*, vol. 2: *Prophetic No. 1*, p. 132.

[35]Ibid., pp. 132-3.

[36]Ibid., pp. 135, 375.

[37]Ibid., p. 135.

[38]Ibid.

[39]Ibid., p. 375.

[40]Ibid., pp. 377-8. Bass makes a serious error here. He represents Darby as saying that "Israel's failures caused it to be incapable of manifesting the principles of the government of God, hence the government was transferred to the *church*, which exercises it by calling out some from the nations to be a heavenly people." See Clarence B. Bass, *Backgrounds to Dispensationalism* (Grand Rapids: Wm. B. Eerdmans Publishing Co., 1960), p. 131 (italics added). Darby nowhere says that the government of the earth was taken from Israel and given to the church. It was given to the Gentile nations (represented first by Nebuchadnezzar), not to those Gentiles who are called out of the nations to form the church.

[41]Darby, *Writings*, vol. 1: *Ecclesiastical No. 1*, p. 127.

[42]Darby, *Synopsis*, 5:392, 396.

[43]The relationship of these two types of government to the full spectrum of dispensations is presented in graphic form in **Appendix D**.

[44]Darby, *Synopsis*, 5:387, 404.

[45]Ibid., 5:399.

[46]Ibid., 5:387-8.

[47]Ibid., 5:388.

[48]Ibid., 5:392.

[49]Ibid., 5:403.

[50]Darby, *Letters*, 2:43.

[51]Darby, *Synopsis*, 5:396.

[52]Ibid.

[53]Darby, *Writings*, vol. 1: *Ecclesiastical No. 1*, p. 127.

[54]Ibid., vol. 5: *Prophetic No. 2*, pp.388-90.

[55]Ibid., vol. 1: *Ecclesiastical No. 1*, p. 38f.

[56]Ibid., vol. 11: *Prophetic No. 4*, p. 47.

[57]Ibid.

[58]Ibid.

[59]Ibid., 5:420, 561.

[60]Darby, *Writings*, vol. 2: *Prophetic No. 1*, p. 141.

[61]Darby, *Synopsis*, 5:420.

[62]Scofield, *Prophecy Made Plain*, p. 24.

[63]Darby, *Writings*, vol. 8: *Prophetic No. 3*, p. 26.

[64]Ibid., vol. 1: *Ecclesiastical No. 1*, p. 238.

[65]Ibid., vol. 4: *Ecclesiastical No. 2*, pp. 278, 284.

[66]Ibid., p. 292.

[67]Ibid., p. 284.

[68]Ibid., vol.26: *Expository, No. 5*, p. 248.

[69]Ibid., pp. 248-9

[70]Ibid., vol. 27: *Expository No. 6*, p. 143.

[71]Darby, *Synopsis*, 3:42.

[72]Darby, *Writings*, vol. 1: *Ecclesiastical No. 1*, p. 289.

[73]Ibid., vol. 32: *Miscellaneous No. 1*, p. 235.

[74]Ibid.

[75]Ibid., p. 236.

[76]Ibid., pp. 236-8.

[77]Ibid., vol. 1: *Ecclesiastical No. 1*, p. 251.

[78]Ibid., vol. 32: *Miscellaneous No. 1*, pp. 238-9.

[79]Ibid., vol. 5: *Prophetic No. 2*, p. 93.

[80]Ibid., p. 86.

[81]Compare *Writings*, vol. 2: *Prophetic No. 1*, pp. 136-7, and vol. 16: *Practical No 1*, pp. 127-30. Darby emphasizes the fact that there was no responsibility under Abraham in order that God's promises might be placed on a solid foundation. But then he says that Abraham had a responsibility which involved getting out of his homeland to the place that God would show him.

[82]Ibid., vol. 1: *Ecclesiastical No. 1*, p. 114.

[83]Ibid., p. 115.

[84]Ibid., vol. 13: *Critical No. 1*, p. 164; cf. vol. 1: *Ecclesiastical No. 1*, p. 245; vol. 11: *Prophetic No. 4*, pp. 47, 119.

[85]Charles Caldwell Ryrie, *Dispensationalism Today* (Chicago: Moody Press, 1965), p. 112. Ryrie cites a statement that Scofield makes in the *Reference Bible*, "The point of testing is no longer legal obedience as the condition of salvation, but acceptance or rejection of Christ..." (p. 1115, note 2).

[86]Lewis Sperry Chafer, "Inventing Heretics Through Misunderstanding," *Bibliotheca Sacra* 102 (January 1945):1.

[87]Ryrie, p. 123 (italics his).

[88]Darby, *Writings*, vol. 1: *Ecclesiastical No. 1*, p. 98.

[89]Scofield, *Reference Bible*, p. 5.

[90]Darby, *Writings*, vol. 1: *Ecclesiastical No. 1*, p. 114.

[91]Ibid., vol. 5: *Prophetic No. 2*, p. 93.

[92]Ibid., vol. 1: *Ecclesiastical No. 1*, p. 180.

[93]Ibid., vol. 2: *Prophetic No. 1*, p. 98.

[94]Ibid., vol. 18: *Doctrinal No. 5*, p. 253.

[95]Darby, *Letters*, 2:274.

[96]Darby, *Writings*, vol. 4: *Ecclesiastical No. 4*, p. 272.

[97]Ibid., vol. 1: *Ecclesiastical No. 1*, p. 115.

[98]Ibid., p. 129.

[99]Ibid., vol. 4: *Ecclesiastical No. 2*, p. 273.

[100]Ibid., vol. 2: *Prophetic No. 1*, p. 98.

[101]Ibid., vol. 1: *Ecclesiastical No. 1*, p. 114.

[102]Darby, *Synopsis*, 4:44.

[103]Darby, *Writings*, vol. 14: *Ecclesiastical No. 3*, pp. 28-29 (italics, boldface and underlining added to identify dispensations and their subdivisions). It should be observed that in this catalog of the dispensations, Darby has added the non-dispensational Adamic period, omitted the dispensations of Noah, Abraham, and the millennium, and given the present dispensation (the church age or assembly) a double treatment. In categorical discussions of the dispensations, Darby does not always follow the same pattern and often omits in one place what he includes in another.

[104]Darby, *Writings*, vol. 1: *Ecclesiastical No. 1*, p. 116.

[105]Ibid., p. 169

[106]John Nelson Darby, *Miscellaneous Writings of J. N. D.*, vols. 4 and 5, reprint ed. (Oak Park, Ill.: Bible Truth Publishers, n.d.), 4:150-1.

[107]Darby, *Writings*, vol. 1: *Ecclesiastical No. 1*, p. 169.

[108]Ibid., p. 175.

[109]Ibid., vol. 2: *Prophetic No. 1*, pp. 377-8.

[110]Darby, *Synopsis*, 4:192-4.

[111]Scofield, *Rightly Dividing the Word of Truth*, pp. 14-15.

[112]Darby, *Writings*, vol. 22: *Doctrinal No. 6*, p. 337.

[113]Ibid., vol. 2: *Prophetic No. 1*, p. 375.

[114]Ibid., vol. 8: *Prophetic No. 3*, p. 26.

[115]Ibid., vol. 11: *Prophetic No. 4*, p. 41.

[116]Ibid., vol. 5: *Prophetic No. 2*, p. 88.

[117]Ibid., p. 384.

[118]Ibid., vol. 11: *Prophetic No. 4*, p. 45.

[119]Ryrie, pp. 46-7, 102-5.

[120]Darby, *Writings*, vol. 1: *Ecclesiastical No. 1*, p. 116.

[121]Ryrie, pp. 102-3.

[122]Scofield, *Reference Bible*, p. iii.

[123]Scofield, *Prophecy Made Plain*, p. 22.

[124]Darby, *Writings*, vol. 1: *Ecclesiastical No. 1*, pp. 129-30; cf. Scofield, *Rightly Dividing the Word of Truth*, p. 16.

CHAPTER 4-PART 1

DARBY'S SYSTEM OF DISPENSATIONS
(CREATION TO CHURCH AGE)

Introduction to the System

THE PERVASIVE AMBIGUITY

Darby is quite ambiguous with respect to a specific system of dispensations. While he discusses the dispensations in a categorical way in a few places, the content of those categories is not always the same and his treatment of the dispensations is not in an altogether systematic fashion. For example, in one instance that we are aware of, Darby includes what he calls the dispensation of the "Spirit."[1] It is obvious that it is a reference to "the present" dispensation, which elsewhere goes by the designation "Christian," "Gentile," or less commonly, "church."

It is evident also that Darby identifies the millennial kingdom as a dispensation in the _particular_ sense, yet it is never included in categorical discussions of the dispensations. In the reference just cited, for instance, he says of the present dispensation of the Spirit, that it is "The last we have to notice..."[2] Yet he asks the question, "Is this dispensation the last?" His answer is that the coming of the Savior will introduce a new dispensation, "another dispensation before the end of the world." He even affirms that among dissenting brethren there is hardly "one who does not believe in this truth."[3] Nevertheless, Darby's categorical treatments of the dispensations usually end with the dispensation of the Gentile nations and thus exclude the dispensations of the church and kingdom.[4]

Darby follows no well-defined outline for the establishment of a specific period of God's dealing with humankind as a dispensation (e.g., governmental arrangement, responsibility, revelation, test, failure, and judgment). While he usually focuses on the characteristics of government, responsibility (to a certain extent), and failure, and gives the others only limited attention if any, it is left to the reader to synthesize the material into some cogent system. This we attempt to do in the following pages. Comparisons and contrasts are also made between Darby and Scofield's specific dispensations.

THE PROPOSED OUTLINE

Even though Darby precludes the possibility of dispensational arrangement for the period prior to the deluge, for the sake of completeness, discussions of the state of innocency from the creation to the fall, and the period in Scofield's system called conscience (from the fall to the flood), are included. The outline followed is: 1. Paradisaical state (innocency); 2. Conscience; 3. Noah; 4. Abraham; 5. Israel: a. Under the Law, b. Under the priesthood, and c. Under the kings; 6. Gentiles; 7. Spirit (Christian, church, etc.); and 8. Millennium. This portion of our study concludes with a brief statement about the nondispensational eternal state.

For each dispensation, the focus is upon the primary characteristics of the governmental principle established by God and the responsibility under which humankind is placed. The revelation of God necessary to implement the new governing relationship with its attendant responsibility is not prominent as Darby gives it little direct attention. While each of the secondary characteristics of test, failure, and judgment are discussed, Darby's major focus is upon humankind's failure in each of the successive dispensations.

The Non-Dispensational Periods

PARADISAICAL STATE (INNOCENCY)

Not a Dispensation

Darby steadfastly affirms that until the deluge "there had not been, so to speak, government in the world."[5] This statement is made within the context of a discussion of the succession or history of the dispensations. Thus for Darby, for lack of government or an administrative arrangement between God and humankind, there could be no dispensation under Adam. He denies completely "that the first or Adamic state is ever called a dispensation, or *oikonomia*, or anything like it."[6] In fact, says Darby, without the aid of government "to maintain it and make it good against the opposition of an adverse nation or the weakness of a failing one," the time before the flood as well as the new heavens and earth, must be viewed as "another world from that in which we live."[7]

Darby does believe that with the fall, a new order of things began. He writes:

> ...when Adam had forfeited his title and was driven out from the place where God had set him, he then became, and not before, the head of a sinful race; and God did deal in new ways with man, as "do these things, and thou shalt live," to prove what his state was. And Christ becomes head of a new race when risen; for the grain of wheat otherwise remains alone. (John 12)[8]

It is clear from this statement that Darby's concept of government and that of the contemporary dispensationalist (i.e., government as a "distinct administration," see p. 26 above) are not the same. If they were, Darby could only have admitted the beginning of a new dispensation with the fall of Adam.

Character of Paradisaical State

Darby says that Adam was created innocent, which is to say that he had neither malice, corruption, nor lust, and was unable to discern good and evil. He had no need for such discernment, Darby maintains, because he was surrounded by good and had only to enjoy it with gratitude to God. Concerning the nature of innocency in the first man, Darby says,

> Man, the first Adam, was neither righteous nor holy. He was innocent, which excludes both righteousness and holiness. He had not the knowledge of good and evil. Righteousness discriminates between good and evil in the relationship in which we stand towards others, whether God or the creature, and acts in the sense of responsibility, according to the claim which such relationships have on us. Holiness hates evil intrinsically in itself; delighting in purity, in God's nature, it abhors all that is discordant with it.[9]

In his assessment of Adam's innocency as excluding holiness, Darby is at odds with most contemporary dispensationalists. Ryrie, for example, maintains that Adam was created not only innocent but with a positive holiness, and it was this which allowed him to communicate with God on a face-to-face basis. Ryrie points out that it was by no means a holiness like God's, for Adam was but a creature whose holiness was unconfirmed pending successful completion of the test of obedience placed before him. "Therefore," concludes Ryrie, "it seems that Adam's moral condition before God in those days of 'innocency' was unconfirmed creaturely holiness."[10]

1. Primary Characteristics.

While Darby denies that the Paradisaical state was a dispensation, he nevertheless contends that there was in this period a definite responsibility with a test, failure and judgment. Furthermore, "as regards the universal failure of man, it is a most important instance."[11] The only thing that seems to be lacking, in his judgment, is a governmental relationship between God and humankind.

a. The Government. According to Darby, the principle of government was not inaugurated until the time of Noah. Until that time, humankind was on its own and left to itself. Darby maintains that it was a different world from our own--a unique probationary period in which humanity was given the perfect chance to prove itself without the interference of God. One of the phases through which humankind had to pass was that of innocence. Darby says in this regard that,

> He must be, on God's part, an innocent and happy creature, by his own will fallen and guilty, and in a state in which all the grace of God displays itself, and in which God unfolds all its riches and righteousness, while His sovereign good-pleasure raises man to a height which depends wholly on this good-pleasure and glorifies God Himself in the result which is produced but glorifies a God of love.[12]

Humankind of course failed miserably in this laissez faire period and finally had to be destroyed. Only then, says Darby, did God interfere and establish the principle of government upon the earth.

An important point here in Darby's understanding of government in the dispensational sense, seems to be headship or a center of focus of God's dealings with the world. He says of Adam that he was the head of creation, but he was not the head of a people. Neither was there a head over the people during the period of conscience. It wasn't until Noah that God appointed a head over humanity and "he was," says Darby, "so to speak, a drunken head over the world."[13]

Darby maintains that following Noah, Abraham, and Israel, the Gentile kings (beginning with Nebuchadnezzar), were all the center of God's dealings with humankind. He says that in the present dispensation, Gentile kings are still in control of government of the earth. But Darby seems to infer that the Holy Spirit was supposed to be the center of God's earthly dealings in this dispensation of the church (see p. 53 above), as Christ will be personally in the millennial dispensation.

b. The Responsibility. Adam's responsibility as the head of creation with his glory and blessing full[14] was to be obedient to God in keeping with his headship status. He had only to enjoy the good with which he was surrounded in obedience to the One who had provided the good. And God supplied a means whereby the first humans' obedience in the responsibility under which they were placed could be proven.[15]

2. Secondary Characteristics.

a. The Test. Whether or not the first humans would obey God, says Darby, was put to the test by the prohibition against eating the fruit of the "one tree alone which was found in the midst of the garden." Eating the fruit was not evil in itself, he points out, it was only evil because forbidden.[16]

b. The Failure. Almost immediately, laments Darby, humankind failed the very first test it faced. Of the importance and consequence of the failure, Darby writes:

> It is too plain, too sadly known, to require much proof in detail, important as shewing that no condition of man set him free from the prevailing act of the great adversary. When he was innocent and untainted, surrounded by every mercy, and at the head of all blessing, he fell immediately....As it was to be shown here in principle, that man in nature could not stand, the first thing we read is of his fall, the first act consequent upon the responsibility in which he was placed, after his being set at the head of creation, and his wife given to him; in a word, after responsibilities were established, and his glory and blessing full.[17]

Prior to the fall, humankind in a state of innocence would have enjoyed direct intercourse with God. In consequence of the fall, however, human beings no longer dwell with God, nor He with them.[18]

c. The Judgment. Darby maintains that it was not fitting that the first human beings in their failure should go unpunished. They must be judged, for the holiness of God abhors sin and is repelled by it. In order that the righteousness of

God according to His holiness might maintain His authority, it is necessary to execute judgment upon those who do evil. Consequently, notes Darby, "Man was banished from paradise, and *the world began*."[19] Elsewhere, Darby extends the judgment on Adam's failure to the flood. He says that "Corruption, disorder, violence, were the consequences of this, until the Lord destroyed the first world created..."[20]

Scofield's Dispensation of Innocence (Creation to the Fall)

Scofield sets forth the dispensation of innocence in the following way:

> This dispensation extends from the creation of Adam, Gen. 2:7, to the expulsion from Eden. Adam, created innocent, and ignorant of good and evil, was placed in the garden of Eden with his wife, Eve, and put under responsibility to abstain from the fruit of the tree of the knowledge of good and evil. The Dispensation of Innocence resulted in the first failure of man, and in its far-reaching effects, the most disastrous. It closed in judgment--"So he drove out the man."[21]

Humanity was placed in a perfect environment, says Scofield, and subjected to the simplest of tests with a forewarning of the consequences that failure would bring. In spite of all, the woman succumbed to pride and fell while the man fell deliberately and thus judgment resulted.[22] Scofield describes the life of unfallen humankind under the Edenic Covenant (Gen. 2:15-17). He writes:

> Made lord of creation, placed in a perfect environment, given absolute liberty in the use of all things needful for his full development, and such occupation as guarded him from the curse of idleness, one, and only one, prohibition limited his freedom, he must not know evil. He deliberately violated that prohibition (1 Tim. 2:14), with consequences disastrous to the race of which he was the father and head (Rom. 5:12; Psa. 14:1,2; 51:5; 1 Cor. 2:14; 15:22).[23]

The Evaluation

It is clear that Scofield's dispensation of innocence is in harmony with his definition of dispensations. It "[was] a period of time during which man [was] tested in respect of obedience to some *specific* revelation of the will of God."[24] For Darby, on the other hand, while his evaluation of the Adamic period shares most points in common with Scofield's dispensation, it nevertheless fails to exhibit the principle of God's government of the world as he understands it.

The major failing of Darby's position is in what appears to be an inconsistent application of his definition of dispensations, or at least the application of an unclear definition. In stating his philosophy of dispensations, Darby says that "the dispensations themselves all declare some leading principle or interference of God, some condition in which He has placed man..."[25] That there was an administrative principle which "placed responsibility in the hands of man for the display and discovery of what he was..." is evident, but as for God's direct interference in the form of government, according to Darby, there was none. It may be this fine distinction which caused Darby to say that the paradisaical state could not "perhaps" properly "be called a dispensation in this sense of the word..."[26]

Apparently, this is all based upon the fact that Adam was the head of creation but not of a people, and therefore there was no government in Darby's understanding of it. In the first place, while Adam may not have been the head of a body of people present in Eden, he was the head of the entire human race. He is not to be viewed as a laboratory subject, somehow hermetically sealed in a world entirely alien from our own. This position seems to come close to mitigating the solidarity of the race in Adam and the impact of original sin upon his posterity.

In the second place, we fail to see how the state of affairs in Eden can be extended all the way to the flood. Darby himself recognizes that there was a dramatic change in humankind's condition brought about by the fall. Conscience comes to the fore in the individual's relationship with God. Yet, according to Darby, because there was no people before the fall over whom Adam could serve as head, nor a head under which the people after the fall could be in a governmental relationship with God, there was no government nor dispensation. Humankind was left to itself with no specific relationship to God. At this point, we find Darby's understanding of government based upon headship and the consequent relationships of God to humanity before and after the deluge to be somewhat contrived and difficult to accept.

It is a curious thing in Darby that while he insists that there was no government of the earth by God during the pre-deluge history of the race, he still speaks of the period in terms of the principles of government. In setting forth the consequences of the fall, for example, Darby distinguishes between God's government of the earth and the result of sin as it affects humankind's relationship with God and the remedy effected for it by salvation and deliverance. He writes:

> As regards government (that is, present effects upon earth--the ways of God), man, instead of paradise, finds an earth of toil and pain, and woman sorrow and grief of spirit in that which was natural joy to her. As regards the full effect of sin, both are alike driven out from God's presence, and the way of the tree of life closed to them.[27]

As we noted previously, Darby uses the terms "government of the earth," "ways of God," and "dispensations" interchangeably. His position, then, seems to be that while there is no center of God's dealings with humanity established before the flood, and therefore no government in that sense, there are nevertheless, manifestations of many of the principles of government (of dispensations)--e.g., responsibility, test, failure, judgment--displayed during that span of human history. We can only wish that Darby had been clearer in his presentation of this important concept of government.

CONSCIENCE

Not a Dispensation

It hardly bears repeating that Darby did not consider the period from the fall of

Adam to the flood to be a dispensation. It was for him, a phase of human history during which the race was left completely to itself without any direct interference of God or established center of God's dealings with it. While some of the principles of government or dispensations were exhibited during this period, there was no government in the technical sense of the term.

Character of Conscience

God, says Darby, has made sure that in his sinful state humankind is accompanied by conscience.[28] When Adam fell, he acquired the knowledge of good and evil and a bad conscience which feared face-to-face discourse with God. He was no longer innocent.[29] Darby explains the nature of conscience this way:

> Conscience has a double character, which we do not always distinguish; the sense of responsibility to another; and the knowledge of good and evil in itself. The latter element was absent from Adam's mind before his fall. The sense of responsibility was there, the debt of obedience; it was in the nature of his relationship with God; but distinguishing things as good and evil in themselves had no place in his mind. To have eaten of the tree was no evil whatever in itself ... God had forbidden it, and all depended on that command. Adam innocent was formed to understand responsibility to obey. To avoid a thing, where there was no command because it was evil, was unknown to him. He was innocent, ignorant of evil to be avoided. In his mind nothing evil in itself existed to be avoided.[30]

As a result of the fall, then, humankind got a bad conscience and in many things became a law unto itself. But if one forgot God, suggests Darby, it was the purpose of conscience to tell him of the wrong he had done. Thus righteousness and holiness were terms that now had meaning for that one who neither needed nor had an understanding of them prior to the fall.[31]

According to Darby, even in this state as "fallen, sinful, disobedient, guilty, and under judgment," humanity is presented with the blessed hope of recovering faith. While the first Adam was destroyed by the serpent's cunning, a second Adam is set up, the seed of the woman, who will bruise the serpent's head and destroy his power. "Such, then," says Darby, "was the position of man; sin, conscience in the sense of knowledge of good and evil, and (sin being there) a guilty and defiled conscience, and the revelation of a deliverer."[32]

Darby maintains that after humankind was driven from God's presence, he was in despair and depended upon "the fruits of his own perverted intellect" to bring order to the world through civilization and the arts. It was all that was left to the human race in the absence of divine holiness and perfections. Yet without the superior power of God to act as a force in the repression of humankind's will, Darby continues, "civilization...cannot arrest the vehemence of lusts, nor the violence of passions..." of a fallen and sinful creature.[33]

1. Primary Characteristics.

   a. The Government. While there was no government during the period of conscience, according to Darby, God nevertheless did not leave Himself without witness or testimony. The prophecy in existence before the flood concerned the fact that Christ, the second Adam who would crush the power of the serpent, was to come.[34] He provided the testimony of righteous Abel, who gained acceptance by God on the basis of a sacrifice which atoned for recognized sin. He furnished the testimony of righteous Enoch, who walked with God and was rewarded for his faithfulness and for his seeking after God.[35]

b. The Responsibility. Darby says next to nothing about responsibility during this period. In almost all categorical discussions of the failure of human-kind throughout its existence, he routinely leapfrogs from Adam to Noah.[36] This is no doubt due to the fact that he tends to think of the entire period from creation to the deluge as a single unit. However, it may be inferred from Darby's state-ment that "if [man] forgot God, conscience was there to tell him of wrong done,"[37] and from Abel's recognition of sin which required a blood sacrifice in atonement, that humankind's responsibility was to obey God on the basis of the dictates of conscience and that this obedience was to manifest itself in the offering of an acceptable sacrifice before God.[38]

2. Secondary Characteristics.

a. The Test. If Darby is unclear about the responsibility of humanity be-fore God during the prominence of conscience, he is of course unclear about the nature of any testing with respect to it. Presumably, God would determine whether or not individuals would obey him on the basis of their response to the conscience and by the nature of the sacrifice offered to Him.

b. The Failure. If Darby is vague about the responsibility and testing of the race at this time, he is perfectly clear about its failure and judgment. He sug-gests that failure began with Cain and his sacrifice of the fruit of the ground which had been cursed.[39] And then humankind, driven from paradise and left to itself without law but not without testimony, degenerated to the point that corruption and violence covered the face of the earth. At this time, sin against one's neigh-bor was consummated as sin against God was consummated in paradise.[40]

c. The Judgment. According to the "principles of divine government," says Darby, judgment became necessary. But a small remnant of only eight people who were willing to listen to God's testimony of coming judgment upon the earth would be safely preserved in an ark. Darby summarizes the situation in the following words:

> During the period which transpired between the expulsion of Adam from the terrestrial paradise and the deluge, man was one family, one race....Man was left to his own ways (not without witness, but without re-straint from without), and the evil became insupportable: the deluge put an end to it.[41]

Scofield's Dispensation of Conscience (Fall to the Flood)

Scofield explains that as a result of disobedience, humanity came to know good and evil personally and experimentally. The good was perceived as obedience and the evil as disobedience "to *the known will of God."* Conscience, he continues, was awakened by this knowledge and in this new state as no longer a resident of Eden, humankind was responsible to do all that it knew to be good and to abstain from all that it knew to be evil. In addition to this, humankind was to approach God on the basis of sacrifice. The result of the testing of the race during the period of conscience (Gen. 6:5)--"while there was no institution of government and of law"--was total corruption and failure with judgment of the flood the consequence.[42]

The life of fallen humanity upon the earth, says Scofield, was conditioned by the Adamic Covenant (Gen. 3:14-19). Life was to be maintained, according to the covenant, only through toil, and would end in physical death. But in stark relief to this dark forecast, was the promise of the "Satan-Bruiser" who was to come. With the awakening of conscience in the human race came the knowledge of good and evil and the dawn of a new moral test which required that each individual do good and abstain from evil. The result was corruption and failure and judgment of the flood, which ended the testing of humankind under conscience, but not conscience itself. "This Adamic Covenant, the testing of humanity under conscience," Scofield maintains, "has still a racial obligation upon those who know neither the law nor the Gospel, but it brings as in the days of the Flood only condemnation (Rom. 2:12, et seq.)."[43]

The Evaluation

Again it is evident that Scofield consistently applies his definition of dispensations to the period in question--from the fall to the flood--whereas Darby denies the existence of a dispensation altogether but allows that some of the principles of dispensations do exist. As to what the principles might be, he is decidedly vague and it is left to the reader to piece together an understanding of the nature of this period and its relation to God's dealings with humankind.

As with Adam, this period too is excluded from the status of "dispensation" on the basis of the absence of some center of God's dealings (i.e., an established government) with the race. That God is in fact dealing with humanity on the basis of some entirely new principle (conscience), involving previously unknown circumstances, even Darby admits. Yet on the strength of some fine point which he fails to fully define, he relegates this period to an "other worldly" status.

Perhaps the most unsatisfactory feature of Darby's treatment of the pre-deluge history of the race is the overall lack of preciseness with which he presents the period. One is often unsure whether to regard statements as applying to the whole period from the creation to the fall or to that only from the fall to the flood. It is clear from Darby's presentation of the facts that each has certain peculiar characteristics of its own, even if we are not always privy to exactly what they are.

The Dispensational Periods

NOAH

Introduction and Importance of the Dispensation

Darby asserts that with Adam and his sin against God which precipitated the fall from innocency, humankind continued in a state of decline exhibited by unrestrained violence of neighbor against neighbor, until an utterly corrupt world had to be cleansed of its pollution.[44] This having been accomplished by the deluge, says Darby, a new world begins. With Noah, "we begin the course of dispensations, or of the manifestation of the ways of God for the final bringing out the full glory of Christ."[45]

Noah was established as the head and chief of the first dispensation in this new world. According to Darby, three features or new principles characterized and accompanied this position: 1. God's pledge of blessing in the form of covenant as long as the earth should last; 2. Sacrifice which turned the curse aside; and 3. Restraint of evil in the world. With respect to dispensation, Noah served as the head of a new system where evil still existed but was under restraint and the curse under which the earth labored was relieved.[46]

With respect to the covenant, points out Darby, the earth is blessed by God more than before and the answer to sacrifice is the assurance that there will never again be a universal deluge. God's pledge to this effect to the creation is in the form of a covenant. And the "Covenant was sure, for God is faithful when He binds Himself."[47]

Concerning the second new principle, that of sacrifice, Darby maintains that "The sacrifice of Christ (in figure) becomes a ground of dealing with the earth, not alone of accepting man, as in Abel..." And the ground upon which faith rests now, says Darby, is covenant. In grace, God has bound Himself so that humankind's faith has a solid guarantee upon which it can count.[48] But for Darby, there can be no doubt that the most important new principle to emerge in this first dispensation and that which gives it its distinctive character is the establishment of government upon the earth.

Character of the Dispensation

1. Primary Characteristics.

a. The Government. In this new world which begins with Noah, says Darby, there are two great principles: *rule* placed in humanity's hands and *separation from the world* by God's call (the latter comes with Abraham).[49] The first of these principles, rule in humanity's hands, he explains, is easily corrupted, "and men may shew themselves in this, and in everything else, unfaithful in maintaining the glory of God..." It was this principle which was first established with Noah. He became the head of humankind and as such the center of God's dealings with the earth. On the basis of Genesis 9:6, "Whoever sheds man's blood, by man his blood shall be shed...," human or self-government was placed in the hands of humankind by virtue of the fact that God's authority over life had been entrusted to it.[50] God sets humanity in power with the right of the sword in order that it might rule, and repress and restrain evil upon the earth.[51]

Darby suggests that the value of this principle of rule for which humankind was now responsible, was in the recalling (by both the governor and the governed) of the authority of the One who had established it. It was "an authority which, thus recognized, would restrain the lust of the flesh, ere they broke out in those acts to which the power of the sword itself was to be applied..." In its most effective application, the principle would even eliminate the effects of desires which were not of such a serious nature as to require the death penalty.[52]

b. The Responsibility. The first dispensation under Noah should have been characterized by restraint and godliness. Humankind's responsibility was to govern effectively with the God-given power of the sword in order that corruption and violence might be repressed.[53]

c. The Revelation. Darby says that "To Noah...the principle of government was communicated, in order to restrain evil in its effects..."[54]

2. Secondary Characteristics.

a. The Test. Darby refers to the effective administration of this new government with its power of the sword as the "new trial" under which humanity was placed. The implication is that God placed the power of the sword in the race's hands to see if it could in fact govern effectively.[55]

b. The Failure. The result, as is always the case when responsibility is placed in the hands of humankind, says Darby, was immediate failure. Noah, the head of this new world, failed when he got drunk and lost the respect of his own son who should have been the first to obey.[56] The consequence of Noah's failure was the continuation of evil unrepressed. In the days of Nimrod, violence and strife were displayed and perhaps, suggests Darby, ambition and pride in those who wished to make a name for themselves were rising against God. Here, the principle of rule was caused to flow from humanity's violence and will by Satan.[57]

c. The Judgment. God's judgment descended upon humankind in the form of confusion of tongues. The projects of rebellious humankind were confounded and the people themselves were dispersed. The race's pride was effectively humbled.[58]

Two great principles, says Darby, grew out of the events at the tower of Babel. The first was different nations, the second the emergence of idolatry. Prior to Babel, there had been a single family of humankind. But now, explains Darby,

> ...in consequence of the judgment of man, who seeks to exalt himself on the earth and to make himself a name or centre which may give him strength, God scatters those who were building the tower, and there are nations, languages, and peoples. The actual form of the world was established in reference to its division into different tribes and different nations....Now that the world is constituted, we arrive at the testimony and ways of God.[59]

This division of humanity into nations, Darby asserts, provided opportunity for the organizations of God's providence. It provides the impetus for the calling of Abraham.[60]

The second great principle to grow out of the judgment at Babel is the introduction of idolatry. Darby believes that prior to the flood, there had been neither government nor idolatry.[61] But after the judgment of Babel, he says, the race's sin is not just against God in the form of corruption and the activity of its independent will. Rather, demons now come in and take God's place in people's eyes and imaginations. Idolatry now holds sway over the nations, including the race of Shem. Each nation had its own gods, and even the system which God had established Himself at the time of Babel's judgment worshipped demons as its gods.[62] Darby somehow sees the failure of Noah and the cursing of his son who[63] mocked him as the events which "issued in idolatry; Joshua 24."

Scofield's Dispensation of Human Government (Flood to Babel)

God saved eight people out of the flood, says Scofield, and gave them sufficient power to govern the new world. The distinctive feature of this new dispensation was the institution of human government--the government of people by their fellow human beings. The judicial taking of human life, Scofield points out, is the highest function of government. Consequently, all other powers of government are implied in this one function. Humankind's responsibility in this new dispensation, then, is to govern the world in accordance with God's principles which includes the power of the sword. The failure of the dispensation became evident, however, upon the plain of Shinar in the race's "impious attempt to become independent of God..." The dispensation ended with God's judgment in the form of confusion of tongues.[64]

Scofield gives a much broader context for the responsibility, failure, and judgment of the race under human government than does Darby. He says:

> That responsibility rested upon the whole race, Jew and Gentile, until the failure of Israel under the Palestinian Covenant (Deut. 28.-30. 1-10) brought the judgment of the Captivities, when "the times of the Gentiles" (See Lk. 21. 24; Rev. 16. 14) began, and the government of the world passed exclusively into Gentile hands (Dan. 2. 36-45; Lk. 21. 24; Acts 15. 14-17). That both Israel and the Gentiles have governed for self, not God, is sadly apparent. The judgment of the confusion of tongues ended the _racial_ testing; that of the captivities the _Jewish_; while the _Gentile_ testing will end in the smiting of the Image (Dan. 2.) and the judgment of the nations (Mt. 25. 31-46).[65]

The Covenant of Noah (Gen. 9: 5, 6), says Scofield, established human government as the principle of God's dealings with humankind in this dispensation, and it still serves as "the charter of all civil government..." After affirming that the responsibility was to "govern righteously," with the result Babel and the judgment the confusion of tongues, Scofield goes on to discuss the division of kind into tribes and then nations. With respect to the nations, he states that:

These, with the single exception of the family of Shem, who had been set apart for a special relation to God in the Noahic Covenant (Gen. 9:26, 27), soon became idolaters, and lost the knowledge of the true God. In Romans 1:21-23 the steps of this utter apostasy are traced, and the moving cause disclosed: "They did not like to retain God in their knowledge,"--literally, "did not approve God" (Rom. 1:28).[66]

The Evaluation

It is obvious here that Darby and Scofield share most elements of the dispensation of human government in common. And as is usually the case, Scofield is the more systematic of the two,[67] while Darby is doubtless the more innovative. Yet while Scofield is very systematic and clear in his treatment of the dispensations, he seldom offers more than a paragraph or two in his discussions of each. Darby's presentations are much fuller.

ABRAHAM

Introduction and Importance of the Dispensation

Up to this time, says Darby, the subjects of Scripture are primarily two: Adam, who stood as the head of natural creation, and Noah, who was installed as the representative head of government upon the earth. Under Adam there was immediate failure in the garden of Eden which resulted in the ultimate corruption and destruction of all humankind save Noah and his family. Under Noah, the principle of government manifested in the power of the sword to restrain evil, proved ineffective when Noah got drunk and showed himself incapable of governing--as indicated by the disrespect of even his own son.[68] As with Adam, there was both immediate and long-range failure. With government proven ineffective against the inroads of evil, pride and the "lust of ambitious selfishness," finally at Babel God brought judgment in the form of confusion of tongues and thus distinct nations were born.[69]

Darby affirms, however, that God's judgments did not end either the principle of "country and kindred," or the principle of human government. No matter how the principle of government might be exercised, righteously or unrighteously, he says, it remained and still remains in all its power. Darby writes:

> As regards this part of the history previous to Abram (that is, the earth under government), we have the fact recorded of the division of the earth amongst its various nations and families; this we find in Genesis 10, where the fact is stated, the origin of which we find explained only in Chapter 11....Thus, whatever may have been the particular changes since, the earth under government assumed the form which it now bears....Indeed...if we take the list of nations spoken of as gathered together under the wilful king in the latter day, and under Gog in Ezekiel we shall find ourselves brought back to the same nations, and tongues and families, which are presented to our view at the outset, as the immediate consequence of the establishment of this principle of government in the hands of Noah, and as formed into actual condition by the sin of Babel.[70]

Even though government continues to the present day, God used the opportunity afforded by the failure of His perverse creatures to introduce another principle which would glorify Himself.[71]

Character of the Dispensation

1. Primary Characteristics.

a. The Government. The next important principle brought out in God's dealings with humanity after Noah, was the principle of calling (and election). Not only had the world become corrupt and violent, explains Darby, but it had chosen to forsake worship of God in order to serve other gods (idolatry). In the face of this, God calls Abraham to separate from the world and follow Him on the basis of promise by faith. Thus we have "election, call, promise, by which the believer is a stranger in a world departed from God."[72] Consequently, Abraham becomes the center of God's dealings with the earth, the root of all of His promises to humankind, and the father of the faithful.

The Biblical account of Abraham's call is Genesis 12. The content of this chapter, Darby maintains, is particularly important in the unfolding of the dispensations. He writes:

> In other parts of scripture may be more fully seen what the means were by which the purposes of God should be accomplished, and the great object in which those purposes found their result; but the principles on which the dealings of God hinge are nowhere more clearly produced. It is, in fact, their first exhibition, and therefore (however succinctly) they are definitely and very completely produced and stated;…that is, in the sovereign acting of God upon the principles in which we were thereby to be instructed.[73]

Darby goes on to say that the great point of Genesis 12 is God's call and the principles upon which that call is based, and this "*calling of God* is a cardinal point of His dispensations."[74]

Darby maintains that in God's call of Abraham as the type of His family and depository of His promises to humankind, He introduces a new principle which will make good His name, character, and grace in a world "withdrawn from His providential judgments." The substance of the call issued to Abraham is contained in Genesis 12:1-2, "Now the Lord said to Abram, 'Go forth from your country, and from your relatives and from your father's house, to the land which I will show you…'" In principle, says Darby, God is calling for Abraham's separation from the world. He is asking Abraham to break the strongest ties and closest relationships that one experiences in the world, and to devote himself "in heart, faith, and confidence" to God alone.[75] Thus it is a principle which places a paramount claim upon the individual in grace. It supersedes all natural relationships and formed associations. Everything else must be left behind as one is called out to follow God alone.[76]

b. The Responsibility. Darby is difficult to follow at this point, for he maintains at the same time that the call to Abraham was above all responsibility on humanity's part and yet, he clearly states that Abraham had a responsibility to obey God. In the first instance, Darby says that "the principle of the call of God maintained His supremacy in a manner which put it beyond the effects of man's responsibility."[77] God's promises to Abraham, Darby explains, were absolute and unconditional. His interference in blessing was conferred on the basis of His faithfulness alone and rested upon His sovereign choice. "It is universal in the sphere of its application," says Darby, "absolute in its character, and its accomplishment dependent on the sole faithfulness of God."[78]

In point of fact, the state of the one to be blessed had nothing to do with the principle of the call. In other words, the question of righteousness was not raised at all. God had made promises in grace to Abraham which He confirmed to his offspring (Isaac and Jacob) and His own faithfulness alone would see that they were fulfilled.[79] Darby maintains that by doing this, God was insuring that prior to the Law, which was to come 430 years later (Gal. 3:16, 17), that the principle of grace would be maintained.[80]

Yet, according to Darby, Abraham had a definite responsibility to be obedient to God. He was called upon to break existing relationships and to leave his country and kindred for a land which God would show him. "Whatever the power which acted on his mind might be," says Darby, "obedience was the result; for in the very terms of the call it was manifest--no obedience, no blessing." It was implied that Abraham was to exhibit faith in God's love, power, and faithfulness.[81]

c. The Revelation. As is always the case with Darby, little is said directly about the revelation necessary to effect change in each dispensational arrangement. That which is said is usually implicit rather than explicit. With respect to God's call of Abraham, Darby does say that "The personal *revelation* of Himself to Abram, as it were, identified him with Himself and with His purpose, and with the blessing of an appointed inheritance."[82] And in another place he says that "God *reveals* Himself to [Abraham] as the God of promise, who separates a people to Himself by a promise which He gives them."[83]

2. Secondary Characteristics.

a. The Test. Darby says nothing directly about a test during this period either. However, it may be inferred by his statement "no obedience, no blessing" that at least individual blessing for Abraham hinged upon his obedience in leaving his homeland and in his continued obedience, faith, and trust in God. God's promises to Abraham as the head of a new race, promises subsequently repeated to Isaac and Jacob, obviously were not affected by obedience or the lack of it and were not, therefore, subject to testing.

b. The Failure. In almost every categorical discussion of the failure of humanity under responsibility, Darby omits the name of Abraham.[84] Yet if one digs long enough he will find that indeed there was failure on Abraham's part and by his descendants. According to Darby, Abraham's personal failure is seen in the fact that he went down into the land of Egypt and while there, he lied to the Pharaoh about Sarah's relationship to him.

When Abraham departed from the land of Canaan for Egypt to avoid famine, says Darby, he displayed a lack of confidence in the God who had led him thus far. Without God, Abraham left the land of faith and promise and thus he could expect no blessing for his unbelief. While Abraham was blessed with riches by the prince of this world, he could expect no blessing from the God of his calling.[85]

But the worst of it as far as Darby is concerned, is that Abraham's lack of faith and confidence in God is illustrated by the fact that he lied about his relationship to Sarah. Fearing that the Pharaoh might take his wife, Abraham, rather than trusting God to preserve him, says that Sarah is his sister and thus Pharaoh takes her into his house.[86] Thus with regard to humankind under the calling of grace, laments Darby, "we find shameful failure."[87]

Darby shows elsewhere that as with the previous periods of human history, there was both an immediate and future failure during the Abrahamic dispensation. After Abraham was escorted from the land of Egypt, he returned to the land of Canaan and received reaffirmation of God's promises to him (Gen. 13,14,17). He lived in the faith and confidence that God would one day fulfill his promises to his descendants. But in time, says Darby, we find a people who have little regard for these promises of God. Far removed from the faith of their father Abraham, they return to the land of Egypt.[88]

c. <u>The Judgment</u>. Darby discusses the judgments pronounced upon humanity for its failures in this period only in an oblique way. With regard to Abraham's untruth about Sarah, the families of the earth (in this case represented by the house of Pharaoh) which were to have been blessed because of him, are the recipients instead of plagues (Gen. 12:17).[89] In the case of Abraham's descendants who had little regard for the promises of God, in time they found themselves "groan[ing] under the yoke of a merciless tyranny."[90] While Darby does not say that this is the direct judgment of God, he implies that it is indeed the direct consequence of unfaithfulness to God and His promises to Abraham.

<u>Abrahamic Dispensation and the Dispensation of the Church</u>

There is a clear parallel in Darby's thinking between the Abrahamic dispensation and that of the Spirit or church.[91] The calling of Abraham has a twofold nature or application--one termed carnal by Darby, the other spiritual. In one sense, as it applies to the earth (the carnal application), Abraham is the father of the nation Israel. Promises are made to Abraham and his descendants concerning an earthly land which will be fulfilled in the millennial dispensation. In this instance, it is the calling out of a man to head a physical family upon the earth.[92]

At the same time, Abraham represents the calling out of a spiritual family to be God's own people separated out of this world, as Abraham was separated from his old homeland. Darby explains that,

> If the nations, the peoples, the families, and the languages took demons for their gods [idolatry under human government], God took a man by His grace to be the head of a family, the stock of a people, who may belong to Him for His own. The fatness of God's olive-tree is found in those who

grow on the root of Abraham, whether it be in a people, the seed according to the flesh, or in a seed which shares in the promised blessings, inasmuch as belonging to Christ the true Seed of the promise.[93]

The great distinguishing feature of the calling of God, Darby asserts, is *"separation from the world."* As it was the character of the call to Abraham who was to separate himself from his country and kindred, so it is the character of the church and the individual believer in the present dispensation. The believer is called by God in faith to come out of the world and to trust in a promise not immediately fulfilled and to take God alone as his security and guide.[94]

Here Darby sets forth a peculiar concept of men and women in the Bible as types. He writes:

> And here I would remark, what will, I believe, simplify the use of many types, and be found (at least I have so found it) that *men* who are types represent the energy of faith, the spiritual energy of the church, under the circumstances in which the type represents it, or perhaps its failure therein; and that *females* who are presented to us as types represent the state and condition of the church.[95]

In other words, says Darby, "the *woman* is the state in which the dispensation is; the *man* is the conduct of faith in it." And after Abram and Sarai are introduced, he continues, it is the conduct not the calling of the church that is brought out.[96]

We are told by Darby that Abraham, acting upon his own reasoning and without reference to God, went down into Egypt. He explains the typical significance of this event for the church as follows:

> If there was not famine for the saint, there was the denial of the blessing and indissoluble bond which subsisted between the church and its bridegroom, represented in faith by those who stood in that relation before God. He came into the regions of the prince of this world for his own comfort to satisfy his present need, not of faith in God. The consequence was, the immediate denial of the holy separation from the world and union with Christ which belonged to the church: she was his sister, not his wife; true, perhaps, in one sense, but deadly in its actual character as to the faith of God's elect. She was very fair to look upon...as well as being the spouse of Christ the Son; she was commended in the world. The faith of the church had denied and disowned its unalterable affiance to Christ. The church was taken into the world's house, the house of the prince of this world; and the prince of this world entreated Abram well for her sake.[97]

Darby maintains that if in the church's state and condition, Satan can get it into his house, he will bless it with the things of the world. And this is the history of the church in its practical conduct--in its departure from faith--but not in its calling.

The result for Abraham was that instead of receiving honor himself, God vindicated Himself through the plagues that He sent because of Sarah. So too the

church as the King's daughter is taken by the world in the lust of its own dominion and thus will be judged. The sin was Abraham's, affirms Darby, and what
should have been his blessings were curses instead.[98]

It would seem that Darby's distinction between conduct and calling is essentially the difference between the intentions and counsels of God.[99] What God intends for a dispensation depends directly upon the faithfulness of humankind in
the responsibility under which it is placed. In this, in the conduct of Abraham and
the church, there is failure as is always the case in every dispensation concerning
the intentions of God. God *intended* for Abraham to dwell in the land of promise
and to exercise complete faith and trust in Him--even in the face of famine. God
intended for the church to be a manifestation of the union of the Body of Christ on
earth. Both Abraham and the church have failed, however, and thus the intentions
of God have failed. With respect to the calling of God on the other hand, whether
concerning the earthly promises to Abraham's physical descendants, the Jews, or
to his spiritual descendants, the church, these are above responsibility and therefore cannot fail.

In both the Abrahamic dispensation and the dispensation of the Spirit or
church, Darby develops a two-tiered concept of God's dealings with humanity.
One level, that which concerns God's call and counsels, is seemingly above all
dispensational characteristics. There is no responsibility or failure, for all depends
upon God's faithfulness and not upon the obedience and faithfulness of the individual. However, on the level concerned with human conduct and God's intentions, God carries out His dispensational dealings with humankind. On this level,
there is responsibility always accompanied by failure.

It is this two-tiered understanding of these two dispensations which seems to
cause Darby to vacillate at times between responsibility and yet no responsibility;
between failure on the one hand and the impossibility of failure on the other. It is
this too in large part which causes him to see no dispensation at the present time
and yet identify the church age (i.e., Christendom) as the failed dispensation in
which we now live. In these respects, then, both the dispensation of Abraham and
the church share a certain kinship and seem to be presented by Darby in something of an italicized if not parenthetical form.

Scofield's Dispensation of Promise (Call to the Law)

From among those dispersed at Babel, says Scofield, God calls one man,
Abram, and enters into covenant with him. The promises made to Abram and his
descendants were of two kinds: some were totally gracious and unconditional
(Gen. 12:1-2), while others were conditioned upon obedience and faithfulness
(Gen. 26:2, 3, blessing hinged upon staying in the land and not going to Egypt).
All of the conditions to be met with regard to the latter class of promises were
violated and thus the failure of Israel (Gen. 47:1, went to Egypt) resulted in the
judgment of the Egyptian bondage.[100] Among the unconditional promises were
those involving: 1. A land; 2. A natural or earthly seed; and 3. A spiritual or
heavenly seed.[101]

Scofield explains that Genesis 11 and 12 outline an important turning point in

God's dealing with humankind. Previously, God had dealt with the whole Adamic race. But now, He had called one man out of the mass of humanity to create a single nation--Israel, and it is this one nation which is the subject of Genesis 12 to Matthew 12:45. It should be kept in mind, says Scofield, that the human race apart from Israel, known henceforth as the Gentiles, continues under the Adamic and Noahic covenants and the dispensations of conscience and human government.[102]

With regard to the covenant established during this new dispensation, Scofield writes:

> ...now God begins to act upon the special promise to Shem: "God shall enlarge Japheth, and he shall dwell in the tents of Shem" (Gen. 9:27). One of the Semitic stock, Abram, is called out of Ur in Chaldea that in and through him and his seed the great redemptive purposes of God toward the whole race might be worked out. In Abraham, and in the Abrahamic Covenant (Gen. 12:1-3; 13:15, 16; 15:18 and preceding) the nation which came to be called Israel, after the grandson of Abraham, to whom the Abrahamic Covenant was confirmed (Gen. 28:13 et seq.) was set apart to a special work on behalf of Jehovah with the whole of humanity as the objective.[103]

All that was required of Abraham's descendants to inherit every blessing, explains Scofield, was to dwell in their own land. So when they went to Egypt, their blessings were lost, but their covenant was not. The dispensation and the covenant, Scofield points out, must be distinguished. "The former is a mode of testing; the latter is everlasting because unconditional." The dispensation of promise itself as a testing of Israel ended, according to Scofield, when Israel accepted the Law (Ex. 19:8), but the covenant continued. The Abrahamic Covenant was not abrogated by the Law, but the Law served as an intermediate disciplinary dealing of God with Israel.[104]

The Evaluation

Digging out the characteristic elements of this dispensation is especially difficult because of Darby's twofold understanding of its nature. He clearly considers this phase of God's dealings with humanity to be a dispensation, but his desire to have it closely mirror the character of the church age results in what appear to be contradictory statements concerning the characteristics of this economy. Humankind is responsible, he says, and yet the dispensation is above all responsibility. There is failure, but it is primarily an individual lapse of confidence in God on Abraham's part and hardly worth mentioning in any catalog of the failures of the race in its sojourn on earth. As to the judgment which followed, it was upon Pharaoh's house and precipitated by Abraham's lie regarding his relationship with Sarah. The Egyptian bondage barely receives honorable mention.

The vagueness and difficulty encountered in Darby's analysis here, is due in part to his pressing the connection between the Abrahamic and church dispensations beyond the limit of the principles of the calling out and spiritual headship of Abraham. It is due to a great extent also to his failure to explicitly distinguish the dispensation from the covenant and the conditional from the unconditional promises. It is a mistake later avoided by Scofield. It seems that Darby is forced into some rather interesting inventiveness to overcome the difficulties caused by the oversight. The distinctions between conduct and calling and between men and women as types, while interesting, fall short in their effort to persuade.

ISRAEL: UNDER THE LAW

One is somewhat hard pressed to determine whether the period from Moses to Nebuchadnezzar is one dispensation or three in Darby's analysis. Is it the single dispensation of Israel or the dispensations of Israel under the Law, Israel under the priesthood, and Israel under the kings? The rationale for the threefold division is the fact that all three periods have their own system under which Israel is placed with a different responsibility and subsequent failure. On the other hand, Darby tends to lump all three divisions together as the "Jewish Dispensation" or "Jewish System" when comparing Israel's history to other dispensations.[105] While each subdivision will be treated separately here, in future discussions of the period, they will be taken as a single dispensation.

Introduction and Importance of Israel Under the Law

Darby suggests that Israel's deliverance from Egyptian bondage provided the opportunity for the introduction of an entirely new principle in the ways of God for the human race. This next important step in God's program involved the deliverance of a people from their enemies by judgments, and their formation into a people who were to be "set apart as a people of dilection to God on the earth"--a prefigure of the church, the Body of Christ.[106] Darby explains that the object of the "Jewish dispensation" which preceded Christ's incarnation, was not to gather the church on earth, but to exhibit God's government through an elect nation.[107]

Concerning the special position of this people, Israel, Darby writes:

> First, it is a people. This till then there had never been: just men by grace, believers, called ones, there had been; now, though according to the flesh, these are a people of God on the earth. This was based on redemption wrought by God. Further, God, as we have seen, dwells amongst His people on earth when redemption is accomplished. That is the distinct fruit of redemption; He had not dwelt with innocent Adam; He had not with called Abraham; He does with redeemed Israel.[108]

It is at this time, Darby says elsewhere, that the holiness of God is set before us for the first time. In Genesis, with the exception of the sanctification of the sabbath in paradise, neither the holiness of God nor anything else is set forth. With the accomplishment of redemption, however, "God takes this character, and establishes it as necessary for everything that is in relation with Himself." This is shown, says Darby, by Exodus 15 and 19, and Leviticus 19:26.[109]

Character of Israel Under the Law

1. Primary Characteristics.

a. The Government. The principle of government had been established under Noah and that of calling (and election) under Abraham. Now the two principles are combined in Israel as the basis and center of God's dealings with humankind and they set the stage for a new trial of its faithfulness under responsibility. The history of these two principles combined, says Darby, whether viewed under the responsibility of the race (government) or the efficacy of the supremacy of God (calling), is synonymous with the history of the Jewish nation. Consequently, writes Darby,

> It is...in the history of this people that we must look for the centre of the administration of government of the world; containing (as it does) in its past history, on the one hand, the witness given by a people called to the knowledge of the only true God against the false gods of the Gentiles...and, on the other hand, the witness afforded to the principles of the government of the true God by *His* conduct towards His chosen people, blessing or punishing them openly according to their proceedings...Amos 3:2.[110]

The directing principle of the history of the Jewish people, says Darby, was the Law, for it was the "expression of the actual terms of God's government."[111] Thus Israel was a called and separated people; separated to enjoy earthly blessings and to enjoy the promise. At the same time, she was to be subject to the function of God's government on the basis of the Law.[112]

Concerning the nature and function of the Law itself, Darby says that it could only convict humankind of its incompetency.[113] God never intended to save the human race on the basis of Law, it was given rather, to convince it of its state of sin by manifesting positive transgressions. The Law was a perfect expression of what humankind ought to be, says Darby, and as such it revealed humanity's lack of native righteousness and therefore condemned it before God and showed its guilt and need for salvation.[114] In general, however, the Law did give the principle of a rule of the will of God which was later to be written in the hearts of God's people, the Jews.[115]

b. The Responsibility. The Law was handed down to Israel at Mt. Sinai, and based upon it, a covenant was established. The express condition of obedience on the part of the Israelites was stipulated as the grounds for their enjoyment of the promises contained in the covenant,[116] and their well-being under it.[117] "Now then, if you will indeed obey My voice and keep My covenant, then you shall be My own possession among all the peoples, for all the earth is Mine" (Ex. 19:5).

The question of righteousness had not been raised with Abraham, says Darby, but here it is. Blessing is made dependent upon the obedience of humankind under the Law. The covenant, Darby points out, was made between two parties and depended not solely upon the infallibility of the one who promised, but upon the obedience of the ones to whom the promises were made. Righteousness in the form of obedience was expected from those under the covenant.[118]

c. The Revelation. Darby says that with the Law there was "the added revelation of all the graciousness and goodness of the character of Him under whose government he [the Israelite] was placed, and who would act in that government on the principles thus revealed."[119]

2. Secondary Characteristics.

a. The Test. Darby refers to the establishment of the Law in this new economy as the means for "the putting of man to the proof on the revealed principles of what he ought to be…"[120] This is of course an obvious reference to the test of whether or not the people would obey the Law in all its parts. But beyond this, Darby sees another test--a test concerning the Messiah.

"Hence there is a double test," says Darby, "applicable in the ways of God in government of Israel." Christ was the Messiah of the Jews, the King who was to reign in righteousness and "to display fully and in perfection God's immediate [i.e., "direct" or "manifested"] government." Would Israel glory in the privileges in which she was placed? Would she meet Jehovah in glory in the Person of the Messiah who was to come?[121]

b. The Failure. Like the other dispensations before, this one too (this subdivision of dispensation of Israel) ends in failure. And as we have come to expect from Darby, that failure has a twofold nature. Before Moses could even bring down the details of God's covenant with His people from Mt. Sinai, they had turned from Him to worship a god of gold--a golden calf. Thus they had broken the very heart of the covenant almost before it had been received (Ex. 32:1).[122]

But, as Darby points out, this was not to be the end of it, for in addition to this failure and those to come in the other subdivisions--Israel under priesthood and kings--the ultimate failure was to come in the rejection of the Messiah. After the division of the nation of Israel and the Babylonian captivity, Christ the Messiah is presented to and rejected by a residue of two tribes. Thus, says Darby, "two things gave occasion to Israel's judgment--idolatry and rebellion against Jehovah, and the rejection of Christ."[123]

c. The Judgment. Darby has little to say about judgment after the failure of Israel under the Law. He does say that God takes the Israelites at their word and no longer acknowledges them as His people under the provisions of the covenant. In proof of the fact that God no longer acknowledges the people as His own, Darby quotes Exodus 32:7, "Go, get thee down; for *thy* people, which *thou* broughtest out of the land of Egypt, have corrupted themselves."[124]

It should be kept in mind, Darby reminds his reader, that the promises given unconditionally to Abraham and repeated to Isaac and Jacob, were in no way abrogated by Israel's failure under the Law. The covenant made to Abraham and to his descendants was not conditioned upon the responsibility of humankind. It rested absolutely and unconditionally upon the calling of God.[125]

God's Relationship with Humanity Through Prophets, Priests, Kings

Before we proceed to Israel under the priesthood, it is necessary to discuss what may be in large part the source of Darby's threefold division of the dispensation of Israel. In the wilderness model, Darby sees three instruments of God's relations to humanity--prophets, priests and kings. The prophets, says Darby, served as the instruments of the communication of God's will. The priests provided the means of humankind's approach to God, while the kings received God's power and functioned as the instruments of His government.[126]

In Moses, Darby sees the representative of royalty and quotes Deuteronomy 33:5, "And He was king in Jeshurun..." in support of this supposition.[127] Unfortunately for Darby's theory, "The subject in ver. 5. is not Moses but Jehovah, who became King in Jeshurun..."[128] According to Darby, at different times, Moses actually functioned in all three positions. Aaron of course held the office of high priest, while Miriam served as "the prophetess" during the Exodus. "During the union of the two principles of government and calling," says Darby, "these things were fully developed. But under responsibility in these things, the Jewish people corrupted themselves in each one of them."[129]

ISRAEL: UNDER THE PRIESTHOOD

Introduction and Importance of Israel Under the Priesthood

Darby both denies that Israel under the Priesthood is a dispensation[130] and yet plainly labels it as such.[131] With respect to the former, he states that in its Aaronic character, the priesthood does not enter into "the ways of God with man." It comes in, rather, under different "dealings of God" in order that individuals might be maintained in their positions, but it is not "positively itself one." The reader will recognize both "the ways of God" and "dealings of God" with humanity as frequent synonyms in Darby's writings for God's dispensational arrangements on earth (see p. 47).

As to the purpose and significance of this arrangement, Darby writes:

> It was the means of approach of man to God, and subsisted in connection with the existence of His people without a king and under the kings. It supposed an accepted earthly people, so far as it was in daily exercise, though there might be particular failure. So far as the acceptance of the people was in question, it was hidden within the veil. In this character it is Christ's present position with regard to Israel, for we know the acceptance, the veil being rent.[132]

Character of Israel Under the Priesthood

1. Primary Characteristics.

   a. The Government. While Israel was under the priesthood, says Darby, God served as her King, and only judges were installed to preserve her inheritance during the periods of misery caused by her unbelief. At this time, Israel was related to God through the mediatorship of the priest.[133] This mediation of the priesthood, which placed Israel under God's immediate (or direct) government on the basis of the principles of government announced to Moses by God, was declared in the Exodus. Therefore, it seems to have co-existed from the start with Israel under the Law, but after failure under the Law, it gained a prominence all its own. The purpose of this priesthood, according to Darby, "was...to maintain the blessing if there was failure, where it was not departure from God, or sinning with a high hand; and Israel, in obedience, would have had their peace flow like a river."[134]

b. The Responsibility. Darby says nothing directly about responsibility during this period, and yet he outlines what certainly appears to be the responsibility of the priests on behalf of the people. He explains that the Law had no element of grace in it. On the contrary, it supposed sin in man and manifested this fact by showing humankind what it ought to be and yet was unable to be because of its lack of righteousness. God's love and grace towards humanity, however, was never brought out by the Law. Consequently, the Law failed completely to bring individuals to God.[135]

Nevertheless, Darby assures us that there was grace in addition to the Law in the form of sacrifices. These partake of the character of grace, he says, because they were offered on the transgressor's behalf. This is of course where the priesthood comes in. In Hebrews 5:1 we read, "For every high priest taken from among men is appointed on behalf of men in things pertaining to God, in order to offer both gifts and sacrifices for sins." This is grace, affirms Darby, for God does not require good on the part of the sinners, rather He makes provision for them.[136]

c. The Revelation. Darby makes no mention of new revelation given in this period.

2. Secondary Characteristics.

a. The Test and Failure. Here again, Darby says nothing directly about "a test," or as he sometimes puts it, humanity being "put to the proof," or "the trial" of humankind. But the nature of the priesthood's failure suggests the nature also of the test. From the brazen altar, as prescribed in Leviticus 6:12-13 and 16:12, coals were to be taken to ignite the incense that ascended to God as part of the ordinance of the Day of Atonement. Instead of following this prescribed procedure (the implied test of obedience), Aaron's sons, Nadab and Abihu, offered "strange fire"--fire from another source--before the Lord (Lev. 10:1).[137] This act was followed by the failure of Aaron's remaining sons, Eleazar and Ithamar, to both eat the sin offering and to bring the blood of it into the holy place in the prescribed manner (Lev. 6:26; 10:16-20).[138] Thus we see, says Darby, that under the priesthood there is complete corruption (e.g., Eli's worthless sons, I Sam. 2 and 3).[139]

Darby sees in Aaron and his sons a definite type of Christ and the failure of the church. In Nadab and Abihu, he explains, service was separated from the power of its acceptance. As one might expect, the race failed under Law, but even in the place of grace humanity had failed. Thus, according to Darby, the sin of these two sons of Aaron, who are "the awful type of the professing church...was sin against the very grace of God, want of respect in the sense of their position, of reverence of God."[140]

With respect to Eleazar and Ithamar, Darby says, "there is, in a certain sense, a priestly way in which we have to bear the sins and sorrows of our brethren; not, of course, as to atonement...but still there is a true sense in which we have to bear them." Darby affirms that in this, above all else, like Eleazar and Ithamar, we fail. He explains that by eating a portion of the sin offering, the priests had a share in bearing the burden of the people of Israel. Darby sees the washing of feet in John 13 as the New Testament counterpart to this practice.[141] He writes:

> Where there is defilement seen in a brother, there should ever be this washing by us; but it is impossible that there can, unless in spirit we bear before the Lord all the burden of the fault and sin we desire to confess (washing the feet is not atonement); and here we all fail--in the use of this priestly service.[142]

As it was Eleazar and Ithamar's privilege to partake of the sin offering, so it is ours. In so doing, God's grace both blesses and uses us. We become fellow-workers under God.[143]

But, maintains Darby, we have all failed. While the professing church has offered strange fire before the Lord, we [the true church] have failed to eat the sin offering on behalf of our brethren. We have failed to intercede on behalf of other believers before the Lord. In this, says Darby, there is among us no sense of the saints' identity with Christ which would place us in an intercessory role.[144]

Darby explains that there is hope, however, as we see in Aaron's response when the sin of these two sons is brought to his attention by Moses. Aaron takes responsibility for their actions by laying it all upon himself, and thus "it seemed good in [Moses'] sight" (Lev. 10:20). Christ, like Aaron, makes Himself responsible for us in the atonement. Thus, when the voice of Aaron (Christ) is lifted up, "God is 'content.'"[145]

b. The Judgment. And how was the sin of Aaron's sons met, asks Darby. As it always must be met--in judgment. In the case of Nadab and Abihu who took a false place before Jehovah, judgment was swift as fire came down from heaven and consumed them (Lev. 10:2).[146] Eleazar and Ithamar, as we have said, were excused on the basis of the explanation offered by Aaron, even though their service had failed.[147] Concerning Aaron, Darby says,

> ... and the Lord said unto Moses, speak unto Aaron, thy brother, that he come not at all times into the holy place within the veil. The consequence was, that the garments of glory and beauty were never worn by the high priest save at his consecration. For he was to wear them only on going into the holy place within the veil, and his going in being now only on the day of atonement, he was desired withal on that day to come in other though holy garments.[148]

While the priesthood had failed like the Law, God would still patiently and mercifully carry it on "till there was no remedy,"[149] and until "He came who could efficiently fill all its functions."[150]

Introduction and Importance of Israel Under the Kings

Samuel, who was a judge over Israel and also a representative of the prophetic line, says Darby, governed Israel as God's witness over against the corrupted state of the priesthood. Yet God's people were not content with His "government by prophets," and desired rather a king like that of their neighbors. In anger, God installed a king (Saul) "according to the flesh..." The desire for such a king when the people experienced the immediate government of God as their king, Darby comments, only served to show the weakness of humanity's actions and the folly of its desires.[151]

Character of Israel Under the Kings

1. Primary Characteristics

a. The Government. Darby observes that Israel's demand for a king gave rise to the establishment of "another principle of God's ways with men..."[152] This "kingly dispensation"[153] features the establishment by grace of a royalty which was to extend not only to Zion, but to the Gentiles as well. The priesthood having lost its place, the king becomes God's anointed. With regard to the principle of royalty, Darby maintains that it,

> ...is on one side the throne of the Lord (Solomon is said to sit on the throne of the Lord), and on the other, it is strength out of weakness. See Hannah's song. It is the re-establishment of Israel in blessing when hopelessly ruined, by the means of the rejected but God-fearing king, who delivers them from their enemies and subdues the heathen. This re-establishment by royalty has a double bearing--the blessing of the people after their ruin, by the deliverance wrought, and then reestablished in accepted worship after the guilt (the temple after Shiloh, and that in a peculiar manner in grace, after the numbering of the people).[154]

Darby suggests that there were three stages to the principle of royalty in Israel: 1. when it was completely rejected in Israel; 2. when David placed the ark on Mt. Zion; and 3. in the victory connected with the covenant under Solomon. He says that all three of these stages--the rejected, powerful, and victorious king--are or will be fulfilled by Christ. In summary, writes Darby, "we have the important additional principle of a human ordained king, in a royalty established by God over His people, said to be seated too on the Lord's throne."[155]

Christ's kingship over His people, Darby maintains, was in God's design from the beginning. The fact of this kingship is presented in type in David and Solomon. The former is typical of Christ in that, after suffering and being completely obedient, he overcame all his enemies (Christ in the incarnation). The typical nature of the latter is seen in his peaceful and glorious reign over a "happy, obedient, and prosperous people" (Christ in the millennial kingdom). The picture ends here, Darby exclaims, for "Man may furnish types, but can never fill the functions of that which is true, and which shall be fulfilled in Christ."[156]

b. The Responsibility. Here as under the priesthood, no direct indication is given of the responsibility of the people under the kings. However, as one looks at the nature of Israel's failure--the divided monarchy--it appears that Israel united was to have submitted to God's appointed representative on earth, the king.

c. The Revelation. Darby indicates that it was Israel's inability to walk by faith and trust in God which precipitated her rejection of Him as King and her demand for a king like other nations. This, however, "gave occasion to the *revelation* of another principle of God's ways with men, the establishment of royalty in Zion..."[157]

2. Secondary Characteristics.

a. The Test and Failure. The dispensation of Israel under the Kings, laments Darby, failed just as that under the "previous ordering" had (Judges 2). While David exhibited royalty in victory and Solomon manifested it in peace, Rehoboam and Jeroboam are witnesses of total failure. God's patience and mercy continue until "the provocations of Manasseh set aside all hope of recovery or way of mercy in that dispensation."[158] They had failed the test of obedience to God's established royal administration.

Nor was Solomon, who Darby regards as a type of Christ in his reign of peace, free of failure as the representative of God on earth. It was indeed the very fact of peace and glory in his reign that caused Solomon's fall. He did not remain faithful in the midst of God's gifts, but chose to follow the false gods of his many wives. Thus, writes Darby,

> Kingship, the last resource of God for maintaining His relationship with His people, was corrupted, just in that particular in which Israel should have been His witness. The kingdom failed, and was divided: nevertheless, the house of David had one tribe, in the wisdom of God, for the love of David His servant, and of Jerusalem, the city which He had chosen among all the tribes of Israel; for the calling of David was a calling according to grace, and the choice of Jerusalem was the choice of God. See I Chron. 21:22; ch. 22:7-14; I Kings 11:13.[159]

After that, concludes Darby, a long-suffering God waited, taught, reproved, and forewarned the people of Israel through the prophets (II Chron. 36:15).[160]

According to Darby, however, the consummation of Israel's failure was yet to come. As evil arose in David's descendants, the major portion of Israel rebelled against him and his family. But two tribes remained, and it was a small remnant from these returned from the Babylonian captivity to whom Christ the Messiah was presented, only to be rejected.[161]

Darby sums up Israel's failure and its result in these words:

> Judaism, according to God's government on earth, promised temporal blessing to the righteous; but all was in disorder: even the Messiah, the head of the system, was rejected. In a word, Israel, looked at as set under

responsibility, and to enjoy earthly blessing could no longer, on that footing, be the means of bearing testimony to the ways of God in government.
There will be a time of earthly judgment, but it was not yet come.[162]

Elsewhere, after he presents Stephen's summary of Israel's history, Darby
says,

> Thus we have the complete summing up of their history, connected with
> the last days of their judgment. They always resisted the Holy Ghost, as
> they had always disobeyed the law. Judaism was judged, after the long
> patience of God and all His ways of grace with man as means were ex-
> hausted. For Israel was man under the special dealings and care of God.
> Man's guilt now is not only sin, but sin in spite of all that God has done.
> It was the turning-point of man's history. Law, prophets, Christ, the Holy
> Ghost, all tried, and man at enmity against God. The cross had really
> proved it, but this had added the rejection of the testimony of the Holy
> Ghost to a glorified Christ. All was over with man and began anew with
> the second Man ever in connection with heaven.[163]

For a history of Israel's rejection of Christ and of their own condemnation with
respect to responsibility, Darby directs the reader to the Gospel of Matthew.[164]

b. The Judgment. Darby is unclear about the nature of the judgment upon
Israel for her failure under the kings. He does make it clear, however, that her
judgment was based upon two things: 1. idolatry (Solomon's worship of his
wives' gods) and rebellion against Jehovah; and 2. rejection of Christ.[165] Darby
seems to sum up the immediate judgment upon Israel for her failure under the
monarchy by saying "the kingdom was made over to the Gentiles."[166] Presumably, Darby means to include in this pronouncement the judgment of the various
captivities under which Israel would suffer. As an expression of judgment upon
the Jews for their rejection of the Messiah, Darby quotes Christ's words in
Matthew 23:37-38. Their house would be left desolate, He says, and they will not
see Him until His second coming.

Scofield's Dispensation of Law (Sinai to Calvary)

Once again, says Scofield, in grace God rescued helpless humanity, the redeemed and chosen people from their bondage in Egypt. At Sinai, He proposed
the Covenant of Law and instead of begging for a continuation of their relationship of grace to God, they willingly took on the yoke of the Law. The history of
the people from that time on, points out Scofield, is one persistent and flagrant
violation of the Law. Finally, after repeated warnings, God closed humankind's
testing under the Law in judgment. Israel first, then Judah, were driven from the
land and dispersed far and wide; a situation which persists to the present. Under
Ezra and Nehemiah, a small remnant returned to the land and provided the source
from which the Messiah came. In due time, He was crucified at the hands of both
Jews and Gentiles alike.[167]

Scofield observes that Israel received the Mosaic Covenant in three parts:
1. the commandments - expressed God's righteous will (Ex. 20:1-26); 2. the

judgments - governed Israel's social life (Ex. 21:1-24); and 3. the ordinances - governed Israel's religious life (Ex. 24:12; 31:18). As a method of God's dealing with humanity, says Scofield, Law characterized the dispensation from the giving of that Law to Christ's death.[168] He maintains that while the testing of Israel ended with the judgment of the captivities, the dispensation itself did not end until the cross.[169]

The Evaluation

Because they draw upon the same Biblical data, it is evident that Darby and Scofield hold some concepts in common. They both discuss the giving of the Law, for example, and the outcome of its effect upon Israel. In their understanding of God's dispensational dealings with Israel, however, there is little point of contact between the two men. Nothing of Darby's threefold dispensational arrangement, or single dispensation with its threefold manifestation, can be found in Scofield.

Scripture itself clearly upholds the giving of the Law as the principle of God's dealings with humanity until the incarnate Christ should come. It was He, Scofield points out in following the teachings of the apostle Paul, who bore the curse of the Law and delivered the believer from both that curse and the dominion of the Law (Gal. 2:16; 3:2, 3, 11, 12). It was not until Christ came that it could be said that the believer is no longer under Law, but under grace (Rom. 6:14; 7:4; Gal. 2:19; 4:4-7; I Tim. 1:8, 9).[170]

We can find no grounds, and neither did Scofield, for the establishment of a dispensation of the Gentiles (discussed below) between the captivities of Israel and the coming of Christ. Nor do we find Darby's amorphous dispensation of Israel in its threefold presentation to be compelling. The priesthood was simply the means by which Israel approached God on the basis of the Law. The kings formed no new method of God's dealings with the human race in the dispensational sense, for they were as much subject to the Law as was the rest of Israel. God simply permitted Israel to be established under the monarchy, even though her motives and timing were all wrong. Consequently, neither the priests nor kings can be regarded in any dispensational sense as constituting the establishment of a new administrative arrangement of God with humankind.

GENTILES

Introduction and Importance of the Dispensation

Darby points out that prior to the captivity, God's glory resided in the temple in Jerusalem. The functions of government were carried out by Him directly as He maintained an immediate relationship with Israel. The people lived under a pure theocracy, though altered somewhat at the end by the monarchy under David.[171]

But it pleased the people, says Darby, not to submit to the direct government of God. They chose, rather, to adopt the worship of idols.[172] David's family, placed in responsibility on the Lord's throne at Jerusalem, had proven unfaithful.

Manasseh's sin made the government of Israel "insupportable to Jehovah," says Darby, and thus Israel was removed from the sight of God as Judah would be also.

After this course of events, asserts Darby, nothing remained of God's direct government of the earth. His glory, which had filled the temple in Jerusalem, was withdrawn from Jerusalem and the earth. He had set the nation Israel aside for a time, for He could no longer identify with her, and had placed Judah under the power of the Gentile nations for chastening.[173]

Darby explains that God could no longer address Himself directly to the people as owned by Him. Therefore, from the time of Israel's setting aside, God's sovereign power ceased to be immediately exercised by Him, but was transferred to those who were not His people--the Gentiles.[174] Nebuchadnezzar, as the representative of the new Gentile regime, takes control of Jerusalem "and the times of the Gentiles begin."[175] It is, says Darby, a governmental arrangement which exists to the present day.[176]

Darby sets forth the importance of this transfer of government in the following way:

> This was a change of immense importance, both in respect of the government of the world, and God's judgment of His people. Both lead the way to the great objects of prophecy developed at the close--the restoration, through tribulation, of a rebellious people, and the judgment of an unfaithful and apostate Gentile head of power.[177]

Character of the Dispensation

1. Primary Characteristics.

a. The Government. With the complete and final fall of the nation Israel, the right of government was transferred to the Gentile nations. But Darby is quick to point out that that right must be kept distinct from God's calling and promise. Darby reminds the reader that government upon the earth had been established under Noah, the calling of God under Abraham, and the two had been united in Israel. But now the two principles have been separated once more.

When Israel failed, explains Darby, she proved that she was incapable of manifesting the principle of God's government upon the earth. God had acted in righteousness in Israel, but Israel's unrighteousness proved that she could no longer serve as the depository of God's power among humankind. Consequently, God's government of the world, which He "transports...where He will," says Darby, was given into Gentile hands. It should be remembered that this government is not the "direct" government of God, for that was set aside at this time. Rather, it is the "general" government of God which is established under the Gentiles.[178]

The calling of God earthward, on the other hand, remains with Israel. As Darby explains, Israel continues to be God's called people, "for the gifts and calling of God are without repentance." While there is a calling of God from among the Gentiles, or nations--the call of the church, a heavenly not earthly call--the calling of God with regard to the earth remains with the Jews and is never transferred to the Gentile nations.[179] The center of God's dealings with the earth, insists Darby, is ever and always Israel.[180]

With God's pronouncement Lo-ammi, "not my people," says Darby, the times of the Gentiles begin with Nebuchadnezzar. Government in the form of civil authority and power is taken from Israel and placed in the hands of her enemies. Darby observes that this constituted a substantial modification of the principle of royalty, "the confiding the power of universal dominion, wherever the children of men dwell, to man on the earth." This dominion was sovereignly conferred beyond the limits of Israel's promise and dominion and acquired by the Gentiles on the basis of "no faithful service in suffering, but divinely bestowed by the God of heaven."[181] Successively, the reins of this dominion or government pass from the Babylonians, to the Medes and Persians, to the Greeks, and then to the Romans.[182] This is the subject, Darby points out, of Daniel and portions of the Apocalypse.[183]

b. The Responsibility. According to Darby, under the leadership of Nebuchadnezzar, Babylon represented the world at the time God had given the empire to the Gentiles. In this capacity, she was responsible to exercise God's power. While Darby does not say so, presumably the exercise of this power was to be under God's authority and in keeping with His divine character and principles of government.[184] In short, says Darby, "God trusts Nebuchadnezzar with power, and he is the head of gold among the Gentiles..."[185]

c. The Revelation. Again, Darby says nothing specifically about revelation in the establishment of this dispensation.

2. Secondary Characteristics.

a. The Test and Failure. While Darby does not specifically address the matter of Gentile testing during this time of their dominion, he is quite specific about their failure. He notes that instead of ruling in accord with the righteous principles of God, Nebuchadnezzar falls into pride, makes a great golden idol, casts God's people into the fiery furnace, and becomes as a beast with a beast's heart. For seven years, the Babylonian monarch is devoid of reason and out of his senses "(a figure of the Gentile empires)," to the extent that he consumes grass like an ox.[186]

The power of the Gentiles becomes violent, corrupt, and ambitious, says Darby. It cannot, as Scripture says, stay at home. It thus likens Gentile powers to "ravening beasts" (an allusion to the prophecies of Daniel, chapter 7).[187]

The failure of the Gentiles, however, was to be consummated as was that of Israel, in the rejection and crucifixion of Christ. "It [Gentile authority] put Christ to death when He came in grace," says Darby, "lusts against the Spirit where He is, and, if one is called to the third heaven, would puff him up about it."[188] Though substituted for the Jewish royalty, observes Darby, the Gentiles united with the Jews in rejecting God's Son and the Jews' King.[189] Darby writes:

The fourth monarchy consummated its crime at the same instant that the Jews consummated theirs, in being accessory, in the person of Pontius Pilate, to the will of a rebellious nation, by killing Him who was at once the Son of God and King of Israel. Gentile power is in a fallen state, even as the called people, the Jews, are. Judgment is written upon power [government] and calling, as in man's hand.[190]

b. The Judgment. The times of Gentile dominion are destined to continue, says Darby, until the judgment of Christ shall fall upon those who have been the oppressors of God's people and they are destroyed.[191] Darby explains elsewhere that prior to the destruction of Gentile power, Judah will be oppressed by its head, a false Christ, in the latter days. God still regards Israel as His, however, and while a remnant of her people shall by grace survive great Tribulation, call upon God's name, and shun the idolatry of the Gentiles and their leader the Antichrist, the false prophet and apostate Gentile government will be judged by God.[192]

Darby points to Revelation 11:18 as closing the general history of the human race. He says,

It is the conclusion of the history of the government and of the judgment of God on earth. There is something progressive in the action of the providential government of God over men. We see, first, things of ordinary occurrence, such as famines, pestilences. After this there are judgments more striking, powers falling; then, in the first four trumpets, men judged in their circumstances. In the last three trumpets the judgments fall on men themselves. After chapter 12 we have the history of the apostasy.[193]

We know of no dispensationalist who would agree with Darby's position here, for the final destruction of Gentile power does not come until Christ's second coming and the battle of Armageddon is completed (to the end of Rev. 19). In fact, elsewhere this is the position that Darby himself sets forth. With the destruction of Antichrist in Revelation 19:20, he says, "This is the end of the times of the Gentiles."[194] This is certainly Scofield's position.[195] In any case, with the destruction of Gentile power, Israel will be established in blessing under Christ upon the earth, and the throne of the Lord will once again reside in Jerusalem as the millennial kingdom begins.[196]

The Faithful Remnant

A very important concept in Darby's understanding of God's dealings with Israel is that of the faithful remnant. In spite of the fact that Israel as a dispensation had failed, and that God no longer had anything to do with Israel in terms of government of the world, He nevertheless had a faithful remnant whom He had chosen. To this remnant, God communicated His intentions and outlined the events to come which would have a bearing upon them. Part of this outline, says Darby, is to be found in the prophetic part of the Apocalypse.[197]

Darby states that such a remnant has always existed, from the time of Israel's apostasy to the formation of the church, and will continue to exist in the days to come. In days of crisis especially, it is those from among the remnant who gain special distinction. This included men like Samuel, David, Jeremiah, Ezekiel, Daniel, the prophets in general, Ezra, Nehemiah, and the apostles among others.[198] "Thus Israel as a whole, under the law," says Darby, "were [sic] put as a dispensation under the responsibility of its observance, and nationally failed, though a remnant all through were of God and saved."[199]

Darby makes it clear that Israel's cutting off and punishment in captivity at the hands of the Gentiles was not a question of the "eternal consequences of sin, but of the government of God with respect to Israel."[200] In other words, as a dispensation, the Jewish branches were broken off and the Gentiles took the place of the Jews "in the enjoyment of the dispensation of the promises" (Rom. 11:12, 13). Darby explains further that in addition to the union of the faithful with Christ, there are privileges to be enjoyed as a dispensation and these may be lost, as they were by Israel.[201]

Darby insists that while Israel may have failed with respect to the intentions of God, with regard to the counsels[202] or purposes[203] of God, there can be no failure. Israel has only temporarily been set aside and she will yet experience the full blessings of God and see the complete fulfillment of the promises contained in the Abrahamic and Davidic Covenants. Darby summarizes the apostle Paul's argument in Romans 11 in proof that God has not rejected His people.[204] He explains that when God said Lo-ammi, "not my people," to Israel, it wasn't that God was giving them up, on the contrary, "They shall be His people at last..."[205]

Scofield holds out similar hopes for God's chosen people. He gives this explantion for the remnant of "spiritual Israel":

> In the history of Israel a "remnant" may be discerned, a spiritual Israel within the national Israel. In Elijah's time 7,000 had not bowed the knee to Baal (1 Ki. 19. 18). In Isaiah's time it was the "very small remnant" for whose sake God still forbore to destroy the nation (Isa. 1. 9). During the captivities the remnant appears in Jews like Ezekiel, Daniel, Shadrach, Meshach, and Abednego, Esther and Mordecai. At the end of the 70 years of Babylonian captivity it was the remnant which returned under Ezra and Nehemiah. At the advent of our Lord, John the Baptist, Simeon, Anna, and "them that looked for redemption in Jerusalem" (Lk. 2. 38), were the remnant. During the church-age the remnant is composed of believing Jews (Rom. 11. 4, 5). But the chief interest in the remnant is prophetic. During the great tribulation a remnant out of all Israel will turn to Jesus as Messiah, and will become His witnesses after the removal of the church (Rev. 7. 3-8). Some of these will undergo martyrdom (Rev. 6. 9-11), some will be spared to enter the millennial kingdom (Zech. 12. 6-13. 9). Many of the Psalms express, prophetically, the joys and sorrows of the tribulation remnant.[206]

It is this remnant of Israel which comes out of the Tribulation, says Scofield, who will be restored as a nation in the land of promise and exalted as the earthly people of God in the millennial kingdom.[207]

Scofield and "Times of the Gentiles"

As indicated in the discussion of Israel under the kings, Scofield does not identify the "times of the Gentiles" as a dispensation. Rather he defines this long period of time as that,

> ...beginning with the Babylonian captivity of Judah, under Nebuchadnez-zar, and to be brought to an end by the destruction of Gentile world power by the "stone cut out without hands" (Dan. 2. 34, 35, 44), i.e. the coming of the Lord in glory (Rev. 19. 11, 21), until which time Jerusalem is politically subject to Gentile rule (Lk. 21. 24).[208]

The overlordship of Israel by the Gentiles, Scofield traces to the effects of God's judgment upon Israel for her failure under the Davidic Covenant. He points out that Psalm 89:32 warns of chastening if there is disobedience in David's royal posterity. The divided kingdom marks the historical beginning of this chastening (I kings 11:26-36; 12:16-20), says Scofield, and it culminates in the captivities which subordinate Israel to Gentile rule.[209] In spite of this chasten-ing process, however, Scofield is in agreement with Darby that Israel remains al-ways the center of the "divine counsels earthwards (Deut. 32. 8)." While the Gentile nations serve as God's chastening instrument in the discipline of His cho-sen people, the retribution of God inevitably comes down upon them.[210]

Concerning God's government of the world, Scofield writes in connection with the establishment of human government under Noah that,

> Man is responsible to govern the world for God. That responsibility rested upon the whole race, Jew and Gentile, until the failure of Israel under the Palestinian Covenant (Deut. 28.-30. 1-10) brought the judgment of the Cap-tivities, when "the times of the Gentiles" (See Lk. 21. 24; Rev. 16. 14) be-gan, and the government of the world passed exclusively into Gentile hands (Dan. 2. 36-45; Lk. 21. 24; Acts 15. 14-17). That both Israel and the Gentiles have governed for self, not God, is sadly apparent.[211]

Scofield, like Darby, observes that Daniel has the distinction of being the prophet of the "times of the Gentiles."[212] He recaps Daniel's visions in which it is revealed that the reins of Gentile power shall pass successively from Babylon, to Medo-Persia, to the Greeks, and then to the Romans. These are the only world powers revealed to Daniel, states Scofield, and any attempt to establish another has always failed. It was the Lord Himself, says Scofield, who gave a name and sign to the period from 610 B.C. to the present--"Jerusalem shall be trodden under foot of the Gentiles, until the times of the Gentiles be fulfilled" (Luke 21:24).[213]

Like Darby too, Scofield sees total failure in the great experiment of Gentile government. He says, "They have never governed for one fraction of a second under the Christian ideal--never once." We are approaching the end of this long period of testing to see whether the natural man could successfully govern the world. "And the experiment certainly has broken down."[214]

According to Scofield, the end of the experiment is near. "We are in the feet, if not the toes, of the image [Dan. 2:31-45];" he maintains, "and the last events will be rapidly fulfilled."[215] And if the end of the period of Gentile world power is near, then so is that of the present age, for they are co-terminus.[216]

The Evaluation

It is apparent in Scofield's analysis of the "times of the Gentiles" that the earthly, civil government of God is turned over to the Gentiles. However, it does not constitute a new dealing of God earthward (i.e., a new dispensation), for Israel continues to be the focus of God's counsels and blessing in the world. The Gentile nations, far from constituting a new economy in God's dealings with humanity, serve rather as only the instruments of His divine judgment upon Israel, His errant people. In the dispensation of Grace, of course, the calling of a people to be God's own--the Body of Christ--includes the Gentiles as well as the Jews.

The institution of the Law under Moses continued to be the established principle upon which God dealt with humankind until He who was to be the perfect fulfillment of the Law should come. Ryrie touches upon this point when he says, "During that extended period [Moses to crucifixion] Israel's change in spiritual condition might seem to indicate a change in dispensation." But if it can be shown that Jesus considered the Mosaic Law "still operative and incumbent on the Jewish people" during His lifetime, then it could not have ended until the cross. Ryrie points to Matthew 8:2-4, 23:2-3, and 5:17 as proof that Christ did indeed live under the Law and expected those who followed Him to do likewise.[217]

Endnotes

[1]John Nelson Darby, *The Collected Writings of J. N. Darby*, 34 vols., ed. William Kelly, vol. 1: *Ecclesiastical No. 1* (Sunbury, Pa.: Believers Bookshelf, n.d.), p. 127. This article entitled "The Apostasy of the Successive Dispensations," pp. 124-30, first appeared in 1836 in *The Christian Witness*, a little paper started by Darby and a few other Brethren. This appears to have been the first published expression of Darby's dispensational views.

[2]Ibid.

[3]Ibid., p. 170.

[4]Ibid., vol. 5: *Prophetic No. 2*, p. 388. Here Darby excludes the present and kingdom dispensations, but includes Adam, a period which he definitely concludes is not in any proper sense a dispensation at all.

[5]Ibid., vol. 2: *Prophetic No. 1*, p. 374.

[6]Ibid., vol. 13: *Critical No. 1*, p. 153, cf. p. 161. The reader is directed also to vol. 1: *Ecclesiastical No. 1*, pp. 124-5 (and the discussion on p. 46 above), where Darby gives the most concise statement of his philosophy of dispensations and then follows it by saying that "The Paradisaical state cannot properly perhaps be called a dispensation in this sense of the word..."

[7]Ibid., vol. 5: *Prophetic No. 2*, p. 384. It is evident, particularly from vol. 1: *Ecclesiastical No. 1*, p. 125, that Darby is including both the state of innocency and that of conscience in the expression "the time before the flood." At times it is difficult to tell where he means to include the two periods together or is referring only to the period of conscience from the fall to the flood.

[8]Darby, *Writings*, vol. 13: *Critical No. 1*, p. 153.

[9]Ibid., vol. 22: *Doctrinal No. 6*, p. 365.

[10]Charles Caldwell Ryrie, *Dispensationalism Today* (Chicago: Moody Press, 1965), pp. 57-8.

[11]Darby, *Writings*, vol. 1: *Ecclesiastical No. 1*, p. 125.

[12]Ibid., vol. 22: *Doctrinal No. 6*, p. 337.

[13]Ibid., vol. 32: *Miscellaneous*, No. 2, p. 233.

[14]Ibid.

[15]Ibid., vol. 22: *Doctrinal No. 6*, p. 337.

[16]Ibid.

[17]Ibid., vol. 1: *Ecclesiastical No. 1*, p.125.

[18]Ibid., vol. 22: *Doctrinal No. 6*, p. 337.

[19]Ibid., p. 338.

[20]Ibid., vol. 1: *Ecclesiastical No. 1*, p. 125.

[21]C. I. Scofield, *Rightly Dividing the Word of Truth* (Fincaste, Va.: Scripture Truth Book Co., n.d.), p. 13.

[22]C. I Scofield, ed., *The Scofield Reference Bible* (New York: Oxford University Press, 1909), p. 5.

[23]C. I Scofield, *What Do the Prophets Say?* (Greenville, S.C.: The Gospel Hour, Inc., 1918), pp. 27-8.

[24]Ibid.

[25]Darby, *Writings*, vol. 1: *Ecclesiastical No. 1*, p. 125.

[26]Ibid., pp. 125-6.

[27]Ibid., vol. 22: *Doctrinal No. 6*, p. 367.

[28]Ibid., p. 337.

[29]Ibid., p. 366.

[30]Ibid.

[31]Ibid., pp. 366-7.

[32]Ibid., p. 367.

[33]Ibid., pp. 338-9.

[34]Ibid., p. 389; vol. 2: *Prophetic No. 1*, p. 374.

[35]Ibid., vol. 22: *Doctrinal No. 6*, p. 338.

[36]For an example of this procedure, see *Writings*, vol. 1: *Ecclesiastical No. 1*, p. 205, where Darby writes: "Adam soon lost his innocence. Noah got drunk...," etc.

[37]Darby, vol. 22: *Doctrinal No. 6*, p. 366.

[38]Ibid., p. 339.

[39]See *Writings*, vol. 16: *Practical No. 1*, pp. 57-8 for a discussion of the nature of the sacrifices offered by Cain and Abel.

[40]Ibid., vol. 22: *Doctrinal No. 6*, pp. 338-40.

[41]Ibid., p. 340.

[42]Scofield, *Reference Bible*, p. 10; cf. *Rightly Dividing the Word of Truth*, p. 13.

[43]Scofield, *What Do the Prophets Say?*, pp. 28-9.

[44]John Nelson Darby, *Synopsis of the Books of the Bible*, 5 vols., reprint ed. (Sunbury, Pa.: Believers Bookshelf, n.d.), 1:23. Darby understands sin against God and violence against one's neighbor to be "the two perpetual characters of sin, amongst men..." In an interesting footnote, he says, "There are three characters of sin--violence, falsehood and corruption. The two first are directly ascribed to Satan; alas, man follows him in them, the third is more properly man's. All three are noticed in Colossians iii. 5-9."

[45]Darby, *Writings*, vol. 5: *Prophetic No. 2*, p. 384.

[46]Ibid.

[47]Darby, *Synopsis*, 1: 23. Darby defines as covenant here "when used in connection with the Lord,...[as] some order established by God and announced to man, according to the terms of which He enters into relationship with man, or according to which man is to approach Him."

[48]Ibid.

[49]Darby, *Writings*, vol. 2: *Prophetic No. 1*, p. 132.

[50]Ibid.

[51]Ibid., vol. 5: *Prophetic No. 2*, p. 14.

[52]Ibid., vol. 2, *Prophetic No. 1*, pp. 132-33.

[53]Ibid., vol. 1: *Ecclesiastical No. 1*, p. 125.

[54]Ibid., vol. 19: *Expository No. 1*, p. 123.

[55]Darby, *Synopsis*, 1:23.

[56]Darby, *Writings*, vol. 2: *Prophetic No. 1*, p. 133.

[57]Ibid., pp. 133-4.

[58]Ibid., p. 134.

[59]Ibid., vol. 22: *Doctrinal No. 6*, p. 340.

[60]Ibid., vol. 2: *Prophetic No. 1*, p. 134.

[61]Darby, *Synopsis*, 1:23.

[62]Darby, *Writings*, vol. 22: *Doctrinal No. 6*, pp. 340-1.

[63]Ibid., vol. 1: *Ecclesiastical No. 1*, p. 125.

[64]Scofield, *Rightly Dividing the Word of Truth*, p. 13; *Reference Bible*, p. 16.

[65]Scofield, *Reference Bible*, p. 16.

[66]Scofield, *What Do the Prophets Say?*, p. 29.

[67]Darby is usually strong on the ruling principle (i.e., government) and failure of humanity in each dispensation. With respect to the other characteristics of the dispensations (responsibility, revelation, test, and judgment), however, one usually has to search several volumes to collect them all and even then any given characteristic may be only inferred or contained in a single sentence or cast in different terms in different places.

[68]Darby, *Writings*, vol. 19: *Expository No. 1*, pp. 122-3.

[69]Ibid., p. 124.

[70]Ibid.

[71]Ibid., vol. 2: *Prophetic No. 1*, p. 134.

[72]Ibid., vol. 5: *Prophetic No. 2*, pp. 384-5.

[73]Ibid., vol. 19: *Expository No. 1*, p. 122.

[74]Ibid.

[75]Ibid., vol. 2: *Prophetic No. 1*, p. 134.

[76]Ibid., vol. 19: *Expository No. 1*, pp. 126-7.

[77]Ibid., vol. 2: *Prophetic No. 1*, p. 135.

[78]Ibid., vol. 22: *Doctrinal No. 6*, p. 368.

[79]Ibid., pp. 368-9.

[80]Ibid., vol. 32: *Miscellaneous No. 1*, pp. 232-3.

[81]Ibid., vol. 19: *Expository No. 1*, pp. 127-8.

[82]Ibid., p. 128 (italics added).

[83]Ibid., vol. 2: *Prophetic No. 1*, p. 375 (italics added).

[84]We could offer several examples of this practice, but the reader is directed to the following as illustrative of the procedure: "In chapter iii. [of Genesis] we find--what, alas! has always happened, and happened immediately when God has set up anything in the hands of responsible man-- disobedience and failure. So it was in Adam, so in Noah, so in Israel with the golden calf, so in the priesthood with strange fire, so in Solomon son of David, and Nebuchadnezzar. So indeed in the church, I John ii. 18, 19, and Jude" (*Synopsis*, 1:16). This is the usual catalog: Adam (non-dispensation), Noah, (Abraham omitted), Israel - under law, priesthood and kings, church, (Kingdom omitted). Cf. *Writings*, vol. 1: *Ecclesiastical No. 1*, p. 205; vol. 11: *Prophetic No. 4*, p. 279.

[85]Darby, *Writings*, vol. 19: *Expository No. 1*, pp. 129-32.

[86]Ibid., p. 131.

[87]Ibid., vol. 1: *Ecclesiastical No. 1*, p. 125.

[88]Ibid., vol. 22: *Doctrinal No. 6*, p. 341.

[89]Ibid., vol. 1: *Ecclesiastical No. 1*, p. 125.

[90]Ibid., vol. 22: *Doctrinal No. 6*, p. 341.

[91]There is a certain overall parallel structure in Darby's dispensations as is shown by **Appendix E**.

[92]Darby, *Writings*, vol. 22: *Doctrinal No. 6*, p. 341.

[93]Ibid.

[94]Ibid., vol. 19: *Expository No. 1*, pp. 128-9.

[95]Ibid., p. 130.

[96]Ibid.

[97]Ibid.

[98]Ibid., p. 132.

[99]See p. 60ff above for a treatment of the intentions of God versus His counsels.

[100]Scofield, *Rightly Dividing the Word of Truth*, p. 14.

[101]C. I. Scofield, *Scofield Correspondence Course* (Chicago: Moody Bible Institute, 1934).

[102]Scofield, *Reference Bible*, p. 19.

[103]Scofield, *What Do the Prophets Say?*, p. 30.

[104]Scofield, *Reference Bible*, p. 20.

[105]See **Appendix C**.

[106]Darby, *Writings*, vol. 5: *Prophetic No. 2*, p. 385.

[107]Ibid., vol. 1: *Ecclesiastical No. 1*, p. 139.

[108]Darby, *Synopsis*, 1:82.

[109]Darby, *Writings*, vol. 22: *Doctrinal No. 6*, p. 343.

[110]Ibid., vol. 2: *Prophetic No. 1*, p. 136.

[111]Ibid.

[112]Ibid., p. 375.

[113]Ibid., vol. 5: *Prophetic No. 2*, p. 386.

[114]Ibid., vol. 22: *Doctrinal No. 6*, p. 344.

[115]Ibid., vol. 5: *Prophetic No. 2*, p. 386.

[116]Ibid., p. 136.

[117]Darby, *Synopsis*, 1:83.

[118]Darby, *Writings*, vol. 22: *Doctrinal No. 6*, pp. 369-70.

[119]Ibid., vol. 5: *Prophetic No. 2*, p. 386.

[120]Ibid.

[121]Ibid., vol. 11: *Prophetic No. 4*, p. 125.

[122]Ibid., vol. 2: *Prophetic No. 1*, p. 138, cf. vol. 1: *Ecclesiastical No. 1*, p. 126.

[123]Darby, *Writings*, vol. 11: *Prophetic No. 4*, p. 48.

[124]Ibid., vol. 2: *Prophetic No. 1*, p. 138 (italics added by Darby).

[125]Ibid., pp. 136-7.

[126]Ibid., pp. 138-9.

[127]Ibid., p. 138.

[128]C. F. Keil and F. Delitzch, *Commentary on the Old Testament*, 10 vols. (Grand Rapids: William B. Eerdmans Publishing Co., n.d.), 1:499.

[129]Darby, *Writings*, vol. 2: *Prophetic No. 1*, p. 139.

[130]Ibid., vol. 5: *Prophetic No. 2*, p. 391.

[131]Ibid., vol. 1: *Ecclesiastical No. 1*, p. 126. Here he says, "The ordinance or dispensation of priesthood failed…"

[132]Darby, *Writings*, vol. 5: *Prophetic No. 2*, p. 391.

[133]Ibid., vol. 2: *Prophetic No. 1*, p. 139.

[134]Ibid., vol. 5: *Prophetic No. 2*, p. 386.

[135]Ibid., vol. 16: *Practical No. 1*, pp. 56-7.

[136]Ibid., p. 57.

[137]Ibid., p. 60.

[138]Ibid., vol. 1: *Ecclesiastical No. 1*, p. 126; vol. 16: *Practical No. 1*, pp. 65-7.

[139]Ibid., vol. 2: *Prophetic No. 1*, p. 139.

[140]Ibid., vol. 16: *Practical No. 1*, pp. 60-1.

[141]Ibid., p. 65.

[142]Ibid., pp. 65-6.

[143]Ibid., p. 66.

[144]Ibid., p. 67.

[145]Ibid., pp. 66-7.

[146]Ibid., p. 61.

[147]Ibid., vol. 1: *Ecclesiastical No. 1*, p. 126.

[148]Ibid.

[149]Ibid.

[150]Ibid., vol. 2: *Prophetic No. 1*, p. 139.

[151]Ibid., pp. 139-40; cf. vol. 5: *Prophetic No. 2*, pp. 386-7.

[152]Ibid., vol. 5: *Prophetic No. 2*, p. 386.

[153]Ibid., vol. 1: *Ecclesiastical No. 1*, p. 126.

[154]Ibid., vol. 5: *Prophetic No. 2*, p. 387.

[155]Ibid.

[156]Ibid., vol. 2: *Prophetic No. 1*, p. 140.

[157]Ibid., vol. 5: *Prophetic No. 2*, p. 387 (italics added).

[158]Ibid., vol. 1: *Ecclesiastical No. 1*, pp. 126-7.

[159]Ibid., vol. 2: *Prophetic No. 1*, p. 140.

[160]Ibid.

[161]Ibid., vol. 11: *Prophetic No. 4*, p. 48.

[162]Darby, *Synopsis*, 3:354.

[163]Ibid., 4:21-2.

[164]Ibid., 3:23.

[165]Darby, *Writings*, vol. 11: *Prophetic No. 4*, p. 48.

[166]Ibid., vol. 2: *Prophetic No. 1*, p. 140.

[167]Scofield, *Rightly Dividing the Word of Truth*, p. 14.

[168]Scofield, *Reference Bible*, p. 1244.

[169]Ibid., p. 94.

[170]Ibid., p. 1245.

[171]Darby, *Writings*, vol. 5: *Prophetic No. 2*, p. 138.

[172]Ibid.

[173]Ibid., vol. 11: *Prophetic No. 4*, p. 50.

[174]Ibid., p. 48.

[175]Ibid., vol. 5: *Prophetic No. 2*, p. 138.

[176]Ibid., p. 14.

[177]Ibid., vol. 11: *Prophetic No. 4*, p. 48.

[178]Darby, *Synopsis*, 5:396. The reader is directed to p. 52ff above for a discussion of the "direct" versus the "general" government of God.

[179]Darby, *Writings*, vol. 2: *Prophetic No. 1*, pp. 377-8.

[180]Ibid., vol. 11: *Prophetic No. 4*, p. 304.

[181]Ibid., vol. 5: *Prophetic No. 2*, p. 387.

[182]Ibid., vol. 11: *Prophetic No. 4*, p. 304.

[183]Ibid., p. 50; cf. *Synopsis*, 3:366.

[184]Darby, *Writings*, vol. 2: *Prophetic No. 1*, p. 151.

[185]Ibid., vol. 11: *Prophetic No. 4*, p. 279.

[186]Ibid.; cf. vol. 14: *Ecclesiastical No. 3*, p. 87, 99; vol. 18: *Doctrinal No. 5*, p. 253.

[187]Darby, *Writings*, vol. 18: *Doctrinal No. 5*, p. 253.

[188]Ibid., vol. 21: *Evangelic No. 2*, p. 119.

[189]Ibid., vol. 5: *Prophetic No. 2*, p. 387.

[190]Ibid., vol. 2: *Prophetic No. 1*, p. 378.

[191]Ibid., vol. 11: *Prophetic No. 4*, p. 304.

[192]Ibid., p. 50.

[193]Ibid., vol. 5: *Prophetic No. 2*, p. 28.

[194]Ibid., p. 82.

[195]Scofield, *Reference Bible*, p. 1345.

[196]Darby, *Writings*, vol. 11: *Prophetic No. 4*, p. 51.

[197]Ibid., vol. 5: *Prophetic No. 2*, p. 139.

[198]John Nelson Darby, *Letters of J.N. Darby*, 3 vols., reprint ed. (Sunbury, Pa.: Believers Bookshelf, 1971), 1:123. For the history of the remnant from the beginning of the Old Testament to the end of the New, see **Appendix F**.

[199]Darby, *Writings*, vol. 1: *Ecclesiastical No. 1*, p. 114.

[200]Ibid., vol. 4: *Ecclesiastical No. 2*, p. 180.

[201]Ibid., vol. 1: *Ecclesiastical No. 1*, p. 180.

[202]Darby, *Synopsis*, 4:192, 194. For a discussion of the intentions or purposes versus the counsels of God, the reader is directed to p. 60 and following above.

[203]John Nelson Darby, *Miscellaneous Writings of J. N. D.*, vols. 4 and 5, reprint ed. (Oak Park, Ill.: Bible Truth Publishers, n.d.), 4:163.

[204]Darby, *Synopsis*, 4:192f. See also Scofield's note on Romans 11:1, *Reference Bible*, p. 1204, note 2.

[205]Darby, *Miscellaneous Writings*, 4:163.

[206]Scofield, *Reference Bible*, p. 1205.

[207]Ibid., p. 1204.

[208]Ibid., p. 1345; cf. p. 816.

[209]Ibid., p. 643.

[210]Ibid., p. 722.

[211]Ibid., p. 14.

[212]Ibid., p. 898; cf. *What Do the Prophets Say?*, pp. 67-70.

[213]Scofield, *What Do the Prophets Day?*, pp.69-70.

[214]C. I Scofield, "The Course and End of the Age," *Bibliotheca Sacra* 108 (January 1951):105-6; cf. "The Times of the Gentiles," *Bibliotheca Sacra* 107 (July 1950):354.

[215]C. I Scofield, "The Times of the Gentiles," *Bibliotheca Sacra* 107 (July 1950):353.

[216]C. I Scofield, "Tested By Grace," *Bibliotheca Sacra* 107 (October 1950):491.

[217]Ryrie, pp. 53-4.

CHAPTER 4-PART 2

DARBY'S SYSTEM OF DISPENSATIONS
(CHURCH AGE TO ETERNAL STATE)

The Dispensational Periods (Cont.)

SPIRIT/CHRISTIAN/GENTILE/CHURCH/PRESENT[1]

Introduction and Importance of the Dispensation

Darby's position on the dispensation of the Spirit may remind the reader of a question Elijah posed to the Israelites. With regard to whether they would worship God or Baal, Elijah asked, "How long *will* you hesitate between two opinions?" (I Kings 18:21). As to whether the present church age is a dispensation or not, Darby seems to have two different opinions. The opinion he follows at any given point depends upon the angle from which he is viewing the subject.

That there is a distinction between the state of things before Christ came and then after, Darby has no doubt. He states that God has in fact suppressed that order of things known as Judaism. We are no longer under the "Jewish economy" or "Jewish Dispensation" the "dispensation of the law," says Darby, for God has substituted the "Christian dispensation" for it. Darby goes so far as to affirm that "Every one knows that..." and anyone who aspires to reinstate the "Jewish dispensation" is guilty of sin.[2]

The reader will note that here, Darby seems to characterize the entire period from the giving of the Law to the coming of Christ as a single dispensation--the "Jewish dispensation," the "dispensation of the law." Darby says that this "dispensation under which the law subsisted in its integrity as a rule of the government of God, and under which the prophets exercised their ministry..." has been replaced by another because of the sins of those who should have lived in conformity to it (the Levitical system).[3] If the "Christian dispensation" immediately followed the "Jewish dispensation...of the Law," one wonders what became of the Gentile dispensation and of those of Israel under the priesthood and kings.

According to Darby, the "Jewish scene" officially closed with the ascension of Christ. With this event, Jewish testimony ceased and would not resume until Israel could say, "Blessed is he that cometh in the name of the Lord..." (i.e., the second coming of Christ). Individuals could be and were converted, says Darby, "but the order of Jewish ministry ceased."[4]

A new scene now opens, Darby observes, that of the church whose portion is the heavenlies in contrast to the earthlies which were the portion of the Jews. He explains that the new scene begins because the Jews had rejected the testimony of the risen Christ and that of Stephen and the apostles. Darby sees Stephen's testimony as the hinge upon which the transition between the Jewish and Christian order of things swings, for Stephen had seen Jesus in the heavenlies (undoubtedly a reference to Acts 7:55). "Thus," says Darby, "he formed the link between Jewish rejection and the position and state of the church which followed."[5] At the death of Stephen, the "Gentile dispensation" began as a distinct thing because that event served as a witness that the Jews were resisting the Holy Ghost just as their fathers had.[6]

If the death of Stephen was the pivotal event which inaugurated the Gentile dispensation, then Paul as the apostle to the Gentiles was its head and chief representative. He is the type, says Darby, of "the regular Gentile form and order of the dispensation..."[7] Darby explains the significance of Paul's headship of this dispensation in terms of the apostle's statement that,

> "Last of all he [Christ] was seen of me also, as of one born out of due time," as an abortion (*ektroma*); and this character attaches to the whole dispensation, an extraordinary arrangement and provision, something born out of due time--*ektromatal*--for the time present, till the earthly system is just ready to be restored, but belonging entirely to the heavenlies, having no earthly derivation or connection in its power with the succession of that order which was first outwardly established.[8]

Distinction Between Jewish and Christian Dispensations

As a dispensation born out of due time, according to Darby, the Christian dispensation is very different from the Jewish dispensation which preceded it. In fact, the failure to distinguish the two leads to the greatest of interpretive problems, he says, for they are "the hinge upon which the subject and the understanding of Scripture turns."[9] What is it exactly that most distinguishes the two dispensations?

To begin with, in Judaism, the Law was given at Sinai to regulate the relationship or direct the conduct of a people already formed and recognized as God's people. Their existence and rights depended upon their descent from Abraham, Isaac, and Jacob. Thus, they already existed as a people when God established a covenant relationship with them, in order that He might determine if, with this privileged status and with every necessary advantage to maintain their position (mediation of the priesthood), they could remain faithful to Him. "The question was not," explains Darby, "how to seek and call those without; but to *order the intercourse* with God of a people already recognized as such."[10]

Darby points out that in the Christian dispensation, the situation is altogether different. The Law had proven that no matter the advantage or privilege afforded humankind, it is impossible for people to stand on their own before God. Thus, upon the proven failure of humanity, God visits a ruined race, Jew and Gentile alike, with grace. In Christianity, a person is first considered and then proven in reality to be lost and then sought as a true worshipper of God through the power of the new life. This accomplished, explains Darby, the worshipper is introduced to God as Father, not through the mediatorship of a priestly class, but directly and without fear. God is not now perceived as terrible and imperfectly known, but as known and loved.[11]

This distinction between the relationship of humanity to God in Judaism and Christianity, raises what Darby perceives to be the great characteristic and distinguishing factor in this dispensation--the concept of ministry. He writes:

> The consequence of this marked difference between the relations in which Jews and Christians stand as toward God is, that the Jews had a priesthood (and not a ministry) which acted outwards, that is, outside the people; while Christianity has a ministry which finds its exercise in the active revelation of what God is--whether within the church or without--there being no intermediate priesthood between God and His people, save the Great High Priest Himself. The Christian priesthood is composed of all true Christians, who equally enjoy the right of entering into the holy places...Ministry, then, is essential to Christianity; which is the activity of the love of God in delivering souls from ruin and from sin, and in drawing them to Himself.[12]

With respect to the relationship subsisting between God and humankind on earth, then, the distinguishing characteristic of the Jewish dispensation was the priesthood, while that of the Christian dispensation is ministry. This is true, says Darby, "because priesthood maintained the Jews in their relations with God; and because by ministry Christianity seeks in this world worshippers of the Father."[13]

The Nature of the Church

1. Heavenly Versus Earthly Nature.

Here we have the introduction of both the church as parenthetical in nature and the distinction between the church (i.e., Christendom) as a dispensational and therefore earthly thing, and the true church (i.e., the Body of Christ) as above the earthly order and therefore a heavenly thing. According to Darby, the departure of the church as an earthly order of things from its heavenly calling was predicted by Paul himself. He writes:

> Paul was the special witness...yet though he sustained it [the Gentile dispensation] by the energy of the Spirit during his life, he knew well that it would end then, that is, as thus corporately held together: "I know this, that after my departing shall grievous wolves enter in, not sparing the flock. Also of your own selves shall men arise speaking perverse things to draw away disciples after them" [Acts 20:29-30].[14]

Perhaps Darby's point is this. From the death of Stephen through Paul's life, the church was united in its heavenly calling and earthly arrangement. However, at the apostle's death, the church in its earthly character (the "professing" church, Christendom) and the church in its heavenly character (the true church, the Body of Christ) would become two distinctly different things.

Clarence Bass says of Darby's distinction between Christendom and the true church, that it is "One of the earliest principles to emerge in [his] thought..." He explains this principle in Darby's ecclesiology in the following way:

> The true church contains only those who have been saved, a limited num-
> ber out of the mass of professing Christians. Ecclesiastical organization
> has corrupted the organized church--the eternal, visible church that is seen
> here on earth. The church, therefore, cannot be described in terms of the
> organized structure which is seen today, but only in terms of the relation
> of the believer to Christ. The church is heavenly, not earthly: the individ-
> ual believer is not baptized into a church here on earth, but into a heavenly
> relation with Christ.[15]

To the extent that he is describing Darby's concept of the nature of the true church, we are in essential agreement with Bass. But he is in error when he says that "The church...cannot be described in terms of the organized structure which is seen today..." What he means of course, is that the true church cannot be so described, but in fact the professing church, Christendom, is described in such terms by Darby and it is in this form that it partakes of God's dispensational dealings earthward.

In this regard, Darby says,

> The Church, properly speaking, the body of Christ, is not a dispensation, it
> does not belong to the earth; but there is an *order of things* connected with
> it during its sojourning here below--an order of things whose existence is
> linked with the Church's responsibility....
> But if, according to the general language of the Christian world, we
> call the present order of things a dispensation or economy, it has not yet
> been rejected, as I have already very plainly said. It does not follow from
> this that Christians have not lost some things which they cannot again re-
> establish, nor that they are not guilty...of that which, in spite of the long-
> suffering of God, will bring down judgment and cause Christ to spue the
> whole system from His mouth [an allusion to the apostate church charac-
> terized by Laodicea in Rev. 3:14-16].[16]

Thus Darby concludes that the church has "a double aspect and character..." While it has no part in the ages and dispensations of the world, it nevertheless "has [its] place and service in time in the world."[17] And because its manifestation in time is on the basis of dispensed service, "it partakes of all the responsibility of a dispensation on earth, as of deeds done *in the body.*"[18]

Brethren after Darby, like H. A. Ironside, follow him in rejecting as unscrip-
tural the designations "visible" and "invisible" church, for Christendom and the true church respectively. They follow him too in making the distinction between the true and professing church, though not always in the same terms. Ironside, for example, says that,

> Every well-instructed man among [the Brethren] distinguishes carefully
> between the Church, according to the mind of God and the Church in its

present outward aspect, or, between the Church as the "Body of Christ," including every saved soul in the present dispensation, and excluding all false professors, and the Church as the "House of God," [here, as we shall see, Ironside is using Darby's terminology] largely committed to man, in which saved and unsaved are sadly mixed together.[19]

While Scofield also makes this twofold distinction with regard to the nature of the church, he has no aversion to the term "visible" to describe professing Christendom in contrast to the true church. In a note on I Timothy 3:15, under the heading, "Church (visible) summary," he says that it is,

> ...that visible body of professed believers called, collectively, "the Church," of which history takes account as such, though it exists under many names and divisions based upon differences in doctrine or in government. Within, for the most part, this historical "Church" has existed the true Church, "which is his body, the fulness of him that filleth all in all" (Eph. 1. 22, 23; Heb. 12. 23, *note*), like the believing Remnant within Israel (Rom. 11. 5, *note*). The predicted future of the visible Church is apostasy (Lk. 18. 8; 2 Tim. 3. 1-8); of the true Church, glory (Mt. 13. 36-43; Rom. 8. 18-23; 1 Thes. 4. 14-17).[20]

In another place, Scofield speaks of the two distinct lines followed by the predictive element in the epistles and the book of Revelation. One concerns the true church, while the other deals with "the mass of profession" known as Christendom. At present, these are intermingled and for the most part indistinguishable, like the wheat and tares of Matthew 13: 24-30 and 36-43. But the future of each, Scofield explains, is quite different, for the "mass of profession... [goes] through the great tribulation--the church which is His body does not."[21] In spite of the fact that their destinies are different, in Scofield's estimation, they are both full participants in this present dispensation of Grace in every sense of the word.

2. Mystery and Parenthetical Nature.

An important point in Darby's understanding of the dispensation of the church and particularly of the heavenly character of the true church, is his concept of this present age as a mystery. As such, it was unknown prior to the coming of Christ, even though it was in the mind of God from eternity. According to Darby, it functions essentially as an interruption in God's dispensational dealings with His earthly people Israel. He says of the present church age that it isn't that Old Testament prophecies say little about it while focusing greater attention upon the millennial dispensation to come, "but that they never speak of the Church at all. It was a hidden mystery."[22] This present age, he says elsewhere, is "the great parenthetic anomaly of the Gentile dispensation..."[23]

Darby maintains that this present church age was God's secret, hidden from the ages and dispensations which preceded it, and was revealed only after the risen and glorified Christ had returned to the Father and had sent the Spirit down (presumably a reference to Pentecost). Because of God's rejection of His earthly people Israel for her unbelief, this "extraordinary break" occurred in the dispensations. This "break" constituted a system which had no part in the earthly system and provided a time during which "a body for Christ--a heavenly people associ-ated with Him in the glory..." could be formed out of the earth.[24]

While Darby refers to this present order of things as a break in the dispensa-tions, he nevertheless speaks of it as a dispensation. Thus at this point he seems to have temporarily amalgamated Christendom and the true church. He writes:

> Looked at as an earthly dispensation, it merely fills up, in detailed exercise of grace, the gap in the regular earthly order of God's counsels, made by the rejection of the Jews on the covenant of legal prescribed righteousness, in the refusal of the Messiah, till their reception again under the new covenant in the way of grace on their repentance; but, though making a most instructive parenthesis, it forms no part of the regular order of God's earthly plans, but is merely an interruption of them to give a fuller charac-ter and meaning to them.[25]

Darby gives two reasons for considering the present order of things a paren-thesis rather than a dispensation. When Christ was upon the earth, He spoke of "this age" (period of His incarnation) as the same as that age (the millennium) which would close in judgment, both of which distinctly connect Christ in the flesh with the Jews. In the interval between the two ages, however, "the Church of the first-born" is being gathered out for heaven.[26]

The age of Christ upon the earth, in other words, was in a manner suspended in order to let in "the heavenly body, the bride the church..." But it will resume "in the dealings of God with the Jews and the kings of the earth [last part of Tribulation], who stand up against the Lord and His anointed, and, as is evident to me," says Darby, "before the manifestation of the Son of man." In addition to the calling out of the true church during this interval, Darby suggests that the apostasy (failure) of professing Christendom (church age as dispensation on earth) will take place also.[27]

The second reason ("and proof that it is so") given by Darby for considering the present time to be a parenthesis rather than a dispensation is "that sixty-nine of Daniel's weeks are run out [ending with Messiah being cut off, i.e., crucified], and then there is an interval of ages [the church age], and the last week [seven-year Tribulation period] begins again to run on and to be counted."[28] Darby explains elsewhere that we are to stop counting for an indefinite amount of time after the sixty-nine weeks conclude with the cutting off of the Messiah. While the seven-tieth week under Antichrist still remains to be fulfilled at some future time, in the meantime, the church has been introduced to fill the gap and has occupied more than eighteen hundred years (in Darby's day) already.[29]

Darby has indicated throughout, that the mystery, the thing revealed at the first advent of Christ which had not been known previously, was the establish-ment of the church, the Body of Christ. But he suggests further that what is also introduced is the calling out of the Body to "obtain the glory of our Lord Jesus Christ." Since the time and place of that glory is not now or here, our calling can-not be for earth, but must await the appearance of Christ who is the source of our life and glory.[30] Darby thus lays out Stephen's death and the calling of Paul, and the rapture of the church as "the boundaries of the full light in standing before God."[31]

Ironside considered this doctrine of the parenthesis church to be "the chief gem in the diadem of the truth of Christianity," but lamented the fact that for centuries it had been lost. It was not, he says,

> ...until brought to the fore through the writings and the preaching and teaching of a distinguished ex-clergyman, Mr. J.N.Darby, in the early part of the last century, it is scarcely to be found in a single book or sermon throughout a period of sixteen hundred years! If any doubt this statement, let them search, as the writer has in measure done, the remarks of the so-called Fathers, both pre- and post-Nicene; the theological treatises of the scholastic divines; Roman Catholic writers of all shades of thought; the literature of the Reformation; the sermons and expositions of the Puritans; and the general theological works of the day. He will find "the mystery" conspicuous by its absence.[32]

Scofield too emphasizes the mystery and parenthetical nature of the present dispensation. In the Acts of the Apostles, he points out, we have the record of the Holy Spirit's descent (at Pentecost) to establish a new thing in the history of humanity--the church. Whereas the division of humankind previously had been between the Jew and Gentile, now there was the church, a combination of Jew and Gentile alike formed into the one Body of Christ. This new organism provides the chief subject from the book of Acts to Revelation chapter 4.[33]

The new Body, the church, was not instituted in Old Testament times, Scofield affirms, but constitutes "a very distinct body of believers, having a distinct mission, a definite point of beginning [Pentecost] and a definite point of ending [the rapture]."[34] It was "a mystery hid in God" (Eph. 3:1-11) and was to fill up the gap between the two advents of Christ. "The present age, in other words," says Scofield, "is a *parenthesis* in the prophetic order, and was hidden from the Old Testament prophets" but revealed after Christ by the apostle Paul.[35]

In proof of the parenthetic nature of the church age, Scofield points not only to Daniel's prophecy of the seventy weeks (Dan. 9),[36] but to Isaiah 61:1 as quotes by Christ in Luke 4:16-21. In the reading of this passage from Isaiah, observes Scofield, Christ stopped at a comma and closed the book. And it is precisely here, between "the acceptable year of the Lord" and "the day of vengeance of God," between Messiah's cutting off at the end of Daniel's sixty-nine weeks and the resumption of God's dealings with Israel again (when "the day of vengeance" or Great Tribulation begins), that the whole period of the church is to be found.[37]

Character of the Present Age

1. As the True Church the Body of Christ.

At this point, perhaps it would be useful to give a brief, summary account of Darby's definition and conception of the true church as originally designed. His position is set forth primarily under two figures: "First, [the true church] is the formation of the children of God into one *body united to Christ Jesus* ascended to heaven, the glorified man; and that by the power of the holy Ghost. In the second place, it is the house or *habitation of God* by the Spirit."[38]

a. The Body of Christ.

The nearest that one is likely to come to a succinct definition of the true church in Darby, is found in an article entitled, "What Is The Church." After stating that he "will shew [the reader] what the church is," he offers the following: "The church of the living God is the body of saints formed on earth in unity with Christ in heaven as the Head, by the Holy Ghost sent down from heaven to form them into unity with Christ at the right hand of God."[39]

It should be noted in passing that Darby disliked the translation "church" for the Greek word *ekklesia*. Consequently, he usually employs the literal rendering "assembly." Nevertheless, the end result is practically the same, for he clearly uses the word "assembly" as a synonym for the word "church."[40]

The Body concept is central to Darby's understanding of the true church. As to its time of conception, its composition, and its time of consummation, Darby is perfectly clear. He says, "The Church...is composed, according to scripture, only of the saints from Pentecost till the Lord comes to receive it to Himself [the rapture]."[41] He explains further that,

> If we turn to I Corinthians [12:12, 13] we are taught how the unity of the body is formed. We are the body of Christ and members in particular; and it is by one Spirit we have been all baptized into one body; and we are expressly taught in the beginning of Acts that this baptism took place at the day of Pentecost. "Ye shall be baptized with the Holy Ghost not many days hence."
> Thus the formation of the body is distinctly revealed to date from the day of Pentecost. The Church according to God did not exist before.[42]

Thus, God has established a people united with Christ under the power of the Holy Spirit and this people includes both Jew and Gentile. Distinctions which existed before Christ's coming have been done away with. Now there is "neither Jew nor Gentile, Barbarian, Scythian, bond nor free."[43]

b. The Habitation of God.

In addition to the church as the Body indwelt by and united with Christ, the church is seen also by Darby as the habitation of God on earth. Ephesians 2:22 says, "in whom ye also are built together for a habitation of God in [the] Spirit" (Darby's translation).[44] Darby notes that God first dwelt among humanity when He had dwelt with His people Israel in the tabernacle in the wilderness, and afterwards "Solomon built him a house." But with the establishment of the church at Pentecost, says Darby, Jews and Gentiles have been "builded together" as "an habitation of God," a dwelling place for God on earth.[45]

This special place of privilege, like that of being placed in the Body of Christ, was accomplished by Christ's redemptive work. Concerning the redemptive basis and nature of this indwelling by God, Darby writes:

> Christ, having wrought this redemption, having ascended to God, having sat down at the right hand of God, having gathered us together, makes us, thus gathered together, "an habitation of God through the Spirit." It is not God merely acting in certain men; it is God dwelling in the church down here, as gathered through the word of the gospel. The church is the place of God's presence on the earth. He has set us in redemption, and He comes and dwells in us. When the church was gathered together with one accord in one place, at Pentecost, the Holy Ghost came down and dwelt there, the result of the accomplished work of Jesus.[46]

Darby suggests that this house which exists on earth as an habitation for God must be looked at on the basis of Scripture in a twofold sense: 1. according to God's purpose and as founded on earth by Him, and 2. as administered under the responsibility of humankind. In the first sense, as the house or church which Christ is building upon the rock of Peter's confession of faith in Him, it is not yet complete, for individuals as living stones are still to be added (I Pet. 2:4, 5; Eph. 2:21). "This is the Lord's work," says Darby, "and it cannot fail, and the stones are living stones, built on Christ the living Stone." The Lord is building His temple and this cannot fail for His work cannot be frustrated.[47]

But, says Darby, the building as the "eternal body, as a house and temple down here in which we are builded together for a habitation of God through the Spirit," has been placed under humankind's responsibility. Paul, as the master builder, laid the foundation, but it was left to those who followed him to raise the superstructure. In this sense, the house is subject to failure, and in fact, says Darby, wood, hay, and stubble have been built into it. Even in Paul's day, the mystery of iniquity had come in and the church was on its way to ruin.

According to Darby, then, as the Body of Christ and habitation of God being built by Christ with living stones, the church cannot fail. But as the house or habitation of God built by humankind and under its responsibility--as a dispensation on earth--the professing church has failed to continue in the goodness of God and will be cut off.[48] This is the principal subject of the following section--the church as a dispensational arrangement of God in His dealings with the earth.

In his understanding of the true church, Scofield begins with the Greek word *ekklesia*, which he translates "church." He rightly states that it is formed from *ek* meaning "out of," and *kaleo* meaning "to call." Thus it has the resultant meaning of the "called out ones," or the "called out assembly." It is used in this sense not only of the New Testament church, but also of Israel in the wilderness (Acts 7:38). Scofield points out that because of its varied usage, the Biblical context itself must determine the "distinctive character, privileges, and responsibilities of the called out assembly" in question. It is only when it is applied to the Body of Christ or to local assemblies of believers in Christ that it can in any sense be translated "church."[49]

Scofield too, points to I Corinthians 12:12, 13, the baptism of both Jews and

Gentiles into one Body by the Holy Spirit, as that which constitutes or serves as the forming agent of the church of which Christ is the Head (Eph. 1:22, 23). It is the Spirit too, who gifts those members united to Christ for the varied activities of ministry in the world (I Cor. 12; Eph. 4). Scofield maintains that this work of building the church began at Pentecost and will continue until the rapture of the saints.[50]

Unlike Darby, Scofield does not bring the concept of the habitation of God into the essential character of the church. Rather, he speaks of it under the subject of the church's relationships. "The 'church which is His body,'" says Scofield, "is related to God as temple and habitation (Eph. ii:19-21; 1 Pet. ii:4-7; 2 Cor. vi:16)." It serves as a connection with the Old Testament type and prophecy of Christ. Scofield explains that,

> The Tabernacle (and afterward the Temple, which was but the Tabernacle made permanent) was primarily the place of Jehovah's *abode* among His people (Ex. xxv:8; xxix:43-46; Lev. xxvi:11, 12; 2 Kings xi:13; Eph. ii:22). *Secondly*, the tabernacle or Temple was a house of *worship* (Eph. ii:21; 1 Pet. ii:5; Heb. xiii:15, 16). Here the figure changes. Seen as one body with Christ, the church is a habitation of God, and also His temple, or spiritual house. Seen as "many members" (1 Cor. xii:20), the church is "an holy priesthood, to offer up spiritual sacrifices, acceptable to God by Jesus Christ" (1 Pet. ii:5). In other words, the "many members" of the one body are an hierarchy of priests, of which Jesus Christ is the High Priest.[51]

Scofield explains that the way in which God takes possession of this "spiritual house" as His habitation and temple, is "through the Spirit." The house is built by the Spirit (I Cor. 12:12, 13) and then He takes up residence in it (Eph. 2:22) "as the manifestation of God."[52]

2. As Dispensation of the Church/Spirit.

Now we take up the subject of the church as a dispensation on earth. The discussion necessarily involves the nature of the true church as first established, but focuses primarily upon that which the church becomes as it forsakes the purpose, according to Darby, for which it had been intended by God. It is here that the nature of the church--as Christendom, the professing church--comes out in its full dispensational sense, while the true church--the Body of Christ--continues above all dispensational arrangements for earth.

a. Primary Characteristics.

1). The Government.

According to Darby, Scripture says three things with regard to the present dispensation. First of all, by the very existence of this dispensation and by the principles set forth in it, the world is placed in a new and unique relationship with God. Salvation has come, not only for the Jew who has failed, but for the Gentile who has failed as well.[53] Thus we see that the nature of the present dispensation can be expressed only in terms of God's sovereign *grace* and the exercise of His love.[54] If the church has proven unfaithful in the use of this grace to benefit the world, "so much the worse for the church."[55]

The second thing that Scripture says about the present dispensation, in Darby's view, is that "those who are called, but not elect, all the baptized, are put in direct relation with the Lord, and are responsible in general...for the privileges of Christianity." If there are those, says Darby, who have enjoyed these privileges and then allowed Satan to corrupt, or if others have been able to come in because of the corruption's prior introduction, then again, "so much the worse...for them and for the aggregate." This, according to Darby, is the state of the professing church--Christendom.[56]

The third thing we learn about this dispensation from Scripture, Darby maintains, is that there is the Body of Christ composed of those who exercise *faith* in Christ and are therefore united to Him. They have not seen the risen Christ themselves, yet they believe the testimony of those who have. And therein lies the principle upon which the believer walks in this dispensation. These are partakers of Christ's life and they will be saved regardless of all that might befall them in this world. This is the state of the true church--the Body of Christ.[57]

According to Darby, in the beginning God established the ideal church to include Jew and Gentile alike--the Body of Christ. But it became apparent that corruption was to come in alongside God's ideal, for Satan was to exert influence upon those who were called but not of the elect. Thus, the apostate ecclesiastical structure to become known as Christendom was to have its genesis. However, there would be those, both of the Jews and the Gentiles, who would have faith in the resurrected Christ and thus combine to form the Body of Christ, the true church, called out of the world to be above all dispensation. But under what circumstances was the corruption known as Christendom to occur?

In Darby's estimation, it can only be understood in terms of the concept of ministry to be exercised under the power and influence of the Holy Spirit in this present dispensation. Darby believes that "there are three great positions of Christ to which our christian thoughts answer: on the cross; at the right hand of God; and coming again." The first of these provides the foundation of everything for the Christian, while the second and third give the church "its present christian character..." In addition to this, Christ's being seated at God's right hand, provides the answer to the Holy Spirit's presence with the church in this dispensation.[58]

"The priesthood of Christ," Darby declares, "is the great characteristic of this dispensation [as a system set up on earth]..." It consists of ministering by the Holy Spirit's power here below to the end that believers "might be a witness to the world of what the power of it is in Christ, to the Father of what He was: they are in His place before the Father and before the world."[59] In this interval between the rejection of Christ and His earthly reign in the millennium, the saints are sustained in the world by the Spirit and bear witness to the Son's exaltation.[60] It is this fact of Christ's sending the Spirit, the Comforter, that "constitutes the essential difference of the present christian state..."[61] and suggests as one of the titles for the present dispensation, the dispensation of the Spirit.[62]

The governing factor, then, the center of God's dealings with humankind as a dispensation at the present time, is ministry through the power of the Holy Spirit. The prototypical expression of this was the power and presence displayed by the Spirit in Acts, chapters two and four.[63] The essence of this ruling factor is seen in Darby's belief that the sin against the Holy Spirit is the substitution of "the notion of a clergyman" for the power and presence of the Spirit which characterizes this dispensation.[64] Darby writes:

> It is a question of the dispensational standing of the church in the world--a statement that that depends wholly on the power and presence of the Holy Ghost, and that the notion of a clergyman contradicts His title and power, on which the standing of the church down here depends. It is the habitation of God through the Spirit.[65]

Every clergyman, Darby affirms, is contributing in this dispensation to the sin against the Holy Ghost. And what is the sin against the Holy Ghost? It is, he says, "the ascribing to the power of evil that which came from the Holy Ghost: and such is the direct operation of the idea of a Clergyman."[66]

The practical effect of allowing the Spirit to fully exercise His influence in the present dispensation, says Darby, is the unrestricted liberty of Christians to preach. The only recognized priesthood in this age is the priesthood of all believers, and since this is the "dispensation of the outpouring of the Spirit," then all believers who can do so are qualified to preach. Darby supports this contention with Acts 1:17. He notes that at Pentecost, Peter quoted Joel's prophecy that in the latter days the Spirit would be poured out upon all mankind.[67]

And what, according to Darby, is the outcome of this sin against the Holy Ghost which is the establishment of professional clergy and the denial of the priesthood of all believers? It is to mistake the power of the dispensation, and consequently, to lose it.[68] Darby writes:

> If the presence of the indwelling Spirit be in the church, it has that which renders it substantially competent to its own edification, and to worship God "in spirit and in truth." If it be not there, nothing else can be recognized, and it is a church no longer; for no makeshift is warranted by Scripture in default of the original constitutive character and endowments of a dispensation.[69]

Before we quit the subject, remember this point regarding government and the true church in the present dispensation. While the church, the Body of Christ, is not connected with God's dispensational arrangements for the earth, according to Darby, there is nevertheless a sense in which it falls under God's "general" government of the earth which commenced with Nebuchadnezzar. The true church is related to this form of God's government of the world, he says, in the sense that it is subjected to suffering at the hands of evil persons for righteousness sake.[70]

2). The Responsibility.

As we pointed out earlier,[71] Darby's concept of responsibility in the successive dispensations takes a peculiar turn when he reaches the present one. He says that with the cross, the whole course of God's dealings with the world ended and thus while humanity was under responsibility from Adam to Christ, that responsibility ended with Christ's death. But Darby does go on to explain that while responsibility in the form of testing to see what is in humankind (i.e., the history of the race under responsibility from Adam to Christ) is over, yet as to moral dealing with each individual, it is still completely operative. Each person must go through the history of responsibility and failure, not to determine if they are lost, but to show that in fact they are.

This present dispensation of the Spirit is assigned more than one responsibility by Darby. One of these is most prominent--purity and unity under the headship of the Holy Spirit--but it will be considered in turn. The first responsibility, however, seems to have been placed upon the apostles themselves.

Darby points to Matthew 28:19 and Christ's command to go and make disciples of all the nations as a direct responsibility placed upon the apostles. This, he says, was the risen and all powerful Christ's special commission to them as those specially chosen by Him. Darby wants to know where the fulfillment of this is, and since it cannot be found recorded in Scripture, he concludes that the apostles failed to carry it out.[72] We mention only the responsibility aspect of this command here, passing over a fuller discussion of the notion until our analysis of failure in this dispensation.

Darby says that the "dispensation of the Holy Ghost's power, or the manifestation of Christ glorified by the Holy Ghost the Comforter,...has its responsibility too." This, he maintains, "is true, effectual salvation..." This appears to be the responsibility incumbent upon each individual in this dispensation, but does not seem to qualify in Darby's assessment as *the* characteristic responsibility of humankind in this economy.[73] That which best fills this position for Darby, is purity and unity under the headship of the Holy Spirit.

Here below, Darby observes, this dispensation has a destiny as did the Jewish economy. And from the standpoint of responsibility, "it is the purity and faithfulness of the church, which are the basis on which this destiny rest." Darby maintains that, "The universal church of the elect manifested on earth was to shew forth in the world the glory of Christ, by the power of the Holy Spirit, as a city situated on the top of a mountain; it was to be the salt of the earth--and all that in its unity, being composed of all those who believe."[74] This display of the glory of the church's Head by the Spirit's power, is the very purpose for which the church as a body in visible unity was placed on the earth.[75]

Darby also speaks in general terms of the responsibility of humankind in this dispensation as being the same as that of the Jews--namely, to continue in the goodness of God. Darby almost always mentions this responsibility in terms of a warning. He asserts that as the Jewish branches were cut off from "the good olive tree of the promises made to the fathers," so also will the Gentile branches which were grafted on be cut off if they do not continue in the goodness of God.[76] In other words, says Darby, as the subject of dispensation, the church is subject to the same responsibility that Israel was and will be cut off if it fails.[77] What Darby

seems to be dealing with here, is not the specific responsibility uniquely characteristic of the dispensation (i.e., unity of the Body, etc.), but the general responsibility of obedience to the revelation of God's will--no matter the specific form,
e.g., to govern righteously, to obey the Law, to maintain unity in the power of the
Holy Spirit, etc.--present in each dispensation.

In keeping with his concept of the dual nature of the church, Darby identifies a
different responsibility for the true church following its failure to carry out its
original purpose. Since righteousness has been established in Christ, he points
out, the Christian's standing is not based upon responsibility as a child of the first
Adam, but upon redemption as a child of God. As Darby explains, there are two
trees in grace--one of life and one of responsibility. Under the Law, it was responsibility first, then life. Under grace, it is life first, then responsibility. Our
responsibility individually now, which flows from our position as heirs of God
and joint heirs with Christ, is to display this character before the world as Christ's
epistles.[78]

3). The Revelation.

Again Darby does not state specifically what *the* revelation of God's will and
principles in this dispensation are. But he does give definite indications as to
what it is that is unique in the progressive unfolding of God's plan for humanity in
this new arrangement of things. In this Christian dispensation, he says, "The
ways of God, and the principles of His dealings with sinners, are here unfolded
with many more details for the conscience, and more distinctness and splendour
as to the accomplishment and the revelation of grace."[79]

Ministry as the chief characteristic of the relation which exists between God
and humankind in the Christian dispensation, according to Darby, "finds its exercise in the active revelation of what God is..."[80] The form which the revelation
of God's grace and nature has taken in this dispensation is rightly seen by Darby
as the incarnation of Christ. It was the incarnate Christ who told us what God is
and who gave the ultimate display of grace in His sacrificial death on the cross. It
was He also who provided the basis of ministry and then sent the Spirit to ener-
gize His Body on earth.

b. Secondary Characteristics.

1). The Test.

Darby, as usual, does not spell out the exact nature of the trial to which humankind is put in this dispensation. He does imply of course, that the test placed
before the apostles was whether they would be obedient in fulfilling the command
in the Great Commission to preach the Gospel to all the world. He implies that
the trial before the church concerns the maintenance of unity in the power of the
Holy Spirit which would result in a testimony to the world of the grace of the
glorified Christ. He implies too that the general test of obedience which Israel
faced, is also faced by the Gentiles in this dispensation. Will individuals in this
economy continue in the goodness of God, or will they fail and be cut off like
Israel?

2). The Failure ("The Church in Ruins").

One of Darby's most prominent and unique themes and consequently one of his best known, is the doctrine of the apostate church--"the Church in ruins." Before we proceed to a discussion of this doctrine, we must first look at what amounts to perhaps the first failure of humanity in this dispensation. The apostles, says Darby, had been commanded to go into all the world and make disciples. Where, he asks, is the fulfillment of this command recorded in Scripture? It isn't, he answers. And thus, like all other dispensations before it, no sooner was it established than it broke down at the very outset. Not only this, but the Gospel has never been preached in all the world, but the church itself "has departed from the faith of the gospel, and gone away backward, so as to be as bad or worse than the heathen."[81]

Now it is incredible that Darby should understand this command in the "Great Commission" as applying to the twelve apostles for complete fulfillment. While he does seem to back off from this position a little with the indictment of the church in its subsequent failure, no dispensationalist that we know of would agree with the primary implication of Darby's position here. All would see the command, rather, as a statement of the missionary task of the whole church, of which the apostles were but the first representatives. In any case, Darby does not view this as the primary failure of humankind in the present dispensation. It is only the initial one.

In order to fully understand the nature of the church's failure in this dispensation, some preliminary concepts must be presented first. These are the intentions versus the counsels of God for this dispensation, and Darby's concept of the church as the Body of Christ versus the church as the habitation of God on earth. An understanding of these two concepts makes it possible to also understand how the church, in Darby's thinking, can both be earthly and fail and be heavenly and above failure at the same time.

The intentions versus the counsels of God. According to Darby, Scripture reveals two great mysteries which are unfolded in the present dispensation. The mystery of Christ is one, and the mystery of lawlessness the other. The counsels of God have to do with the first, while the intentions of God relate to the second.[82]

The counsels of God for the church, says Darby, will be accomplished in heaven when the union of the Body of Christ with Himself will take place.[83] The first step in this union and the full accomplishment of the counsels of God is the resurrection of the church, followed by the marriage of the Lamb.[84] After this, the church will be fully glorified in its union with Christ. The counsels of God with regard to the church, Darby assures us, are above all dispensations and responsibility of humankind and therefore beyond failure.[85]

Darby explains, on the basis of Ephesians 1:1-4, II Timothy 1:9-10, and Titus 1:2-3, that before the world even existed, God had counsels about a people destined to have this special relationship with Christ. But these counsels, he continues, were not revealed by the Gospel until Christ died and provided atonement, for this was the ground upon which their accomplishment rested. This people specially related to Christ, says Darby, were chosen independently of the world, and thus they are not of the world (John 17:16).[86]

But according to Darby, when the world was created, an entirely new thing came in--not a counsel, but a responsibility. This is related to the intentions of God for humankind on earth, and the mystery of lawlessness. The intentions of God for this dispensation, Darby explains, were for the church to be a manifestation of the union of Christ's Body on earth. This was the church's responsibility, but it failed when it substituted a manmade clerical system for the priesthood of all believers under the power and presidency of the Holy Spirit.[87] Thus the mystery of lawlessness had begun to work in the church, even in Paul's time, and would continue until the lawless one and the apostate church (this dispensation) are judged by Christ at His second coming.

The church as the Body of Christ versus the church as the habitation of God. Darby further explains the failure of Christendom as a dispensation and the future glory of the true church in terms of the two characters of the church found in Ephesians, chapters one and two. The church is both the Body of which Christ is the Head (its heavenly character) and a building which serves as the habitation of God through the Spirit (its earthly character). The church as the Body united to Christ its Head, cannot and never will fail, Darby states, for it is the fulness of the One who fills all things.[88]

The church as a building on earth for the habitation of God, however, requires the responsibility of the maintenance of unity to serve as a witness. Here there can be and is failure. Darby asserts that in its earthly, dispensational character as Jews and Gentiles "builded together for an habitation of God through the Spirit," the church has ignored God's principles for unity and is now in a state of ruin.[89] At this point we can proceed to a detailed discussion of Darby's doctrine of "the church in ruins"--its total failure in this dispensation.

The statement of apostasy. Clarence Bass offers a good summary statement of Darby's belief in the fact and nature of the apostasy and ruin of the church. He writes:

> It is not merely that the church has become corrupted, and has lost its effectiveness. *The church is in ruins!* It has become a corrupt mass, an apostasy hastening to its final consummation, rather than the symbol of a dispensation which God is sustaining through His faithful grace. The holy Spirit is not owned as its power; unity in the sense of a visible body on earth is lost; the sense of responsibility to be one as a testimony on the earth has been erased; its spiritual character has been replaced; its principle of action as to the workings of the Spirit has been laid aside and replaced by a human system, which does not recognize the action of the members of the body.[90]

In his explanation of the church's ruined state, Darby says,

> I fully recognize that there was an organization in apostolic and scriptural times, but affirm that what exists now is not the scriptural organization at

all, but mere human invention, each sect arranging itself according to its own convenience, so that, as an external body, the Church is ruined; and though much may be enjoyed of what belongs to the Church, I believe from scripture that the ruin is without remedy, that the professing church will be cut off. I believe that there is an external professing Christendom, holding a most important and responsible place, and which will be judged and cut off for its unfaithfulness.

The true body of Christ is not this. It is composed of those who are united to Christ by the Holy Ghost, who, when the professing church is cut off, will have their place with Him in heaven.[91]

The definition of apostasy. Darby defines the word *apostasy* in the Biblical sense as both the "moral and real abandonment of the true principles of Christianity." He says that it applies to people who call themselves Christians, but act under Satan's influence (I Tim. 4). Darby notes that Satan corrupts what he cannot hinder. He explains further that this "outward form of Christianity" (i.e., Christendom), is composed of persons who have abandoned the true principles of Christianity, but pretend not to have done so. Consequently, what the Word calls "apostasy," has a hidden and deceptive quality.[92]

The cause of apostasy. The great lesson of this dispensation with respect to righteousness, says Darby, is that people are willing to trust in a person who is present and visible to the eye, but unwilling to trust in God, who to the eye, is absent.[93] As was the case with Israel, the tendency of the human heart today is to forego faith in God, while choosing instead to go down into Egypt in search of help. The end result of this practice, Darby warns, is always judgment.[94]

In the same way, in this dispensation humankind has failed to produce the unity that God intended through the power of the Holy Spirit and the glorified Christ. While that unity was visible at the beginning of this dispensation, the manifestation of the glory of Christ by the church in unity no longer exists.[95] The cause of this state of things, according to Darby, is humanity's desire to go down into Egypt, so to speak, in that it has rejected the presidency of the Holy Spirit in favor of a manmade clerical system.[96] Thus, asserts Darby, the church,

> ...has not been faithful to the command of Christ to glorify Him; has not sought the wisdom and guidance of the Holy Spirit; has not committed itself to the task of obedient service in His kingdom, but rather has contented itself with the luxuries of a vast and complex system of orders instead of freedom in the Spirit; pastoral supervision instead of the priesthood of all believers; governing bodies and boards instead of the presidency of the Holy Spirit; ritual instead of simple and direct exercise of the soul toward God; ecclesiastical ethics instead of obedience to God's command; pomp and pretense instead of humbleness of soul; and derived authority instead of the gift of God to minister.[97]

The extent of apostasy. Darby believes that the "public apostasy" of the end times has not yet come, but that "in the spirit of the thing, it took place long ago..." This follows the analogy, he says, of the many antichrists who would come, although there was to be *the* Antichrist, who would be associated with *the* apostasy. Thus apostasy in the fullest and completest sense has not yet arrived. But Darby concludes that "we have reached such a point in that direction that the distance which separates us from it is scarcely appreciable..."[98] In any case, the extent of the present ruin of the church is not to be understood merely in the existence of independent churches (denominationalism), he says, but as the complete perversion of the purpose and character of the church as it was originally established by God.[99]

The Biblical proof of apostasy. Darby regularly appeals to the following passages in proof that, first, there was the possibility of failure and cutting off, and second, that there were prophetic declarations that there was an apostasy to come, and finally, that the mystery of iniquity was already present and working in the earliest times. The passages cited and what they teach are: Matthew 13, the parable of the wheat and tares; Romans 11, that if the church did not continue in the goodness of God, it would be cut off like Israel was; II Thessalonians 2, that the "mystery of iniquity" was already at work and would continue until its culmination in the wicked one who would be judged at Christ's second coming; II Timothy 3, that in the last days "perilous times" would come and grow worse and worse; and finally, in Jude 4 and 14, notes Darby, "the declension and falling away is still more palpable..."[100]

All these passages, says Darby, testify that the result of this dispensation would be "apostasy," "perilous times," "departure from the faith," and that the "mystery of iniquity," those principles of evil responsible for producing this, were already working.[101] If this testimony is correct, asserts Darby, it is the most solemn consideration for the children of God, "the failure from the outset, through man's folly and evil, of the economy of the church in the world." He says that his,

> ...object here is not to shew the degree of maturity to which the apostasy may be generally or locally arrived, but the fact of its existence from the commencement in the judgment and by the revelation of God, applicable to the entire course and condition of the dispensation as a whole; and instructing us in the true character of pretension to succession and continuance.[102]

The remedy of apostasy. If the church has lost its unity, power, and holiness, and has become "the center and the power of evil and corruption in the world,"[103] what can be done about it? Nothing at all can be done to restore the dispensation, says Darby. This dispensation's testimony in public power is gone and will never be recovered.[104] A fallen dispensation is never restored, for it is neither in the Father's will nor in humankind's power to effect restoration. Furthermore, observes Darby, God always replaces a failed economy with a better one. God replaced the kingdom of Saul, for example, with that of David, and He replaced Judaism with Christianity.[105]

What is left for Christians to do then? They can and should, advises Darby, separate from the apostate mass of Christendom (II Tim. 3:5). This separation will not, however, prevent the dispensation from being entirely marred, nor God's judgment of it by ending it in preference for the kingdom of Christ to come.[106] In the parable of the wheat and tares (Matt. 13), for example, we are taught that the Sower's (Christ's) work in the world has been marred and cannot be repaired by humankind. The counsels concerning the wheat cannot fail, "it will be in the barn," but the work entrusted to humanity was carelessly handled so that it was corrupted by the enemy. And it is a corruption for which there is no remedy as long as the dispensation lasts.[107]

3). The Judgment.

The final result of apostasy (Antichrist/judgment). Darby assures all true believers that they will meet the Lord in the air and remain forever with Him.[108] They have no part in this unfaithful, corrupt dispensation, and therefore face no judgment for its failure. On the contrary, they will enter a better state in heaven as they are conformed to the image of the Son of God. And then they will take part in the kingdom of the Son when it is established on earth.[109]

With regard to the professing church or apostate Christendom, however, it will end in judgment says Darby.[110] Just as Romans 11 threatens (as is taught also in Matt. 13; Rev. 19; II Thess. 2, I Thess. 5, the end of Rev. 13; and Isaiah 66), if the Gentiles do not continue in the goodness of God, their system will end just as that of the Jews did. Darby observes that the subject of the Apocalypse is this truth that the apostasy which will give birth to the Antichrist will be judged at the second coming of Christ and a new dispensation of glory will be established.[111]

Darby affirms that Christ's second coming "has for its object the execution of judgment on the apostasy, which has ripened into open revolt against Himself," and is consummated by the revelation of the man of sin. At this time the mark of the beast will be required if any wish to buy or sell. Finally, the kings of the earth will gather to make war against the Lamb. "But the most terrible part of this terrible day, from which the Lord will return having His garments dyed with blood," states Darby, "will be the judgment of the apostates and rebels."[112] The most severe judgments will be visited upon the earth and will end with the Antichrist's consignment to the lake of fire. Nevertheless, Darby assures the reader, that even during this terrible time, access to the throne of grace will yet be open and faithful ones will emerge even under Antichrist.[113]

End of the Present Age

The end of the present dispensation, according to Darby, is marked by two events at the second coming: *the judgment* of a ruined church and the corrupt nations, and *the harvest* of the saints. On the basis of Mark 4:26-9, Darby maintains that "the time which elapses from the seed-sowing till the harvest is what is generally called *the present dispensation*." He calls this "the church dispensation," he explains, because the church is called and exists here below during this time in contrast with the Jews and their legal system.[114] Thus the harvest of wheat, which is to take place at the end of this age or dispensation (Matt. 13:39), marks its end for the saints. During the same general period of time that the wheat is gathered into the barn, the tares (the corrupt mass of humanity, including the professing church), are bundled together and burned.[115] When this is completed and the dispensation is ended, says Darby, God's throne will once again become the center of relations with the earth as He resumes direct dealings with humankind.[116]

Scofield's Dispensation of Grace (Calvary to Second Coming)

The dispensation of grace, says Scofield, begins with the death and resurrection of Christ (Rom. 3:24-26; 4:24, 25).[117] This introduced the concept of grace, "which means undeserved favor, or God GIVING righteousness, instead of God REQUIRING righteousness, as under Law."[118] The twofold manifestation of grace is salvation (Rom. 3:24), and the daily walk and continued service of those saved (Rom. 6:15). Scofield maintains that the form of testing, therefore, is no longer legal obedience to the Mosaic legislation, but the acceptance or rejection of Christ, followed by good works which is the fruit of salvation (John 1:12, 13; 3:36; Matt. 21:37; 22:42; John 15:22, 25; Heb. 1:2; I John 5:10-12).[119] Two results are predicted for this testing of humanity, notes Scofield, the salvation of those who believe (Acts 16:31), and apocalyptic judgments upon the apostate professing church and unbelieving world (Matt. 25:31-46; II Thess. 1:7-10; I Pet. 4:17, 18; Rev. 3:15, 16).[120]

According to Scofield, three great events will mark the end of this dispensation--the rapture, the Tribulation, and the second coming of Christ. First, Christ will return from heaven to raise the dead saints who together with those still living, will be caught up to meet the Lord in the air and remain forever with Him (I Thess. 4:16, 17). This will be followed by the seven-year period known as the Tribulation (Matt. 24:21, 22; Dan. 12:1; Jer. 30:5-7; Zeph. 15-18). Then the Lord will return in power and glory to judge the earth and prepare the way for the last dispensation, the dispensation of the kingdom (Matt. 24:29, 30; 25:31-46).[121]

Concerning the nature of the apostasy that will result in judgment at the end of this dispensation, Scofield says, it is a "falling away" and "is the act of professed Christians who deliberately reject revealed truth (1) as to the deity of Jesus Christ, and (2) redemption through His atoning and redeeming sacrifice (1 John 4. 1-3; Phil. 3. 18; 2 Pet. 2. 1)." Apostasy, Scofield explains, is different from mere error regarding truth, for the latter may result simple from ignorance (Acts 19:1-6). And it is different from heresy which may result from Satan's snares (II Tim. 2:25, 26). Both error and heresy may "consist with true faith." Apostates on the other hand, while holding to an outward profession of Christianity, depart from the true faith (II Tim. 3:5). Scofield points to II Timothy 4:3, 4, as a perfect description of the apostate and II Timothy 4:3, II Peter 2:1-19, and Jude 4, 8, 11-13, and 16, as descriptions of apostate teachers. In conclusion, Scofield asserts that as in Israel (Isa. 1:5, 6; 5:5-7), apostasy in the church "is irremediable and awaits judgment (2 Thes. 2. 10-12; 2 Pet. 2. 17, 21; Jude 11-15; Rev. 3. 14-16)."[122]

The Evaluation

As is generally the case in a comparison between Darby and Scofield's dispensations, there are points of similarity in their descriptions of the present one. Both emphasize the work of the incarnate Christ as that which makes this age unique in God's dispensational dealings with humanity. Both see the dispensation ending in apocalyptic judgments upon the failure of a corrupt and apostate church.

And they agree that ultimately there will be salvation and glorification for all true believers at the return of Christ. While they both agree that the church has a responsibility to maintain unity within its ranks, for Darby, this is clearly *the* distinguishing responsibility during this dispensation. For Scofield, on the other hand, it is each individual's call to either accept or reject the salvation offered in Christ.

The most glaring dissimilarities between the two men's systems at this point, however, are in their concept of "dispensation" as it applies to the present age, and in their understanding of "apostasy" as it applies to the established church, and the remedy for it. As stated previously, Darby's conception of the church as both a dispensation and yet above all dispensations is totally foreign to Scofield. While Scofield makes a distinction between the true church as the Body of which Christ is the Head, and the apostate church as that composed of professing Christians who have departed from the true faith, he nowhere makes the Body of Christ in any sense exempt from participation in the present dispensation. He rightly makes the placement of "Christians" into one camp or the other contingent upon individual acceptance or rejection of the offer of salvation, an offer made on the basis of grace (the ruling principle in this dispensation).

Darby is correct in saying that the church has a heavenly calling and that it must await its residence in that realm, where it will be glorified with Christ, for the realization and fulfillment of its true destiny. But it is also true that the church is a genuine participant in this present dispensation and has responsibilities in it. It seems that Darby, in his zeal for the true calling of the church, is not content to await the harvest for the separation of the wheat and tares, but seeks rather to begin the process in the absence of the Sower.

This tendency is seen in Darby's concept of the apostasy of the professing church and in what he believes the Christian's response to it ought to be. The Bible certainly teaches that there will be false teachers in the church, and Paul does indeed indicate that they will come in early. But nowhere does Scripture suggest that the visible, organized church on earth, is at present an apostate mass to be abandoned by all true believers. This obviously was not the belief of Brookes, Scofield, and others, for none of them abandoned their denominations in answer to Darby's call for separation. We heartily agree with Charles Feinberg's "clarification" on this point. He asserts that,

> ...dispensationalism *does not teach* that the entire church in any century is apostate. It does teach that the last days of the church age will witness a great apostasy from the ranks of the church, and that is abundantly attested by Scripture (see 2 Cor. 11:14-15; 2 Thess. 2:1-12; 1 Tim. 4:1-3; 2 Tim. 3:1-9, 13; 4:3-4; James 5:1-5; 2 Pet. 2:1-3; 1 John 2:18-29; 4:1-6; Jude 3-4; Rev. 2-3).[123]

The Church Versus the Kingdom of Heaven

One last point warrants some consideration before we leave the Christian dispensation. What is the relationship between the kingdom of heaven and the church? Or put another way, are the church and the kingdom of heaven one and the same?

"It is of great importance," says Darby, "to distinguish between the kingdom and the church."[124] When the Messiah was rejected by the Jews, the kingdom of heaven was introduced and "this present age becomes purely and simply *this present evil world (age)*, from which Christ delivers us..."[125] The kingdom of heaven, Darby explains, is a government or reign and the King and His authority are there. He defines the word *kingdom* as "the government of a king over his sphere of rule."[126]

Perhaps the term "kingdom of heaven" is best defined and understood in relation to the term "kingdom of God." Darby writes:

> Observe, that Matthew only uses the expression, "kingdom of heaven." It is often, in a general sense, capable of being interchanged with "kingdom of God," as we see by comparing Luke. Notwithstanding, the two phrases cannot always replace each other, and Matthew uses "kingdom of God" in a few passages where "kingdom of heaven" could not be used (Matt. 6:33; 12:28; 21:43). Thus "the kingdom of God" was there when Christ the King was there; "the kingdom of heaven" began with Christ going to heaven. By-and-by, when Satan ceases to rule, it will be the "kingdom of heaven" (and "of God" too, of course), not in a mystery, but in manifestation. "The kingdom of God" has also a moral force which "kingdom of heaven" has not; and in this way it is frequently used by Paul, and was peculiarly suitable to the Spirit's design in Luke.[127]

Darby explains elsewhere that "The kingdom of God is the exercise or exhibition of the ruling power of God under any circumstances in the wisdom of God," while "The kingdom of heaven is the kingdom of God in its heavenly character."[128]

Concerning the kingdom and the order of events surrounding its establishment, Darby says that Israel, "the whole system into which the Lord had come," was provisionally set aside in order that the assembly (the church) and the kingdom in its heavenly character, might be brought in.[129] After Christ is dispensationally rejected (Matthew 12), the kingdom of heaven is substituted (Matthew 13). Humankind and its responsibility are set aside in this arrangement of things, and now God in grace acts above all dispensations in calling out the true church.[130] Afterwards, the assembly comes in in glory and the kingdom in power and glory--the millennium.[131]

In Darby's thinking, the kingdom of heaven has a direct relation to the present dispensation, while the true church does not. Darby writes:

> It is true that the enemy works in the kingdom while men sleep [parable of wheat and tares], because they are put there under responsibility; and there you see the importance of using the word dispensation, that everybody understands, because it is only a question of man and his position when God has placed him under responsibility, while the kingdom, or the reign, embraces also the government of the King, the sovereignty of God Himself.[132]

In other words, explains Darby, the authority of the kingdom of heaven was established over God's government on the earth and His work in respect to it, but not over the church united in heaven to Christ.[133]

According to Darby, the kingdom of heaven was in fact supposed to have been "that new dispensation which was to take the place of the one which, properly speaking, belonged to Sinai, where the Lord had spoken on the earth." This new dispensation (long expected Messianic kingdom), was to have been characterized by heavenly rule under God's authority in Christ.[134] This was not to be, however, for the King was rejected. Therefore the establishment of the kingdom was postponed until the King should return a second time at the conclusion of the present church age.

How is the church to be understood then, in its relation to this kingdom of heaven? Darby maintains that it "has no relation nor any contact with the kingdom, save that it exists down here in the field, over which the authority of the kingdom is exercised." In this point alone there is a connection between the kingdom and the church. The kingdom "is the administration of the power and authority of the Lord Jesus Christ, though it is invisible or in mystery now." It is characterized by a reign of righteousness and judgment, not grace. Therefore, any attempt to identify it with the church simply will not do,[135] for it does not have "the same character as the church of the living God." The church is above the kingdom, associated now with Christ in love, and will one day reign over the kingdom with Christ the King who it owns as such now by right.[136]

Scofield defines the term, "kingdom of heaven," as "signifying the Messianic earth rule of Jesus Christ, the Son of David." It is given this name, he explains, because "it is the rule of the heavens over the earth (Mt. 6. 10)." As the source of the term, he points to Daniel 2:34-36, 44, and 7:23-27, where it is seen as the kingdom to be set up by "the God of heaven" after the Gentile world system is destroyed by "the stone cut out without hands..." It is the kingdom of the covenant to David's descendants (II Sam. 7:7-10), described by the prophets (Zech. 12:8), and confirmed to Christ through Gabriel (Lk. 1:32, 33). This kingdom, according to Scofield, has three aspects in Matthew: 1. as "at hand"--from John the Baptist's ministry (Mt. 3:2) to virtual rejection of Christ and beginning of new brotherhood (Mt. 12:46-50); 2. in mystery form--to be fulfilled in the present age are the seven parables of Matthew 13:1-52, and those following related to the sphere of Christian profession in this age; and 3. the future aspect--the millennial kingdom to be established at Christ's glorious return (Mt. 24:29-25:46; Lk. 19:12-19; Acts 15:14-17).[137]

Scofield maintains that the kingdom of God (Mt. 6:33), which is the larger word,[138] is distinct from the kingdom of heaven in five ways:

> (1) The kingdom of God is universal, including all moral intelligences willingly subject to the will of God...of past or future dispensations (Lk. 13. 18, 19; Heb. 12. 22, 23); while the kingdom of heaven is Messianic, mediatorial, and Davidic, and has for its object the establishment of the kingdom of God in the earth (Mt. 3. 2, *note*; 1 Cor. 15. 24, 25). (2) The kingdom of God is entered only by the new birth (John 3. 3, 5-7); the kingdom of heaven, during this age, is the sphere of a profession which

may be real or false Mt. 13. 3, *note*; 25. 1, 11, 12). (3) Since the kingdom of heaven is the earthly sphere of the universal kingdom of God, the two have almost all things in common. For this reason many parables and other teachings are spoken of the kingdom of heaven in Matthew, and of the kingdom of God in Mark and Luke....(4) The kingdom of God "comes not with outward show" (Lk. 17. 20), but is chiefly that which is inward and spiritual (Rom. 14. 17); while the kingdom of heaven is organic, and is to be manifested in glory on the earth....Zech. 12. 8, *note*; (N.T.), Lk. 1. 31-33; 1 Cor. 15. 24, *note*; Mt. 17. 2, *note*.) (5) The kingdom of heaven merges into the kingdom of God when Christ, having "put all enemies under His feet," "shall have delivered up the kingdom to God, even the Father" (1 Cor. 15. 24-28).[139]

Scofield understands the Sermon on the Mount (Matt. 5-7) as setting forth the principles of the kingdom of heaven as "at hand," and these principles as a whole as providing "the divine constitution for the righteous government of the earth."[140]

Like Darby, Scofield is insistent that the church and the kingdom are not one and the same. The confusion of the two, he laments, "is the irremediable disaster which the wild allegorising of Origen and his school has inflicted upon exegesis." He cites the intermingling of the purposes of the church and kingdom as the principal cause of a thirteen hundred year period of "palsied evangelis[m]" which is even "today the heavy clog upon the feet of those who preach the glad tidings."[141]

Scofield maintains that while the church is not the kingdom of God, it is part of it. While it is not the kingdom of heaven, it is related to it. At the return of Christ when the kingdom is set up, the church will be the Bride of the King (Eph. 5:29-32; II Tim. 2:12; Rev. 6:10), and thus associated with Him in rule. "It cannot be too clearly held," says Scofield, "that the work of God in this dispensation is not the gathering of *subjects* of the coming kingdom, but the outcalling of the *ekklesia*, the co-ruler with Christ of the coming kingdom."[142]

MILLENNIAL KINGDOM

Introduction and Importance of the Dispensation

Darby asks the question: "Is this dispensation [church age] the last?" His answer is an emphatic, no! After commenting upon the large amount of material written about the subject of Christ's second coming to establish a new dispensation, Darby affirms that, "A large number of Christians of all denominations...believe fully, as a truth of the Christian faith, that there will be another dispensation before the end of the world."[143]

On the basis of Psalm 96, 99, Ezekiel 36:9-11, I Corinthians 6:2, and Zephaniah 3:8, 9, 19, 20, Darby concludes that "It is evident that there will be a dispensation in which the Lord shall reign in righteousness; now He is dealing in the patience of grace."[144] In Isaiah 32, says Darby, there is a clear change of dispensation. Then the Spirit will be poured out on the nation Israel, and Christ as King will reign in righteousness.[145]

Not only does Scripture teach that there will be a new dispensation after this one, says Darby, but statements about the character of the age to come clearly signify that it cannot be identical to the one in which we now live. In the age to come, according to Ephesians 1:9-10 for example, Christ will gather all things in heaven and earth together in one. This cannot be the present dispensation, Darby maintains, for Satan, as the ruler of the world now, sows tares among the wheat. It is under these circumstances that God calls out a people for His name. Thus we see that rather than gathering all things in heaven and earth into itself, the church is being gathered out of the earth.[146]

Furthermore, points out Darby, the present dispensation is one of "testimony and instruction," while the economy to come is one "of universal knowledge" of the glory of the Lord. Concerning the Jews, at present there is only a remnant according to God's grace, but then all Israel shall be saved as a body. Thus this dispensation is characterized by "the saving of the body," while that one which is to come is characterized by "the rescuing of the remnant."[147]

Darby explains further that this is uniquely a dispensation of grace, while the dispensation to come relates to righteousness and judgment. Grace acts now to draw the human heart to heavenly things. But in the millennial kingdom, Christ's reign will be one of righteousness. And as we see in the Psalms, it will be one of justice as well.[148] Under Christ's reign too, the heirs of salvation shall have full enjoyment of the inheritance of all things, while now, the heirs are only being gathered together.[149]

According to Darby, another strong argument for the distinction between this age and the one to come, has to do with the events surrounding the actual close of this dispensation and the commencement of the next. First, Christ must quit the Father's throne and begin the harvest which is to take place at the end of the age (Matt. 13:39). This harvest of the wheat and tares, in Darby's reckoning, begins with the rapture of the saints and ends with the destruction of Antichrist. The rapture of the saints and the destruction of Antichrist, he explains, belong to this age, because the former is a part of the harvest at the end of this age. The destruction of Antichrist on the other hand, belongs to Daniel's seventieth week, "which clearly [does] not belong to the new age" and does not close until Antichrist is destroyed.[150] In other words, it is not until the end of the times of the Gentiles when Christ comes to execute judgment upon the nations (which culminates in the battle of Armageddon, Rev. 19:17-21), that the dispensation will evidently close.[151]

Character of the Dispensation

Before proceeding to the specifics of the primary and secondary characteristics of the millennial dispensation, we shall first look at some of what might be termed the general characteristics of the period. "One of the principal characters of the dispensation to come," says Darby, "is that Satan is bound." That is an entirely new thing for the earth and one can hardly imagine what a difference it will make in the world. Creation fell and was taken away from humanity under Adam and Eve, but the corrupting power of the wicked one will be neutralized in the kingdom.[152]

During this time of Satan's ineffectiveness, there will also exist a glory heretofore unknown. It will in fact, be "a dispensation of glory..."[153] Here is a very distinct point of contact between Darby and contemporary dispensationalists. The millennium is seen as the culmination of earthly history and the time during which the glory of God is manifested in the personal reign of Christ as it never was before.[154] It is a time when a righteous God will be vindicated before a corrupt, Christ-rejecting world. Darby suggests that on the basis of the evidence, if there were no such dispensation to come, "God's glory is defeated and destroyed in the world, and that instead of the Lord destroying the works of the devil, the devil, as far as this world goes...has destroyed the work of the Lord."[155]

Darby observes that one of the most prominent characteristics of the dispensation of the kingdom will be unparalleled blessing and righteousness upon the earth. God will gather all things together in Christ, and the church will share in full measure the glory of the King as His righteous rule covers the earth. "In a word," says Darby, "whilst now we have to follow Jesus in His humiliation and rejection--precious participation in His sufferings, so that we may be glorified together, then it will be the presence of Jesus reigning in power."[156]

Darby believes that the kingdom age will be distinctly the time of Israel's full blessing and restoration, for that is one of the primary purposes of the millennial period. "If there be a direct testimony that Israel shall be planted again in their own land, and never plucked up," Darby points out, "it is plain it has never been fulfilled."[157] On the other hand, it is just as certain that "the promises to Israel shall be fulfilled to the letter: for when," asks Darby, "has God failed in His promises?"[158]

Israel may have failed miserably with regard to God's intentions for her, says Darby, nevertheless, the counsels of God with respect to His earthly people never fail. Although the Jewish dispensation was set aside because of the unfaithfulness of the Jews--until the fulness of the Gentiles (the church) had come in[159]--a remnant of Israel will escape that great day of trouble spoken of by the prophet Jeremiah (30:7). The remnant will be saved when the Deliverer out of Zion comes, and He will form of this people the nucleus of a new nation and make their city Jerusalem the metropolis of the world (Isa. 2:1-2; 60:1-3; 27:6; Zeph. 3:8-9; Ps. 71; Zech. 8:20-23; Rom. 11).[160] "In a word," concludes Darby, "the millennium may be considered as a restoration of Paradise under the second Adam..."[161]

1. Primary Characteristics.

a. The Government. In the millennial dispensation, Darby sees the principles of calling and government combined once again as they were in Israel. It is, he says, the manifestation of God's incomparable wisdom and power when God in Christ personally takes control of the government of the world.[162] Darby maintains that in the future of the Jewish people, who are the center of God's government of the world, we see that,

...the sovereignty and efficacy of the calling of God will be clearly and openly manifested, and the government of all the earth be put into the hands of the king whom God has established, and conducted according to the principles of a law which God shall, in the meantime, have written on the hearts of His people; a covenant teeming with rich and sovereign blessings, and proving at once the riches of His goodness and the faithfulness of His promises, and of which the obedient Gentiles shall partake, according to their measure, in a world filled with the knowledge of the glory of God, as the waters cover the sea.[163]

Darby explains that at the present time, while Christ has all power in heaven and earth, as regards the government of the earth, His power in judgment is not exercised. He does not now act in the public government of the earth as He will when He takes up His great power as sovereign and reigns over the world.[164] It is when the Lord returns the second time and executes judgment upon the earth "that the ways of God in government--of which the Jews were the earthly centre--shall be fully manifested."[165]

The reader will recall[166] that in Darby's understanding of the matter, the direct, immediate, or manifested government of God ceased with the cutting off of Israel, and the general government of God commenced for the present age. Darby says that sin brought everything into disorder so that "we are not under the manifested government of God as Israel was..."[167] In the days of Nebuchadnezzar, this form of government was set aside. But it was not until its sovereign (the Messiah) was rejected, and its seat (Jerusalem) was destroyed, that all traces of it were completely eliminated.[168] However, when Christ returns, He will not be rejected by Israel, and Jerusalem will be rebuilt. Thus the basis of the direct government of God will once again be in place.[169]

b. The Responsibility. Darby says next to nothing about responsibility in connection with the dispensation of the kingdom. The reason for this will become evident when we discuss the nature of testing and failure during this economy. At any rate, Darby would probably agree that humankind's responsibility as subjects of the King is simply to live righteously and in obedience to the principles of the King's direct government.

c. The Revelation. Darby says of the "direct manifestation of Christ, of the judicial power of the Lamb," that it is quite distinct from that which the rejectors of the study of prophecy presently expect. He writes:

When John saw heaven opened and beheld a white horse, and He that sat upon him called Faithful and True, and in righteousness doth He judge and make war--when he saw the Person and glory of the Word of God, it was the revelation of something wholly different from the secret operations of the Spirit of God; and it was something characteristically different from previous providential judgments. These had been hail, and thunder, and lightning, and earthquake; but this was a manifestation of Him who had been long hid behind instruments, who had governed the world as one that apparently suffered His church to grow up and spring He knew not how, because the harvest of the earth was ripe.[170]

Until His return, Darby continues, Christ had ruled His church through the ordained government of the earth and the operation of the Spirit, and therefore it was a suffering church. With the manifestation of Christ in power, however, the church becomes triumphant.[171]

2. Secondary Characteristics.

a. The Test. Even in the millennium, according to Darby, humankind (the nations, not the redeemed of the church or Old Testament saints) has not been completely delivered from the "yoke of corruption." "It would be extraordinary in a dispensation," says Darby, "for man not to be subject to trial and temptation in the ways of God." Consequently, those in their unglorified bodies who have come out of the Tribulation are subject to temptation like those of past dispensations.[172]

The interesting thing about Darby's understanding of this trial, is that it does not take place during the course of the thousand years. It occurs only at its conclusion, after Satan is released from the bottomless pit.[173] This would account for his silence concerning responsibility during the millennium. Responsibility naturally involves testing, and apparently, as far as Darby is concerned, in the absence of the corrupter of humanity, there can be no temptation or trial. In this, he seems not to have taken account of the references in the prophets to individual rebellion against the King and His government (Isa. 11:3-4; 29:20-21; Jer. 31:29-30).[174] In any case, the nature of the test clearly involves the question of whether humankind will continue to follow the righteous King, or Satan, who has been freed from his bottomless prison (Rev. 20:7).

b. The Failure. As always, laments Darby, the failure of the race is immediate. He says,

> Not even having seen Christ and enjoyed the fruits of His glory--no mere means can secure the heart of man, if it is to be depended upon; and men fall, in number as the sand of the sea, into Satan's hands as soon as tempted; enjoying blessing, where unfaithfulness would have been present loss (perhaps cutting off) and there was nothing to tempt them, but unfaithful as soon as they are tempted, as soon as the heart is tried.[175]

Darby explains that this final testing was necessary because humankind could not have enjoyed God with natural hearts unless first successfully tested under the present blessing of a personal, visible, glorious Christ.[176]

c. The Judgment. Darby explains that the great multitude of rebels from "the breadth of the earth" go up against the saints and surround the city of Jerusalem, but that Christ is absent from the scene. He suggests that this is in some way a final test of the faithfulness of the saints. This conclusion, based on Revelation 20:9, is without warrant. In any case, God's judgment from heaven falls upon the rebels and they are destroyed. Their leader the devil, is cast into the lake of fire with the beast and false prophet "and they will be tormented day and night forever and ever."[177]

Scofield's Dispensation of Kingdom (Second Coming to Eternal State)

The seventh and "last of the ordered ages which condition human life on earth," that of the kingdom or "Fulness of Times," says Scofield, is identical to the Davidic kingdom (II Sam 7:8-17; Zech. 12:8; Lk. 1:31-33; I Cor. 15:24).[178] It will be established after Christ returns and purifies the earth by means of judgments. At that time, He will begin a thousand-year reign, commonly known as the millennium, during which time He will rule over a restored Israel. Jerusalem will serve as the seat of government and all the saints, including the church, will partake of the glory of the King (Acts 15:14-17; Rev. 19:11-21; 20:1-6; Isa. 2:1-4).[179]

At the conclusion of the thousand years, says Scofield, Satan is loosed and easily gathers an army of those whose hearts are prone to evil, to do battle with Christ and His saints. This dispensation, like all others before it, closes in judgment.[180] The kingdom is then delivered up to the Father and the millennial dispensation ends (I Cor. 15:24).[181]

Scofield summarizes the Scriptural evidence concerning the age to come as follows: 1). "Such an age is definitely foretold in the following Scriptures: Matthew 12:32; Mark 10:30, with Luke 18:30; Luke 20:35; Ephesians 1:21; Hebrews 6:5." 2). "The age to come is introduced by the return of the Lord in power and glory." Five events signal the beginning of the coming age: a. the rapture of the church (I Thess. 4:14-17); b. the judgment of the living Gentile nations (last half of Tribulation; Matt. 25:31-46); c. the regathering of Israel (Deut. 30:1-10; Matt. 24:30-31); d. the conversion of Israel (Zech. 12:10; Ezek. 20:33-38; Rom. 11:25-27); and e. the earth's filling with the knowledge of the glory of Christ (Isa. 11:9; Hab. 2:14; Acts 15:16-17). 3). "The 'righteousness' which is the ethical keyword of the age to come is simply right *doing*." 4). "The unseen powers of evil, headed up in Satan, are removed from the scene (Rev. 20:1-3) during the entire period." 5). "At His first advent, while preaching to Israel the kingdom as 'at hand' (Matt. 4:17; 10:5-7), our Lord demonstrated in seven great miracles His power to deal with all the temporal (as well as the eternal consequences of sin." He healed leprosy, palsy, fever, stilled a storm, cast out demons, raised the dead and healed the blind. 6). "…that age is to witness the 'manifestation [*apokalupsis* = unveiling] of the sons of God.' The sons of God, partakers of the Divine nature through the new birth (2 Pet. 1:4)…"[182]

The Evaluation

Darby and Scofield share a great deal in common in their understanding of the dispensation of the kingdom. With the exception of Darby's concept of the combination of the ruling principles of government and calling, which is uniquely his, the two men are generally in agreement with regard to the characteristics of the millennial kingdom. Scofield would agree that the principle of rule during the dispensation is the personal government of Christ Himself on the throne in Jerusalem, but he makes no distinction between the general and direct or manifested government of God on earth. Neither does he set forth a principle of calling as part of the ruling principle during the millennial kingdom. More will be said about the details of end-time events which precede and follow the millennial period, and both men's views concerning them, in chapter six, which deals with Darby's essential eschatological events.

<u>THE ETERNAL STATE</u>

In speaking of Ephesians 1:10, Darby says that he does not believe that it is a reference to the post-millennial state, "which cannot properly be called a dispensation, for it is eternity."[183] Following the millennial kingdom, righteousness will reign in the new heavens and earth. It is with the commencement of the eternal state, according to Darby, that the government of God will come to an end. The government, he says, "that has brought all things into order, will terminate, and unhindered blessing will flow from God, the kingdom being given up to God the Father."[184]

Endnotes

[1]In reconstructing Darby's dispensational system, one is hard pressed to know exactly what to call this dispensation in which we now live--that which extends from the first to the second coming of Christ. In his first published work on the subject of dispensations, "The Apostasy of the Successive Dispensations," Darby calls it the "dispensation of the Spirit," (*Writings*, vol. 1: *Ecclesiastical No. 1*, p. 127). Seldom is the title used thereafter. On pp. 180-1, a number of references are given for the designation, "Christian dispensation." Darby affirms elsewhere, however, that the "present dispensation" (probably his most common designation), or "the Gentile dispensation, as a distinct thing, took its rise on the death of Stephen..." (vol. 1: *Ecclesiastical No. 1*, p. 130). The major problem with this last name for the present dispensation is that Darby already has a dispensation of the Gentiles commencing with Nebuchadnezzar after Israel's failure under the monarchy. As for the designation "church *dispensation on earth*," Darby says that "as to time" it takes "the place of the broken-off Jewish branches..." (vol. 2: *Prophetic No. 1*, p. 174, note*).

[2]John Nelson Darby, *The Collected Writings of J. N. Darby*, 34 vols., ed. William Kelly, vol. 4: *Ecclesiastical No. 2* (Sunbury, Pa.: Believers Bookshelf, n.d.), p. 272.

[3]Ibid., pp. 275-7.

[4]Ibid., vol. 1: *Ecclesiastical No. 1*, p. 96, 97.

[5]Ibid., p. 97.

[6]Ibid., p. 130.

[7]Ibid., pp. 97-99.

[8]Ibid., p. 99.

[9]Ibid., vol. 2: *Prophetic No. 1*, p. 18.

[10]Ibid., vol. 1: *Ecclesiastical No. 1*, pp. 206-7.

[11]Ibid., pp. 207-8.

[12]Ibid., p. 208.

[13]Ibid.

[14]Ibid., pp. 104-5.

[15]Clarence B. Bass, *Backgrounds to Dispensationalism* (Grand Rapids: Wm. B. Eerdmans Publishing Co., 1960), p. 46.

[16]Darby, *Writings*, vol. 4: *Ecclesiastical No. 2*, pp. 328-29 (italics added).

[17]Ibid., vol. 20: *Ecclesiastical No. 4*, p. 329.

[18]Ibid., vol. 3: *Doctrinal No. 1*, pp. 110-11.

[19]H. A. Ironside, *A Historical Sketch of the Brethren Movement*, rev. ed. (Grand Rapids: Zondervan Publishing House, 1942; reprint ed., Neptune, N.J.: Loizeaux Brothers, 1985), p. 207.

[20]C. I. Scofield, *The Scofield Reference Bible* (New York: Oxford University Press, 1909), p. 1276.

[21]C. I. Scofield, *What Do the Prophets Say?* (Greenville, S.C: The Gospel Hour, Inc., 1918), pp. 118-19; cf. pp. 86-7 and *Reference Bible*, p. 1018.

[22]Darby, *Writings*, vol. 13: *Critical No. 1*.

[23]Ibid., vol. 33: *Miscellaneous No. 2*, p. 2.

[24]Ibid., vol. 1: *Ecclesiastical No. 1*, pp. 93-4.

[25]Ibid., p. 94.

[26]Ibid., vol. 13: *Critical No. 1*, p. 155.

[27]Ibid., vol. 5: *Prophetic No. 2*, p. 389.

[28]Ibid., vol. 13: *Critical No. 1*, p. 155.

[29]Ibid., vol. 5: *Prophetic No. 2*, pp. 173-5. Darby actually believes that the first half of the seventieth week (three and one half years) was fulfilled in the ministry of Christ, while only the last half of the week is related to the time of Antichrist's power on earth (see p. 169 below for a discussion of Darby's interpretation of Daniel's seventieth week and the duration of the Tribulation period).

[30]Ibid., vol. 1: *Ecclesiastical No. 1*, p. 94.

[31]Ibid., vol. 5: *Prophetic No. 2*, p. 389.

[32]H. A. Ironside, *The Mysteries of God* (New York: Loizeaux Brothers, 1946), pp. 50-1.

[33]Scofield, *Reference Bible*, p. vi.

[34]C. I. Scofield, *Prophecy Made Plain: "Addresses on Prophecy "* (Glasgow: Pickering and Inglis; London: Alfred Holness, n.d.), p. 42.

[35]Scofield, *What Do the Prophets Say?*, pp. 79-80, 102-3.

[36]For a classic dispensational interpretation of Daniel's prophecy of the seventy weeks, the reader is directed to Sir Robert Anderson's, *The Coming Prince* (Grand Rapids: Kregel Publications, n.d.), and Alva J. McClain's, *Daniel's Prophecy of the 70 Weeks* (Grand Rapids: Zondervan Publishing House, 1969).

[37]Scofield, *Prophecy Made Plain*, pp. 130-32.

[38]Darby, *Writings*, vol. 14: *Ecclesiastical No. 3*, p. 76.

[39]John Nelson Darby, *Miscellaneous Writings of J. N. D.*, vols. 4 and 5, reprint ed. (Oak Park, Ill.: Bible Truth Publishers, n.d.), 4:157.

[40]Darby, *Writings*, vol. 14: *Ecclesiastical No. 3*, p. 16f. Compare this reference, p. 21, where Darby quotes Jesus in Matthew 16:18, as saying that it was His "assembly" which He was going to build upon the rock, with *Miscellaneous Writings*, 4:158, where it is His "church" which He is going to build upon the rock.

[41]Ibid., vol. 10: *Doctrinal No. 3*, p. 83.

[42]Ibid., p. 85.

[43]Darby, *Miscellaneous Writings*, 4:159.

[44]John Nelson Darby, *The Holy Scriptures*, A New Translation from the Original Languages, 1967 ed. (Oak Park, Ill.: Bible Truth Publishers, 1967), p. 1412.

[45]Darby, *Writings*, vol. 12: *Evangelic No. 1*, pp. 240-1.

[46]Ibid., pp. 245-6.

[47]Ibid., vol. 29: *Doctrinal No. 8*, p. 352.

[48]Ibid., pp. 352-4.

[49]C. I. Scofield, *Things New and Old*, comp. and ed. Arno C. Gaebelein (New York: Publication Office "Our Hope," 1920), p. 257-8.

[50]Ibid., pp. 260-3.

[51]Ibid., pp. 265-6.

[52]Ibid., p. 266.

[53]Darby, *Writings*, vol. 1: *Ecclesiastical No. 1*, p. 293.

[54]Ibid., p. 206.

[55]Ibid., p. 293.

[56]Ibid., pp. 293-4.

[57]Ibid., p. 294, and vol. 5: *Prophetic No. 2*, p. 4.

[58]Darby, *Writings*, vol. 10: *Doctrinal No. 3*, p. 257.

[59]Ibid., vol. 1: *Ecclesiastical No. 1*, p. 105.

[60]Ibid., vol. 2: *Prophetic No. 1*, p. 63.

[61]Ibid., vol. 10: *Doctrinal No. 3*, pp. 234, 255.

[62]Ibid., vol. 1: *Ecclesiastical No. 1*, p. 127.

[63]Ibid.

[64]Ibid., p. 38.

[65]Ibid., p. 37.

[66]Ibid., p. 39. Neither Scofield nor any dispensationalist that we know of on the contemporary scene would agree with Darby's position on this point concerning clergymen.

[67]Darby, *Writings*, vol. 1: *Ecclesiastical No. 1*, pp. 75-6.

[68]Ibid.

[69]Ibid., p. 71.

[70]For a full discussion of the distinction between the direct and general government of God and the church's relation to each, see p. 52ff above.

[71]Refer to p. 54ff above, where Darby's concept of responsibility as it is connected with the present dispensation is treated and for full documentation for this paragraph.

[72]Darby, *Writings*, vol. 1: *Ecclesiastical No. 1*, pp. 128-9.

[73]Ibid., p. 114.

[74]Ibid., p. 251; cf. p. 186.

[75]Ibid., p. 236.

[76]Ibid., pp. 180-2.

[77]Ibid., p 117.

[78]Ibid., vol. 32: *Miscellaneous No. 1*, pp. 238-9.

[79]Ibid., vol. 1: *Ecclesiastical No. 1*, p. 206.

[80]Ibid., p. 127.

[81]Ibid., pp. 128-9.

[82]Ibid., p. 175.

[83]Ibid.

[84]Ibid., vol. 5: *Prophetic No. 2*, p. 75.

[85]Ibid., vol. 1: *Ecclesiastical No. 1*, p. 175.

[86]Ibid., vol. 32: *Miscellaneous No. 1*, pp. 231-2.

[87]Ibid., vol. 1: *Ecclesiastical No. 1*, p. 175.

[88]Ibid., vol. 20: *Ecclesiastical No. 4*, p. 331.

[89]Ibid.

[90]Bass, p. 103.

[91]Darby, *Writings*, vol. 14: *Ecclesiastical No. 3*, pp. 274-5.

[92]Ibid., vol. 1: *Ecclesiastical No. 1*, p. 246.

[93]Ibid., p. 92.

[94]Ibid., p. 93.

[95]Ibid., p. 201.

[96]Ibid., pp. 38-9.

[97]Bass, p. 104; cf. Darby, *Writings*, vol. 1: *Ecclesiastical No.* 1, pp. 92-111.

[98]Darby, *Writings*, vol. 20: *Ecclesiastical No. 4*, pp. 302-3.

[99]Ibid., pp. 298-9.

[100]Ibid., vol. 1: *Ecclesiastical No. 1*, pp. 153-5; vol. 5: *Prophetic No. 2*, pp. 120-1.

[101]Ibid., vol. 1: *Ecclesiastical No. 1*, pp. 119-20.

[102]Ibid., p. 123.

[103]Ibid., vol. 3: *Doctrinal No. 1*, p. 278.

[104]Ibid., vol. 5: *Prophetic No. 2*, p. 349.

[105]Ibid., vol. 3: *Doctrinal No. 1*, p. 278; cf. vol. 1: *Ecclesiastical No. 1*, p. 145.

[106]Ibid., vol. 3: *Doctrinal No. 1*, p. 278.

[107]Ibid., vol. 1: *Ecclesiastical No. 1*, p. 176.

[108]Ibid., vol. 4: *Ecclesiastical No. 2*, p. 278.

[109]Ibid., vol. 14: *Ecclesiastical No. 3*, p. 87.

[110]Ibid.

[111]Ibid., vol. 4: *Ecclesiastical No. 2*, pp. 278-9.

[112]Ibid., p. 278.

[113]Ibid., vol. 1: *Ecclesiastical No. 1*, p. 172.

[114]Ibid., p. 289.

[115]Ibid., vol. 12: *Evangelic No. 1*, p. 46.

[116]Ibid., vol. 5: *Prophetic No. 2*, p. 176.

[117]Scofield, *Reference Bible*, p. 1115; cf. p. 1044.

[118]C. I. Scofield, *Rightly Dividing the Word of Truth* (Fincastle, Va.: Scripture Truth Book Co., n.d.), p. 14.

[119]Scofield, *Reference Bible*, p. 1115.

[120]Ibid., pp. 1044, 1115.

[121]Scofield, *Rightly Dividing the Word of Truth*, p. 15.

[122]Scofield, *Reference Bible*, pp. 1280-1.

[123]Charles L. Feinberg, *Millennialism: The Two Major Views*, rev. ed. (Chicago: Moody Press, 1980), p. 80.

[124]Darby, *Writings*, vol. 12: *Evangelic No. 1*, p. 372. The importance of the issue is set forth by Ryrie: "If [the kingdom] is the Church, then dispensationalism is unwarranted. If the present form of the kingdom is not the Church and if the future form is the Davidic kingdom on earth, then dispensational premillennialism is the only answer" (*Dispensationalism Today*, p. 171).

[125]Darby, *Writings*, vol. 24: *Expository No. 3*, p. 12.

[126]Ibid., vol. 11: *Prophetic No. 4*, p. 360.

[127]Ibid., vol. 25: *Expository No. 4*, p. 47.

[128]Ibid., vol. 2: *Prophetic No. 1*, p. 55.

[129]John Nelson Darby, *Synopsis of the Books of the Bible*, 5 vols., reprint ed. (Sunbury, Pa.: Believers Bookshelf, n.d.), 3:241.

[130]Ibid., p. 112.

[131]Ibid., p. 241; cf. p. 112.

[132]Darby, *Writings*, vol. 1: *Ecclesiastical No. 1*, pp. 186-7. Darby says that the expression "kingdom of heaven" is "specially occupied with dispensations, and the dealings of God with the Jews" (*Synopsis*, 3:30).

[133]Ibid., vol. 24: *Expository No. 3*, p. 6.

[134]Darby, *Synopsis*, 3:30-1.

[135]Darby, *Miscellaneous Writings*, 4:169; cf. *Writings*, vol. 1: *Ecclesiastical No. 1*, p. 287.

[136]Darby, *Miscellaneous Writings*, 4:169-71.

[137]Scofield, *Reference Bible*, p. 996.

[138]Ibid., p. 1029.

[139]Ibid., p. 1003.

[140]Ibid., pp. 999-1000.

[141]Scofield, *Prophecy Made Plain*, pp. 34-5.

[142]Scofield, *Things New and Old*, pp. 263-4.

[143]Darby, *Writings*, vol. 1: *Ecclesiastical No. 1*, p. 170.

[144]Ibid., p. 173.

[145]John Nelson Darby, *Letters of J.N. Darby*, 3 vols., reprint ed. (Sunbury, Pa.: Believers Bookshelf, 1971), 1:516.

[146]Darby, *Writings*, vol. 2: *Prophetic No. 1*, p. 90.

[147]Ibid., p. 92.

[148]Ibid., vol. 5: *Prophetic No. 2*, p. 72. It should be borne in mind that Darby is not saying that there will be no grace in the millennial dispensation, quite the contrary is true. While he does maintain that the coming dispensation will be one of judgment on the earth in contrast with grace

(Ps. 72, 96-99; Isa. 32), he nevertheless states that "it [is] always true that it is only grace which saves individuals in every dispensation" (*Writings*, vol 1: *Ecclesiastical No. 1*, p. 245). It must be added that Darby's statements about judgment as a characteristic of the millennial dispensation are misleading. The judgment spoken of, as in Psalm 96:13, means judgment in the sense of righteous government. It is true of course that there will be swift judgment upon those who rebel under the righteous reign of the King (Isa. 11:3-4; 29:20-21; Jer. 31:29-30), but this is not the judgment to which Darby is referring. There is only one place that we are aware of where Darby does seem to hint at this type of instantaneous millennial judgment. He says, "if evil appear, it will be at once judged and banished from the earth" (*Writings*, vol. 22: *Doctrinal No. 6*, p. 363).

[149]Ibid., vol. 2: *Prophetic No. 1*, p. 290.

[150]Ibid., vol. 8: *Prophetic No. 3*, pp. 13-14.

[151]Ibid., vol. 1: *Ecclesiastical No. 1*, p. 173.

[152]Ibid., vol. 5: *Prophetic No. 2*, p. 83.

[153]Ibid., vol. 1: *Ecclesiastical No. 1*, p. 189.

[154]Charles Caldwell Ryrie, *Dispensationalism Today* (Chicago: Moody Press, 1965), p. 18.

[155]Darby, *Writings*, vol. 2: *Prophetic No. 1*, p. 96.

[156]Ibid., vol. 1: *Ecclesiastical No. 1*, p. 182.

[157]Ibid., vol. 2: *Prophetic No. 1*, p. 28.

[158]Ibid., p. 162.

[159]Ibid., vol. 1: *Ecclesiastical No. 1*, pp. 181-2.

[160]Ibid., vol. 5: *Prophetic No. 2*, pp. 121-2.

[161]Ibid., vol. 2: *Prophetic No. 1*, p. 24.

[162]Ibid., pp. 136, 141.

[163]Ibid., p. 136.

[164]Ibid., vol. 13: *Critical No. 1*, p. 161.

[165]Darby, *Synopsis*, 5:392, 403.

[166]See p. 52ff above for an account of the distinction between the "general" and "direct," or "manifested" government of God.

[167]Darby, *Letters*, 2:43.

[168]Darby, *Synopsis*, 5:396.

[169]Ibid., 5:561.

[170]Darby, *Writings*, vol. 2: *Prophetic No. 1*, p. 29.

[171]Ibid. Refer to p. 52 above for the concept of the suffering church under the general government of God.

[172]Ibid., vol. 5: *Prophetic No. 2*, p. 93.

[173]Ibid., p. 86.

[174]See footnote 148.

[175]Darby, *Synopsis*, 5:557.

[176]Ibid.

[177]Ibid., 5:557-8.

[178]Scofield, *Reference Bible*, p. 1250; cf. *What Do the Prophets Say?*, p. 163f.

[179]Scofield, *Rightly Dividing the Word of Truth*, p. 16.

[180]Ibid.

[181]Scofield, *Reference Bible*, p. 1341.

[182]Scofield, *What Do the Prophets Say?*, pp. 164-73.

[183]Darby, *Writings*, vol. 8: *Prophetic No. 3*, p. 222.

[184]Darby, *Synopsis*, 5:420.

CHAPTER 5

DARBY'S VIEW OF PROPHECY

Interest in Prophecy

It is difficult to determine the exact genesis of Darby's interest in prophecy. As we have said, Darby's earliest doctrinal interests were ecclesiological rather than eschatological. An unpublished letter entitled, "Considerations Addressed to the Archbishop of Dublin [Magee] and the Clergy Who Signed the Petition to the House of Commons for Protection,"[1] written in 1827, is a polemic against the state church. In the following year, Darby's first published tract, "Considerations on the Nature and Unity of the Church of Christ,"[2] appeared. His first published work on prophecy, "Reflections upon the Prophetic Inquiry and the Views Advanced in It,"[3] is dated 1829.

THE POWERSCOURT CONFERENCES

It appears, however, that Darby's serious involvement in prophetic inquiry was not to come until after the commencement of the prophetic conferences under Lady Powerscourt's sponsorship in October of 1831. It was at these conferences that Darby was to become acquainted with George V. Wigram, who became a friend and collaborator in the years ahead. A chairman was chosen at these meetings and it was his responsibility to select the individual who was to speak on the evenings topic. "It became soon evident," says Ironside, "that Mr. Darby's enlightenment on prophetic themes was considerably in advance of most of the others…"[4]

A number of clergymen attended these meetings, including some connected with Edward Irving's Catholic Apostolic Church. This, says Ironside, has given the "erroneous impression" that the Brethren movement was somehow linked with this group. But the Irvingites, he notes, "soon dropped out, because the teaching was so contrary to what they held."[5]

With regard to the significance of doctrinal developments in the Powerscourt conferences, Ironside writes:

> It was in these meetings that the precious truth of the rapture of the Church was brought to light; that is, the coming of the Lord in the air to take away His church before the great tribulation should begin on earth.

The views brought out at Powerscourt castle not only largely formed the views of Brethren elsewhere, but as years went on obtained wide publication in denominational circles, chiefly through the writings of such men as Darby, Bellett, Newton, S. P. Tregelles, Andrew Jukes, Wigram, and after 1845 William Kelly, whose name was then linked with the movement, C. H. Mackintosh, Charles Stanley, J. B. Stoney and others.[6]

One observes in Darby's prophetic discussions, that his interest is almost exclusively in that prophecy which is unfulfilled. He devotes little space and attention to fulfilled prophecy. This he seems to view in the overall context of history as interesting and informative, but not of the same value as those prophetic utterances which concern the future.[7]

Nature of Prophecy

Darby closely associates the nature and function of prophecy with the grace of God and the failure of humanity in the various dispensations. He maintains that,

> Prophecy is the intervention of God's sovereign grace in testimony, in order to maintain His relationship with His people when they have failed in their responsibility to God in the position they held, so that their relationship with God in this position has been broken; and before God has established any new relationship by His own power in grace.[8]

According to Darby, prophecy clearly involves the revelation of God's thoughts and counsels with regard to current failure and future events, whether for the Jewish remnant or for the church.[9]

The prophet, then, is looked upon by Darby as the one through whom God maintained a relationship with Israel and the rest of the world when there was failure. Thus prophecy is a characteristic of every dispensation, and employed by God in the periods of emergency throughout humankind's history. Darby explains further that,

> It revealed God and foretold Christ, but evidently was to cease when the things it spoke of were accomplished, for then it had no place. Its character was the sovereign intervention of God, not the development of His ways. Hence it was in exercise at all times, when, as regards those ways, man had failed. It shewed and reproved the failure, and encouraged the faith of the Jew, faithful among the faithless, in the enduring fidelity of the Lord, pointing out with an increasing fulness the intervention of God in power...Hence we find it in Enoch before the flood, in Noah, in the patriarchs, and, in a particular manner, in Samuel when Israel had failed under the theocracy, and in Israel departed from God, and in Judah become unfaithful in her kings.[10]

Scofield too, notes that prophets were God's people raised up "in times of declension and apostasy in Israel." They served primarily, he says, as "revivalists and patriots," who spoke to the hearts and consciences of the people on God's behalf. Scofield concludes that the prophetic messages had a twofold character.

The first was local and contemporary, while the second involved the prediction of God's purpose for the future. He points out that the prediction often grew directly out of the local circumstance (e.g., compare Isa. 7, verses 1-11, with verses 12-14).[11] Scofield cautions the reader that,

> It is necessary to keep this Israelitish character of the prophet in mind. Usually his predictive, equally with his local and immediate ministry, is not didactic and abstract, but has in view the covenant people, their sin and failure, and their glorious future. The Gentile is mentioned as used for the chastisement of Israel, as judged therefor, but also as sharing the grace that is yet to be shown toward Israel.[12]

Purpose of Prophecy

Darby offers several answers to the question, "What is the purpose and end of prophecy in Scripture?" He says that it shows the divinity of the Bible. It is a guide to the remnant and the church with regard to coming events. It detaches us from the world and reveals the character of God. And finally, it throws light upon the dispensations.

IT SHOWS THE DIVINITY OF THE BIBLE

Darby observes that in his day, one of the major uses of fulfilled prophecies was to demonstrate the divinity of the Bible. He agrees that this is indeed one of their legitimate uses, but maintains that this "is not the special object for which they [were] given." He asserts that prophecy was not given for the benefit of the world in general, but for the benefit of the church and remnant in particular.[13]

IT SERVES AS A GUIDE TO THE CHURCH AND REMNANT

According to Darby, one of the primary purposes of prophecy is to serve as the church and remnant's "guide and torch" before the arrival of the events which the prophecies predict. Prophecy communicates the intentions of God for the purpose of directing "us in our present walk in the ways of the Lord, and to be our comfort in enabling us to see that it is God who disposes of all events, and not man."[14] The way to know what God intends for the future, says Darby, "is certainly the study of that prophecy which He has given to us."[15]

IT DETACHES US FROM THE WORLD AND REVEALS THE CHARACTER OF GOD

In Darby's estimation, the study of prophecy, with the understanding of God's intentions for the future that it brings, has two results. The first is our detachment from the world. Darby says that while every part of Scripture when applied by the Spirit can accomplish this, it is a function for which "prophecy is peculiarly adapted; its tendency must be to 'deliver us from this present evil age.'"[16]

The second end of prophecy, says Darby, is that it instructs us in the character of God and His dealings with us. It is one of the primary ways in which the char-

acter of God is "fully unveiled." The double end of prophecy, then, the detachment from the world and the revelation of God's character, constitute what Darby
calls "two precious and wholesome fruits, which spring from the acquirement of
the knowledge of prophecy."[17]

IT THROWS LIGHT UPON THE DISPENSATIONS

Darby maintains that another important function of prophecy is to shed light
upon dispensational distinctions. He suggests that it is through a study of
prophetic truths that these distinctions are made clear. Thus, it does a great deal
to bring freedom of the soul towards God. Darby illustrates this point with a reference to the confusion that often surrounds the relationship between the Law and
the Gospel. "For what hinders it [freedom of the soul] more than the error so
often committed," he says, "of confounding the law and the gospel, the past
economies or dispensations with the existing one?"[18] He explains further that,

> If we insist on the difference which exists between the position of the
> saints of old, and that of the saints during the actual dispensation, this
> again troubles the minds of many. Now the study of prophecy clears up
> such points, and at the same time enlightens the faithful as to their walk
> and conversation; for, whilst it always maintains free salvation by the
> death of Jesus, prophecy enables us to understand this entire difference
> between the standing of the saints now and formerly, and lights up with all
> the counsels of God the road along which His own people have been con-
> ducted, whether before or after the death and resurrection of Jesus.[19]

Scofield asserts that what God revealed through the prophets "of the mind of
God, and of the divine nature and motives has a permanent and altogether ines-
timable value." He says that while prophecy refuses to cater to the mere human
curiosity, it does "give in broad and clear outline the program of the future of the
earth and of human life and destiny thereon." In light of the tremendous value of
prophecy, then, Scofield is mystified at the seemingly total indifference to the
subject on the part of "those whom God would fain take into his confidence..."
This neglect and willful ignorance of prophetic literature by even ministers of the
Word, he says, "has no parallel in our attitude toward any other great and serious
literature." Scofield concludes that "It is impossible to overstate the loss to spiri-
tuality, to comprehension of God in himself and in his immutable purposes toward
the earth and the race of men, resulting from this stupid neglect of nearly one-
fourth in bulk of the Bible."[20]

Approach to Prophecy

FUTURISM AND PROPHECY

In the course of the Powerscourt conferences on prophecy, it became apparent
that there was marked difference of opinion on the interpretive approach to be
taken with prophetic books, particularly the books of Daniel and Revelation.
Some participants, like Henry Drummond, held to the historicist position while
others, like Darby and almost all of the Plymouth Brethren, advocated a futurist

interpretation of the books.[21] The historicist maintains that apocalyptic disclosures pertained to events which, at the time they were made, were yet future. However, they have occurred and are still occurring within the church's life span.[22]

The futurist, on the other hand, believes that the prophetic and apocalyptic portions of Scripture relate "primarily" (often there is both an immediate and a long-range fulfillment of a prophecy) to an "end time" (i.e., the end of this present age and prior to the commencement of the eternal state). According to this view, end-time events are still future as they were for those to whom they were first revealed.[23] Darby says in this regard, that "The greater part of the prophecies, and, in a certain sense, we may say, all the prophecies, will have their accomplishment at the expiration of the dispensation in which we are."[24]

On September 27, 1832, the topic of discussion at Powerscourt was "An Inquiry into, and a connection between Daniel and the Apocalypse." While the millenarians present agreed that the chronologies of eschatological events in Daniel and Revelation were related though independent, there was sharp controversy over how much they overlapped. Sandeen says of the historicist party, that almost all of them,

> ...judged that much of Daniel was recapitulated in the book of Revelation and that the two accounts could and should be used to interpret each other. They believed that the events described in the Apocalypse were being fulfilled in European history (thus the name of the party). Henry Drummond went so far as to state that all of the first fifteen chapters of Revelation had already been fulfilled and that in 1827 European history was hovering somewhere between the twelfth and seventeenth verses of Revelation 16.[25]

The futurists, on the other hand, maintained that with the exception of the first three chapters of Revelation, which depict in a moral sense the history of the church on earth, the events described in the Apocalypse are all future. Darby, for example, says that in the fourth chapter of Revelation "we see *the things which are to come afterwards* [Rev. 1:19]." Here, the subject is no longer *the things which are* (events which take place in the history of the church), but the events which occur after the church age has ended. Thus, observes Darby, we see that there is a "double interpretation of the Apocalypse..." He explains that,

> If the seven churches are taken as a sketch of the history of the church, Laodicea, the last one, receives this sentence--"*I will spue thee out of my mouth.*" Consequently, the church is then no more recognised on earth; and what follows in the Revelation is the history of the government of God, and the chastisements sent on the earth from that time, until Christ comes to establish His kingdom. If the churches are taken in a literal sense, the types of the prophecy must be applied to events which have for the greater part already taken place; but in any case the church in the Revelation is neither recognised nor presented on earth from chapter 4, from the time that the scene changes, and that John, leaving "things which are," is introduced into heaven to see "things which are to come."[26]

Scofield too, sees a threefold division of the book of Revelation based upon Revelation 1:19. He asserts that "The three major *divisions* of Revelation must be clearly held if the interpretation is to be sane and coherent." The first division consisted of things which John had already seen (the Patmos vision, Rev. 1:1-20). The second division, "the things which are," says Scofield, is "obviously the churches." He explains that "The temple had been destroyed, the Jews dispersed: the testimony of God had been committed to the churches (1 Tim. 3:15). Accordingly we have seven messages to seven representative churches, 2. 1-3. 22." Scofield observes that the church is not mentioned in chapters 5-18. The final period, "the things which are to come," says Scofield, are the events to occur after the church age ends. He points out that the length of this dispensation of the church is indeterminate, but will be marked by the rapture spoken of in I Thessalonians 4:14-17.[27]

Sandeen maintains that "The divergence between the historicists and the futurists remained the only serious source of dissent among the millenarians during the first generation of the movement." He goes on to explain that with regard to the "basic tenets of the millenarian creed," there was a "surprising degree of unanimity..." These "basic tenets" are identified by Sandeen as,

> ...the belief that acceptance of the divine authority of Scripture required that the believer expect a literal rather than a spiritual fulfillment of the prophecies; the belief that the gospel was not intended nor was it going to accomplish the salvation of the world, but that, instead, the world was growing increasingly corrupt and rushing toward imminent judgment; the belief that Christ would literally return to this earth and the Jews be restored to Palestine before the commencement of the millennial age; and the belief that his whole panorama of coming glory and judgment was explicitly foretold in the prophecies where one could, if taught by the Spirit, discover the truth and be ready for the coming of the bridegroom.[28]

It is Sandeen's belief that with few exceptions, the British millenarians of the early nineteenth century "would have given ready consent to these statements."[29]

<u>CONTROL OF SCRIPTURE AND PROPHECY</u>

Darby expresses great concern about the divisions in his day--over the subject of prophecy--among "both those who hold and those who strenuously oppose views, which, for convenience' sake, we may call Millenarian..." He writes:

> Many have written on one side and the other ignorant of each other's views, and precipitate and unwarranted in their inferences from them; and, while those who hold the views of prophecy, which have occasioned the controversy, have indulged in language utterly inconsistent with the spirit of their Master, those who are unconvinced by them, though charging this exclusively on the Millenarians, are themselves, it appears to me, in no way free from blame. Superciliousness, distrust, and animosity...have marked their conduct and language; while those who sought instruction...have been hindered, perplexed, and repelled in their inquiries by the

selfish precipitancy of the one...and the uncandid uninquiring rejection and denouncement of the other.[30]

Darby traces this sorry state of affairs in prophetic interpretation to the lack of control of Scripture. There ought to be a disposition, he says, to try the soundness of those views which we claim come from Scripture, before the value and veracity of the Bible itself is "brought into question, perplexity, and disgrace, by the presumptuous and hasty pursuit, not of scriptural truth, but of our own untried thoughts..."[31] Darby explains the crux of the problem in these terms:

> I confess I think the modern writers on prophecy justly chargeable with following their own thoughts hastily, and far too much removed from the control of Scripture. They have got some general view, perhaps sound, of God's purpose. They take some text or prophecy as a starting point, pursue the suggestions of their own minds in connection with their general views previously adopted, but leave the results almost entirely untried by the direct testimony of the word, affording us theories, often enlarging when by a writer much imbued with Scripture, often of general soundness of view though replete with false statements; but, when not by such a writer, diverging into absurdities calculated to awaken the impatience of many and bring the truth of all into dishonour. In the meanwhile the Church is distracted. There is not a single writer whose writings I have seen (unless it be the author of one short inquiry) who is not chargeable with this fault.[32]

Darby upholds the norm of Scripture not only for those who teach and write on prophetic themes, but for the Bible student in general who must evaluate their works and views. He urges everyone to seek the testimony of Scripture and to "draw ideas simply and directly from this..." He warns the reader, at the same time, to neither place trust in any individual's mind, "whether millenarian or antimillenarian," nor to adopt or reject anything unexamined. For Darby, the "bottom line" is the Scriptural injunction "to prove all things, and hold fast that which is good [I Thess. 5:21]..."[33]

With regard to the subject of the control of Scripture and the Biblical scholarship of others, the comparison and contrast between Darby and Scofield is most interesting. There is no question whatsoever that Scofield would agree with Darby that prophetic views, as well as all nonprophetic theological concepts, must stand or fall on the basis of the teachings of Scripture itself. In his biography of Scofield's life, Charles Trumbull asks how the phenomenal success of the *Scofield Reference Bible* among Christians of all levels of learning can be explained. The answer, he says, is that,

> The man who gave his lifetime study to the making of the notes and comments in the Scofield Reference Bible was concerned only to *find and state exactly what the Bible itself had to say* on any and every point....It is the undiluted Scripture basis of its notes and comments that makes the Scofield Reference Bible so invaluable and so almost unique.[34]

Obviously, Scofield would also agree with Darby that no view should be accepted or rejected without first proving it on the basis of Scripture and then holding fast to that which is good.

When it comes to the question of past scholarship, however, the two men are worlds apart. Unlike Darby, who could scarcely find a righteous individual in the Sodom of prophetic interpretation (Gen. 18:32), Scofield seems to have found many. Trumbull tells us that "the editor of the Scofield Reference Bible was too reverent and too thorough to imagine that he alone had been taught of the Spirit," and thus he was driven to the great task of studying the writings of others.[35]

Scofield himself says, "I hold no new or peculiar theories of prophetic interpretation, nor have I any novel doctrine in the interests of which I might be tempted to force favorable applications or obscure predictions." He laments the fact that II Peter 1:20, "the great inspired rule governing prophetical interpretation," has not been followed. This rule, explains Scofield, states that no prophecy is to be interpreted independently of the entire body of prediction on the subject in question. After affirming that this rule is a "safeguard of sanity," he suggests that "It is not too much to say that, had Peter's rule been observed we should have had, with some minor disagreements no doubt, a majestic consensus of interpretation of the body of predictive prophecy."[36]

Interpretation of Prophecy

<u>LITERALISM AND THE HOPES OF THE CHURCH AND ISRAEL</u>

One of the most important underlying principles in Darby's understanding of prophecy is his hermeneutical principle of literal interpretation. George M. Marsden says of dispensationalist teachers like Darby, Blackstone, Brookes, and Scofield, that they held "that the Bible was absolutely reliable and precise in matters of fact, that its meanings were plain, and that whenever possible it should be taken literally."[37] Brookes maintained for example, that "The language in which prophecy is written is as simple and easy to understand as any other part of the Scriptures, and all that is needed in reading it is a submissive disposition, ready to take God at His word without any theory of our own to establish."[38]

In 1878, a Methodist minister named William E. Blackstone, published a book entitled *Jesus is Coming*. Loraine Boettner says of this work, "with the exception of the Scofield Bible this book undoubtedly has done more than any other to popularize the dispensational system."[39] In his book, Blackstone asks,

> What is the *purpose of language*, if not to convey definite ideas? Surely the Holy Spirit could have chosen words to convey His thoughts correctly. Indeed it is all summed up in the inquiry of a little child, "If Jesus didn't mean what He said, why didn't He say what He meant?" But we believe that He did mean what He said, and that His words will "not pass away." Mat. 24:35.[40]

Scofield expresses the same idea with respect to prophecy in particular. He encourages his reader to,

> Approach [prophetic] writings as all other writings are approached; give these great preachers enough reverence to suppose that they were as capable of using language in its ordinary meaning as other preachers and writers; follow Peter's great rule of interpreting every prediction in harmony with all the other predictions on that subject (2 Pet. 1:19-21)...[41]

As we have come to expect from Darby, there is no systematic presentation of his hermeneutical concept of literal interpretation. He makes few direct statements on the subject of hermeneutics proper. His position is revealed more incidentally in relation to what he sees as the hopes of the church and Israel. With regard to the study of prophecy, Darby lays down two principles. He says,

> First, in prophecy, when the Jewish church [i.e., assembly] or nation (exclusive of the Gentile parenthesis in their history) is concerned, i.e., when the address is directly to the Jews, there we may look for a plain and direct testimony, because earthly things were the Jews' proper portion. And, on the contrary, where the address is to the Gentiles, i.e., when the Gentiles are concerned in it, there we may look for symbol, because earthly things were not their portion, and the system of revelation must to them be symbolical. When therefore facts are addressed to the Jewish church as a subsisting body, as to what concerns themselves, I look for a plain, common-sense, literal statement as to a people with whom God had direct dealings upon earth, and to whom He meant His purposes concerning them to be known. On the other hand, as the church was a system of grace and heavenly hopes (though God indeed overruled by providence in respect of His ultimate purposes concerning it, it was neither the visible object of His dealings upon earth, nor had an admitted interest in, though acted on by them), it is addressed by an exhibition of their moral character, and is symbolised by analogous agencies.[42]

While it is clear that in contemporary dispensationalism, "the distinction between Israel and the Church is born out of a system of hemeneutics...called literal interpretation,"[43] the order in Darby is not so clear. At times, as here, Darby's hermeneutics seem to be based upon the dispensational distinction between Israel and the church, rather than the other way around. As a dispensation related to earth, Israel's future has to do with earthly and therefore literal things. As that which is heavenly, and therefore above all dispensational and earthly things, the true church must be viewed in symbolic rather than literal terms. While in theory this hermeneutical application seems to conform nicely to Darby's understanding of the Israel-church distinction, in practice it appears to lose its way.

That Darby applies the principle of literal interpretation to prophecies concerning Israel is evident enough. For example, in speaking of the promise of an earthly dominion for Abraham's physical seed, the Jewish people, Darby says that it "was an expectation which every Jew (taking prophecy literally, as every Jew must), because he was a Jew, must have justly held upon belief in the prophetic declaration."[44] But how prophecies concerning the church are to receive a symbolical interpretation is not so clear.

The only clue that Darby offers is in the statement of the second of his principles of prophetic interpretation. He writes:

> Secondly, intimately connected with this [the first principle] (because
> the history of the Bible is the history of the Jews--for history is the relation
> of facts on earth, of which the Jews are the portion of GOD'S agency and as
> to whom we know it was ordered), is another principle, viz., that wherever
> Scripture affords the history of a fact, there we may expect it to be dis-
> tinctly and literally declared or predicted in prophecy. When the Scrip-
> tures do not extend to the giving the history (which is evidently the case
> after the fact of the restoration of the Jews from Babylon, save the fact of
> the Lord's coming to offer Himself, and perhaps we may add the outpour-
> ing of the Spirit), then, we must expect it to be declared only symbolically,
> i.e., appropriately in its moral character; and hence, partly, the partial ob-
> scurity of the seventy weeks of Daniel, because they were no regular
> recognised portion of the Jewish history, but a sort of anomalous period
> for the coming of the Lord.[45]

Perhaps here too, Darby means to include the anomalous church age, the parenthesis between Daniel's sixty-ninth and seventieth weeks.

In any case, what is clear is that Darby does indeed understand key predictions
related to the church in a very literal sense. With regard to the predicted rapture
of the church at the end of the present dispensation, for example, he says that
there is "Nothing clearer, then, than we are to go up to meet Him, and not await
His coming to earth..."[46] Even more to the point is Darby's position on the interpretation of one of the key prophetic passages related to the church, Revelation
20. Concerning this passage, he says that,

> We read of God and Christ, of the devil and Satan, the first resurrection and
> the second death. This is not symbolical, but plain; and (what is very impor-
> tant to remark) it is not a state of things described, but a reward of per-
> sons.... We do not (though figures may be used to express them) believe that
> the things here spoken of are figures; we do not believe, that, when the Lord
> said that people who suffered with Him should also reign with Him, He
> meant that the principles which they suffered for should prevail in persons
> who were reigned over... His word has declared it...we shall be priests of
> God and of Christ, reigning a thousand years with Him, a Priest upon His
> throne, reigning upon, or rather over, the earth.[47]

Darby goes on to say elsewhere that if the first resurrection which precedes this
thousand-year reign of Christ is not to be taken literally, then why should the
second resurrection (of the unjust) at the end of the millennial period be so understood?[48]

Darby's conclusion on the question of interpretation, not only of prophecy, but
of all of the Bible, is that to "resist the plain testimony of Scripture," brings persons into "awful error."[49] He contends that the difficulty that people encounter in
understanding the Bible, "[does] not arise from the word of God not being simple,
clear, and convincing..." The problem, rather, is that preconceived ideas and
opinions "rob us of its natural sense."[50]

Darby makes it clear that what also prevents us from understanding Scripture in its natural sense, is the "mystifying of the Old Testament" and spiritualization in general. The task of the interpreter, he asserts, is simply to seek the purpose and meaning of the one writing or speaking, and nothing further. Darby says, "when I seek the meaning of a passage, I seek simply what God meant, where it is His testimony; or in what light He seeks to put man's conduct, if it is a history of this, or what is His purpose, as a whole, in the narration."[51]

Scofield knows nothing of Darby's theoretical principle of a literal under-standing of prophecy related to Israel, but a symbolic interpretation for the church. As Israel and the church are the respective subjects of prophecy, he understands it in a literal way in either case. While Scofield says nothing about this Darbyite distinction, he does express great concern over the serious problems caused by the use of the allegorical method of interpreting Bible prophecy.

Scofield is convinced that the spiritualization or allegorization of prophecy is that which, more than anything else, has led to the neglect of prophetic writings. These writings, he says, "have been wounded in the house of their friends." Sane and thoughtful individuals have turned in disgust from the "wild interpretations of well-meaning but ill-taught men." These are interpretations which find fulfill-ment of prophecy in any historical (e.g., "the so--called 'historical' interpretation of the Apocalypse") or current event, no matter how remote the connection. These are interpretations too, says Scofield, "which find in the Christian Church the fulfillment of the numerous and explicit predictions which the prophets them-selves declare relate to Israel, and to the kingdom covenanted to David and his seed..."[52]

How can it be, asks Scofield, that the Jews were so slow to believe the many predictions concerning the coming of the Messiah? Their blindness, he answers, was for the same reason that many Christians have been blinded today to the "equally evident meaning of a far greater number of predictions" of Christ's sec-ond coming and earthly glory--"the process of 'spiritualizing' Scripture." "In other words," says Scofield, "the ancient scribes told the people that the prophe-cies of Messiah's *sufferings* were not to be interpreted literally, just as some mod-ern scribes are telling people that the prophecies of Messiah's *earthly glory* are not to be literally interpreted."[53]

LITERALISM AND THE USE OF SYMBOLS AND FIGURES

The foregoing is not given to suggest that Darby and Scofield fail to recognize symbols and figures in Scripture in general. Neither is it to suggest that they ad-here to a rigid, unyielding literalism in prophetic interpretation which is devoid of any recognition of symbolism, as Bass implies of Darby.[54] Darby states in a di-rect manner what he believes to be an important principle in our understanding of the prophets. He maintains that "Whatever figures the Spirit of God may use in depicting the ways of God or those of the enemy, the subject of the prophecy is never a figure."[55] Darby goes on to explain the difference between a symbol and a figure. He says,

I am not speaking of those prophecies in which all is symbol; this remark could not be applied to them. Moreover a symbol is not the same thing as a figure. It is a collection of the moral or historical qualities, or of both, which belong to the prophetic object, in order to present God's idea of that object. Certain elements which compose this symbol may be figures; but a striking whole, made up of the qualities that morally compose the thing described. Accordingly nothing is more instructive than a well-understood symbol. It is the perfect idea which God gives us of the way in which He looks upon the object represented by the symbol--His view of its moral character.[56]

It seems to us that this is essentially the same point that Ryrie makes when he says that "Figures often make the meaning plainer, but it is the literal, normal, or plain meaning that they convey to the reader." He maintains that symbols and figures of speech are not at all contrary to literal interpretation. However, they must be interpreted in accordance with the recognized laws of language "as any other utterances are interpreted--that which is manifestly figurative being so regarded."[57]

Darby further shows his desire to understand Scripture in its plain, normal sense, even where figures are concerned, in his evaluation of Paul's instructions for the Lord's Supper. While it is literal bread which is broken, he points out, when it is said that the cup was blessed, it is a reference to that which is a figure of the blood of Christ, and not to the cup itself. "Proper literality in the strict sense," says Darby, "would make nonsense of all language--is not its known sense." In other words, he explains, giving the physical sense of something is not the same as giving the literal sense. For example, drinking a glass of wine implies the consumption of the contents of the glass, not the glass itself. In the same way, asks Darby, when Ezekiel speaks of "these bones" as the house of Israel, "Does any one doubt what it means?" Darby affirms that there are many such figures in Ezekiel,[58] all of which carry a plain or normal meaning beyond the figure used.

Scofield also refers to Ezekiel's valley of dry bones when he is asked to "Give an illustration of the statement, 'Figures are often found in the prophecies, but the figure invariably has a literal fulfillment.'" Scofield explains that,

> It would be, perhaps, more accurate to say, the things figured, or the meaning hidden in the figure, has a literal fulfilment. For instance, in the 37th chapter of Ezekiel the prophet sees a vision of a valley full of dry bones. Then he views the bones, he sees them covered with flesh and skin; and they stand up, an exceeding great army. This is the figure. Verses 11-14 explain the figure. These bones are the whole house of Israel, and the meaning of the new life given to the bones is explained to be a future restoration of Israel to their own land--the land of Palestine. The thing figured by the vision of the valley of dry bones will be literally fulfilled....In other words, we have but to ascertain the meaning of the figure, and we have then something that in the plan of God will be fulfilled literally.[59]

We might add in passing before leaving this subject, that Darby makes an interesting statement about types in Scripture. He writes:

The types which are presented to us in the scriptures are of different characters; [1] partly, of some great principle of God's dealings, as Sarah and Hagar of the two covenants; [2] partly, they are of the Lord Jesus Himself, in different characters, as sacrifice, priest, &c.; [3] partly, of certain dealings of God, or conduct of men, in other dispensations; [4] partly, of some great future acts of God's government.

Though no strict rule can be given, we can say in general that Genesis furnishes us with the chief examples of the first class; Leviticus, of the second, though some remarkable ones are found in Exodus; Numbers, of the third class; those of the fourth class are more dispersed.[60]

Scofield comments in regard to the lifting up of the bronze serpent (Num. 21:9), that it had a literal significance for the Israelites who looked upon it then and lived, but a typical significance for Christians to come who would look upon Christ as He was lifted up to make atonement for sins.[61]

Subjects of Prophecy

PRELIMINARY CONSIDERATIONS

Object of Prophecy

The "great subjects" of prophecy, according to Darby, are the hope of the church and the hope of Israel.[62] These in turn grow out of the "great object" of prophecy and the distinction between Israel and the church. In keeping with the concept that "The divine glory is ever the end of all things," Darby maintains that Christ Himself is the object of all prophecy. He explains that neither the church, nor Jerusalem, nor the Gentiles, much less Nineveh or Babylon, is the object of prophecy. It is only in their connection with Christ that they take on any importance. In this fact, says Darby, we find "the true scope and intelligence of the real importance and place of each subject; namely, as Christ is to be the centre in which all things in heaven and earth are to be united, various subjects become the sphere of His glory..." It is in this connection, Darby maintains, that we get the means by which these subjects may be understood.[63]

After suggesting that we are not to limit our knowledge of Christ to Him crucified, but that we are to know Him glorified and at the Father's right hand, Darby goes on to say that,

> Revelation 12 presents to us the great object of prophecy, and of all the word of God, that is, the combat which takes place between the last Adam and Satan. It is from this centre of truth that all the light which is found in Scripture radiates. This great combat may take place either for the earthly things (they being the object), and then it is in the Jews; or for the church (that being the object), and then it is in the heavenly places. It is on this account that the subject of prophecy divides itself into two parts: the hopes of the church, and those of the Jews; though the former be scarcely, properly speaking, prophecy, which concerns the earth and God's government of it.[64]

Darby explains elsewhere that the subject of prophecy is not providence, which he defines as "the ordering of the course of all things by divine power, in such sort that all results which happen in the world are according to the divine purpose and will." The earth, rather, and God's government of it, is "the proper subject of prophecy." Concerning the "heavenly company," says Darby, it becomes "a collateral subject of prophetic revelation" only in so far as it is connected with God's government of the earth.[65]

And what is the consequence of failing to see the distinctness of the church's hopes or of combining them with the hopes of Israel? Darby "implore[s] [the] brethren to weigh anxiously this point: [for] they may be assured it is of the greatest practical importance." Darby explains that,

> The life and spiritual energy of a saint depends on his faith in what is proper to his own dispensation. This is so true, that, if he only believed what belonged to the last, it would not be life to him; it has ceased to be the test of faith to him. To Abraham, faith in Almighty God was living faith: is this (though living faith surely owns it) what living faith consists in now? A Jew, not owning Jehovah, would have failed from the covenant. And it is true of power too. If the Holy Ghost be not fully owned, no general idea of salvation, however true, will give the power, nor form and guide for Christ's glory those who neglect the former. What is special to the dispensation is the power and testimony of the dispensation, and not what is said to be common to all.[66]

Extra-Darby Distinction Between Church and Israel

One of the common fallacies set forth by nondispensationalists like Bass[67] and Fuller,[68] is that the distinction between Israel and the church and their respective hopes, and the idea that the former should never be confused with the latter, was invented by Darby and is therefore confined to dispensational theology. The postmillenarian, Charles Hodge (1797-1878), says John Walvoord, "insisted that Israel always means the nation Israel, and is not a synonym for the church."[69] Furthermore, Hodge contends, as does Darby, that Israel will experience a future conversion and restoration. In a commentary on Romans 11:26, he writes:

> Israel, here, from the context, must mean the Jewish people, and *all Israel*, the whole nation. The Jews, as a people, are not rejected; as a people, they are to be restored. As their rejection, although national, did not include the rejection of every individual; so their restoration, although in like manner national, need not be assumed to include the salvation of every individual Jew. *Pas Israel* is not therefore to be here understood to mean all the true people of God, as Augustin, Calvin, and many others explain it; nor all the elect Jews, *i.e.*, all that part of the nation which constitute "the remnant according to the election of grace;" but the whole nation, as a nation.[70]

Walvoord concludes that it is correct to say that Darby made new distinctions, but it is "a factual error" to claim that those distinctions are completely novel. "Many modern scholars who are not dispensationalists," Walvoord points out, "have abandoned the equation of Israel and the church, much as Hodge did a century ago."[71]

The Hopes of the Church

1. Her Calling: Heavenly--not the subject of prophecy. According to Darby, the church properly speaking (i.e., the true church) is not the subject of prophecy.[72] Prophecy, he maintains, applies to things on earth, not heaven, and the failure to understand this has misled the church. The church has been under the mistaken notion, says Darby, that it had in its power the ability to accomplish earthly blessing, when in fact it has been called to enjoy heavenly blessings.[73] Indeed, the church sits in heavenly places where prophecy does not reach. And the government of God will never establish the church on earth as it did Israel, insists Darby, for this is not the church's calling.[74]

Darby asserts that "The church is something altogether apart--a kind of heavenly economy..."[75] Concerning Old Testament prophecy, the New Testament "declares in the most absolute and positive manner that it was a mystery hidden in all ages, and now revealed to the apostles and prophets by the Spirit."[76] Thus, during the time of Israel's rejection as God's earthly people, God has chosen a people who will enjoy heavenly glory with Christ.[77]

Darby holds the interesting notion that with Christ's rejection by the Jews, He became "wholly a heavenly person." He says that according to this doctrine, especially taught by the apostle Paul, "It is no longer the Messiah of the Jews, but a Christ exalted, glorified; and it is for want of taking hold of this exhilarating truth, that the church has become too weak."[78] In Darby's view, the consequence of this (i.e., the heavenly character of Christ) for the church, is that as the Body of Christ, the church belongs to heaven. And as long as Christ is seated in heaven, the church is seated there too.[79]

The question that naturally arises is, how can this completely heavenly Body of Christ, the church, which has nothing to do with earth (the proper sphere of prophecy), be one of the great subjects of prophecy? One would expect "church" in the earthly context to mean the apostate professing church--Christendom. But the professing church is not in view here, for Darby affirms that a portion of the Apocalypse applies to "what has the name of the church, but is the power of evil in the world...but this does not make the church a subject of prophecy."[80]

Darby explains that only when the church takes part in the government of the earth, does it relate to prophecy. And it is "the marriage of the Lamb and the description of the heavenly Jerusalem [which] give the epoch from which dates the character of this relationship with the earth."[81] Darby writes:

> Here it is we find the church in prophecy. The marriage of the Lamb having taken place with the church already gone up on high, the saints come forth with the Lord on the white horse to the triumphant destruction

of the beast and the false prophet. And then the church is seen in her relationship with the earth in blessing, as the heavenly Jerusalem...[82]

It is still difficult to determine how the church is actually related to prophecy in Darby's understanding of it. That it participates in the prophetic events just cited and profits by prophetic utterances (see pages 143-44 above), is clear enough. But beyond this, after he has said that the subject of prophecy is divided into two parts, the hope of Israel and the hope of the church, Darby staunchly denies that the church is in any way the subject of prophecy, for all of the reasons stated above.

Perhaps that which comes closest to Darby's actual position is his statement, "I do not believe the church is the subject, though it is the recipient and depository of prophecy, as Abraham was of what should happen to Lot." After affirming that the church is not earthly and that "Prophecy gives the career of *earthly* events, the wickedness of man, or the dealings of God," Darby repeats what he believes to be the church's direct relation to prophecy. He says, "what relates to it is, as I have said, only seen when it comes down out of heaven having the glory of God. Hence it has no place in prophecy."[83]

2. Her Hope: Second coming--glory of Christ. Darby observes that "There is not an epistle in the New Testament in which the coming of the Lord Jesus is not made the prominent object of the faith and hope of believers..."[84] Thus it is seen that salvation ("that is, to escape the wrath of God") alone is not the hope of the church, but participation in the Son's glory.[85] Darby writes:

> During the period which separates the first coming of the Lord from the second, the church is gathered by the action of the Holy Spirit to have part in the glory of Christ at His return.
> These, in a few words, are the two great subjects which I have been opening; namely, that Christ, having done all that is needful for the salvation of the church--having saved all those who believe, the Holy Ghost now acts in the world to communicate to the church the knowledge of this salvation. He does not come to propose the hope that God will be good, but a fact...that Jesus has already accomplished the salvation of all those who believe; and when the Holy Spirit communicates this knowledge to a soul, it knows that it is saved. Being then put in relationship with God as His children, we are His heirs...All that concerns the glory of Christ belongs to us, and the Holy Spirit...make[s] us understand that we are children of God....[and] teaches the children of God what their inheritance is. As they are one with Christ, all the truth of His glory is revealed to them...[86]

Thus the hope of the church, says Darby, is seen as identified with and founded upon its relationship as united with Christ in heaven. The church is both a pilgrim and the Bride of Christ on earth, but its hope is to be married to the Bridegroom Who is in heaven. While the church will "see things set right in the kingdom," its glory is heavenly, not earthly. Darby says that "we may come forth from heaven, for the kingdom and the glory, but our place is in heaven, in the unity with Christ as one with Him."[87]

Following the marriage supper of the Lamb, observes Darby, the church will become a partaker of all the glory of Christ. In this position, the saints will receive honors such as Christ Himself receives. And in association with "the Lord of glory," they will judge the world and angels. The saints too, "will be the servants and instruments who will dispense the light and the blessings of His kingdom over an earth delivered of all its sorrows, and where Satan is no longer." Darby exclaims, "Happy those believers!"[88]

The Hopes of Israel

1. Her Calling: Earthly--proper subject of prophecy. At this point, we come to what is apparently for Darby the real subject of prophecy. Darby says that at the close of this dispensation there will be a Jewish remnant, delivered and blessed on the earth at Christ's second coming. This truth, he asserts, "is, beyond all controversy, the doctrine of Scripture." The Scripture cited by Darby is, Zechariah 13:8, 9; Ezekiel 20:33-38; 37:11-28; Daniel 11:32-5; 12:1-3; Hosea 2, 3; Jeremiah 30:4-9, and chapters 31-33. Among other things, according to Darby, these passages show that "This remnant has neither the church's heavenly blessings nor the church's hope."[89] By means of the new covenant, Israel will be brought in again when the church is in heaven. Darby explains that by taking the church to heaven and by rejecting the earthly order of things connected with it, God can deal with Israel on the basis of this covenant founded on the blood of Christ.[90]

The subjects of prophecy, then, according to Darby, are the following: 1. "The dealings of God in government upon the earth, in the midst of Israel;" 2. "The moral details of the conduct of the people which led to their ruin;" and 3. "God's intervention at the end [millennial period] in grace by the Messiah to establish His people in assured blessing by God's own power, according to His purpose." There are, Darby adds, two things which must be considered in connection with these leading subjects. The first thing is the judgment of the nations, which was necessary for Israel's establishment in her own land. The second thing is the Jew's rejection of Christ at His first coming as the Messiah.[91]

Darby indicates that due to their association with Israel in her failure, the nations are also treated in prophecy. He explains that after the judgment upon Noah's descendants at Babel, Israel became the center and keystone of the new order of things. In this new system, the throne of God at Jerusalem became "the seat of divine authority over all nations," and the temple of God at Jerusalem became "the place where they should go up to worship Him who dwelt between the cherubim."

But when Israel failed in that obedience which was the condition of her blessing and dispensational standing on earth, according to Darby, God set up "another system of human supremacy" headed by Nebuchadnezzar. Thus prophecy deals also with this Gentile system and its relationship with God's earthly people. Darby maintains that, "Guilty of rebellion against God, and associated with Israel in the rejection of Christ, and at the close rising in revolt against Him, this power is associated with the Jews in the judgment, as being united with them in evil."[92]

All of the foregoing, according to Darby, primarily involves Old Testament prophecy. So, he asks, what is the difference between Old Testament and New Testament prophecy? He repeats the position that since the Assembly (the church) is heavenly and thus has nothing to do with earthly government, it has no direct relation to prophecy. He explains that,

> The communications are direct from the Father and from the Lord according to the relationship in which it stands to them, just as prophecy was with the Jews. But the Spirit can look forward in the assembly to the time when the decay of the outward system [Christendom, the professing church] will prepare the way for the introduction of the direct government of God again in the Person of Christ [millennial dispensation]. This in general we find in the Apocalypse, from the beginning of the assembly's declension until it is rejected, and then in the world. Hence we have also the prophecies which announce the decay and ruin of the assembly after the departure of the apostles, as in 1 Timothy iv. 1; 2 Timothy iii, and 2 Thessalonians ii. The decay itself is spoken of in the Epistles of John, Jude, and 2 Peter.[93]

Darby also points to Matthew 24 (with parallel passages in Mark and Luke) as another prophetic subject introduced by Christ Himself, namely, "the connection of Christ as minister of the circumcision with the Jewish people..." In Matthew 10:15-42, he says, "the portion of the residue in their service in Israel is traced on to the Lord's coming." Darby concludes this summary of New Testament prophecy by saying "that in the moral ruin of the assembly on earth, and the history of the residue, we have the connecting links of these days and Christ's mission to Israel, with His coming in the last days."[94]

Now we begin to see something of Darby's understanding of prophecy and how the church is related to it. For Darby, prophecy really is connected only with earth, and therefore applies primarily to the nation of Israel. Even the prophecies concerning the apostate church in the end times serve only to show how these present days are connected with Israel and Christ's dealings with her in the last days.

Apparently, Darby views subjects like the rapture of the church and the first resurrection as simply parenthetical statements of what has happened to the true church while the real business of prophecy is being conducted in other more earthly contexts. In fact, at one point, he says that the Lord's coming is the hope of the church, not the subject of prophecy.[95] Why, in Darby's view, can it not be both at the same time? His only argument seems to be that prophecy relates to earth (particularly failure on earth) and not heaven. Christ's coming is viewed as the hope of the true church on the heavenly plane, not the divine response to failure in this present earthly dispensation.

2. <u>Her Status: Owned and not owned--the two characters of prophecy to the Jews</u>. All of the prophecy concerning Israel is finally explained by Darby in these terms. There is a class of prophecy which concerns Israel as owned of God, and one which concerns Israel while she is no longer owned as the people of God. Darby says that,

This distinction flows from the fact that the throne of God, sitting between the cherubim, has been taken away from Jerusalem, and the dominion of the earth committed to the Gentiles. The period of this dominion is called "the times of the Gentiles." The former class of prophecies [Israel owned by God] applies to that which precedes [dispensation of Israel] and that which is subsequent to this period [millennial dispensation]. The latter refers to this period itself [dispensations of the Gentiles and church].[96]

3. Her Hope: Restoration--earthly kingdom and inheritance. Darby maintains that in the latter days, the remnant of Israel out of the Tribulation will once again be owned by God. Israel may have failed in her dispensational responsibility and suffered temporary cutting off for it, says Darby, but God's counsels are sure and beyond failure. It has ever been the divine plan to fulfill the unconditional covenantal promises to Abraham and his posterity, and thus there is ample testimony in Scripture to "the certainty of the restoration of Israel to their own land to be blessed under Christ and the new covenant."[97]

Consequently, the hope of Israel is the return of her King to establish a literal earthly kingdom. During this time, the Jews will look upon the Christ they had rejected and pierced, and mourn. The city of Jerusalem will be rebuilt and reinhabited,[98] sacrifices will once again be offered in the restored temple,[99] and Christ will reign upon the throne of David. Furthermore, writes Darby,

> ...the glory of Jehovah being thus manifested in the midst of the nations, Israel from this day forth shall know that it is Jehovah Himself who is their God, and the nations shall know that it was the iniquity of Israel that brought judgment upon them, and not that Jehovah had failed either in power or in the stability of His counsels. ([Ezek. 38] Vers. 22-24.) In a word, Jehovah and His government should be fully known in Israel, and by means of this people in the world; and from that time God would no more hide His face from them. His Spirit should be poured out upon His people.[100]

And such, says Darby, "is the establishment of God's divine government at the close." Israel is the center of this government in proof of God's "fixed purpose and unchangeable calling..." And while Israel rejects the Gospel now, the beloved of the Father "will believe when they see."[101]

SCOFIELD AND THE SUBJECTS OF PROPHECY

An evaluation of Scofield's position as it relates to Darby's concepts, reveals very evident similarities as well as very distinct dissimilarities. In the latter instance, unlike Darby, Scofield considers Israel and the church alike to be the chief subjects of prophecy,[102] and he brings the Gentiles into the subject in their own right as well. He writes:

> The Scriptures separate the human family into three grand divisions, each having a distinct place in the counsels and purposes of God. (1 Cor. 10:32) To apply indiscriminately to all, the promises, prophecies and re-

sponsibilities of each is to wholly lose sight of the divine order and beauty of the plan of God, and to hopelessly confuse the interpretation of His word.[103]

Concerning the distinction between the church and Israel and the hopes of each, there is basic agreement between Scofield and Darby. Scofield says that anyone who attentively reads the Bible "cannot fail to perceive that more than half of its contents relate to one nation--the Israelites." And in this perception too, according to Scofield, it is evident that in God's dealings and counsels, Israel's place is a very distinct one. This is seen in their separation from the mass of humankind, and in their special covenant with and promises from Jehovah, which are not enjoyed by other nations. It is their history alone, says Scofield, which is the subject of Old Testament narrative and prophecy. Other nations are mentioned only as they come into contact with God's chosen people. In addition to Israel's distinctness in these respects, Scofield observes that,

> It appears, also, that all the communications of Jehovah to Israel *as a nation* relate to the Earth. If faithful and obedient, the nation is promised earthly greatness, riches and power; if unfaithful and disobedient, it is to be scattered "among all people, from the one end of the earth even unto the other" (Deut. 28:64). Even the promise of the Messiah is of blessing to "all the families of the *Earth*."[104]

With regard to the distinction between Israel and the church, Scofield explains further that predictions concerning the future of the church call for its entire removal from the earth (the rapture), while "restored Israel is yet to have her greatest earthly splendor and power."[105] This is not to imply, explains Scofield, that the godly Jew did not go to heaven at death. "The distinction," he continues, "is that the *incentive* to godliness in his case was *earthly* blessings, not heavenly."[106]

As the student of Scripture continues his researches, says Scofield, he discovers that yet another distinct body is mentioned, namely the church. Like Israel, this body has a peculiar relation to and specific promises from God. "But similarity ends there," he says, "and the most striking contrast begins." He observes that,

> Instead of being formed of the natural descendants of Abraham alone, it is a body in which the distinction of Jew and Gentile is lost. Instead of the relation being one of mere *covenant*, it is one of *birth*. Instead of obedience bringing the reward of earthly greatness and wealth, the Church is taught to be content with food and raiment, and to expect persecution and hatred, and it is perceived that just as distinctly as Israel stands connected with temporal and earthly things, so distinctly does the Church stand connected with spiritual and heavenly things.
> Further, Scripture shows him that neither Israel nor the Church always existed. Each had a recorded beginning.[107]

After giving several Scripture citations for "The comparative position of the Jew, the Gentile, and the Church," Scofield concludes that in comparing what Scripture says with respect to Israel and the church, one "finds that in origin, calling, promise, worship, principles of conduct, and future destiny--all is contrast."[108]

While Darby almost places the true church above all prophetic utterances as he places it above all dispensational arrangements, Scofield asserts that "the **Christian's hope** is peculiarly the theme of New Testament prophecy."[109] If the hope of Israel is to be realized in the earthly millennial kingdom, then what is it that constitutes the heavenly hope of the church. Scofield is in agreement with Darby that it is not salvation. He says, rather, that "'Looking for that blessed hope and *the glorious appearing of the great God and our Saviour Jesus Christ.'* That is the blessed hope."[110]

After stating that salvation is a present reality, Scofield asks, "Then where does hope come in, 'and rejoice in the hope of the glory of God?'" It is not the salvation of God, he answers, but the glory of God. Scofield explains that in Colossians we see that at Christ's appearing, the glory of God is brought unto the church. "The glorious appearing of the Lord," he maintains, "is pointed to as the believer's hope. It is the first to be fulfilled of all the unfulfilled prophecies."[111] Darby too, views the rapture as the next event for the church, but he fails to classify it as unfulfilled prophecy per se.

Scofield is as adamant as Darby in viewing the confusion of the hopes of the church with those of Israel as resulting in the most serious of consequences. He writes:

> It may safely be said that the Judaizing of the Church has done more to hinder her progress, prevent her mission, and destroy her spiritually, than all other causes combined. Instead of pursuing her appointed path of separation from the world and following the Lord in her heavenly calling, she has used Jewish Scriptures to justify herself in lowering her purpose to the civilization of the world, the acquisition of wealth, the use of an imposing ritual, the erection of magnificent churches, the invocation of God's blessing upon the conflicts of armies, and the division of an equal brotherhood into "clergy" and "laity."[112]

At this juncture, a point made previously bears repeating. In light of such statements as, "The Jew was promised an earthly inheritance, earthly wealth, earthly honour, earthly power,"[113] and "Israel's distinction, glory and destiny will always be earthly,"[114] Scofield, as well as Darby and other dispensationalists, have given the impression that for Israel there is no heavenly hope or future. As Ryrie points out, however, "Any apparent dichotomy between heavenly and earthly purposes is not actual." While the "earthly-heavenly, Israel-Church distinction" is true, Ryrie explains, "it is not everything that dispensationalists teach about the ultimate destiny of the people included in these groups."[115]

Endnotes

[1]John Nelson Darby, *The Collected Writings of J. N. Darby*, 34 vols., ed. William Kelly, vol. 1: *Ecclesiastical No. 1* (Sunbury, Pa.: Believers Bookshelf, n.d.), pp. 1-19.

[2]Ibid., pp. 20-35.

[3]Ibid., vol. 2: *Prophetic No. 1*, pp. 1-31.

[4]H. A. Ironside, *A Historical Sketch of the Brethren Movement* (Grand Rapids: Zondervan Publishing House, 1942; reprint ed., Neptune, N.J.: Loizeaux Brothers, 1985), p. 23.

[5]Ibid.

[6]Ibid.

[7]Darby, *Writings*, vol. 2: *Prophetic No. 1*, p. 179.

[8]John Nelson Darby, *Synopsis of the Books of the Bible*, 5 vols., reprint ed. (Sunbury, Pa.: Believers Bookshelf, 1971), 2:462.

[9]Darby, *Writings*, vol. 2: *Prophetic No. 1*, p. 281.

[10]Ibid., vol. 5: *Prophetic No. 2*, p. 390.

[11]C. I. Scofield, *The Scofield Reference Bible* (New York: Oxford University Press, 1945), p. 711.

[12]Ibid.

[13]Darby, *Writings*, vol. 2: *Prophetic No. 1*, p. 279.

[14]Ibid., p. 280.

[15]Ibid., p. 371.

[16]Ibid., p. 370.

[17]Ibid., pp. 370, 382.

[18]Ibid., pp. 382, 371.

[19]Ibid., p. 371.

[20]C. I. Scofield, *What Do the Prophets Say?* (Greenville, S.C.: The Gospel Hour, Inc., 1918), pp. 24-5. For Scofield's sixfold reasons for the study of prophecy, see *Dr. C. I. Scofield's Question Box*, comp. Ella E. Pohle (Chicago: The Bible Institute Colportage Association, 1917), pp. 119-20.

[21]Ernest R. Sandeen, *The Roots of Fundamentalism* (Chicago: University of Chicago Press, 1968; reprint ed., Grand Rapids: Baker Book House, 1978), p. 36.

[22]Millard J. Erickson, *Contemporary Options in Eschatology* (Grand Rapids: Baker Book House, 1977), p. 30.

[23]Ibid.

[24]Darby, *Writings*, vol. 2: *Prophetic No. 1*, p. 279.

[25]Sandeen, pp. 36-7.

[26]Darby, *Writings*, vol. 5: *Prophetic No. 2*, pp. 12-13.

[27]Scofield, *Reference Bible*, p. 1330.

[28]Sandeen, p. 39.

[29]Ibid.

[30]Darby, *Writings*, vol. 2: *Prophetic No. 1*, pp. 1-2.

[31]Ibid., p. 2.

[32]Ibid., pp. 4-5.

[33]Ibid., p. 10.

[34]Charles Gallaudet Trumbull, *The Life Story of C. I. Scofield* (New York: Oxford University Press, 1920), pp. 80-81 (italics his).

[35]Ibid., p. 84.

[36]Scofield, *What Do the Prophets Say?*, p. 9. See Scofield's further remarks on this interpretative rule in II Peter 1:20 in "The Times of the Gentiles," *Bibliotheca Sacra* 107 (July-September 1950):343.

[37]George M. Marsden, *Fundamentalism and American Culture* (New York: Oxford University Press, 1980), p. 51. For the position of contemporary dispensationalism on the hermeneutical principle of literal interpretation, see p. 31ff above.

[38]James H. Brookes, *Maranatha*, 10th ed. (New York: Fleming H. Revell Co., 1889), p. 35.

[39]Loraine Boettner, *The Millennium* (Philadelphia: The Presbyterian and Reformed Publishing Co., 1957), p. 368.

[40]W[illiam] E. B[lackstone], *Jesus Is Coming* (Chicago: Fleming H. Revell Co., 1908), p. 23. See Charles C. Ryrie's *Dispensationalism Today* (Chicago: Moody Press, 1965), pp. 87-8, where he also takes up the question of the purpose of language and the need for literal interpretation.

[41]Scofield, *What Do the Prophets Day?*, p. 26.

[42]Darby, *Writings*, vol. 2: *Prophetic No. 1*, p. 35.

[43]Ryrie, p. 45.

[44]Darby, *Writings*, vol. 2: *Prophetic No. 1*, pp. 55-6.

[45]Ibid., p. 36.

[46]Ibid., vol. 11: *Prophetic No. 4*, p. 153.

[47]Ibid., vol. 2: *Prophetic No. 1*, p. 81.

[48]Ibid., p. 309; see p. 158ff above for a further discussion of Darby's concept of prophecy and the church's relation to it.

[49]Ibid., p. 82.

[50]Ibid., p. 301.

[51]Ibid., vol. 9: *Apologetic No. 1*, pp. 256-7.

[52]Scofield, *What Do the Prophets Say?*, pp. 25-6.

[53]C. I. Scofield, *Rightly Dividing the Word of Truth* (Fincastle, Va.: Scripture Truth Book Co., n.d.), p. 18. See also *Prophecy Made Plain* (Glasgow: Pickering and Inglis; London: Alfred Holness, n.d.), p.75f, where Scofield discusses "a school of interpretation having disciples among both Jews and Christians which insists that, unlike all other writings, unfulfilled prophecy is to be interpreted, not in the natural and unforced sense of the words themselves, but in an allegorical or so-called 'spiritual' sense." Here too, he discusses at length what he calls "a Divine law of prophetical interpretation." According to this law, the total and literal fulfillment of all past prophecies is the guarantee that all future prophecies will be fulfilled in like manner. Scofield quotes several prophecies in proof of this contention.

[54]Clarence B. Bass, *Backgrounds to Dispensationalism* (Grand Rapids: Wm. B. Eerdmans Publishing Co., 1960), p. 130.

[55]Darby, *Synopsis*, 2:278.

[56]Ibid.

[57]Ryrie, p. 87.

[58]John Nelson Darby, *Letters of J.N. Darby*, 3 vols., reprint ed. (Sunbury, Pa.: Believers Bookshelf, 1971), 3:100-1.

[59]Scofield, *Question Box*, pp. 65-6.

[60]Darby, *Synopsis*, 1:128.

[61]Scofield, *Reference Bible*, p. 198.

[62]It will soon become apparent, that while Darby clearly states that the hopes of the church is one of the great subjects of prophecy, this is true more in theory than in fact. It is a puzzling contradiction in Darby for which a satisfactory explanation is never given. In any case, the concept is followed through to its conclusion.

[63]Darby, *Writings*, vol. 11: *Prophetic No. 4*, pp. 41-2.

[64]Ibid., vol. 2: *Prophetic No. 1*, pp. 372-3.

[65]Ibid., vol. 11: *Prophetic No. 4*, p. 43.

[66]Ibid., vol. 8: *Prophetic No. 3*, pp. 112-13.

[67]Bass, pp. 24-7.

[68]Daniel P. Fuller, *Gospel and Law: Contrast or Continuum?* (Grand Rapids: William B. Eerdmans Publishing Co., 1980), pp. 8-9.

[69]John F. Walvoord, review of *Backgrounds to Dispensationalism*, by Clarence B. Bass, in *Bibliotheca Sacra* 118 (January 1961), p. 69.

[70]Charles Hodge, *Commentary on the Epistle to the Romans*, rev. ed. (Grand Rapids: Wm. B. Eerdmans Publishing Co., 1886), p. 374.

[71]Walvoord, p. 69.

[72]Darby, *Writings*, vol. 11: *Prophetic No. 4*, p. 45.

[73]Ibid., vol. 2: *Prophetic No. 1*, p. 376.
[74]Ibid., vol. 11: *Prophetic No. 4*, p. 46.
[75]Ibid., vol. 2: *Prophetic No. 1*, p. 376.
[76]Ibid., vol. 11: *Prophetic No. 4*, p.45.
[77]Ibid., vol. 2: *Prophetic No. 1*, p. 376.
[78]Ibid.
[79]Ibid., vol. 11: *Prophetic No. 4*, p. 45.
[80]Ibid., pp. 46-7.
[81]Ibid.
[82]Ibid., p. 53.
[83]Darby, *Letters*, 1:131.
[84]Darby, *Writings*, vol. 2: *Prophetic No. 1*, p. 25.
[85]Ibid., p. 283.
[86]Ibid., pp. 373-4.
[87]Ibid., vol. 12: *Evangelic No. 1*, p. 381.
[88]Ibid., vol. 2: *Prophetic No. 1*, pp. 275-6.
[89]Ibid., vol. 11: *Prophetic No. 4*, pp. 120-1.
[90]Ibid., vol. 4: *Ecclesiastical No. 2*, p. 328.
[91]Darby, *Synopsis*, 2:462.
[92]Ibid., 2:462-3.
[93]Ibid., 2:463. In the case of the book of Revelation, Darby says that "the part fully and properly prophetic [chaps. 4-22] treats of the world and the apostasy, or of the Jews ..." (*Writings*, vol. 5: *Prophetic No. 2*, p. 391).
[94]Darby, *Synopsis*, 2:463.
[95]Darby, *Letters*, 1:329-30.
[96]Darby, *Synopsis*, 2:276.
[97]Darby, *Writings*, vol. 11: *Prophetic No. 4*, p. 278.
[98]Ibid., p. 277.
[99]Darby, *Synopsis*, 2:405-8; cf. *Letters*, 2:468.
[100]Darby, *Synopsis*, pp. 404-5.
[101]Darby, *Writings*, vol. 11: *Prophetic No. 4*, p. 278.
[102]In the starkest contrast to Darby's attempt to almost completely disassociate the church from prophetic subjects, Scofield asks, "Did you observe in your study of the Bible that more than three-fourths of prophecy is yet unfulfilled, and that there is absolutely nothing in all the purpose of God, as it unfolds itself in the prophetic Word concerning the illimitable future, with which we who are Christians do not stand in some way connected?" (*Prophecy Made Plain*, p. 15).
[103]C. I Scofield, *Scofield Bible Study Leaflet* (Philadelphia: Philadelphia School of the Bible, 1935), Series C, Lesson 4.
[104]Scofield, *Rightly Dividing the Word of Truth*, p. 6.
[105]Ibid., p. 9.
[106]Ibid., p. 8.
[107]Ibid., p. 6.
[108]Ibid. For a full discussion of and Scriptural support for these distinctions, see pp. 6-12 in *Rightly Dividing the Word of Truth*.
[109]Scofield, *Prophecy Made Plain*, p. 16 (emphasis Scofield's).
[110]Ibid., pp. 16-18 (italics his).
[111]Ibid., pp. 17-19.
[112]Scofield, *Rightly Dividing the Word of Truth*, p. 12.
[113]Scofield, *Prophecy Made Plain*, pp. 52-3.
[114]Scofield, *Question Box*, p. 70.
[115]Ryrie, pp. 146-7. See Ryrie's further comments and pp. 30-1 above.

CHAPTER 6

DARBY'S ESSENTIAL ESCHATOLOGY

Introduction to His Eschatology

It is clear from the preceding chapter that Darby's eschatology is an outgrowth of his hermeneutical principle of literal interpretation and the dichotomy between Israel and the church. With respect to literal interpretation, as we have seen, the impact upon Darby's prophetic views is one more of practical application than stated doctrine. While he affirms that references to the church in prophecy must be interpreted symbolically, and that those referring to Israel must have a literal application, he nevertheless renders all predictions of end-time events involving the church in a literal way.

While not always clearly expressed, it is probably true also that Darby's dichotomy between Israel and the church stems largely from the application of the principle of literal interpretation. Again, this is more his practice in fact, rather than a statement of doctrinal principle. Darby seems to imply the principle that all areas of the Bible are to be interpreted in a plain, normal, literal sense, unless something in the text itself indicates otherwise. On this basis, he concludes that one cannot but distinguish Jewish and Christian dispensations and the corresponding destinies and hopes peculiar to each.

Beyond this, however, the distinction between Israel and the church seems to take on a life of its own. It almost becomes a principle of interpretation in its own right. This comes out, for example, in Darby's understanding of the bearing of prophecy and end-time events on the church. Also, in his view, prophecy is connected with the judgment of the Jews and Gentiles (nations) in the Tribulation and the blessings of the Jews in the millennial period when righteousness reigns. But what of events involving the church during this time?[1]

The church, says Darby, has a higher thing "the affections which flow out of relationships with Christ..." Darby explains further that,

> ...these affections do form morally, and in the sweetest way, more than in mere righteousness. And to this I take it, the coming of the Lord and the marriage of the Lamb is the answer, not judgment: still, the other is true and hence I distinguish between the coming of the Lord and prophecy (though this last by the way), though one acts on the other, because He has associated us with His competency to judge the world and all, though the authority is with Him. But this shews what a very high place the church is in.[2]

Darby adds elsewhere that "to me the Lord's coming is not a question of prophecy, but my present hope. Events before His judging the quick are the subject of prophecy; His coming to receive the church is our present, heavenly hope."[3]

In any case, Darby sees predictions of eschatological events as a sure guide to the believer of that which is to come. They are given to him to encourage and comfort him in his present walk and to enable him to see that it is God who controls and orders all human affairs. Darby says,

> Altogether separated from these worldly things, I can study beforehand the profound and perfect wisdom of God; I get enlightened, and cleave to Him instead of following my own understanding. I see in the events which take place around me the unfolding of the purpose of the most High, and not a field abandoned to the struggle of human passions. Thus, and specially in the events which come to pass at the end, it is, that prophecy opens out to us the character of God--all that God would have us know of Himself--His faithfulness, His justice, His power, His longsuffering, but at the same time the judgment which He will certainly execute on proud iniquity, the public and fearful vengeance which he will take on those who corrupt the earth--in order that His government may be established in peace and blessing for all.[4]

Prophetic studies, Darby asserts, is no mere speculation. If that were so, he asks, what was the use of the Lord forewarning the disciples to flee under this or that circumstance? What was the point of prophetic utterances if they had no understanding of what He spoke about, and no belief beforehand in the truth of Christ's word? But just as it was their knowledge and faith concerning the truth of predicted events that distinguished the disciples from the unbelievers among the Israelites, so it is with the church.[5] And what is it that God has said with regard to those events which must "have their accomplishment at the expiration of the dispensation in which we are"?[6]

Structure of His Eschatology

DARBY'S OUTLINE[7]

Darby places the events to occur at the end of the present age in the following sequence:

1. The rapture. Darby says, "There is no event between me and *heaven*."[8] The Holy Spirit causes the church to wait for the Bridegroom and the marriage of the Lamb (Rev. 22:17; chap. 19). While this can only take place in heaven, Darby points out, the church with its heavenly calling is already there and united to Christ by the Spirit (Eph. 2:6; Phil. 3:21, 22).[9] But after all the church is assembled, it will physically go up to meet Christ in the air (I Thess. 4:15-17).[10]

2. The first resurrection and change. At the moment that Christ comes to take the saints "according to His promise," says Darby, He will both change those who

are living, and raise those who have died. This He does in order that they may ever be with the Lord (I Thess. 4:17) where He Himself is in the Father's house (John 14:2). As children of the Father in glory, these believers "together form the bride and body of Christ."[11]

Darby hastens to point out that the rapture does not establish the kingdom. Rather it is the gathering of the "coheirs who are to reign with Christ, and gives their place to them with Him, infinitely above all reign (whatever it be) over the earth." Darby maintains, however, that the earthly reign is "the necessary, blessed and glorious consequence" of the gathering of the saints and their coheirship with Christ.[12]

3. The post-rapture events in heaven. For reasons which will become apparent, it is difficult to place the following events in precise sequence, but this seems to be the logical order:

a. The expulsion of Satan. Darby holds that as soon as the church is raptured, a battle will take place in heaven "in order that the seat of government may be purged of those fertile sources, and of those active agents, of the ills of humanity, and of all creation." Christ's aim in this, says Darby, is to dispossess Satan and to drive him from power so that everything might be restored to its proper order.[13] The result of this battle will be the expulsion of Satan from heaven forever (Rev. 12:12; 16:13, 14; 18:13, 14; 19:18f).[14] Satan, not yet bound, will be cast down to earth. The situation then, Darby maintains, will be "the created heavens occupied by Christ and His church; and Satan in great wrath upon the earth, having but a short time."[15]

b. The judgment seat of Christ. Darby discusses Romans 14 and II Corinthians 5 as the only places in Scripture where these expressions may be found. The first of these passages, he says, has as its purpose the prevention of individual judgments and the second the provocation to do good. Darby maintains that at this time, "the whole of our acts will be detailed there, before the judgment-seat, not for us however, as if we were in the flesh, and thus to our condemnation, but to make evident to our own eyes the grace that occupied itself with us--regenerate or unregenerate."

Darby believes that his own history detailed before the judgment seat will be paralleled by the history of God's grace and mercy toward him. The scene, in other words, "will be declarative, not judicial." Darby considers this event to be that which makes the bride ready (presumably for the marriage supper), and thus it is a wondrous moment.[16]

c. The marriage of the Lamb. Darby maintains that the corporate church is not yet married to Christ for it is not yet formed. Its present position, rather, is one "of fidelity of hope to one long absent from His pledged love--as a stranger therefore in the midst of all that knows Him not..." But after the marriage supper, observes Darby, "She shall reign queen over all her Lord's goods, and rule in His house with Him..."[17] In Revelation 19, Darby sees a picture of the celebration as well as an indication of when the event will occur. Darby writes:

This is after the judgment of Babylon. And again, in chapter 21:9, "I will shew thee the bride, the Lamb's wife." Here we have then the Church confessedly not married to the Lamb; and I believe this to be a most important difference: error as to which has produced as much mistake as any other at all concerning scripture. It may be said to be espoused or destined for him, but the marriage is not yet come. This takes place on being united to Him in that day when He shall appear in His glory, when He calls them up into the air; then shall He "present it to himself a glorious church, without spot or wrinkle or any such thing."[18]

Darby's sequence of events is inconsistent at this point. The above remarks seem clearly to place the marriage of the Lamb in close proximity to the rapture ("when he calls them up into the air"),[19] which occurs at the very end of the present dispensation and prior to the commencement of the Tribulation period. Yet at the same time, Darby has the marriage occurring after the "the judgment of Babylon," which takes place well into the Tribulation (Rev. 18). Indeed, the latter sequence of events is that of the book of Revelation, for the marriage of the Lamb is pictured in chapter 19. It would seem here that as a result of simple confusion or oversight, Darby failed to make his usual distinction between the rapture, when Christ will come *for* the saints, and the second coming proper, when He will come *with* the saints for the battle of Armageddon at the end of the Tribulation. More will be said about this distinction below.

4. The post-rapture events on earth.

a. The Tribulation. Satan, having been cast down from heaven, will be "in open and public rebellion against God,"[20] says Darby. Under the control of the Antichrist, the fourth monarchy--the revived Roman empire--will provide the backdrop for the enactment of Satan's final drama.[21] He will be joined in this drama, this rebellion against God, by the Gentiles and the great majority of the Jews.[22] Darby maintains that Satan "will excite the whole earth, and will raise up in particular the apostate part of it, which has revolted against the power of Christ coming from heaven."[23] Darby writes that,

> This rebellion will bring in a time of extraordinary tribulation on the land of Judah, and in general there will be a temptation which shall put to the proof all the Gentiles. But the testimony of God will go throughout the world, and the judgment will come, and will be executed upon the apostates from among Christians, upon rebellious Jews, and upon all nations which shall have rejected God's testimony. This will be the judgment of the quick, the first resurrection having already taken place. The fulness of times begins at this period.[24]

Darby understands the first beast of Revelation 13, to be the temporal, imperial or secular power of the Gentiles,[25] who receives his power directly from Satan.[26] The second beast of Revelation 13, and the false prophet of Revelation 16:13 and 19:20, he takes to be references to Antichrist. Darby considers the Antichrist to be "the vessel of evil, religious energy, rather than that of evil public government."[27] Thus the first beast and the Antichrist, according to Darby, are "the heads of evil among the Gentiles and among the Jews, the secular and spiritual heads of mischief and rebellion on the earth."[28]

It should be noted here that Darby is not followed by contemporary dispensationalists in his interpretation of Daniel's seventieth week and the duration of the Tribulation period. He writes in this regard that,

> The seventy weeks, or 490 years, include the great gap which has already lasted more than 1800 years--these coming in between the end of the 483rd and the end of the 490th--only that Christians know that half the 70th week was really fulfilled in Christ's ministry; therefore we get a half week in Daniel vii. [v.25] and in the Revelation [12:14].[29]

On this basis, Darby places "the entire deliverance of the heavenly saints from [Satan's] power...," the rapture in other words, "at the moment of the commencement of the great rage of Satan for the three times and a half..."[30]

Scofield, on the other hand, reckons the duration of the seventieth week to be seven years on the basis of the fact that "Each of the sixty-nine 'weeks' up to the crucifixion was seven years long."[31] While the full seven years constitutes the Tribulation period, according to Scofield, the last half of the week, or three and a half years, are termed "The great tribulation..." This is "the time of Jacob's trouble" (Jer. 30:7), of unparalleled woe for Israel.[32] Scofield clearly pictures the church as having been translated prior to the commencement of the seven-year period.[33]

b. Christ's second coming and Armageddon. Darby maintains that at the conclusion of the Tribulation period, Christ will return with the saints (Rev. 19; Col. 3:4; Jude 14; Zech. 14:5) to destroy Satan's power on earth and to deliver the world from his evil influence.[34] This He will accomplish by first destroying Satan's governmental power of earth (which had been confided to the Gentiles) in the person of the Antichrist. "This wicked one," says Darby, "having joined himself to the Jews, and having placed himself at Jerusalem, as the centre of government of the earth will be destroyed by the coming of the Lord of lords and King of kings..."[35]

The second phase of the campaign, according to Darby, is the clearing and purifying of the land ("which belongs to the Jews") of those who still refuse to "acknowledge the rights of Christ," and "desire to possess His heritage." This includes "the Tyrians, the Philistines, the Sidonians; of Edom, and Moab, and Ammon--of all the wicked, in short, from the Nile to the Euphrates."[36] After a short interval of peace and security in the land, another enemy, Gog (identified by Darby as Russia),[37] comes "only for his destruction"[38] (Ezek. 38-39; Rev. 20:8).

Darby maintains that the final phase of the returning King's renovation and purification program involves Satan himself. Prior to the commencement of the thousand-year millennial kingdom, the author of evil and ruler of the earth is bound and cast into the bottomless pit (Rev. 20:1-3). No longer, says Darby, is he the prince of this world. The result, observes Darby, is that,

...blessing will be without interruption until "he is loosed for a short season." Instead of the adversary in the heavenly places; instead of his government, the seat of which is now in the air; instead of that confusion and misery which he produces, as much as is allowed him to do; Christ and His church will be there, the source and instrument of blessing ever new.[39]

5. The millennial kingdom. It is at this time, says Darby, that the remnant of the Jews is delivered, and the kingdom of God is established in power (Matt. 16:28; 17; Mark 9; Luke 9). Righteousness reigns (Eph. 1:10), and there is in the fruit of this reign by Christ "the realization of all that the prophets have spoken of peace and blessing on the earth." More will be said later about the nature of the kingdom.

6. The post-millennial events.

a. The final revolt. After the inhabitants of earth have enjoyed a thousand years of peace and repose under Christ's righteous rule, says Darby, Satan will be released from his bottomless prison to test the nations by his temptation. And what is the result of this testing? When temptation comes, those not truly united to Christ fall.[40] Once the testing is completed, God's judgment falls from heaven and destroys Satan's army, while he himself is cast into the lake of fire to suffer eternal torment with the beast and false prophet.[41]

b. The second resurrection. With Satan and his followers finally disposed of, the wicked dead are now raised to face judgment. This is the second resurrection, the first having been completed prior to the beginning of the millennial age.[42] The subject of the double resurrection is elaborated upon below.

c. The great white throne judgment. Judgment of the unjust dead follows their resurrection to life. "A great white throne is set," Darby notes, and "judgment is carried on according to the purity of God's nature." As the dead, great and small, stand before the throne, the secrets of their hearts are judged by an all-knowing God. This judgment is based on men's works, says Darby, "as it was written in the books of record." And those whose names are not found written in the book of life, are cast into the lake of fire. This having been accomplished, death and hades, the power of Satan, are likewise cast into the lake of fire and thus destroyed judicially forever.[43]

7. The eternal state. Now begins the eternal state in which righteousness continues to dwell. Darby says that the kingdom, "the existence of which supposed evil to be subjugated," will end having been delivered up to the Father, but he believes that the church does not "[lose] its place as the bride of Christ and the habitation of God." In any case, the judgment on the earth at the conclusion of the millennium brings "better and higher blessings."[44]

Darby's explanation of the significance of the New Jerusalem which descends out of heaven is interesting. The number twelve, he points out, often "denotes perfection and governmental power." The twelve gates which represent the twelve tribes of Israel, says Darby, "are full of human perfectness of governmental power." The twelve apostles represented by the twelve foundations, furnish by their work the foundation of the heavenly city. "Thus," concludes Darby, "the creative and providential display of power, the governmental (Jehovah) and the assembly once, founded at Jerusalem, are all brought together in the heavenly city, the organised seat of heavenly power....new and now heavenly capital of God's government."[45]

In the character of the city, we see that "the dispensational Ruler, the true God, and the Lamb...has made good His glory." Darby explains that,

> His servants shall have the fullest privilege of His constant presence, shall see His face, and their belonging to Him as His own be evident to all. There is no night there, nor need of light, for the Lord God gives it; and, as to their state, they reign, not for the thousand years, as they do over the earth, but for ever and ever.[46]

<u>SCOFIELD'S OUTLINE</u>

While there is variation in the interpretation of details, Darby and Scofield are in basic agreement concerning the order of end-time events. However, Scofield begins his timetable with the apostasy of the professing church (II Thess. 2:3).[47] Darby certainly agrees that the church will not be raptured and the Antichrist make his appearance before the "falling away" or apostasy occurs. But he does not usually group the apostasy with eschatological events as such. He discusses it, rather, primarily in relation to the failure of the present dispensation.[48]

The second event in Scofield's prophetic schedule is "The Taking Away of the True Church"--the rapture. He bases this on John 14:3; I Corinthians 15:51, 52; and I Thessalonians 4:16, 17.[49] This involves the transformation of those still living and the resurrection (first resurrection) of all saints of past dispensations.[50]

In Scofield's understanding of it, this event is followed by the judgment of the believer's works "in the air" (II Cor. 5:10; I Cor. 3:8, 13-15; cf. I Cor. 9:18; Col. 2:18; 3:24; Rev. 22:12). Scofield says that "The sins of believers were judged in the Cross; the works are judged that due rewards may be given."[51] He summarizes this event as follows: "Time: when Christ comes. Place: 'in the air.' Result to the believer: 'reward' or 'loss'--'but he himself shall be saved.'"[52]

Shortly after the rapture and judgment of the saints, according to Scofield, "The Manifestation of the Man of Sin, and of Anti-Christ" will take place (II Thess. 2:3-10; Matt. 24:15; Rev. 13:1-8, 11-18; I Jn. 2:18).[53] This begins the first half (three and a half years) of the Tribulation period. Scofield follows Darby in his identification of the two Beasts of Revelation 13 and the false prophet. He says that "*the* Antichrist...is 'the Beast out of the earth' of Rev. 13. 11-17, and the 'false prophet' of Rev. 16. 13; 19. 20; 20. 10. He is the last ecclesiastical head, as the Beast of Rev. 13. 1-8 is the last civil head."[54]

After three and a half years of relative peace for the Jews, the Great Tribulation (last three and a half of the seven years of Daniel's seventieth week) begins (Dan. 9: 24, 27; Matt. 24:15, 21). While this period involves the whole earth to a certain extent (Rev. 3:10), says Scofield, "it is yet distinctively 'the time of Jacob's trouble' (Jer. 30. 7), and its vortex Jerusalem and the Holy Land." Toward the end of this period, the marriage of the Lamb occurs, just prior to the Lord's return (Eph. 5:31, 32; II Cor. 11:2; Rev. 19:1, 7).[55]

Scofield maintains that at the conclusion of the Great Tribulation and the marriage of the Lamb, "The Return of the Lord in Glory" takes place (Matt. 24:29, 30; Acts 1:11; Rev. 19:11-16).[56] It is at this time that Christ engages in the great battle of Armageddon (Rev. 19) "to deliver the Jewish remnant besieged by the Gentile world-powers under the Beast and False Prophet (Rev. 16. 13-16; Zech. 12. 1-9)."[57] This having been accomplished, says Scofield, the thousand-year "kingdom of heaven in its mediatorial form" begins.[58]

Scofield holds that at the conclusion of the dispensation of the kingdom, there will be one final revolt of the nations (Rev. 20:7-9). Here, unlike Darby, Scofield sees the participation of Gog and his army. He says of the prophecy in Ezekiel 38, that "The whole prophecy belongs to the yet future 'day of Jehovah' (Isa. 2. 10-22; Rev. 19. 11-21), and to the battle of Armageddon (Rev. 16. 14; 19. 19, *note*), but includes also the final revolt of the nations at the close of the kingdom-age (Rev. 20. 7-9)."[59]

According to Scofield, with the final revolt having been put down, the scene now shifts to the resurrection of the unjust (the second resurrection) and their judgment. This is a resurrection unto judgment.[60] Scofield gives this summary of the "judgment of the wicked dead": "Time: a determined day, after the Millennium (Acts 17:31; Rev. 20:5, 7). Place: before 'the great white throne' (Rev. 20:11). Result: Rev. 20:15."[61] Finally, with the judgment completed, the eternal state begins.[62]

Main Features of His Eschatology

The two eschatological events which are of most importance to Darby and his dispensational theology, are those which relate directly to the hopes of the church and those of Israel--the rapture and the millennial kingdom respectively. In Darby's view, the heavenly hope of the church is the coming of Christ to receive His own unto Himself and to share with it all aspects of His own glory. The earthly hope of Israel (the Jewish remnant), on the other hand, is the fulfillment of the promises made to Abraham and to his posterity of an earthly land, and of an earthly throne and kingdom from the lineage of David.

DOCTRINE OF THE RAPTURE

The Believer and Interest in the Rapture

Darby says that "The rapture of the saints to meet the Lord in the air...and the existence of a Jewish remnant...is happily attracting the attention of Christians." Indeed, interest in the subject has grown to such an extent, he observes, that it has generated "renewed opposition." Darby believes that this can only have a salutary affect upon Christians because it encourages them to examine the Scriptures on the subject. It is, says Darby,

> ... an examination, which will, under grace, spiritually enlarge their apprehensions on many most important points, full of blessing and interest for their souls. The true character of the church of God will appear, and the nature of its connection with Christ, on the one hand, and the ways of God in the government of the world on the other--the first of all concerns, the reconciling of the soul with God. On this last also, indeed, a right intelligence of the other two casts abundant light.[63]

Darby says of the subject of the second coming of Christ, that it is presented in almost every page of the Bible. If the Scriptures are read with "an unprejudiced mind" one cannot fail to see it.[64] He observers that the question of Christ's second coming was "one which exercised the brethren early in their career, but I think they have all settled pretty positively in the conviction that all the saints will be with Christ at His coming."[65] Darby's doctrine of the rapture is best revealed by examining a series of events and concepts with which the doctrine is related.

The Appearing of Christ and the Rapture

1. Darby's Position.

It becomes immediately apparent in a study of Darby's doctrine of the second coming of Christ, that he makes a distinction between Christ's coming *for* the saints (the rapture), and His coming ("appearing," "manifestation," or "public epiphany") *with* the saints at the end of the Tribulation period to engage in the battle of Armageddon. Thus, on the basis of Scripture (especially II Thess. 2), we have two things, maintains Darby, "which we know to be distinct...the coming of Christ and the public epiphany of His presence, with one of which the saints are directly connected, by being gathered together to Him; with the other, the day, because at His appearing He will execute judgment against the ungodly." Darby contends that when Christ appears, we will be with Him, therefore, "we *must* be with Him before even He appears at all..." He writes:

> Now it is quite certain they will not appear with Him when they are caught up to meet Him in the air. Thus it is not merely particular expressions, though these are clear and forcible, but the bearing, and object, and course of reasoning of the whole chapter [II Thess. 2], which shews the distinction of the rapture of the saints before Christ appears, and the coming of the day when He is admired in them.
> What is important to remark is, the entire difference of relationship in which the saints are put with Christ: we belong to Him, go to meet Him, appear with Him, are glorified together. The practical result is, not merely to clear up a question of dates and of time, but to change the whole spirit and character of our waiting and Christ's coming. We wait for Him to come and take us to Himself, the full realisation of our heavenly calling.[66]

Darby points out that the apostle Paul had taught the Thessalonian believers in his first epistle to them, that they would be caught up into the air to meet Christ.

Thus, with this truth established, in his second epistle he could drive home the fact that rather than waiting for the coming of "the day of the Lord on earth," the saints were waiting to meet Him in the air to ever be with Him. If Christ appeared, they would also appear with Him. In this, says Darby, Paul "speaks of what they ought to have remembered, that they would go up before the day, and hence they could not possible be there in their actual state on earth, if the day was."[67]

In general, we find in Darby the following order of end-time events surrounding the rapture and the appearing: 1. Present age. At the present time "Christ is secretly exercising the power of God's throne" (kingdom in mystery form). 2. The rapture of the saints. "Christ cannot receive the power of His own peculiar kingdom below, till this has taken place. Nor can this rapture take place till after He has left the throne, from whence it is evident the harvest cannot either..."[68] 3. The Tribulation (existence of Jewish remnant). There will be "a Jewish remnant waiting for deliverance after the rapture and before the appearing..."[69] 4. The appearing (the day of the Lord). "Neither could the day therefore come before...An apostasy would come, and the man of sin would be revealed, whom the Lord would consume with the breath of His mouth, and destroy by the appearing of His presence."[70] 5. The millennial kingdom. Then will Christ be "coming forth in the exercise of the power of His own peculiar kingdom."[71]

2. Scofield's Position.

Scofield too, makes the distinction between the rapture of the church and the appearing of Christ at the end of the Tribulation to set up the kingdom. His argument for this, however, does not at all involve Darby's main line of reasoning, that in order for the church to appear with Christ after the Tribulation, it must first have been caught up by Him prior to its commencement. Scofield's approach is strictly exegetical.

We know what the end of the church will be (the rapture), says Scofield, because there is "in two notable passages in the Epistles, written through Paul, a succinct but satisfying prophecy of that ending." The passages cited are I Corinthians 15:22-23, 51, 52 and I Thessalonians 4:13-17. Scofield asserts that,

> It is this event, and this only, which is before us in this article. That there is a vast body of prophecy which has to do with the return of Christ *to the earth*, in connection with the setting up of the Messianic kingdom, the resumption of the divine dealings with Israel, and the blessing of the whole world, we are well aware. But the coming, of which the quoted passages speak, is not *to the earth*, but into "the air"; it does not establish anything on the earth, but takes a people away from the earth.[72]

Scofield explains further that Christ's descent into the air for the church cannot then be the second coming spoken of by the Old Testament prophets (e.g., Zech. 14:1-9). Neither can it be the aspect of Christ's coming of which He spoke in the Olivet discourse (Matt. 24), and in the eschatological parables (presumably Matt. 13). Rather, "It is part of what Paul calls 'my gospel'--part of the truth concerning the church."[73]

Scofield discusses three words in Scripture which have reference to the return of the Lord: 1. *"Parousia*, 'personal presence,'... is used of the return of the Lord as that event relates to the blessing of saints (1 Cor. 15. 23; 1 Thes. 4. 14, 17), and to the destruction of the man of sin (2 Thes. 2. 8)." 2. *"Apokalupsis*, 'unveiling,' 'revelation.' The use of this word emphasizes the *visibility* of the Lord's return. It is used of the Lord (2 Thes. 1. 7; 1 Pet. 7. 13; 4. 13), of the sons of God in connection with the Lord's return (Rom. 8. 19), and of the man of sin (2 Thes. 2. 3, 6, 8), and always implies visibility." 3. *"Epiphaneia*, 'appearing,' trans. 'brightness' (2 Thes. 2. 8, A.V.; 'manifestation,' R.V.), and means simply an appearing. It is used of both advents (2 Tim. 1. 10; 2 Thes. 2. 8; 1 Tim. 6. 14; 2 Tim. 4. 1, 8; Tit. 2. 13)."[74]

The Day of the Lord and the Rapture

1. Darby's Position.

Much of Darby's argument here hinges upon his understanding of "the day of the Lord" and the distinction he makes between it and the rapture. Walvoord says, "There are few prophetic subjects about which there is more confusion than the theme of the day of the Lord."[75] Darby apparently understood the day of the Lord to begin with the appearing of Christ to establish the kingdom and perhaps to include the kingdom period itself. Note that according to Darby, the day of the Lord relates to Christ's coming to the earth and the execution of judgment upon the ungodly (Armageddon at the close of the Tribulation). He asserts that,

> They will be punished with everlasting destruction from the presence of the Lord, and from the glory of His power. But He will come to be glorified in His saints, and admired in all them that believe; that is, they will be in the display of this glory in that day. They will appear with Him in glory--be like Him.[76]

The mistake made by the Thessalonian believers, Darby points out, was the identification of tribulation with the day of the Lord.[77] He writes:

> This passage [I Thess. 4-5] says nothing of not being in the tribulation...but the objection confounds the tribulation and the day which really closes it. The tribulation is Satan's power (though of God's judgment in woe); the day is Christ's, who makes it and binds him. But the passage speaks not at all of the tribulation, though it supposes nothing of the kind; but it does speak of the day of the Lord, and with instruction as to the portion of the saints, which shews that it can have in no way whatever to do with them. They are of it and to come in its power.[78]

Walvoord maintains that placing the day of the Lord after the Tribulation created difficult problems for Brethren writers. For instance, how could the day of the Lord come like "a thief in the night" (I Thess. 5:2) if it is to be preceded by notable events and signs like those associated with the Tribulation? It also adversely affected the teaching that the rapture of the church is imminent and preceded by no intervening events. Walvoord offers the following solution to the problems:

The day of the Lord as presented in the Old and New Testaments *includes* rather than follows the tremendous events of the tribulation period (cf. Isa. 2:12-21; 13:9-16; 34:1-8; Joel 1:15-2:11; 2:28-32; 3:9-21; Amos 5:18-20; Obad. 15-17; Zeph. 1:7-18). There seems some evidence that the day of the Lord begins at once at the time of the translation of the church (cf. 1 Thess. 5:1-9)....In a word, the day of the Lord begins *before* the Great Tribulation. When the day of grace ends with the translation of the church, the day of the Lord begins at once.[79]

In any case, Darby believes that the confusion of the rapture and the day of the Lord constitutes a very grave error. It is not merely a mistake in terms, he maintains, but "a subversion of the whole nature of the relationship between Christ and the church, and Christ and...an apostate world; and a losing sight wholly of the great moral bearing of a day coming on the world, of which the Old Testament is full as well as the New."[80] It not only denies the fact and distinctiveness of the rapture, says Darby, but the hope of the church to be glorified with Christ when He appears at the second coming. The appearing of Christ, he suggests, will fully establish divine power in government and result from responsibility. The rapture of the church and its entrance into the Father's house, on the other hand, will be "the accomplishment of sovereign grace towards the saints in their full individual blessedness--of the hopes which communion with the Father and the Son has them."[81]

2. Scofield's Position.

Like Darby, Scofield identifies the day of the Lord with the return of Christ at the conclusion of the Tribulation. He says, "This promise of a second advent of Christ [John 14:3] is to be distinguished from His return in glory to the earth; it is the first intimation in Scripture of 'the day of Christ' (1 Cor. 1. 8, *note*)." In the first instance, explains Scofield, Christ comes for His saints (I Thess. 4:14-17), but in the second (the day of Christ), He comes in judgment of the nations, etc. (e.g., Matt. 24:29-30).[82] Like Darby too, Scofield sees the same teaching in I Thessalonians 4 and 5. In chapter 4, he says, the rapture of the saints in the first resurrection is presented, while in the following chapter we have the day of the Lord and the beginning of judgment.[83]

Scofield seems definitely to include the millennium in his definition of the day of the Lord. He says, "The day of Jehovah (called, also, 'that day,' and 'the great day') is that lengthened period of time beginning with the return of the Lord in glory, and ending with the purgation of the heavens and the earth by fire preparatory to the new heavens and the new earth (Isa. 65. 17-19; 66. 22; 2 Pet. 3. 13; Rev. 21. 1)." He follows this definition with the seven signs which will precede "The day of the Lord."[84]

The Issue of Secrecy and the Rapture

1. Darby's Position.

One of the important issues in the distinction between the rapture and the day of the Lord or second coming proper, is whether the former is private or secret and known only to those involved, or like the latter, readily visible to all. Both Bass[85] and Sandeen[86] indicate that Darby taught the secrecy of the rapture of the saints. In point of fact, Darby was ambivalent about the question. Rowdon quotes Darby as saying, "As to any secret coming [of Christ] I have no conviction about it and the proofs to me are certainly very feeble and vague."[87] Darby says elsewhere:

> A point connected with this has been insisted on by the adversaries of the truth, to which I advert here only to leave it aside, as not touching the main point, *even if true*, and used by them only to obscure the great and vital truth of the rapture of the church--I mean the secrecy of the rapture. The two points on which it is important to have the clear testimony of Scripture are--first that there will be a Jewish remnant at the end, with a place belonging to itself as such; secondly the true character of the church of God.[88]

2. Scofield's Position.

Scofield denies that the rapture will be a secret event. In a catalog of the contrasts between the rapture of the church and the return of Christ at the close of the Tribulation, he notes that at the former "only the sleeping and living 'in Christ' are concerned," while at the latter "His coming is visible to 'every eye'..." But Scofield hastens to point out that "It is by no means to be implied that the departure of the church will be a 'secret rapture.'" Rather, "It will doubtless shake humanity to its center."[89]

On the face of it, it appears that Scofield has missed the point here. The term "secret" does not imply that no one but those involved will know that the event has taken place. For when people are suddenly reported missing en masse all over the world, it cannot go unnoticed or lack impact. What the term "secret" does imply is that Christ's return *for* the saints will not be an event observable by the mass of unbelievers as His return *with* the saints at the end of the Tribulation will be. In any case, Scofield does in fact take note of the visibility of the latter event while omitting it in reference to the former.[90]

The Issue of Imminency and the Rapture

1. Darby's Position.

While Darby is ambivalent about the issue of secrecy and the manner in which Christ will return for the saints, he has no such hesitancy concerning the time of Christ's return. In this regard, Darby has two things to say. First, the exact time of His return is unknown, and second, it could occur at any time. Concerning the first point and Christ's words in Luke 21:32, that "this generation will not pass away until all things take place," Darby comments that "The length of time that has elapsed since then, and that must elapse until the end, is left in darkness." "Heavenly things," he continues, "are not measured by dates." The moment of Christ's return "is hidden in the knowledge of the Father."[91] He alone knows when the last member of the church will be gathered in and thus the time is right for the Son's return.[92]

What Darby is certain of, is that Christ will come, for He "is not slack concerning his promise," and that His coming could be at any moment. In fact, says Darby, "It may be to-night, but this is known only to the Lord."[93] He affirms that, while there may be events between the rapture and Christ's judgment of the earth (at the appearing), "There is no event between me and *heaven*."[94] In light of this fact, Darby explains the difference between the rapture and the appearing of Christ in these terms:

> As to the time of this rapture, no one, of course, knows it. But the difference, in this respect, between it and the appearing is very marked, in what is most important. At the appearing comes the judgment of this world: hence it connects itself with, and closes, its history; and before it that history must have run on to its revealed result, revealed events must have occurred, and the objects of judgment must have appeared on the scene and accomplished what is predicted of them. The church is associated with Christ already gone, is not of the world as He was not, is risen with Him, has its life hid with Him in God. There is no earthly event between it and heaven.[95]

When the Bridegroom comes, says Darby, "No events, no earthly circumstances, intervene or modify the direct summons" to join Him.[96] Darby explains that the saints have no need of judgment before they can participate in the blessings of Christ. But since the Jews and the world, on the other hand, are delivered by judgments, they must await the day of the Lord which will not come before the proper "course of events and the full ripening of earthly evil for judgment."[97] And "When is the Christian to expect the Lord?" Darby answers, "Always."[98]

2. Scofield's Position.

Scofield too, affirms that, "There is no predicted event which must be fulfilled before that coming [for the saints]." He argues that those are wrong who attempt to establish intervening conditions, or see the Tribulation or millennium running their course before the church can be caught up to be with Christ.[99] He writes:

> The characteristic attitude of the believer, all down the ages, is that of constant expectation of our Lord's coming into the air for us. We look not for signs, but for Him. His coming is absolutely signless, timeless, unrevealed. It is not a phase of something else nor an aspect of something else. Beware of these words. They bewitch you. This thing in the counsels of God is not a phase of some other thing in the counsels of God.[100]

Scofield concludes that "We, therefore, answer the question: 'May the Lord come at any time?' affirmatively--He may."[101]

The Hopes of the Church and the Rapture

1. Darby's Position.

Darby maintains that nothing can be clearer in Scripture than that we will go up to meet Christ in the air, and not await His return to earth following the Tribulation. According to Colossians 3, when Christ appears, then we shall appear with Him also in glory. "This identification of the church's hope and glory with Christ Himself," says Darby, "is of the essence of the church's blessing." Darby expresses the heart of the matter this way:

> He is our life, our righteousness; the glory given to Him He has given us: we are members of His body, we are of His flesh and of His bones. We reign with Him, suffer with Him, are glorified together, being like Him--conformed to His image. He is hid in God: our life is hid with Him in glory; but for this we must be caught up to meet Him, and that before He appears at all when He does, we are already with Him and appear with Him....it does clearly shew the entire difference of relationship of the heavenly saints with Christ, and of those who only see Him when He appears. The one are blessed under His reign, and are connected with earth; the others are identified with Himself--with Him who reigns--appear and reign with Him. Wherever this is enfeebled, Satan is at work.[102]

For Darby, the whole argument is quite logical. The hope of the church is to fully participate in the glory of Christ. Christ will appear in full glory in the day of the Lord at the close of the Tribulation. If we are to be with Him to share in this glory, then we must have been raptured, caught up to join Christ prior to His coming back to earth in power and judgment and glory. This concept is so important to Darby, that he says that the one who awaits Christ's appearing (at the end of the Tribulation) as the time in which we will go to be with Him, "has denied the proper hope and proper relationship of the church with Christ." "On this point," asserts Darby, "there can be no compromise." It is one thing to be ignorant of privilege, he notes, but to deny it is quite another. Darby concludes that,

> Such is the general doctrine of the rapture of the church--a doctrine of the last importance; because it is immediately connected with the relationship of the church to Christ, its entire separation from the world and its portion. It is the act which crowns its perfect justification. This rapture before the appearing of Christ is a matter of express revelation, as we have seen from Colossians 3:4.[103]

2. Scofield's Position.

With regard to Scofield's views here, see pp. 159-61, where his teaching on the hopes of the church and those of Israel are treated at length. Suffice it to say that Scofield also regarded the rapture of the church to be its true hope. He points to the teaching of Paul on the doctrine of the rapture, where "the characteristic attitude of the believer is 'waiting'--not for the millennium, nor for the great tribulation, but for 'His Son from heaven, whom He raised from the dead, Jesus'; and, 'looking for that blessed hope.'"[104]

Scofield, like Darby, also connects the hope of the saints in Christ's return with His glory. He refers to Colossians 3, where at Christ's appearing, the glory of God is brought into the church. He says, "The glorious appearing of the Lord is pointed to as the believer's hope. It is the first to be fulfilled of all the unfulfilled prophecies."[105]

What appears to be the greatest difference here between Scofield and Darby, is that the former does not emphasize the importance of the rapture in terms of its necessity for the saints to participate in the return of Christ in glory and judgment. For Scofield, the rapture itself is the blessed hope of the church. It is not predominantly a vehicle for the believer's participation in Christ's later public epiphany. Instead, Scofield emphasizes the role the translated church will play in reigning with Christ in the millennium. After noting that the rapture of the church involves exemption from the Tribulation, Scofield observes that the church will share with Christ,

> ...in the onus, the responsible and highly interesting business of governing the millennial earth. The elders representing the church in the Revelation have this thing to say, "And we shall reign on the earth."
> We go to Him. We come back with Him. We share everything He has. All things were made by Him and for Him, and He is before all things and in Him all things consist, and He is appointed heir of all things and takes us in with Him. Everything He has he shares with His bride.[106]

The Hopes of Israel and the Rapture

1. Darby's Position.

Darby maintains that the whole issue of the rapture leads indirectly to the question of what the church is. This is due to the fact, in Darby's view, that the rapture of the saints prior to Christ's appearing is connected to "the existence of a Jewish remnant waiting for deliverance after the rapture and before the appearing..." The rapture, in other words, is an event of great consequence not only for the church, but for Israel as well. Darby explains that,

> Those who believe in the rapture of the church before the appearing of Christ hold that the church has a special and peculiar character and connection with Christ, in virtue of its being formed into one body by the descent of the Holy Ghost from heaven; and that, while salvation is always necessarily the same, the relative condition of the saints previously was a distinct one. They are convinced that in the Psalms a Jewish remnant is found, and that thoughts, feelings, hopes, fears, into which the Spirit of Christ enters prophetically with and for them, are there expressed in their behalf. This remnant is believed to be continually spoken of in the prophets, as existing before the appearing of the Lord, and waiting for that appearing, and delivered by it.[107]

The interpretation of many New Testament passages became involved in the question of the remnant, Darby goes on to explain, because Christ, as the Savior and minister of the circumcision, presented Himself to Israel on the basis of Old Testament promises. Thus, He became associated with the remnant as its leader "as far as it was awakened to know Him." Consequently, the whole order of the dispensations become involved in the question. But most important, says Darby, is "the question of the church and its privileges, as formed by the Holy Ghost sent down from heaven... and a right understanding of it a key to the interpretation of the word of God."[108]

While the question of the church and its privileges is of the utmost importance, according to Darby, the denial of the Jewish remnant's existence "involves the most grave and, indeed fatal consequences." In fact, says Darby, the Psalms connect the Spirit of Christ directly "with the ungodly and unconverted Jews...with the hopes proper to Israel." Darby asserts that the fact of "a Jewish remnant at the close, delivered and blessed by the Lord at His coming, blessed on earth, is, beyond all controversy the doctrine of Scripture." The Scripture cited by Darby is: 1. "As regards the Jews" (Zechariah 13:8, 9); 2. "As regards the ten tribes of Israel...the rebels will not enter into the land" (Ezekiel 20:33-38). "Still they will be united in the land" (Ezekiel 37:11-28); 3. "As regards Judah" (Daniel 11:32-5; 12:1); 4. "Then general blessing and promise to Israel" (Hosea 2 and 3; Jeremiah 30-33). The conclusion of all of this, Darby maintains, is that it,

> ...shews that it is the *remnant* of Israel which is blessed with Israel's blessings. As it is said in Isaiah 10: "For though the number of the children of Israel be as the sand of the sea, a remnant shall return"; and verse 21, "the remnant shall return, even the remnant of Jacob, to the mighty God." The points thus made clear are that it is the remnant which is blessed, and blessed with Israel's blessings, according to promise, in the land, with Jehovah as their God. The next and capital point (for what precedes is generally admitted), is their previous state; is it a Christian or church state? And now I pray the reader to mark one most important consequence of any supposition that this remnant of Israel is previously in a Christian or church standing. Their blessings are, the earthly glory, under Christ, in the land, according to the promises made to them.[109]

Darby believes that to confuse the hopes of Israel and those of the church is mutually detrimental. If the spiritual condition and hopes of Israel are the same as the church's, they are disappointed in them for they have no fulfillment. If, on the other hand, their hopes are the church's hope, then our hopes have been lowered to temporal and Jewish earthly ones. Darby explains further that,

> In denying a distinct Jewish remnant, having Jewish faith, Jewish hope, and resting on Jewish promises, it reduces the church to the level of these; and the value and power of spiritual blessings in heavenly places in Christ, and the place of Christ's body in union with Him, is denied and lost. It is this which makes the question vital for Christians themselves. The great object of the enemy in denying the rapture of the saints before the appearing of the Lord, and in the consequent rejection of a distinct Jewish remnant, with Jewish hopes and Jewish piety, is to deny and destroy the proper faith of the church of God, and to set the church itself aside.[110]

2. Scofield's Position.

Scofield also teaches that Israel's setting aside was only temporary and that Romans 11:1 distinctly teaches that there is a Jewish remnant which, as the nation Israel, will yet "have its greatest exaltation as the earthly people of God."[111] Scofield explains that it is impossible to understand the prophetic testimony concerning "the period of unexampled Tribulation," unless we understand that at the close of the church age "after the true believers, according to the doctrine of the

15th of First Corinthians and 4th of First Thessalonians, are taken away from the earth--**God takes up Israel again**." He goes on to state that, "Indeed, to understand that is fundamental to the understanding of all unfulfilled prophecy. There is a widespread impression that Israel is cut off for ever. We have fallen into an evil habit of so-called 'spiritualising' the prophecies."[112]

The Subjects of the Tribulation and the Rapture

1. Darby's Position.

In Darby's estimation, the whole issue of the hopes of the church and of Israel involves the question of who the subjects of the Tribulation will be. Of particular importance is the question, "Will the saints be in the Tribulation?" Darby says that "it connects intimately with the gravest and most vital points of prophetic enquiry; or rather of the true character of the church of God and its condition at the close."[113]

The first question with which Darby is concerned, is "How do I know there will be a Tribulation?" His answer is that Scripture clearly teaches that there will be a time of Tribulation at the close such as has never been, and that it will last until the Lord brings deliverance at His appearing. According to Darby, there are four direct passages of Scripture on the subject (Jer. 30:7; Dan. 12:1; Matt. 24:21; Mark 13:19), two more general passages (Rev. 3:10; 7:14), and one indirect supporting passage (Rev. 12:14).[114]

Darby asserts that the first of the direct passages of Scripture, Jeremiah 30:7, "is as clear as possible in announcing those to whom it [the Tribulation] applies…the trouble spoken of is Jacob's trouble." The testimony of Daniel 12:1, is no less clear, Darby suggests, for it declares that "The tribulation is the tribulation of Daniel's people." In Matthew 24:21, the Lord not only speaks of the same event in Daniel's terms (compare Matt. 24:15 and Dan. 12:11), but the language of the passage itself confirms this. In Darby's view, the references to those in Judea, those on the housetops, the holy place, the sabbath, the seduction of the Jewish people with their special hopes by false Christs and prophets, are "all local and Jewish [having] no application to hopes which rest on going to meet Christ in the air." The Mark 13-19 passage relates the same event in practically the same terms. Darby concludes, then, that "these four passages, which speak of the unequalled tribulation, apply it distinctly to Jacob, Jerusalem, and Judea, and the Jews, not to the church. It is entirely another order and sphere of things from the church, and professedly so."[115]

What then of the two more general passages of Revelation 3:10 and 7:14? Darby asks, "Do these, then, apply to the Church?" He answers in the affirmative, and points out that when the church is here addressed, it is declared that she will be kept from that hour which will bring a time of trial to others. Thus, says Darby, "the testimonies of Scripture declare that the unequalled tribulation is for Jacob, and that, when the time of temptation is spoken of in addressing the church, it is to declare that the faithful shall be kept out of it."

Darby states that the same truth is taught in Revelation 7:14. Here, one of the elders explains to John that the class of those who have survived the great Tribulation are a distinct class of people from themselves. "The crowned elders are not at all represented as having been in it [the Tribulation]," explains Darby, "but as pointing out others as those that come out of it. Every element of the description of these persons confirms this distinction."[116]

On the issue of the Tribulation, there is one final passage with which Darby deals, Revelation 12:7-12. While it does not directly refer to the subject, says Darby, it does speak of the epoch in which it occurs. Darby believes that when Satan is expelled from heaven by Michael and cast down to earth, the effect is "That the trial of the heavenly saints is ended, and that of the inhabiters of the earth and the sea just about to begin in its most formidable shape, because Satan is cast down there."

Darby notes that this may not be the exact time of the rapture, but he suggests that at the moment of the commencement of Satan's great rage on the earth (beginning of the three and a half years of the great Tribulation), the heavenly saints will be delivered from his power and their triumph celebrated. In other words, they are not subjected to Satan's last time of rage. Thus, asserts Darby, this chapter, indeed the whole teaching and structure of the entire book of Revelation, fully confirms the exempt status of the church from the last, dreadful time of trial.

With all of these passages of Scripture taken together, then, says Darby, "We have found that the passages which speak of the tribulation first apply it directly to the Jews on one side, and then exclude the church from it on the other. I do not see how such a point as this could be made clearer by scripture."[117] In summary, Darby writes:

> There are six passages which speak of tribulation, and by which we know there will be tribulation. Four are clear and positive in applying it to the Jews; one declares that the faithful church saints will be kept out of it; and the last, speaking of Gentiles, distinguishes them, in the most marked way, from those who represent the church, and saints in heaven, the crowned and enthroned elders. Thus direct Scripture is as clear as clear can be. We have seen that, indirectly, Revelation 2 [apparent misprint for 12] confirms this view. What remains? General principles. Hence the attempt to bring the church into the tribulation; and this is the secret of the whole matter-- the confounding the church of God with the Jews and with the world, their hopes, and the trials that come upon them.[118]

2. Scofield's Position.

That there will be a time of "unexampled Tribulation," according to Scofield, is the clear teaching of Scripture. We read of it in the Olivet Discourse (Matt. 24:21, 22), in Jeremiah 30:7-9, Isaiah 34:1, 2 and "many others of like import." It is the "yom Jehovah" or "day of the Lord" frequently spoken of by the prophets (e.g., Joel 2: 1, 2; Zech. 14:1-3). Thus, while this age ends in catastrophe, judgment, and "awful ruin," as we have seen in I Thessalonians 4:16-18, it will be preceded by "the taking away from the earth of all who are Christ's ..."[119]

In addition to what he believes to be the clear teaching of specific passages of Scripture on the rapture of the saints and their exemption from the Tribulation (I Thess. 4; I Cor. 15), Scofield also believes that the sequence of events suggests it. He says, "We know that the great tribulation follows the descent of the Lord to receive the sleeping and living saints in the air, from the order in which these events are taken up in the Scriptures, in which truth is always progressive."[120]

In I Thessalonians 4 and 5, for instance, we have the rapture of the saints in the first resurrection followed by judgment in the day of the Lord. The comfort of the Thessalonian believers (I Thess. 4:18; 5:11) was in the fact that they had not been appointed for wrath but to obtain salvation. What comfort could there be, asks Scofield, in the prospect of enduring the Tribulation?[121]

The same sequence, Scofield points out, is seen in Revelation 3:10. The Philadelphian church, "representing, historically, the godly remnant in this age," is promised that it will be kept *from* the hour of testing to come. Scofield observes that "if they are to be kept from it, they must necessarily have been taken out of the way previous to this time of tribulation or testing."[122]

In Revelation 4, too, explains Scofield, the church, represented by the twenty-four Elders, is in heaven and preparing to witness the judgments shortly to fall upon the earth. "These scriptures," Scofield concludes, "all indicate most clearly that the great tribulation follows and does not precede the first resurrection, and the rapture."[123] Elsewhere, Scofield points out that never once is the Tribulation mentioned in connection with the first resurrection, the rapture, or "in the Epistles, which were written for the instruction of the church!" "On the contrary," Scofield continues, "the great tribulation is both judgment and wrath, and the church is promised exemption from both (Rev. 14:15, 16; 15:7, 8; 16:1-21; 1 Thess. 5:1-9; John 5:24)."[124]

The Subjects of the First Resurrection and the Rapture

1. Darby's Position.

If the church is not to participate in the Tribulation, but rather to be raptured before it begins, the question of how it will be accomplished remains. Who are the subjects of the rapture and in what manner will they participate? These are questions necessarily involving the doctrine of the resurrection of the saints.[125]

Darby explains that the manner in which the church will participate in Christ's coming is "the subject of the first resurrection."[126] He points out, however, on the basis of I Corinthians 15:51, that at the time of the rapture, all believers will be changed alike and equally as a necessary prerequisite to entrance into God's kingdom, though not all will sleep. The procedure as outlined in I Thessalonians 4:13, is "that when Christ shall come, *the dead in Christ* shall rise first, before we are caught up, and then we, the living who remain, shall be caught up together with them."[127]

The question for Darby is not whether the just and unjust will be raised, but whether they will be raised at the same time. His answer to the question is that,

In the word of God, two resurrections are always spoken of, and never one general resurrection, of which one finds neither the expression nor the idea. God does not thus confound the just and the unjust: and nothing will separate them more than the resurrection. Now, they are mixed and confounded in the world; but the resurrection shall separate them. There is a resurrection from amongst the dead; therefore, there are some dead that do not rise in that resurrection, whereas others do rise.[128]

For Darby, a major part of the justification for a twofold resurrection of humankind is that while they are both accomplished by the same power, the principles upon which they are based are different. The principle which is peculiar to the church, "namely the habitation of the Holy Ghost in them," is totally foreign to the resurrection of the unjust (Rom. 8:11). Darby explains that, "The virtue of the resurrection embraces the life, the justification, the confidence, the glory, of the church." The just are raised because they are united with Christ and thus one with Him. In proof of this principle of the resurrection of the just, Darby cites II Corinthians 1:9; Romans 4:23-25 (cf. I Peter 1:21); 8:11; Colossians 2:12; Ephesians 1:18f; 2:4-6.[129] The principle upon which the wicked are raised, on the other hand, is that of judgment. Consequently, this resurrection is to take place at a different time.[130]

Furthermore, says Darby, the passages concerning the resurrection directly, never speak of the just and unjust rising simultaneously, and those which deal specifically with the resurrection of the just always treat it as a distinct thing. Darby maintains that the concept of a resurrection of the just was known by the apostles, for Luke 14:14 says, "Thou shalt be recompensed at the resurrection of the just." Furthermore, notes Darby, we learn from Luke 20:35, 36, that the children of God alone are accounted as worthy to experience the resurrection which Christ experienced. As the sons of resurrection, explains Darby, they are the sons of God and these two facts signify the "title and inheritance of the same persons."[131]

Darby cites John 5:25-29, as setting forth the concept that there is a period during which souls are quickened and one during which bodies are raised. Darby maintains that at the beginning of the "hour" which is coming, when all in the graves shall hear Christ's voice and rise, there will be a resurrection of life for the righteous. At the end of the hour, the resurrection of judgment for the wicked will occur. Darby explains that there will be no need to judge the children of God to cause them to honor Him for they do so now by virtue of the fact that He has given them life (Jn. 5:25). The wicked, on the other hand, will be forced to honor Him against their will, and thus, the resurrection to judgment will serve as a summons to judgment by virtue of the fact that they have no part in Him.[132] In both cases, Darby concludes, we see how Christ is glorified in the double resurrection.[133]

The connection between the coming of Christ and the resurrection of the dead, says Darby, is very clearly set forth in I Corinthians 15:20, 23. At Christ's coming, the saints will rise and then the end will come. When Christ comes He will take the kingdom, but at the end, He will judge the wicked to purify the kingdom and then deliver it up to the Father.[134]

As discussed previously, Darby cites I Thessalonians 4:14-16, as teaching the sequence of events at the coming of Christ to receive the saints unto Himself. It is the filling up of our hopes when the righteous dead are first raised, followed by the changing of the righteous living. Together, they are caught up to meet the Lord in the air. Darby observes that "All this is a matter which belongs exclusively to the saints--to those who, sleeping or living, are Christ's, and who will be, from that moment, for ever with the Lord."[135]

According to Darby, the "resurrection from among the dead" spoken of in Philippians 3:10, 11, was in Paul's eyes the first resurrection. It was Paul's desire to arrive at the resurrection of the just, regardless of the cost. "Evidently," says Darby, "the resurrection from among the dead was a thing that concerned the church exclusively."[136]

As for the interval between the two resurrections, Darby states that it is an issue "altogether independent of the principle itself . . ." The only place in which the interval between the two resurrections is addressed, he observes, is the book of Revelation, and there it is said to be a thousand years.[137] Darby cites Revelation 20:5, as placing the thousand-year earthly reign of Christ between the resurrection of the just and that of the unjust.[138] Of Revelation 20, Darby says, "The statement is simple, and the language plain. We read of God and Christ, of the devil and Satan, the first resurrection and the second death. This is not symbolical, but plain…"[139]

Darby maintains that on the basis of all of this revelation concerning the first resurrection when Christ returns, we can see that the hope of the church is the coming of Christ. If we fail to understand the truth that the coming of the Lord is the hope of the church, he asserts, "we cannot be bearing a true and faithful testimony to God…" The one question remaining here is, if the resurrection and rapture of the saints at Christ's coming is the hope of the church, what part if any do the Old Testament saints play in it?

Darby apparently includes the saints of the Old Testament in the resurrection and rapture of the church. In connection with this event, he says "the Old Testament saints were saved by the blood, and will be in resurrection glory with the Lord. I assume all this as acknowledged truth…"[140] Contemporary dispensationalists are generally in disagreement with this position. Walvoord, for example, points out that,

> Most of the Old Testament passages of which Daniel 12:1-2 is an example do indeed seem to set up a chronology of Tribulation first, then resurrection of the Old Testament saints. On the other hand, the passages dealing with the resurrection of the church in the New Testament seem to include only the church. The expression "the dead in Christ will rise first" (I Thess. 4:16) seems to include only the Church.[141]

Walvoord states further that the phrase "in Christ" is never used to describe Old Testament saints and that the sound of the "voice of the archangel" (Israel's defender) at the rapture, is not sufficient proof of Israel's resurrection at that time. Walvoord warns that,

The tendency of followers of Darby to spiritualize the resurrection of Daniel 12:1-2 [and Isaiah 26:19] as merely the restoration of Israel, thereby refuting its posttribulationism, is to forsake literal interpretation to gain a point, a rather costly concession for premillenarians who build on literal interpretation of prophecy.[142]

With regard to what happens to the Old Testament saints after they have been raised with the church and raptured, Darby has little to say. His primary concern is the hope of the church and its glorification with Christ.

2. Scofield's Position.

In his treatment of the twofold resurrection, Scofield quotes the same passages of Scripture that Darby does. He begins by saying that the resurrection of all the dead, just and unjust alike, is taught "in the clearest and most positive terms" in the Bible. "No doctrine of the faith," he continues, "rests upon a more literal and emphatic body of Scripture authority than this, nor is any more vital to Christianity [e.g., I Cor. 15:13, 14]."[143]

While it is true that all shall be raised, says Scofield, "the notion, somewhat prevalent in these days, that the resurrection is the simultaneous coming forth of all who have gone into the grave is, from the standpoint of the Scripture, a mistake."[144] First of all, he points out, a partial resurrection of the saints following Christ's resurrection has already occurred (Matt. 27:52, 53). Furthermore, says Scofield, "Two resurrections, differing in respect of time and of those who are the subjects of the resurrection, are yet future. These are variously distinguished as 'the resurrection of life' and 'the resurrection of damnation'; as 'the resurrection of the just and the unjust,' etc." In support of his position, Scofield cites John 5:28, 29; Luke 14:13, 14; I Corinthians 15:22, 23; I Thessalonians 4:13-16; Philippians 3:11 and Revelation 20:4-6 (which gives the interval between the two); 20:12, 13. Scofield concludes that "The testimony of Scripture, then, is clear that believers' bodies are raised from among the bodies of unbelievers, and caught up to meet the Lord in the air a thousand years before the resurrection of the latter."[145]

Scofield's position on the Old Testament saints and the first resurrection, as revealed in the prophets, is not quite the same as Darby's interpretation. On Ezekiel's "dry bones" vision (37:1-12), he says, "The 'bones' are the whole house of Israel who shall then be living. The 'graves' are the nations where they dwell."[146] This is in agreement with Darby's interpretation of the passage.[147] But on the basis of Isaiah 26:19, Scofield maintains that,

> ... the restoration and reestablishment of Israel as a nation is also spoken of as a resurrection (Ezek. 1-11), and many hold that no more than this is meant in Isa. 26. 19. But since the first resurrection is unto participation in the kingdom (Rev. 20. 4-6), it seems the better view that both meanings are here.[148]

Then in the *Reference Bible*, in the heading to Daniel 12:2-3 (which also speaks of Israel's resurrection), Scofield makes a direct connection to the first

resurrection and rapture of the church by referring to I Corinthians 15:52.[149]
Darby, on the other hand, allows no literal resurrection for either Isaiah 26:19 or
Daniel 12:2. In any case, Scofield, like Darby, includes the Old Testament saints
in the first resurrection. However, Scofield's note at Isaiah 26:19, could be interpreted to mean that Israel's resurrection (i.e., "restoration and re-establishment")
takes place at the end of the Tribulation, while the heading at Daniel 12:2-3,
would seem to place it earlier, at the resurrection and rapture of the church.

Scofield's position on this point is cleared up by his notes at I Corinthians
15:52 and I Thessalonians 4:17. At I Corinthians 15:52, Scofield says that the
first resurrection will occur at the coming of Christ (to rapture the church) and
will include the Old Testament saints. But the resurrection of Tribulation martyrs,
who also take part in the first resurrection (Rev. 20:4), will occur at the end of the
great Tribulation.[150] With regard to the I Thessalonians passage, he writes, "Not
church saints only, but all bodies of the saved, of whatever dispensation, are included in the first resurrection (see 1 Cor. 15. 52, *note*), as here described, but it is
peculiarly the 'blessed hope' of the church (cf. Mt. 24. 42; 25. 13; Lk. 12. 36-48;
Acts 1. 11; Phil. 3. 20, 21; Tit. 2. 11-13)."[151]

The Origin of the Rapture Doctrine

Few would argue that Darby was the first to give a systematic presentation of
the doctrine of a pretribulation rapture. With regard to the question of where
Darby himself got the doctrine, however, there is not the same harmony of opinion. A fairly wide range of sources are suggested, most of them contemporaneous
with Darby.

For any possible extra-Biblical historical antecedents for the doctrine, we must
go back to Rabbinic and early patristic sources. While there are hints in these
sources of the translation of the saints prior to the Tribulation, it must be said that
the evidence is meager and inconclusive.[152] Henry C. Thiessen sums up the
matter well. He writes:

> Let us first note that, according to Moffat, 'Rabbinic piety (*Sanh.* 98b) ex-
> pected exemption from the tribulation of the latter days only for those who
> were absorbed in good works and in sacred studies.' Thus there was a
> Jewish background for the expectation that some men would not pass
> through the Tribulation. When we come to the early Fathers we find an
> almost total silence as to the Tribulation period. They abundantly testify
> to the fact of tribulations, but they say little about the future period called
> by preeminence The Tribulation. This fact should cause us no perplexity.
> These writers lived during the second and third centuries, and we all know
> that those were the centuries of the great Roman persecutions. The
> Church was passing through sore trials and it did not much concern itself
> with the question of Tribulation yet to come. Perhaps it did not under-
> stand the exact nature of the period.[153]

In a word, the early church was clearly premillennial, but not clearly either pretribulational or posttribulational by contemporary definition. On the whole, the
eschatology of the Fathers was embryonic and incomplete.

While the Protestant Reformation brought pronounced changes in the doctrine of soteriology, the same was not true in the area of eschatological studies. The Reformers accepted the amillennial eschatology of Augustine, rather than the premillennialism of the early Fathers. Consequently, there was little advance in the interpretation of prophecy until after the Reformation era. Thus, it is to Darby's contemporaries that most nondispensationalists look for the source of his pretribulational views.

It should be apparent from all that has been said previously that Darby's concept of the pretribulation rapture grows out of his understanding of the church as a special work of God, completely distinct from His purpose and plan for Israel. Darby's studies bring him to the conclusion that the church will be removed from the earth to set the stage for her glorification with Christ. And after this is accomplished, he believes that God can turn His attention to the remnant of Israel in the Tribulation and to her hopes associated with the millennial kingdom to follow. While Darby consistently refers to Scripture as the source of his views, a number of his detractors maintain that he got them elsewhere, either from the heretic Edward Irving (perhaps at the Powerscourt conferences), or a young Scottish woman named Margaret Macdonald, or someone else.[154]

Edward Irving (1792-1834), an eloquent and popular Scottish preacher, at first attracted many famous and influential people. But the novelty soon wore off and the unbalanced emphases in his preaching, his treatment of prophecy and eschatology, high view of the sacraments, encouragement of speaking in tongues during worship services, and writings (which led to the charge that he held to the sinfulness of Christ's humanity), eventually resulted in his downfall. Due primarily to the latter charge, in 1833 he was deposed from the Church of Scotland.[155]

Ryrie correctly observes that,

> At best, the Irvingite eschatology is unclear. One of their group drew a time distinction between the epiphany (the Lord's appearing and rapture) and the parousia (the Lord's coming to earth), but it was not seven years. Another placed the rapture at the same time as the last bowl judgment of Revelation 16 (which is the last judgment of the Tribulation period) and *after* the setting up of the ten-nation federation. Still another wrote that the rapture will take place as the Lord is on His way down to earth, which is standard posttribulationism (see R. A. Huebner, *The truth of the Pre-Tribulation Rapture Recovered* [Morganville, N.J.: Present Truth Publishers, n.d.], pp. 21-25).[156]

It is clear, then, that unlike Darby, the Irvingites did not teach the imminency of Christ's return, nor that Daniel's seventieth week (the Tribulation period) would occur between the Rapture and second coming.[157] This is evident from what is said in Edward Miller's authoritative account of Irvingite doctrines. Note the order of events in the following:

> ...those who are alive at the time of His coming, together with the dead who have risen, will be caught up to meet Him in the air, *before* His descent upon the earth. *By this time* the fourth empire has assumed its com-

plete form, as having ten horns. The man of sin, or Antichrist, who is the eighth and last head of the beast, has *now* appeared, accompanied by the false prophet.[158]

A little further on Miller says,

> ...the restoration of the Jews is to take place in successive states. Some of them will repair to the holy city *before* His second Coming, *after* the first-fruits are "caught up." and *before* the Lord descends. *Then* Antichrist and his hosts will besiege Jerusalem.
> *At this moment* the Lord appears, delivers His city and people, and destroys Antichrist and his hosts ...[159]

In a note, Miller says, "The exact time of these [establishment of fourth empire and appearing of Antichrist], however, whether antecedent or consequent upon the good being caught up into the air, appears not to be settled."[160] Indeed, in Miller's sequence of events just cited, either the rapture is posttribulational or it occurs at some time during the Tribulation, perhaps close to the end. At best, this teaching is unclear. Sandeen's assessment of the matter seems accurate. He observes that,

> Darby's opponents claimed that the doctrine [of the rapture] originated in one of the outbursts of tongues in Edward Irving's church about 1832. This seems to be a groundless and pernicious charge. Neither Irving nor any member of the Albury group advocated any doctrine resembling the secret rapture. As we have seen, they were all historicists, looking for the fulfillment of one or another prophecy in the Revelation as the next step in the divine timetable, anticipating the second coming of Christ soon but not immediately.[161]

Daniel P. Fuller also suggests that "since it will be demonstrated that the pretribulation rapture must be granted if the concept of the two people of God be accepted, it is concluded that the safest course to take is that Darby originated the idea from his own hermeneutical premises."[162]

Another candidate for the source of Darby's pretribulation rapture doctrine is Margaret Macdonald (c.1815-c.1840). According to Dave MacPherson, the young mystic from Port Glasgow, Scotland, had a great deal to do with the pretribulational views of both Darby and Irving.[163] The source of Macdonald's information was a vision she supposedly had of Christ's second coming. Her own handwritten account of the vision, later printed in several publications, is completely reproduced by MacPherson.[164]

The first important point in Macdonald's vision is her reference to "look[ing] out for the sign of the Son of man" (line 7). This is apparently a reference to Matthew 24:30. Thus, here, Macdonald places the rapture at the time of the coming of the Son of Man "immediately after the tribulation of those days..." (Matt. 24:29). Ryrie says that Macdonald "reveals by this statement complete confusion, though taken at face value, her vision equated the sign at the end of the Tribulation with the rapture--hardly pretribulationism!"[165]

The second thing that one notices in Macdonald's vision is that she makes a distinction between spiritual and non-spiritual believers. She says "that those who were filled with the Spirit could see spiritual things...while those who had not the Spirit could see nothing--so that two shall be in one bed, the one taken and the other left..." (lines 55-60).[166] The most that can be made out of what Walvoord rightly calls a "garbled" view of prophecy,[167] is that Macdonald may have held to a partial rapture of the church. In other words, only those spiritual Christians who are watching and waiting for the Lord's return are counted worthy to participate in the rapture.

Macdonald goes on to speak of "the fiery trial which is to try us" for "the purifying of the real members of the body of Jesus..." (lines 60-67). She explains that those "who will be counted worthy to stand before the Son of man" will pass through this trial and that "The trial of the Church is from Antichrist. It is by being filled with the Spirit that we shall be kept" (lines 81-87).[168] Here, the "us" to which Macdonald refers is clearly Christians. The definite indication is that believers will endure "fiery trial" at the hands of Antichrist *during* the Tribulation. Ryrie concludes that, "As for the very young and chronically ill Margaret Macdonald, we can only truthfully label her as a 'confused rapturist,' with elements of partial rapturism, posttribulationism, perhaps midtribulationism, but never pretribulationism."[169]

That Darby himself claimed no source for the doctrine, other than Scripture, is beyond question. In a paper entitled, "The Rapture of the saints: who suggested it, or, rather, on what Scripture?," William Kelly quotes Darby as saying, "It is this passage (2 Thess. ii. 1, 2) which, twenty years ago [i.e., from 1850 when he wrote], made me understand the *Rapture* of the saints before--perhaps a considerable time before--*the Day of the Lord* (that is, *before the judgment of the living*)."[170] If the chronology here is correct, it lends credence to Ironside's assertion that it was in the Powerscourt "meetings that the precious truth of the rapture of the Church was brought to light..."[171]

In the final analysis, the question of Darby's source for the rapture doctrine comes to rest more on the development of his own theology and exposition of Scripture than on any superficial similarities to the positions of others. Walvoord is correct in saying that,

> In his many works, any careful student of Darby soon discovers that he achieved his eschatological views from the study of the Bible itself and from his conclusion that the church is the body of Christ rather than having derived it from some human source. Darby's views were only gradually formed, but they are based on the Bible and his doctrinal position.[172]

It is interesting to note that Scofield too goes straight to the Bible as his source for the doctrine of the pretribulation rapture of the saints. In the February, 1902, issue of A. C. Gaebelein's publication, *Our Hope*, Scofield asserts that "We cannot...allow the statement to stand that 'until the days of Edward Irving, who was excluded from the Presbyterian Church for heresy, no one ever heard of this 'coming for' and 'coming with His saints.'" Scofield suggests that if the editor of *Watchword and Truth* (the publication in which this statement appeared), would turn to Zechariah 14:4, 5, "he will learn of a statement concerning the *coming with* which considerably antedates Edward Irving." Scofield goes on to cite I Thessalonians 4:15-18 in further proof of the Biblical origin of the doctrine.[173]

It is instructive to observe that here was a ready opportunity for Scofield to cite Darby as one of the spiritual forebears of the doctrine, but he fails to do so. Instead he refers to "those men of fragrant memory, Dr. James H. Brookes and Dr. A. J. Gordon...two great exegetes," whose writings offer "abundant testimony that they, too, knew of the coming of the Lord for His saints and with His saints." Gaebelein points out that when the Niagara Bible Conference broke up over the distinction between "the coming of the Lord *for* His saints and... *with* His saints," that Scofield "continued to uphold the truth" because he "had been too firmly established in it by his first teacher, Dr. James H. Brookes."[174]

DOCTRINE OF THE MILLENNIUM

The Promises of Blessing

According to Darby, while the rapture primarily involves the hopes and destiny of the church, the millennial reign of Christ focuses predominantly upon the nation Israel and her hopes. There were two principles operative in the history of the Jewish people. On the one hand, unconditional promises had been made to Abraham (Gen. 12), and repeated to Isaac (Gen. 26: 3, 4) and Jacob (Gen. 35:10, 12). On the other hand, Israel had received promises under the condition of obedience (the giving of the Law at Sinai), and in this, failed miserably. Israel's failure, however, did not abrogate the unconditional covenantal promises made to Abraham some four hundred years before, for they rest solely upon the faithfulness of God. While the unconditional promises to Abraham included both earthly and spiritual elements, prominent among them is "an absolute gift of the country."[175]

The principle upon which the people are related to the promised land is set forth, says Darby, in Deuteronomy 29. The condition upon which the people might remain in the land was obedience to God's commands. But Israel failed and was expelled from the land and ultimately the people were dispersed throughout the nations. However, God's unconditional promises and covenants to Israel regarding the land had been made prior to the giving of the Law. Thus, there remains to be fulfilled their reestablishment in the land and all the promises made to Abraham.[176]

The Promises of Restoration

1. Darby's Position.

Darby indicates that even after Israel had taken the Law upon herself and failed, abundant promises of future restoration were forthcoming through the prophets. All of these promises are founded upon the covenant with David (I Chron. 17:11-13). Darby observes that "In Hebrews 1:5, application is made of these words to Christ; that is, all the promises made to Abraham and to his seed--

all the promises made to Israel--are placed in the safe keeping, and gathered together in the Person, of the Son of David."[177]

Concerning the predictions of restoration, says Darby, Isaiah 1:25-38 "decrees the full restoration of the Jews, but by judgments which cut off the wicked." Darby also cites Isaiah 4:2-4; 6:9-13; 11:10 ; 33:20, 24; 49:14-23; chap. 62 and 65:10-25. With regard to the last reference, he says, "there can be no question, but of earthly blessings--such as are hitherto unknown on earth. In that day God Himself will rejoice over Jerusalem."[178]

According to Darby, the above promises "plainly announce the forthcoming glory of the Jewish people and of Jerusalem." But, he says, there are others which are even more direct. In Jeremiah 3:16-18, for example, we see three things occurring simultaneously which as yet have not occurred: "namely, Jerusalem the throne of Jehovah; Judah and Israel united; and the nations assembled to the throne of God." Other passages which also speak of Israel's future glory are Jeremiah 30:7-11; 31:23, 27, 28, 31; 32:37-42; 33:6-11, 15, 25, 26; Ezekiel 34:22-end; 36:22-32; chap. 37; 39:22-25. With reference to Ezekiel 37, Darby says,

> ...[it] gives a detailed history of the re-establishment of Israel--the joining together of the two parts of the nation, their return into the land, and their state of unity and fidelity to God in this same land; God being their God, and David their king being present--present for ever, in such a way as that the nations shall know that their God is the Lord, when His sanctuary shall be in the midst of them for evermore.[179]

Darby closes this section with a recapitulation of the principles upon which these prophecies are based. He writes:

> The restoration of the Jews is founded upon the promises made to Abraham *without* condition; their fall is the result of their having undertaken to act in their own strength. After having exercised the patience of God in every possible way "until there was no remedy," judgment is come upon them; but God reverts to His promises.[180]

2. Scofield's Position.

Like Darby, Scofield sees two main lines of promise to the nation Israel. The first is that she would have a King--the Messiah. And when He comes, He will be a priest after the order of Melchizedek and a king on the throne of David. The second line of promise concerned the regathering and restoration of Israel in her own land after her dispersion in judgment.[181]

Scofield cites Deuteronomy 28-30, as a "foreview, so to speak, of the history of Israel in the land into which they were just ready to enter." Israel received the promise of blessing in the promised land if she obeyed the statutes and commandments of God. If she failed to do so or became apostate, she was warned of chastisement as the first line of punishment and in the face of continued disobedience, expulsion from the land. Israel failed of course, Scofield points out, but in her greatest hour of Tribulation to come, she will return to God and experience regathering and restoration in the land.[182]

Scofield also makes reference to the many predictions of Israel's restoration and blessing in the land. While he informs the reader that he passes over many passages "for lack of time," he does focus on Isaiah 11, Jeremiah 16, and Ezekiel:20, as representative of predictions of the future fulfillment of promises to Israel of blessing in the promised land, and the reestablishment of the throne of David in the person of Christ.[183] Elsewhere, Scofield speaks of the "beautiful order... discernible in [Ezek. 36] and the succeeding prophecies: (1) Restoration of the land (36. 1-15); (2) of the people (36. 16-37. 28); (3) judgment on Israel's enemies (38. 1-39. 24). Afterward follows that which concerns the worship of Jehovah that He may dwell amongst His people."[184]

The Means of Restoration

Darby suggests that while there are prophecies which promise the restoration of Israel, there are also prophecies which indicate the means by which restoration will be accomplished. But first, he reminds the reader of the important fact that the history of the Jews "is especially the manifestation of the glory of Jehovah." Darby explains that,

> It is in this people, by the ways of God revealed to them, that the character of Jehovah is fully revealed, that the nations will know Jehovah, and that we shall ourselves learn to know Him.
> The same person may be king of a country, and father of a family; and this is the difference between God's actings towards us and the Jews, it is the character of Jehovah, the King. His faithfulness, unchangeableness, His almighty power, His government of the whole earth--all this is revealed in His relationship towards Israel; it is in this way that the history of this people lets us into the character of Jehovah.[185]

As for the means by which Jehovah will deliver and restore His people, says Darby, Ezekiel 39:6, 7, 28, reveals that He will destroy her enemies. He will console His people and reestablish them in earthly glory "by the direct acting of His righteousness in their favour (see Psalm 65:5)." Yet, points out Darby, the people will be delivered through "a time of trouble such as never was since there was a nation" (Dan. 12:1). Thus, in a summary of Daniel 12, we see "on the one hand, God standing up for His people in a time of distress; and, on the other, a remnant delivered..."[186]

Darby notes that Hosea 2:14-end and 3:4, 5, reveal that Israel will be brought back into the land and blessed after she has first been humbled. In Joel 3:1, 16-18, 20, 21, says Darby, we learn that after God's judgment upon the nations, Jehovah will dwell in Zion as the hope and strength of Israel and that Jerusalem will be a holy city. Amos 9:14, 15, indicates that after God's people have suffered captivity, they will be planted in the land never again to be removed. Then Israel, who is victorious against all her enemies, will have possession of a restored Jerusalem (Micah 4:1-8) and with Jehovah in her midst, will be disturbed by nothing (Zeph. 3:12). Those who once scattered Israel, will themselves be scattered by the judgments of God (Zeph. 1:15, 17-21).[187]

The Participants in Restoration

1. Darby's Position.

In addition to predictions of restoration and the means by which it will be accomplished, Darby points out that there are predictions which indicate that it is only a remnant of the people of Israel who will be restored to the land. In Zechariah 12:2, 9, says Darby, we see that Jerusalem is beset by enemies. But God defends the city and destroys Israel's enemies, and then pours out "the spirit of grace and supplication" upon the "remnant of Israel..." Again, in Isaiah 18, observes Darby, it is a picture of Israel's return to the land and initial suffering at the hands of the nations, followed by divine deliverance.[188]

As for the identify of those who compose the remnant of Israel, Darby sees three classes of people. He describes these classes as follows:

> First, the Jewish nation, properly speaking--namely, Judah, and those allied with her in the rejection of the true Christ: They will be in connection with the Antichrist, and of them two thirds will be cut off in the land [Zech. 13:8, 9]. Secondly, those of the ten tribes coming up, of whom some will be cut off in the wilderness on their way into the land [Ezek. 20:32-39].[189]

In addition to these "two classes of Israelites who will return by providential agency, but still of their own free accord," after His appearance, the Lord will gather and greatly bless the elect of the Jewish nation (the third class of the remnant of Israel) who are still scattered among the Gentiles (Matt. 24:31; compare Isaiah 27:12, 13, with Isaiah 11:10, 12).[190]

Darby distinguishes the blessings associated with this return from those associated with others (as the return from Babylon for instance), on the basis of two principles. In the first place, he says, these blessings flow from the presence of Christ Himself, the Son of David. And in the second place, they issue from a new covenant. Darby notes that neither of these conditions has yet been fulfilled.[191] This will take place in the millennial kingdom.

2. Scofield's Position.

In his assessment of the participants in the millennial kingdom, Scofield first quotes Matthew 25:31-34, concerning the judgment of those Gentiles who survive the Tribulation. He observes that the "class upon His right hand...forms the Gentile nucleus of the population of the Millennial earth." But when Christ returns at the conclusion of the Tribulation, asserts Scofield, it is first of all for the purpose of delivering the remnant of the Jews, then for the judgment of the Gentiles on the basis of their treatment of Israel.[192]

In his summary of the Jewish remnant, Scofield says that the chief interest in it is prophetic. He points out that,

> During the great tribulation a remnant out of all Israel will turn to Jesus as

Messiah, and will become His witnesses after the removal of the church (Rev. 7. 3-8). Some of these will undergo martyrdom (Rev. 6. 9-11), some will be spared to enter the millennial kingdom (Zech. 12. 6-13. 9). Many of the Psalms express, prophetically, the joys and sorrows of the tribulation remnant.[193]

The Nature of Restoration

1. Darby's Position.

With the victory of Christ over the Antichrist and his followers, says Darby, a remnant of the Jews will be delivered and established in security in the land promised to their fathers. Christ will descend upon the Mount of Olives (Zech. 14:3, 4) and reveal Himself, "not as the Christ from heaven, but as the Messiah of the Jews." As a consequence of the Lord's presence and the Jews' restoration, blessing will fall upon the Gentiles. The church will be blessed, the fourth monarchy (revived Roman Empire) destroyed, and the wicked one and unbelieving Israelites cut off.[194] War and oppression will be no more.[195] In short, the Jews will be at peace in their own land during the millennial reign of Christ.[196]

This, according to Darby, is the realization of the hopes of Israel. The kingdom of God will be established in power, and righteousness will reign. Israel's temporal King will have destroyed her enemies. The kingdom of the Son of David has come. Darby affirms that,

> All the promises of God with regard to Israel shall be accomplished in favour of that people; the law being written on their hearts, the grace and power of God shall accomplish the blessing of the people, blessing which they could not obtain when it depended on their faithfulness, and when they were placed on the principle of their own responsibility. At the same time the dominion over the Gentiles will be in the hands of the Lord, while they will be subordinate to Israel, the supreme people on the earth. Thus all things will be gathered together under a single head--Christ: angels, principalities, the church in heaven, Israel, the Gentiles, and Satan will be bound.[197]

Elsewhere, Darby speaks of the blessings that will flow to all humankind by virtue of the blessings which have been bestowed upon Israel in the kingdom. He writes:

> Those who shall have seen the glory manifested in Jerusalem will go and announce its arrival to the other nations. These will submit themselves to Christ; they will confess the Jews to be the people blessed of their Anointed, will bring the rest of them back into their land, and will themselves become the theatre of glory, which, with Jerusalem as its centre, will extend itself in blessing wherever there is man to enjoy its effects. The witness of the glory being spread everywhere, the hearts of men, full of goodwill, submit themselves to the counsels and glory of God in response to this testimony. All the promises of God being accomplished, and the throne of God being established at Jerusalem, this throne will be-

come to the whole earth the source of happiness. The re-establishment of the people of God will be to the world "as life from the dead."[198]

2. Scofield's Position.

In his note at Micah 4:1, Scofield offers the following "General predictions concerning the kingdom." He says, "The prediction asserts (1) the ultimate establishment of the kingdom, with Jerusalem for the capital (v. 1); (2) the universality of the future kingdom (v. 2); (3) its character--peace (v. 3); (4) its effect--prosperity (v. 4). Cf. Isa. 2. 1-5; 11. 1-12."[199]

Scofield explains further that the rule in the millennium will be a theocracy. "It will be the ruling of God Himself in the Person of Jesus Christ, the Son of David, over the earth" (Jer. 23:5; Luke 1:30-33; cf. Isa. 1:26; Matt. 19:28 and Luke 19, for the way in which the theocratic rule of Christ is made effective). The seat of that government will be a rebuilt Jerusalem (Isa. 2:1-4). "As to the national order," says Scofield, "I will not weary you with quotations. Suffice it to say that Israel has the first place among nations during the Millennium."[200]

Concerning the blessings of the millennial period (described extensively in Isaiah), Scofield says that there will be "a condition of tranquility, blessedness, and peace..." And even the nature of the animal kingdom will undergo change. It will be a time, exclaims Scofield, of "Creation delivered! Creation set free!"[201]

In this time of Israel's restoration and blessing in the land promised to her fathers, says Scofield, the manner of worship will be distinctly Jewish as well. Not only does Ezekiel describe the distribution of land to the tribes of Israel, but also the erection of the millennial temple and the form of worship to be engaged in (chaps. 40-48). Scofield maintains that this worship will involve, "offerings, memorial sacrifices, not expiatory sacrifices," and "Pilgrimages out of all the nations of the earth wending their way annually to that most magnificent city, as it will then be the centre of the Millennial earth's splendour, civilisation, and worship. Every eye directed there to the worship of the King, the Lord of *Hosts*."[202]

Endnotes

[1]John Nelson Darby, *Letters of J.N. Darby*, 3 vols., reprint ed. (Sunbury, Pa.: Believers Bookshelf, 1971), 1:138.

[2]Ibid.

[3]Ibid., 1:329-30.

[4]John Nelson Darby, *The Collected Writings of J. N. Darby*, 34 vols., ed. William Kelly, vol. 2: *Prophetic No. 1* (Sunbury, Pa.: Believers Bookshelf, n.d.), p. 280.

[5]Ibid.

[6]Ibid., pp. 279-80.

[7]See **Appendix G**, for a graphic presentation of Darby's chronology of end-time events.

[8]Darby, *Letters*, 1:330.

[9]Darby, *Writings*, vol. 22: *Doctrinal No. 6*, pp. 361-2.

[10]Ibid., p. 362.

[11]Ibid. Darby does not limit the first resurrection to the saints who have died in the church age only, but includes all saints of all times.

[12]Ibid.

[13]Ibid., vol. 2: *Prophetic No. 1*, p. 379.

[14]Ibid., vol. 22: *Doctrinal No. 6*, p. 362.

[15]Ibid., vol. 2: *Prophetic No. 1*, p. 379.

[16]Ibid., vol. 23: *Doctrinal No. 7*, pp. 369-70.

[17]Ibid., vol. 13: *Critical No. 1*, pp. 13-14.

[18]Ibid., p. 12. Cf. John Nelson Darby, *Synopsis of the Books of the Bible*, 5 vols., reprint ed. (Sunbury, Pa.: Believers Bookshelf, 1971), 5:552.

[19]See *Writings*, vol. 2: *Prophetic No. 1*, p. 378, for another example of this placement of the marriage of the Lamb. Here Darby says that after the church is assembled, "It will go immediately to meet the Lord, and the marriage of the Lamb will take place."

[20]Darby, *Writings*, vol. 22: *Doctrinal No. 6*, p. 363.

[21]Ibid., vol. 2: *Prophetic No. 1*, p. 379.

[22]Ibid., vol. 22: *Doctrinal No. 6*, p. 363.

[23]Ibid., vol. 2: *Prophetic No. 1*, p. 379. It should be noted that Darby never commits himself to the concept of a "secret" rapture. He seems to hold the opinion that Christ's coming in the air to receive the saints unto Himself will be an event observable by the unbelieving world at large. More will be said about this subject in the proper place.

[24]Darby, *Writings*, vol. 22: *Doctrinal No. 6*, p. 363.

[25]Ibid., vol. 13: *Critical No. 1*, p. 362.

[26]Ibid., vol. 11: *Prophetic No. 4*, p. 324.

[27]Ibid., vol. 13: *Critical No. 1*, pp. 362-3.

[28]Ibid., vol. 2: *Prophetic No. 1*, p. 380.

[29]Darby, *Synopsis*, 2:293; cf. 2:446-7; *Writings*, vol. 11: *Prophetic No. 4*, pp. 320-1.

[30]Darby, *Writings*, vol. 11: *Prophetic No. 4*, p. 113.

[31]C. I. Scofield, *Prophecy Made Plain* (Glasgow: Pickering and Inglis; London: Alfred Holness, n.d.), p. 130.

[32]C. I. Scofield, *The Scofield Reference Bible* (New York: Oxford University Press, 1945), p. 1337.

[33]C. I. Scofield, *Dr. C. I. Scofield's Question Box*, comp. Ella E. Pohle (Chicago: The Bible Institute Colportage Association, 1917), pp. 129-30.

[34]Darby, *Writings*, vol. 22: *Doctrinal No. 6*, p. 362.

[35]Ibid., vol. 2: *Prophetic No. 1*, p. 380.

[36]Ibid. What Darby bases this on is not clear. Perhaps it is simply the assumption that the nations which were the ancient occupiers of the promised land will be those Gentile peoples who will constitute Satan's fighting force in the battle of Armageddon.

[37]Ibid., p. 340f. Darby suggests that "The power designated by 'Gog' is that of the north, outside of the territory of the beasts in Daniel" (*Synopsis*, 2:403).

[38]Ibid., p. 380. Here Darby appears to take into account only the Ezekiel references to Gog, and not the Revelation reference to Gog's participation in the battle to follow the millennial period.

[39]Ibid., p. 381.

[40]Ibid., vol. 22: *Doctrinal No. 6*, p. 363; cf. *Synopsis*, 5:557. For a full account of the testing and failure during this final dispensation, see p. 134 above.

[41]Darby, *Synopsis*, 5:558.

[42]See *Writings*, vol. 5: *Prophetic No. 2*, p. 90f.

[43]Darby, *Synopsis*, 5:558-60.

[44]Ibid., 5:560-1.

[45]Ibid., 5:561.

[46]Ibid., 5:564.

[47]C. I. Scofield, *Scofield Bible Study Leaflets* (Philadelphia: Philadelphia School of the Bible,

1935), Series C, Lesson 20.

[48]Darby, *Writings*, vol. 1: *Ecclesiastical No. 1*, pp. 117-20.

[49]Scofield, *Leaflets*, Series C, Lesson 20.

[50]Scofield, *Reference Bible*, pp. 1228, 1269.

[51]Scofield, *Leaflets*, Series C, Lesson 20.

[52]C. I. Scofield, *Rightly Dividing the Word of Truth* (Fincastle, Va.: Scripture Truth Book Co., n.d.), p. 30.

[53]Scofield, *Leaflets*, Series C, Lesson 20.

[54]Scofield, *Reference Bible*, pp. 1342-3. There is some disagreement among contemporary dispensationalists as to the identity of these Beasts. J. Dwight Pentecost asserts that "John is not trying to identify either of these Beasts as antichrist, but to warn any who would deny the person of Christ that they are walking in that system which eventually would culminate in the manifestation of the lawless system in the activities of both Beasts. They, in their corporate unity, culminate lawlessness." See, *Things to Come* (Grand Rapids: Zondervan Publishing House; copyright 1958 by Dunham Publishing Company, used by permission of Zondervan Publishing House), p. 339. Charles Ryrie, on the other hand, equates the first Beast with the Antichrist, and the second he calls the "Antichrist's lieutenant," who is also to be identified with the False Prophet. See the *Ryrie Study Bible* (Chicago: Moody Press, 1978), pp. 1910-11, 1914. Pentecost and Ryrie are in agreement in identifying and equating the False Prophet with the second Beast (*Things to Come*, pp. 336-7).

[55]Scofield, *Leaflets*, Series C, Lesson 20.

[56]Ibid.

[57]Scofield, *Reference Bible*, pp. 1348-9.

[58]Ibid., p. 1349.

[59]Ibid., p. 883.

[60]Ibid., p. 1228.

[61]Scofield, *Rightly Dividing the Word of Truth*, p. 33.

[62]C. I. Scofield, *What Do the Prophets Day?* (Greenville, S.C.: The Gospel Hour, Inc., 1918), p. 174.

[63]Darby, *Writings*, vol. 11: *Prophetic No. 4*, p. 118.

[64]Ibid., vol. 32: *Miscellaneous No. 1*, p. 245.

[65]Darby, *Letters*, 2:230. It will become evident that Darby includes not only the saints of the church age in the rapture, but those of the Old Testament as well. Here, however, the context reveals that it is those who are members of the Body of Christ to which Darby is specifically referring.

[66]Darby, *Writings*, vol. 11: *Prophetic No. 4*, p. 115.

[67]Ibid., pp. 114-15.

[68]Ibid., vol. 8: *Prophetic No. 3*, p. 16.

[69]Ibid., vol. 11: *Prophetic No. 4*, p. 118.

[70]Ibid., p. 115.

[71]Ibid., vol. 8: *Prophetic No. 3*, p. 16.

[72]C. I. Scofield, *Things New and Old* (New York: Publication Office "Our Hope," 1920), pp. 298-9.

[73]Ibid., p. 299.

[74]Scofield, *Reference Bible*, p. 1212.

[75]John F. Walvoord, *The Rapture Question*, rev. and enl. ed. (Grand Rapids: Zondervan Publishing House, 1979), p. 174. Used by Permission.

[76]Darby, *Writings*, vol. 11: *Prophetic No. 4*, p. 115. It is difficult to determine exactly what elements Darby includes in the "day of the Lord." It is clear that for him it does at least encompass the appearing of Christ with the saints to execute judgment at the end of the Tribulation, and to some extent, the manifestation of Christ's glory. But whether it actually includes the entire millennial period remains uncertain. The same can be said of other Brethren writers like C. H.

Mackintosh (*The Mackintosh Treasury* [Neptune, N.J.: Loizeaux Brothers, 1976], pp. 873-81), William Trotter (*Plain Papers on Prophetic and other Subjects*, new ed.-rev. [Kansas City: Walterick Publishers, n.d.], pp. 288, 527), and William Kelly (*The Epistles of Paul the Apostle to the Thessalonians* [Oak Park, Ill.: Bible Truth Publishers, n.d.], pp. 55-65).

[77]Darby, *Writings*, vol. 11: *Prophetic No. 4*, pp. 114-15.

[78]Ibid., p. 117.

[79]Walvoord, *The Rapture Question*, pp. 174-6.

[80]Darby, *Writings*, vol. 11: *Prophetic No. 4*, p. 161.

[81]Ibid., pp. 161-2.

[82]Scofield, *Reference Bible*, p. 1135.

[83]Scofield, *Question Box*, p. 130.

[84]Scofield, *Reference Bible*, p. 1349.

[85]Clarence B. Bass, *Backgrounds to Dispensationalism* (Grand Rapids: Wm. B. Eerdmans Publishing Co., 1960), p. 134.

[86]Ernest R. Sandeen, *The Roots of Fundamentalism* (Grand Rapids: Baker Book House, 1970), pp. 62-3.

[87]*Fry Letters*, 1845, folio I, quoted in Harold H. Rowdon, *The Origins of the Brethren, 1825-1850* (London: Pickering and Inglis, 1967), p. 233.

[88]Darby, *Writings*, vol. 11: *Prophetic No. 4*, p. 120 (italics added).

[89]Scofield, *What Do the Prophets Say?*, p. 124.

[90]See, "The Appearing of Christ and the Rapture," pp. 173-74 above.

[91]Darby, *Synopsis*, 3:367.

[92]Darby, *Writings*, vol. 32: *Miscellaneous No. 1*, p. 244.

[93]Ibid.

[94]Darby, *Letters*, 1:330.

[95]Darby, *Writings*, vol. 11: *Prophetic No. 4*, pp. 155-6.

[96]Ibid., p. 157.

[97]Ibid., pp. 115-16.

[98]Ibid., p. 156.

[99]Scofield, *Things New and Old*, p. 299.

[100]C. I. Scofield, "The Return of Christ in Relation to the Church," *Bibliotheca Sacra* 109 (January 1952):88-9.

[101]Scofield, *Things New and Old*, p. 300.

[102]Darby, *Writings*, vol. 11: *Prophetic No. 4*, pp. 153-4.

[103]Ibid., pp. 154-5.

[104]Scofield, *Things New and Old*, p. 300.

[105]Scofield, *Prophecy Made Plain*, pp. 18-19.

[106]Scofield, "The Return of Christ in Relation to the Church," p. 88.

[107]Darby, *Writings*, vol. 11: *Prophetic No. 4*, p. 119.

[108]Ibid.

[109]Ibid., pp. 121.

[110]Ibid., p. 122.

[111]Scofield, *Reference Bible*, p. 1204; cf. p. 879.

[112]Scofield, *Prophecy Made Plain*, p. 122.

[113]Darby, *Writings*, vol. 11: *Prophetic No. 4*, p. 110.

[114]Ibid; cf. pp. 164-7, for a discussion of the same passages.

[115]Ibid., pp. 110-11.

[116]Ibid., pp. 111-12. For Darby's interpretation of Revelation 3:10, in light of the "Difference of *apo* and *ek*," see vol. 13: *Critical No. 1*, p. 376. A fuller treatment of Darby's exegesis of Revelation 7 and the elders may be found on pp. 165-6 of *Writings*, vol. 11: *Prophetic No. 4*.

[117]Darby, *Writings*, vol. 11: *Prophetic No. 4*, pp. 112-13. Darby follows this discussion of

the Tribulation passages with his views on the distinction between the rapture and the appearing of Christ based on II Thessalonians 1, 2 (see p. 172ff above).

[118]Ibid., p. 167.

[119]Scofield, *Prophecy Made Plain*, pp.117-20.

[120]Scofield, *Question Box*, pp. 129-30.

[121]Ibid., p 130.

[122]Ibid.

[123]Ibid.

[124]Scofield, *What Do the Prophets Say?*, pp. 136-7.

[125]For a good summary treatment of the doctrine of "The Resurrections Associated with the Second Advent," see J. Dwight Pentecost, *Things To Come*, pp. 395-411.

[126]Ibid., vol. 2: *Prophetic No. 1*, p. 301.

[127]Ibid., pp. 16-17.

[128]Ibid., vol. 5: *Prophetic No. 2*, p. 90.

[129]Ibid., vol. 2: *Prophetic No. 1*, pp. 303-5.

[130]Ibid., vol. 5: *Prophetic No. 2*, p. 112.

[131]Ibid., vol. 2: *Prophetic No. 1*, pp. 305-6.

[132]Ibid., vol. 5: *Prophetic No. 2*, pp. 113-14.

[133]Ibid., p. 91.

[134]Ibid., vol. 2: *Prophetic No. 1*, p. 308.

[135]Ibid., pp. 308-9.

[136]Ibid., p. 309.

[137]Ibid.

[138]Ibid., vol. 5: *Prophetic No. 2*, p. 114.

[139]Ibid., vol. 2: *Prophetic No. 1*, p. 81.

[140]Darby, *Miscellaneous*, 4:155-6.

[141]Walvoord, *The Rapture Question*, p. 171.

[142]Ibid. Darby says on this subject: "The resurrection (Dan. 12:2) applies to the Jews. 'Many of them that sleep in the dust of the earth shall awake.' You find the same expression in Isaiah 26: 'Thy dead shall live...' and in Ezekiel 37:12. It is a figurative resurrection of the people, buried as a nation among the Gentiles" (*Writings*, vol. 2: *Prophetic No. 1*, p. 364). For another example of a posttribulation resurrection of the Old Testament saints as presented here by Walvoord, see Charles L. Feinberg, *Millennialism: The Two Major Views* (Chicago: Moody Press, 1980), p. 294, and Pentecost, *Things To Come*, pp. 407-11.

[143]Scofield, *Rightly Dividing the Word of Truth*, p. 26.

[144]Scofield, *Prophecy Made Plain*, p. 120.

[145]Scofield, *Rightly Dividing the Word of Truth*, pp. 26-7.

[146]Scofield, *Reference Bible*, p. 881.

[147]Darby, *Writings*, vol. 2: *Prophetic No. 1*, p. 364.

[148]Scofield, *Reference Bible*, p. 735.

[149]Ibid., p. 919.

[150]Ibid., p. 1228. Obviously, Scofield is suggesting that the "first resurrection" has more than one stage. Here, two stages are seen as separated by the time of the great Tribulation.

[151]Ibid., p. 1269.

[152]For example, Irenaeus says, "And therefore, when in the end the Church shall be suddenly caught up from this, it is said, 'There shall be tribulation such as has not been since the beginning, neither shall be'" (*Against Heresies* 5.29.1). Yet, elsewhere, he speaks of "the resurrection of the just, which takes place after the coming of Antichrist, and the destruction of all nations under his rule..." (*Against Heresies* 5.35.1). Cf. *Hermas the Shepherd* Visions 4.2, for another example of pretribulational language, and *The First Epistle of Clement* 23, for the sure belief in the imminent return of Christ.

[153]Henry C. Thiessen, "Will the Church Pass Through the Tribulation?" *Bibliotheca Sacra* 92 (April 935):189-90.

[154]See Dave MacPherson, *The Great Rapture Hoax* (Fletcher, N.C.: New Puritan Library, 1983), pp. 43-180; Robert H. Gundry, *The Church and the Tribulation* (Grand Rapids: Zondervan Publishing House, 1973), pp. 186-7; George Eldon Ladd, *The Blessed Hope* (Grand Rapids: Wm. B. Eerdmans Publishing Co., 1956), p. 36 (on Irving). While Irving and Macdonald are most frequently named, and therefore the most important, Arnold D. Ehlert says that "Half a dozen sources have been put forth for the origin of this doctrine, including...the Devil himself!" (*Brethren Writers: A Checklist with an Introductory Essay and Additional Lists* [Grand Rapids: Baker Book House, 1969], p. 38). Thomas Croskery suggests the Jesuit priest Pierre Lambert as the source of the doctrine (*Plymouth-Brethrenism: A Refutation of its Principles and Doctrines* [London and Belfast: William Mullan and Son, 1879], p. viii), while LeRoy Froom offers another priest, Francisco Ribera, as the source (*The Prophetic Faith of Our Fathers*, 4 vols. [Washington, D.C.: Review and Herald Publishing Association, 1946-1954], 3:655f).

[155]J. D. Douglas, ed., *The New International Dictionary of the Christian Church* (Grand Rapids: Zondervan Publishing House, 1974), p. 517.

[156]Charles C. Ryrie, *What You Should Know About the Rapture* (Chicago: Moody Press, 1981), pp. 69-70.

[157]Ibid., p. 70.

[158]Edward Miller, *The History and Doctrines of Irvingism, or of the So-called Catholic and Apostolic Church* (London: C. Kegan Paul and Co., 1878), p. 6 (italics added).

[159]Ibid., p. 7 (italics added).

[160]Miller, p. 6. Rowdon says that the rapture was not conceived of as secret, "for it was expected to take place at the same time as the epiphany which would be visible, though unexpected. It was, nevertheless, separated from the actual advent of Christ to the earth" (*The Origins of the Brethren*, p. 17).

[161]Sandeen, pp. 64-5.

[162]Daniel P. Fuller, "The Hermeneutics of Dispensationalism" (Th.D. dissertation, Northern Baptist Seminary, 1957), p. 54.

[163]MacPherson, p. 129.

[164]Ibid., pp. 125-8.

[165]Ryrie, *What You Should Know*, p. 72.

[166]MacPherson, p. 127.

[167]Walvoord, *The Rapture Question*, p. 154.

[168]MacPherson, p. 127.

[169]Ryrie, *What You Should Know*, p. 72.

[170]Quoted in Napoleon Noel's, *The History of the Brethren* (Denver: W. F. Knapp, 1936), p. 73.

[171]H. A. Ironside, *A Historical Sketch of the Brethren Movement*, rev. ed. (Grand Rapids: Zondervan Publishing House, 1942; reprint ed, Neptune, N.J.: Loizeaux Brothers, 1985), p. 23.

[172]Walvoord, p. 154.

[173]Arno C. Gaebelein, "The Story of the Scofield Reference Bible: Part IV-Remarkable Providential Leadings and the Beginning of a New Testimony," *Moody Monthly* 43 (January 1943):278. Scofield was not alone in this position of course, and neither was his recourse to Scripture confined to the doctrine of the rapture. Feinberg asks, "what do the millenarians say as to the basis of their doctrine? Surely they should know their own position. Everyone of them to a man declares unreservedly and unequivocally that he builds the doctrine on the entire Word of God" (Charles Feinberg, *Millennialism: The Two Major Views*, p. 35).

[174]Ibid.

[175]Darby, *Writings*, vol. 2: *Prophetic No. 1*, p. 348.

[176]Ibid., p. 352.

[177]Ibid., pp. 356-7.

[178]Ibid., pp. 357-8.

[179]Ibid., pp. 358-61.

[180]Ibid., p. 361.

[181]C. I. Scofield, "The Return of Christ in Relation to the Jew and the Earth," *Bibliotheca Sacra* 108 (October 1951):478.

[182]Ibid., pp. 478-9.

[183]Ibid., pp. 480-7.

[184]Scofield, *Reference Bible*, p. 879.

[185]Darby, *Writings*, vol. 2: *Prophetic No. 1*, pp. 362-3.

[186]Ibid., pp. 363-5.

[187]Ibid., pp. 365-6.

[188]Ibid., pp. 367.

[189]Ibid., pp. 368-9.

[190]Ibid., p. 369.

[191]Ibid., pp. 369-70.

[192]Scofield, *Prophecy Made Plain*, pp. 142-4.

[193]Scofield, *Reference Bible*, p. 1205.

[194]Darby, *Writings*, vol. 2: *Prophetic No. 1*, pp. 380-1.

[195]Ibid., vol. 22: *Doctrinal No. 6*, p. 362.

[196]Ibid., vol. 2: *Prophetic No. 1*, pp. 381.

[197]Ibid., vol. 22: *Doctrinal No. 6*, p. 363.

[198]Ibid., vol. 2: *Prophetic No. 1*, p. 381.

[199]Scofield, *Reference Bible*, p. 948.

[200]Scofield, *Prophecy Made Plain*, pp. 145-8.

[201]Ibid., pp. 148-50.

[202]Ibid., pp. 150-1.

CHAPTER 7

DARBY'S LASTING LEGACY

Dispensationalism's Debt to Darby

Hopefully, on the basis of this study, the reader has gained a clearer understanding of Darby's dispensational theology and the premises upon which it is based. And in the process, it is hoped too, that the reader has gained more insight into the relationship between Darby's concept of dispensations and that of contemporary dispensationalists in the tradition of C. I. Scofield. In our opinion, there are two errors that should be carefully avoided in this regard. The first error, is the essential denial by some dispensationalists of any debt to Darby. The second error, common among nondispensationalists, is that of making Darby the sole source and fountainhead of dispensational theology.

That Darby's teachings have had a tremendous influence upon the formulation and systematization of many contemporary dispensational concepts, is beyond dispute. His employment of the hermeneutical principle of literal interpretation for all of Scripture, including prophecy, naturally led to the distinction between Israel and the church. And this in turn naturally led to the conclusion that the hopes of Israel and those of the church were of a different nature. While contemporary dispensationalists would not agree with Darby in many of his details, they do indeed agree that all of Scripture must be taken in its plain, normal, literal sense, and that this results in the need for maintaining a distinction between the church and Israel.

Ryrie understands these two principles to be at the heart of dispensational theology. So important is the principle of literal interpretation, consistently applied, that Ryrie calls it "the basis of dispensationalism."[1] And with regard to the distinction between Israel and the church which results from this principle of interpretation, Ryrie says, it is "probably the most basic theological test of whether or not a man is a dispensationalist, and it is undoubtedly the most practical and conclusive."[2]

It is out of the principle of literal interpretation also, that the most important eschatological features of dispensationalism grow. On this basis, one can only assume, as Darby, and Scofield after him did, that many promises were made to Israel in the Old Testament which have not been fulfilled, and therefore, must have some future time (the millennium) in which they will have their fulfillment. This understanding of the how and when of the fulfillment of the promises to Israel, and the hopes and destiny of the church--in other words the distinction between the church and Israel--leads naturally to the doctrine of the pretribulation rapture of the church as the hope and destiny of the one, and the literal earthly millennial kingdom as the hope and destiny of the other.[3]

We believe that the rudiments of this theology may be traced to the patristic period.[4] That most of the early Fathers were premillennialists (or chiliasts), is certainly true. That some of them understood God's dealings with humankind in a dispensational way is also true. And it may even be granted that there are in the writings of the early Fathers the "seeds, from which the doctrine of the pretribulational rapture could be developed..."[5] But one must nevertheless look to Darby for the first, full, systematic expression of a dispensational interpretation of Scripture. Therefore, the debt owed by contemporary dispensational theology to John Nelson Darby as the pioneer, systematizer, and popularizer of this approach to Scripture, can in no way be minimized.

Scofield's Debt to Darby

If there is one assertion that begs refutation it is that Scofield and those who followed him borrowed wholesale--jot and tittle--from Darby. It has been clearly shown that Darby pointed the way in the application of the principle of literal interpretation. It has been demonstrated also that Darby taught in a systematic way that God has had different dispensational dealings with humankind at different times and in progressive stages.[6] But it has also been revealed in this study that while there are definite points of agreement between Darby and Scofield in many particulars, there are major differences in several areas as well.

With regard to the similarities, it is clear that some of the basic structure and understanding of the characteristics of the various dispensations is shared in common by Darby and Scofield. That their outlines of end-time events and basic understanding of the hopes of the church and Israel also have much in common is evident as well. The question is, how are these similarities to be accounted for? Did Scofield borrow his theology directly from Darby? Is it true, as Sandeen suggests, that "Americans raided Darby's treasuries and carried off his teachings as their own"?[7]

If Sandeen's assertion is true, it would appear that Scofield robbed the treasury at night and overlooked some important goods. Chief among these is Darby's concept of the government of God. This doctrine permeates the whole of Darby's dispensational theology. So central is it to his understanding of God's dealings with the earth, that for want of it, he sees no dispensations prior to the deluge. So important is the concept, that it, as much as anything else, results in an earthbound Israel and heavenbound church, so that the latter scarcely has anything at all to do with the earthly subjects of dispensations and prophecy. The result is a dispensational system which bears only sporadic resemblance to that of Scofield. And perhaps the most prominent difference is that the latter's system knows nothing of the former's particular concept of the government of God.

In this last regard, if Scofield robbed Darby's treasuries, he took his dispensational diadem, melted it down and cast it as something quite different from the original. Scofield, as we have said, forges two dispensations where Darby has none (creation to the flood), has one dispensation where Darby has three (or at least three subdivisions of the dispensation of Israel), has none where Darby has one (dispensation of the Gentiles), and views the church and millennial ages as dispensations in their own right, while Darby only grudgingly grants them dispensational status, and that only in an appended way. It becomes apparent, then, that Darby's philosophy of dispensations--including his concept of the government of God--and Scofield's, are not cut from the same bolt of material even though of a similar weave.

Ryrie is correct in his statement that "only one comment is necessary concerning Darby's teachings--it was obviously not the pattern which Scofield followed." "If Scofield parroted anybody's scheme," concludes Ryrie, "it was Watts', not Darby's."[8] In light of such differences and in view of the similarities cited above, what are we to make of the relation between Darby and Scofield?

It has already been demonstrated that there appears to be little evidence to connect Scofield directly with the works and influence of Darby. But that there was an indirect link to his works through Gaebelein and perhaps Brookes, seems also fairly sure.[9] At any rate, Darby seems to have set the stage and guided the way for the dispensational theology which was to follow him.

Darby once told his staunch friend and admirer, William Kelly, that "He was but a miner [who]...left it to others to melt the ore, and circulate the coin..."[10] This, perhaps better than anything else, describes the contribution of Darby to the development of dispensational theology. Using the spade of literal interpretation, he worked the Biblical mine. By his own account, it was work which, for the most part, had not already been done. To those who followed, like Scofield, he demonstrated the use of the tools and left a great deal of what may be viewed primarily as raw ore. The question before us is whether Scofield simply refined Darby's ore, or excavated the mine for himself while using the same tools. There is little doubt in anyone's mind that at the least, Scofield was the master circulator of the coin produced from the ore.

If Ryrie is correct, anyone who applies the principle of literal interpretation to Scripture, and does so consistently, will be a dispensationalist. He must also come to the conclusion that Israel and the church are distinct, and that they have divergent hopes and destinies. The implication is that this must be the ultimate result, regardless of external influences. It must be borne in mind that Darby, Scofield, and all other like dispensationalists, have worked the same mine with the same interpretive tool.

Since Darby and Scofield both make copious references to Scripture in support of their positions, there is little mystery in the fact that their conclusions are similar in many cases. Thus Bass' charge that "The parallel between Scofield's notes and Darby's works only too clearly reveals that Scofield was not only a student of Darby's works, but that he copiously borrowed ideas, words, and phrases,"[11] appears to us to be a gratuitous assumption, seemingly made with a measure of malicious intent.

Scofield agrees with Darby (on the basis of Scripture) that the church will become apostate in the end-times--so where is his emphasis on the "church in ruins" doctrine? Scofield follows Darby (and Watts and others) in viewing God's dealings with the human race dispensationally--so where is the imprint of Darby's outline of the ages on his dispensational scheme? Scofield holds that God deals with humanity on the basis of an administrative principle unique in each dispensation--but where is Darby's doctrine of the government of God? While Scofield believes that the church has a heavenly calling and hope, where is his insistence that it has little or nothing to do with God's dispensational dealings with the earth?

There is little doubt that Scofield benefited from Darby's labors, in at least a predigested form. There is little doubt too, that some of the metal from Darby's ore, as well as that from other scholars, is intermingled with Scofield's theological sculpture. But it cannot be fairly denied that Scofield first gave the ore, whatever its source, the acid test of Scriptural scrutiny before refining and integrating it into his own work.

A Plea for Courtesy

In the final analysis, we may never know for sure where Darby got the ideas for some of his concepts, if in fact they did not come directly from Scripture. We may never know for sure to what extent, either directly or indirectly, Scofield was the beneficiary of Darby's theological labors. But ultimately, for each man, it is "To his own master he stands or falls..." (Romans 14:4). In the meantime, let us examine the views of others, differing as they may from our own, with civility and a ready ear to hear, for,

> See ye not, courtesy
> Is the true alchemy,
> Turning to gold all it touches and
> tries?
> George Meredith,
> *The Song of Courtesy, IV*

Endnotes

[1]Charles Caldwell Ryrie, *Dispensationalism Today* (Chicago: Moody Press, 1965), p. 97.

[2]Ibid., p. 45.

[3]Ibid., pp. 158-61.

[4]See Larry V. Crutchfield, "Israel and the Church in the Ante-Nicene Fathers: Part 1 of Rudiments of Dispensationalism in the Ante-Nicene Period," *Bibliotheca Sacra* 144 (July-September, 1987):254-276, and "Ages and Dispensations in the Ante-Nicene Fathers: Part 2 of Rudiments of Dispensationalism in the Ante-Nicene Period," *Bibliotheca Sacra* 144 (October-December 1987):377-401.

[5]Millard J. Erickson, *Contemporary Options in Eschatology* (Grand Rapids: Baker Book House, 1977), p.131.

[6]Others, like Isaac Watts and Pierre Poiret, also taught the concept of God's dispensational dealings with humanity. See Arnold D. Ehlert, *A Bibliographic History of Dispensationalism* (Grand Rapids: Baker Book House, 1965), for several examples of similar teachings, most of which were propounded before Darby, but not with the same attention to system.

[7]Ernest R. Sandeen, *The Roots of Fundamentalism* (Grand Rapids: Baker Book House, 1970), p. 102.

[8]Ryrie, p. 76. See **Appendix A**, for a comparison of the dispensational schemes of Watts, Scofield, and Darby.

[9]See **Appendix B**.

[10]W. G. Turner, *John Nelson Darby* (London: C. A. Hammond, 1944), p. 73.

[11]Clarence B. Bass, *Backgrounds to Dispensationalism* (Grand Rapids: Wm. B. Eerdmans Publishing Co., 1960), p. 18.

APPENDIX A

A Comparative Chart of the Dispensational Systems
of Poiret, Watts, Darby and Scofield

Pierre Poiret (1646-1719)	Isaac Watts (1674-1748)	J.N. Darby (1800-1882)	C.I. Scofield (1843-1921)
Infancy (Creation to Flood)	Innocency (Before the Fall)	Paradisaical State to Fall (Not a Dispensation)	Innocency (Creation to Fall)
	Adamical (After Fall to Noah)	Conscience, Fall to Flood (Not a Dispensation)	Conscience (Fall to Flood)
Childhood (Flood to Moses)	Noahical (Flood to Abraham)	Noah (Flood to Call of Abraham)	Human Gov't (Flood to Babel)
	Abrahamical (Call of Abraham to Moses)	Abraham (Call of Abraham to Law at Mt. Sinai)	Promise (Call of Abraham to Law at Mt. Sinai)
Adolescence (Moses to Prophets)	Mosaical (Mosaic Law to Christ)	Israel: Under Law, Priesthood, & Kings	Law (Law at Mt. Sinai to Calvary)
Youth (Prophets to Christ)		Gentiles	
Manhood	Christian (Christ to Millennium)	Spirit/Christian Gentile/Church	Grace (Calvary to Second Coming)
Old Age			
Renovation of All Things (Millennium)	Millennium (Not a Dispensation)	Millennium (Second Coming to End of Millennium)	Kingdom (Second Coming to End of Millennium)

■ Represents approximately equal dispensations on the horizontal spectra.

▨ Represents periods of Biblical history not considered to be dispensational in nature.

Poiret, Pierre. *The Divine Oeconomy; or, An Universal System of the Works and Purposes of God Toward's Men, Demonstrated.* 6 vols. London, 1713.

Watts, Isaac. *The Works of the Reverend and Learned Isaac Watts, D.D.* 6 vols. Compiled by Rev. George Burder. London: J. Barfield, 1810. Vol. 4, pp. 1 - 40.

Darby, J. N. *The Collected Works of J. N. Darby.* Edited by William Kelly. 34 vols. Reprint ed. Sunbury, Penn.: Believers Bookshelf, 1971. Vol. 1, p. 124f; vol. 2, pp. 92, 98, 374f; vol. 5, p. 384f.

Scofield, C. I. *Rightly Dividing the Word of Truth.* Fincastle, Va.: Scripture Truth Book Co., n.d. pp. 12 - 16.

APPENDIX B

Illustration of the Interrelationships Among the
Brethren, Darby, Brookes, Gaebelein and Scofield

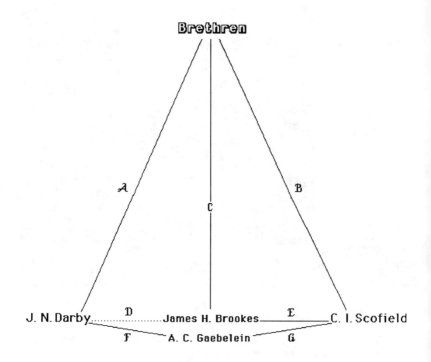

A. Darby and Brethren – Bass, pp. 64-99.
B. Scofield and Brethren – Gaebelein, "Story of Scofield Bible", part 4, pp. 277-79; Trumbull, pp. 108, 116-18.
C. Brookes and Brethren – Kraus, p. 47.
D. Darby and Brookes – Sandeen, pp. 74-5, Ironside, pp. 196, 204.
E. Scofield and Brookes – Trumbull, pp. 35-6; Gaebelein, "Story of Scofield Bible", part 2, pp. 128-9.
F. Gaebelein and Darby – Gaebelein, *Half a Century,* pp. 85, 243.
G. Gaebelein and Scofield – Gaebelein, "Story of Scofield Bible", part 4, p. 279.

APPENDIX C

General Versus Particular Dispensations

General Dispensations

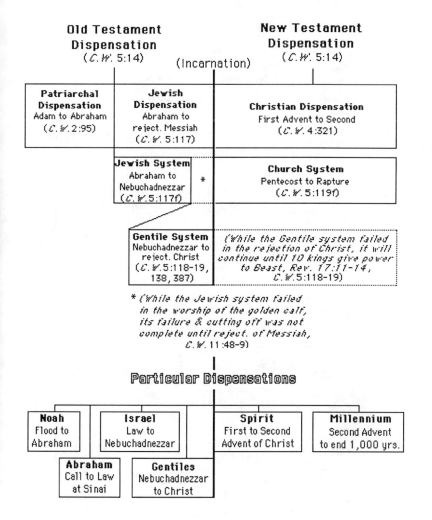

* (*While the Jewish system failed in the worship of the golden calf, its failure & cutting off was not complete until reject. of Messiah, C. W. 11:48-9*)

Particular Dispensations

Noah	Israel	Spirit	Millennium
Flood to Abraham	Law to Nebuchadnezzar	First to Second Advent of Christ	Second Advent to end 1,000 yrs.

Abraham	Gentiles
Call to Law at Sinai	Nebuchadnezzar to Christ

APPENDIX D

Dispensations and the Government of God

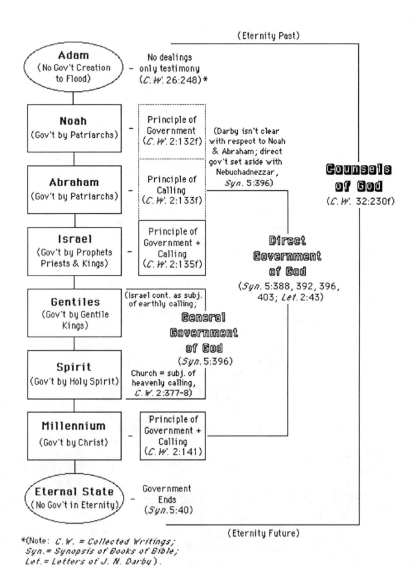

(Eternity Past)

Adam (No Gov't Creation to Flood) — No dealings only testimony (*C.W.* 26:248)*

Noah (Gov't by Patriarchs) — Principle of Government (*C.W.* 2:132f)

(Darby isn't clear with respect to Noah & Abraham; direct gov't set aside with Nebuchadnezzar, *Syn.* 5:396)

Abraham (Gov't by Patriarchs) — Principle of Calling (*C.W.* 2:133f)

Counsels of God (*C.W.* 32:230f)

Israel (Gov't by Prophets Priests & Kings) — Principle of Government + Calling (*C.W.* 2:135f)

Direct Government of God (*Syn.* 5:388, 392, 396, 403; *Let.* 2:43)

Gentiles (Gov't by Gentile Kings) (Israel cont. as subj. of earthly calling;

General Government of God (*Syn.* 5:396)

Spirit (Gov't by Holy Spirit) Church = subj. of heavenly calling, *C.W.* 2:377-8)

Millennium (Gov't by Christ) — Principle of Government + Calling (*C.W.* 2:141)

Eternal State (No Gov't in Eternity) — Government Ends (*Syn.* 5:40)

(Eternity Future)

*(Note: *C.W.* = *Collected Writings*; *Syn.* = *Synopsis of Books of Bible*; *Let.* = *Letters of J. N. Darby*).

APPENDIX E

Parallel Structure of Darby's Dispensations
As They Relate to the Government of God

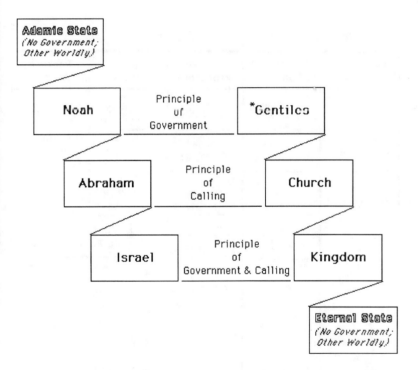

*It is the true Church which is in view here and not the profess-
ing church or Christendom which for Darby fulfills the function
of dispensation in the present age. But at the same time, the
Abrahamic dispensation, with Darby's lack of emphasis on responsibility and failure, is almost lifted above dispensational
status as is the true Church.

APPENDIX F

History of the Jewish Remnant

Old Testament		New Testament		
Post–Eden to Israel	Israel to Pentecost	Before Pentecost	On Pentecost	Rapture to Appearing
Abel (*C. W.* 32:257)*	Joshua/Caleb (*C. W.* 4:180–1)	Simeon (*Syn.* 3:279)	120 Added to Church (*C. W.* 14:25)	144,000 (*Syn.* 5:542–3)
Noah (*Syn.* 5:326)	Samuel (*C. W.* 1:114)	Anna (*Syn.* 3:282)		Faithful in Tribulation (*C. W.* 11:120)
Abraham (*C. W.* 32:257)	David & his Companions (*Let.* 1:123)	Mary & Joseph (*Syn.* 3:282; *C.W.* 11:143–4)		
	Jeremiah (*Let.* 1:123)	Elizabeth & Zacharias (*C.W.* 11:143–4)	Pentecost to Rapture	
	Ezekiel (*Let.* 1:123)	The Disciples (*Let.* 1:123)	(None, all added to Church; *Syn.* 4:9)	
	Daniel (*Let.* 1:123; *C. W.* 5:139)			
	Prophets (in general) (*Let.* 1:123)			
	Ezra & Nehemiah (*Let.* 1:123)			

*C.W. = Collected Writings;
Syn. = Synopsis of Books of the Bible;
Let. = Letters of J.N. Darby

APPENDIX G

Darby's Chronology of End-Time Events

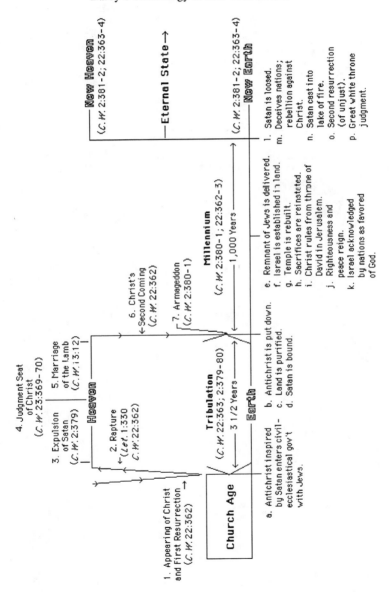

SELECTED BIBLIOGRAPHY

I. BIBLIOGRAPHIES

Ehlert, Arnold D. *A Bibliographic History of Dispensationalism.* Grand Rapids: Baker Book House, 1965.
_____. *Brethren Writers: A Checklist with an Introductory Essay and Additional Lists.* Grand Rapids: Baker Book House, 1969.

II. PRIMARY SOURCES

A. John Nelson Darby

Darby, John Nelson. *The collected Writings of J. N. Darby.* Edited by William Kelly. 34 vols. Reprint ed. Sunbury, Pa.: Believers Bookshelf, 1971.
_____. *The Holy Scriptures: A New Translation from the Original Languages,* 1967 ed. Oak Park, Ill.: Bible Truth Publishers, 1967.
_____. *Letters of J. N. Darby.* 3 vols. Reprint ed. Sunbury, Pa.: Believers Bookshelf, 1971.
_____. *Miscellaneous Writings of J. N. D.* Vols 4 and 5 (follow Miscellaneous No. 3 of the *Collected Writings*). Reprint ed. Oak Park, Ill.: Bible Truth Publishers, n.d.
_____. *Notes and Comments on Scripture.* 7 vols. Reprint ed. Sunbury, Pa.: Believers Bookshelf, 1971.
_____. *Notes and Jottings from Various Meetings with J. N. Darby.* Reprint ed. Sunbury, Pa.: Believers Bookshelf, 1971.
_____. *Synopsis of the Books of the Bible.* 5 vols. Reprint ed. Sunbury, Pa.: Believers Bookshelf, n.d.

B. C. I. Scofield

1. Books

Scofield, C. I. *Dr. C. I. Scofield's Question Box.* Compiled by Ella E. Pohle. Chicago: The Bible Institute Colportage Association, 1917.
_____. *In Many Pulpits with Dr. C. I. Scofield.* New York: Oxford University Press, 1922.
_____. and Gaebelein, Arno C. *The Jewish Question.* New York: Publication Office *Our Hope*, 1912.
_____. *Prophecy Made Plain.* Glasgow: Pickering and Inglis; London: Alfred Holness, n.d.
_____. *Rightly Dividing the Word of Truth.* Fincastle, Va.: Scripture Truth Book Co., n.d.
_____. *Scofield Bible Correspondence Course.* Chicago: Moody Bible Insti-

tute, 1934.

_____. *Scofield Bible Study Leaflets*. Philadelphia: Philadelphia School of the Bible, 1935.

_____. ed. *The Scofield Reference Bible*. New York: Oxford University Press, 1909.

_____. *Things New and Old*. New York: Publication Office *Our Hope*, 1920.

_____. *What Do the Prophets Say?* Philadelphia: Philadelphia School of the Bible, 1918.

_____. *Will the Church Pass Through the Great Tribulation?* Philadelphia: Philadelphia School of the Bible, 1917.

2. Periodicals

Scofield, C. I. "The Course and End of the Age." *Bibliotheca Sacra* 108 (January 1951):105-116.

_____. "The Last World Empire and Armageddon." *Bibliotheca Sacra* 108 (July 1951):355-62.

_____. "The Return of Christ in Relation to the Church." *Bibliotheca Sacra* 109 (January 1952):77-89.

_____. "The Return of Christ in Relation to the Jews and the Earth." *Bibliotheca Sacra* 108 (October 1951):477-87.

_____. "Tested by Grace." *Bibliotheca Sacra* 107 (October 1950):488-96.

_____. "The Times of the Gentiles." *Bibliotheca Sacra* 107 (July 1950):343-55.

III. SECONDARY SOURCES

A. History of Plymouth Brethren

1. Books

Beattie, David J. *Brethren, The Story of a Great Recovery*. Kilmarnock: John Ritchie, Ltd., 1937.

Broadbent, E. H. *The Pilgrim Church*. 2nd ed. London: Pickering and Ingles, 1942.

Carson, James C. L. *The Heresies of the Plymouth Brethren*. Coleraine: John McCombie, 1862.

Coad, F. Roy. *A History of the Brethren Movement*. Sydney, Australia: The Paternoster Press, 1968.

Croskery, Thomas. *Catechism of the Doctrines of the Plymouth Brethren*. London: James Nisbet Co., 1866.

_____. *Darbyism, or the Separationist Theory of a Pure Church*. London: James Nisbet Co., n.d.

_____. *Plymouth-Brethrenism: A Refutation of Its Principles and Doctrines*. London and Belfast: William Mullen and Son, 1879.

D. A. *Darbyism: An Attack Upon J. N. D.* London: Cookhead, Bayswater, 1881.

Dennet, Edward. *The Plymouth Brethren: Their Rise, Division, Practice, and Doctrine*. London: Elliot Stock, n.d.

G. *An Enquiry as to the Scriptural Position of the Plymouth Brethren*. London: G. Morrish, 1875.

Gilmore, William. *These Seventy Years*. Kilmarnock, 1954.

Grant, James. *The Plymouth Brethren, Their History and Heresies*. London: W. H. Guest, 1876.

Ironside, H. A. *A Historical Sketch of the Brethren Movement*. Grand Rapids: Zondervan Publishing Co., 1942; reprint ed., Neptune, N.J.: Loizeaux Brothers, 1985.

Latimer, W. T. *Lectures on the Doctrines of the Plymouth Brethren*. Belfast: James Cleeland, 1890.

Macintosh, Duncan. *The Special Teachings, Ecclesiastical and Doctrinal, of the Exclusive Brethren, or Plymouth Brethren, Compiled From Their Own Writings, With Strictures*. 4th ed. London: Houlston and Sons, 1872.

Mallott, Floyd E. *Studies in Brethren History*. Elgin, Ill.: Brethren Publishing House, n.d.

Mearns, Peter. *Christian Truth Viewed in Relation to Plymouthism*. 2nd ed. Edinburgh: William Oliphant and Co., 1875.

Neatby, W. Blair. *The History of the Plymouth Brethren*. London: Hodder and Stoughton, 1901.

Noel, Napoleon. *The History of the Brethren*. Denver: W. F. Knapp, 1936.

Pickering, Hy. *Chief Men among the Brethren*. London: Pickering and Inglis, 1918.

Reid, William. *Plymouth Brethrenism Unveiled and Refuted*. Edinburgh: William Oliphant and Co., 1880.

Rowdon, Harold H. *The Origins of the Brethren, 1825-1850*. London: Pickering and Inglis, 1967.

Stokes, G. T. *Plymouth Brethrenism: Its Ecclesiastical and Doctrinal Teachings: With a Sketch of Its History*. London: Hodder and Stoughton, 1874.

Teulon, J. S. *The History and Teachings of the Plymouth Brethren*. London: Society for Promoting of Christian Knowledge, 1883.

Turner, W. G. *John Nelson Darby*. London: C. A. Hammond, 1944 [new enl. ed., edited by E. N. Cross. London: Chapter Two, 1990].

Veitch, Thomas Stewart. *The Story of the Brethren Movement*. London: no publisher given, n.d.

Whately, E. J. *Plymouth Brethrenism*. London: Hatchards, 1879.

2. Unpublished Works

Goddard, John Howard. "The Contribution of John Nelson Darby to Soteriology, Ecclesiology, and Eschatology." Th.D. dissertation, Dallas Theological Seminary, 1948.

Gray, Clifton Doggett. "The Meaning of Membership as Perceived by Plymouth Brethren." Ph.D. dissertation, Boston University, 1963.

Hagan, Michael Robert. "The Concept of Christian Ministry Revealed in the Writing of John Nelson Darby, (1800-1882)." Ph.D. dissertation, University of Washington, 1967.

Shinn, Robert Worcester. "The Plymouth Brethren and Ecumenical Protestantism." Th.D. dissertation, Union Theological Seminary, 1968.

Sturgeon, Howard E. "The Life of John Nelson Darby." Th.M. thesis, Southern Baptist Theological Seminary, 1957.

Woodcock, Gordon B. "The Plymouth Brethren." B.D. dissertation, McMaster University, 1948.

B. Dispensational Works

1. Books

Anderson, Robert. *The Coming Prince.* Grand Rapids: Kregel Publications, 1969.

Blackstone, William E. *Jesus is Coming.* rev. ed. Chicago: Fleming H. Revell, 1908.

Brookes, James H. *Maranatha.* 10th ed. New York: Fleming H. Revell, 1889.

_____. *Till He Come.* Chicago: Gospel Publishing Co., 1891.

Chafer, Lewis Sperry. *Dispensationalism.* Dallas: Dallas Seminary Press, 1936.

_____. *The Kingdom in History and Prophecy.* Philadelphia: Sunday School Times, 1919.

_____. *Major Bible Themes.* Revised by John F. Walvoord. Grand Rapids: Zondervan Publishing House, 1974.

_____. *Systematic Theology.* 8 vols. Dallas: Dallas Seminary Press, 1947.

_____. *Must We Dismiss the Millennium?* Crescent City, Fla.: Biblical Testimony League, 1921.

English, E. Schuyler, chairman of the editorial committee. *Holy Bible: New Scofield Reference Edition.* New York: Oxford University Press, 1969.

_____. *Re-Thinking the Rapture.* rev. ed. Neptune, N.J.: Loizeaux Brothers, 1954.

_____. *Studies in the Gospel According to Matthew.* New York: Publication Office *Our Hope*, 1943.

Feinberg, Charles L. *Millennialism: The Two Major Views.* 3rd enlarged ed. Chicago: Moody Press, 1980.

Gaebelein, Arno C. *The Harmony of the Prophetic Word.* New York: Publication Office *Our Hope*, 1907.

_____. *Hath God Cast Away His People?* New York: Gospel Publishing House, 1905.

_____. *The Hope of the Ages.* New York: Publication Office *Our Hope*, 1938.

_____. *The Prophet Daniel.* New York: Publication Office *Our Hope*, 1911.

_____. *The Prophet Ezekiel.* New York: Publication Office *Our Hope*, 1918.

_____. *The Return of the Lord.* New York: Publication Office *Our Hope*, 1925.

_____. *The Revelation.* New York: Publication Office *Our Hope*, 1915.

_____. *Studies in Prophecy.* New York: Publication Office *Our Hope*, 1918.

Gray, James M. *Prophecy and the Lord's Return.* New York: Fleming H. Revell, 1917.

_____. *A Textbook of Prophecy.* New York: Fleming H. Revell, 1918.

Haldeman, I. M. *The Coming of Christ: Both Premillennial and Imminent.* New York: Charles C. Cook, 1906.

_____. *The History of the Doctrine of Our Lord's Return.* New York: First Baptist Church, n.d.

_____. *The Kingdom of God.* A review of Philip Mauro's book *The Gospel of the Kingdom.* New York: Francis Emory Fitch, Inc., 1931.

_____. *The Secret and Imminent Coming of Christ.* New York: Charles C. Cook, 1917.

Hoyt, Herman A. *The End Times.* Chicago: Moody Press, 1969.

Ironside, H. A. *The Great Parenthesis.* Grand Rapids: Zondervan Publishing House, 1943.

_____. *The Lamp of Prophecy.* Grand Rapids: Zondervan Publishing House, 1940.
_____. *Looking Backward over a Third of a Century of Prophetic Fulfillment.* New York: Loizeaux Brothers, 1930.
_____. *Lectures on the Book of Revelation.* New York: Loizeaux Brothers, 1919.
_____. *The Mysteries of God.* New York: Loizeaux Brothers, 1946.
_____. *Not Wrath, but Rapture.* Neptune, N.J.: Loizeaux Brothers, n.d.
_____. *Wrongly Dividing the Word of Truth.* 3rd ed. New York: Loizeaux Brothers, 1938.
Kelly, William. *Daniel's Seventy Weeks.* Los Angeles: Berean Bookshelf, n.d.
_____. *The Epistles of Paul the Apostle to the Thessalonians.* 3rd ed. Oak Park, Ill.: Bible Truth Publishers, 1974.
_____. *Lectures on the Book of Revelation.* London: G. Morrish, n.d.
_____. *Lectures on the Second Coming and Kingdom of the Lord and Saviour Jesus Christ.* Sunbury, Pa.: Believers Bookshelf, 1970.
_____. *Notes on Ezekiel.* Addison, Ill.: Bible Truth Publishers, 1977.
_____. *The Revelation Expounded by William Kelly.* Winschoten, Netherlands: H. L. Heijkoop, 1970.
_____. *Three Prophetic Gems.* Sunbury, Pa.: Believers Bookshelf, 1970.
Lindsey, Hal. *The Late Great Planet Earth.* Grand Rapids: Zondervan Publishing House, 1970.
_____. *The Terminal Generation.* Old Tappan, N.J.: Fleming H. Revell, 1976.
_____. *There's a New World Coming.* Santa Ana, Calif.: Vision House, 1973.
Mackintosh, C. H. *The Mackintosh Treasury.* Neptune, N.J.: Loizeaux Brothers, 1976.
McClain, Alva J. *Daniel's Prophecy of the Seventy Weeks.* Grand Rapids: Zondervan Publishing Co., 1940.
_____. *The Greatness of the Kingdom.* Winona Lake, Ind.: BMH Books, 1959.
Pache, Rene. *The Return of Jesus Christ.* Translated by William S. LaSor. Chicago: Moody Press, 1955.
Pentecost, J. Dwight. *Prophecy for Today.* Grand Rapids: Zondervan Publishing House, 1961.
_____. *Things to Come.* Grand Rapids: Zondervan Publishing House; copyright 1958 by Dunham Publishing House.
Peters, George N. H. *The Theocratic Kingdom of Our Lord Jesus, the Christ.* 3 vols. Grand Rapids: Kregel Publications, 1957.
Poiret, Pierre. *The Divine Oeconomy; or, An Universal System of the Works and Purposes of God Toward's Men, Demonstrated.* 6 vols. London: 1713.
Price, Walter K. *The Coming Antichrist.* Chicago: Moody Press, 1974.
Ryrie, Charles Caldwell. *The Basis of the Premillennial Faith.* Neptune, N.J.: Loizeaux Brothers, 1953.
_____. *The Best Is Yet to Come.* Chicago: Moody Press, 1981.
_____. *Biblical Theology of the New Testament.* Chicago: Moody Press, 1959.
_____. *Dispensationalism Today.* Chicago: Moody Press, 1965.
_____. *The Final Countdown.* Wheaton, Ill.: Victor Books, 1982.
_____. *The Ryrie Study Bible: New American Standard Translation.* Chicago: Moody Press, 1978.
_____. *What You Should Know About the Rapture.* Chicago: Moody Press, 1981.

Sauer, Eric. *The Dawn of World Redemption*. Grand Rapids: Wm. B. Eerdmans Publishing Co., 1955.

_____. *From Eternity to Eternity*. Grand Rapids: Wm. B. Eerdmans Publishing Co., 1955.

_____. *The Triumph of the Crucified*. Grand Rapids: Wm. B. Eerdmans Publishing Co., 1952.

Showers, Renald E. *There Really Is a Difference: A Comparison of Covenant and Dispensational Theology*. Bellmawr, N.J.: The Friends of Israel Gospel Ministry, 1990.

Stanton, Gerald B. *Kept from the Hour*. Grand Rapids: Zondervan Publishing House, 1956.

Thiessen, Henry C. *Introductory Lectures in Systematic Theology*. Grand Rapids: Wm. B. Eerdmans Publishing Co., 1949.

_____. *Will the Church Pass Through the Tribulation?* New York: Loizeaux Brothers, 1941.

Walvoord, John F., and Walvoord, John Edward. *Armageddon: Oil and the Middle East Crisis*. Grand Rapids: Zondervan Publishing House, 1976.

Walvoord, John F. *The Blessed Hope and the Tribulation*. Grand Rapids: Zondervan Publishing Co., 1976.

_____. *The Church in Prophecy*. Grand Rapids: Zondervan Publishing Co., 1964.

_____. *Daniel: The Key to Prophetic Revelation*. Chicago: Moody Press, 1971.

_____. *Israel in Prophecy*. Grand Rapids: Zondervan Publishing House, 1962.

_____. *Matthew: Thy Kingdom Come*. Chicago: Moody Press, 1974.

_____. *The Millennial Kingdom*. Grand Rapids: Zondervan Publishing House, 1959.

_____. *The Nations in Prophecy*. Grand Rapids: Zondervan Publishing House, 1967.

_____. *The Rapture Question*. rev. and enl. ed. Grand Rapids: Zondervan Publishing House, 1979.

_____. *The Return of the Lord*. Grand Rapids: Zondervan Publishing House, 1955.

_____. *Revelation of Jesus Christ*. Chicago: Moody Press, 1966.

_____. *The Thessalonian Epistles*. Findlay, Ohio: Dunham, 1955.

Wood, A. Skevington. *Signs of the Times*. Grand Rapids: Baker Book House, 1971.

Wood, Leon J. *The Bible and Future Events: An Introductory Survey of Last-Day Events*. Grand Rapids: Zondervan Publishing House, 1973.

_____. *A Commentary on Daniel*. Grand Rapids: Zondervan Publishing House, 1973.

_____. *Is the Rapture Next?* Grand Rapids: Zondervan Publishing House, 1956.

2. Periodicals

Aldrich, Roy L. "An Apologetic For Dispensationalism." *Bibliotheca Sacra* 112 (January 1955):46-54.

Blaising, Craig A. "Development of Dispensationalism by Contemporary Dispensationalists: Part 2 of Developing Dispensationalism." *Bibliotheca*

Sacra 145 (July-September 1988):254-80.

Brookes, James H. "Kept Out of the hour." *Our Hope* 6 (November 1899):153-57.

Chafer, Lewis Sperry. "An Introduction to the Study of Prophecy." *Bibliotheca Sacra* 100 (January 1943):98-133.

_____. "Dispensational Distinctions Challenged." *Bibliotheca Sacra* 100 (July 1943):337-45.

_____. "Dr. C. I. Scofield." *Bibliotheca Sacra* 100 (January 1943):4-6.

_____. "Dispensational Distinctions Denounced." *Bibliotheca Sacra* 101 (July 1944):157-60.

_____. "Dispensationalism." *Bibliotheca Sacra* 93 (October 1936):390-449.

_____. "The Scofield Bible." *Bibliotheca Sacra* 109 (April 1952):97-9.

Crutchfield, Larry V. "Ages and Dispensations in the Ante-Nicene Fathers: Part 2 of Rudiments of Dispensationalism in the Ante-Nicene Period." *Bibliotheca Sacra* 144 (October-December 1987):377-401.

_____. "C. I. Scofield." In *Twentieth-Century Shapers of American Popular Religion*, pp. 371-381. Edited by Charles H. Lippy. New York: Greenwood Press, 1989.

_____. "Israel and the Church in the Ante-Nicene Fathers: Part 1 of Rudiments of Dispensationalism in the Ante-Nicene Period." *Bibliotheca Sacra* 144 (July-September 1987):254-276.

Ehlert, Arnold D. "A Bibliography of Dispensationalism." *Bibliotheca Sacra* 102 (January 1944):95-101; 102 (April 1944):199-209; 102 (July 1944):319-28; 102 (October 1944):447-60; 103 (January 1945):84-92; 103 (April 1945):207-19; 103 (July 1945):322-34; 103 (October 1945):455-67; 104 (January 1946):57-67.

English, E. Schuyler. "E. Schuyler English Looks at Dispensationalism." *Christian Life* 17 (September 1956):24-27.

_____. "The New Scofield Reference Bible." *Bibliotheca Sacra* 124 (April 1967):125-32.

_____. "The Judgment of the Nations." *Our Hope* 51 (February 1945):561-65.

_____. "The Judgment Seat of Christ." *Our Hope* 51 (December 1944):416-22.

_____. "The Two Witnesses." *Our Hope* 47 (April 1941):665-75.

Govett, R. "One Taken and One Left." *The Dawn* 12 (February 1936):515-18.

Harrison, William K. "The Time of the Rapture as Indicated in Certain Scriptures." *Bibliotheca Sacra* 114 (October 1957):316-25; 115 (January 1958):20-26; 115 (April 1958):109-19; 115 (July 1958):201-11.

Ironside, Harry A. "Setting the Stage for the Last Act of the Great World Drama." *Our Hope* 55 (April 1949):589-97; 55 (May 1949):661-66; 55 (June 1949):722-29.

Kellogg, S. H. "Premillennialism: Its Relation to Doctrine and Practice." *Bibliotheca Sacra* 99 (April 1942):235-44; 99 (July 1942):364-72; 99 (October 1942):486-99; 100 (April 1943):301-8.

Kelly, William. "The Future Tribulation." *The Bible Treasury* 4 (December 1902):206-8; 4 (January 1903):222-23.

Lewis, Gordon. "Biblical Evidence for Pretribulationism." *Bibliotheca Sacra* 125 (July 1968):216-26.

_____. "Theological Antecedents of Pretribulationism." *Bibliotheca Sacra* 125 (April 1968):129-38.

Lightner, Robert P. "Theonomy and Dispensationalism: Part 1 of Theological

Perspectives on Theonomy." *Bibliotheca Sacra* 143 (January-March 1986):26-36.

Mason, Clarence F. "A Review of 'Dispensationalism' by John Wick Bowman." *Bibliotheca Sacra* 114 (January 1957):10-22.

MacRae, Allan A. "The Millennial Kingdom of Christ." *Our Hope* 53 (February 1947):463-80.

McClain, Alva J. "The Greatness of the Kingdom." *Bibliotheca Sacra* 112 (January 1955):11-27; 112 (April 1955):107-24; 112 (July 1955):209-24; 112 (October 1955):304-10.

Ryrie, Charles C. "Dispensationalism Today." *Moody Monthly* 66 (November 1965):58-9.

Saucy, Robert L. "The Critical Issue between Dispensational and Non-Dispensational Systems." *Criswell Theological Review* 1 (Fall 1986):149-65.

Thiessen, Henry C. "The Place of Israel in the Scheme of Redemption as Set Forth in Romans 9-11." *Bibliotheca Sacra* 98 (January 1941):78-91; 98 (April 1941):203-17.

_____. "Will the Church Pass Through the Tribulation?" *Bibliotheca Sacra* 92 (January 1935):39-54; 92 (April 1935):187-205; 92 (July 1935):292-314.

Unger, Merrill F. "Ezekiel's Vision of Israel's Restoration." *Bibliotheca Sacra* 106 (July 1949):312-24; 106 (October 1949):432-45; 107 (January 1950): 51-70.

_____. "The Temple Vision of Ezekiel." *Bibliotheca Sacra* 105 (October 1948):418-42; 106 (January 1949):48-64; 106 (April 1949):169-77.

Walden, J. W. "The Kingdom of God--Its Millennial Dispensations." *Bibliotheca Sacra* 102 (October 1945):433-41; 103 (January 1946):39-49.

Walvoord, John F. "Amillennialism." *Bibliotheca Sacra* 106 (July 1949): 291-302; 106 (October 1949):420-32; 107 (January 1950):42-50; 107 (April 1950):154-67; 107 (July 1950):281-90; 107 (October 1950):420-29; 108 (January 1951):7-14.

_____. "Dispensational Premillennialism." *Christianity Today* 15 (September 1958):11-13.

_____. "The Doctrine of Grace in the Interpretation of Prophecy." *Bibliotheca Sacra* 140 (April 1983):99-107.

_____. "The Doctrine of the Millennium." *Bibliotheca Sacra* 115 (April 1958): 97-119.

_____. "Does the Church Fulfill Israel's Program?" *Bibliotheca Sacra* 137 (January 1980):17-31; 137 (April 1980):118-24; 137 (July 1980):212-222.

_____. "The Fulfillment of the Abrahamic Covenant." *Bibliotheca Sacra* 102 (January 1945):27-36.

_____. "The Fulfillment of the Davidic Covenant." *Bibliotheca Sacra* 102 (April 1945):153-66.

_____. "Interpreting Prophecy Today, Part 1: Basic Considerations in Interpreting Prophecy." *Bibliotheca Sacra* 139 (January 1982):3-11.

_____. "Interpreting Prophecy Today, Part 2: The Kingdom of God in the Old Testament." *Bibliotheca Sacra* 139 (April 1982):111-28.

_____. "Interpreting Prophecy Today, Part 3: The New Testament Doctrine of the Kingdom." *Bibliotheca Sacra* 139 (July 1982):205-15.

_____. "Interpreting Prophecy Today, Part 4: The Kingdom of God in the New Testament." *Bibliotheca Sacra* 139 (October 1982):302-11.

_____. "Is Moral Progress Possible." *Bibliotheca Sacra* 101 (April 1944):149-

63.
_____. "Is Satan Bound?" *Bibliotheca Sacra* 100 (October 1943):497-512.
_____. "Is the Church the Israel of God?" *Bibliotheca Sacra* 101 (October 1944):403-16.
_____. "Is the Seventieth Week of Daniel Future?" *Bibliotheca Sacra* 101 (January 1944):30-49.
_____. "Israel's Blindness." *Bibliotheca Sacra* 102 (July 1945):282-91.
_____. "Israel's Restoration." *Bibliotheca Sacra* 102 (October 1945): 405-16.
_____. "The Kingdom Promised to David." *Bibliotheca Sacra* 110 (April 1953):97-110.
_____. "The Millennial Issue in Modern Theology." *Bibliotheca Sacra* 106 (January 1949):34-47.
_____. "The New Covenant with Israel." *Bibliotheca Sacra* 103 (January 1946):16-27.
_____. "The New Covenant with Israel." *Bibliotheca Sacra* 110 (July 1953): 193-205.
_____. "New Testament Words for the Lord's Coming." *Bibliotheca Sacra* 101 (July 1944):283-89.
_____. "Postmillennialism." *Bibliotheca Sacra* 106 (April 1949):149-68.
_____. "Premillennialism." *Bibliotheca Sacra* 108 (October 1951):414-22.
_____. "Premillennialism and the Abrahamic Covenant." *Bibliotheca Sacra* 109 (January 1952):37-46; 109 (April 1952):136-60; 109 (July 1952):217-25; 109 (October 1952):293-303.
_____. "Premillennialism and the Church." *Bibliotheca Sacra* 110 (October 1953):289-98; 111 (January 1954):1-10; 111 (April 1954):97-104.
_____. "Premillennialism and the Tribulation." *Bibliotheca Sacra* 111 (July 1954):193-202; 111 (October 1954): 289-301; 112 (January 1955):1-10; 112 (April 1955):97-106; 112 (July 1955):193-208; 112 (October 1955): 289-303.
_____. "Premillennialism and the Tribulation." *Bibliotheca Sacra* 113 (January 1956):1-15.
_____. "A Review of *The Blessed Hope* by George E. Ladd." *Bibliotheca Sacra* 112 (April 1955):97-106.
_____. "A Review of *Crucial Questions About the Kingdom of God*." *Bibliotheca Sacra* 110 (January 1953):1-10.

C. Non-Dispensational Works

1. Books

Allis, Oswald T. *Prophecy and the Church*. Phillipsburg, N.J.: Presbyterian and Reformed Publishing Co., 1947.
Bass, Clarence B. *Backgrounds to Dispensationalism*. Grand Rapids: Wm. B. Eerdmans Publishing Co., 1960.
Berkhof, Louis. *The Kingdom of God*. Grand Rapids: Wm. B. Eerdmans Publishing Co., 1951.
_____. *The Second Coming of Christ*. Grand Rapids: Wm. B. Eerdmans Publishing Co., 1953.
_____. *Systematic Theology*. Grand Rapids: Wm. B. Eerdmans Publishing Co., 1941.

Berkouwer, G. C. *The Return of Christ.* Grand Rapids: Wm. B. Eerdmans Publishing Co., 1972.

Boettner, Loraine. *The Millennium.* Philadelphia: Presbyterian and Reformed Publishing Co., 1957.

Brown, David. *Christ's Second Coming: Will It Be Pre-Millennial?* 6th ed. Edinburgh: T. and T. Clark, 1867.

Cohn, Norman. *The Pursuit of the Millennium.* New York: Oxford University Press, 1970.

Cox, William E. *Amillennialism Today.* Philadelphia: Presbyterian and Reformed Publishing Co., 1971.

_____. *An Examination of Dispensationalism.* Philadelphia: Presbyterian and Reformed Publishing Co., 1971.

_____. *Biblical Studies in Final Things.* Philadelphia: Presbyterian and Reformed Publishing Co., 1967.

_____. *Why I Left Scofieldism.* Phillipsburg, N.J.: Presbyterian and Reformed Publishing Co., 1978.

Edersheim, Alfred. *Prophecy and History.* Grand Rapids: Baker Publishing Co., 1955.

Elliott, E. B. *Horae Apocalypticae; or a Commentary on the Apocalypse, Critical and Historical.* 4 vols. London: Seely, Burnside, and Seely, 1847.

Erickson, Millard J. *Contemporary Options in Eschatology.* Grand Rapids: Baker Book House, 1977.

Fairbairn, Patrick. *Prophecy Viewed in Respect to Its Distinctive Nature, Its Special Function, and Proper Interpretation.* Edinburgh: T. and T. Clark, 1856.

Froom, LeRoy Edwin. *The Prophetic Faith of Our Fathers.* 4 vols. Washington, D.C.: Review and Herald Publishing Association, 1946-1954.

Frost, Henry W. *The Second Coming of Christ.* Grand Rapids: Wm. B. Eerdmans Publishing Co., 1934.

Fuller, Daniel P. *Gospel and Law: Contrast or Continuum?* Wm. B. Eerdmans Publishing Co., 1980.

Guinness, H. Grattan. *The Approaching End of the Age.* New York: A. C. Armstrong, 1884.

Hamilton, Floyd E. *The Basis of Millennial Faith.* Grand Rapids: Wm. B. Eerdmans Publishing Co., 1942.

Harnack, Adolf von. "Millennium." In *Encyclopaedia Britannica*, 9th ed., 16:314-18. New York: Charles Scribner's Sons, 1883.

Hendriksen, William. *And So All Israel Shall Be Saved.* Grand Rapids: Baker Book Store, 1945.

_____. *More Than Conquerors.* Grand Rapids: Baker Book House, 1939.

Hodge, Charles. *Systematic Theology.* 3 vols. New York: Charles Scribner's Sons, 1887.

Kellogg, S. H. *Are Premillennialists Right?* New York: Fleming H. Revell, 1923.

_____. *The Jews, or Prediction and Fulfillment.* New York: James Nisbet Co., 1883.

Kik, J. Marcellus. *An Eschatology of Victory.* Nutley, N.J.: Presbyterian and Reformed Publishing Co., 1974.

Kraus, C. Norman. *Dispensationalism in America.* Richmond, Va.: John Knox Press, 1958.

Kromminga, Diedrich H. *The Millennium in the Church: Studies in the History of Christian Chiliasm.* Grand Rapids: Wm. B. Eerdmans Publishing Co., 1945.

Kummel, W. G. *Promise and Fulfillment: The Eschatological Message of Jesus.* Naperville, Ill.: Alec R. Allenson, Inc., 1967.

Kuyper, Abraham. *Chiliasm, or the Doctrine of Premillennialism.* Grand Rapids: Zondervan Publishing House, 1934.

Ladd, George E. *The Blessed Hope.* Grand Rapids: Wm. B. Eerdmans Publishing Co., 1956.

_____. *A Commentary on the Book of the Revelation of John.* Grand Rapids: Wm. B. Eerdmans Publishing Co., 1972.

_____. *Crucial Questions About the Kingdom of God.* Grand Rapids: Wm. B. Eerdmans Publishing Co., 1952.

_____. *The Gospel of the Kingdom.* Grand Rapids: Wm. B. Eerdmans Publishing Co., 1959

_____. *Jesus and the Kingdom.* New York: Harper and Row, 1954.

_____. *The Last Things.* Grand Rapids: Wm. B. Eerdmans Publishing Co., 1978.

_____. *The Presence of the Future.* Grand Rapids: Wm. B. Eerdmans Publishing Co., 1974

Lenski, R. C. H. *The Interpretation of St. Paul's Exposition of Revelation.* Columbus, Ohio: Lutheran Book Concern, 1936.

MacPherson, Dave. *The Great Rapture Hoax.* Fletcher, N.C.: New Puritan Library, 1983.

_____. *The Incredible Cover-Up.* Medford, Ore.: Omega Publications, n.d.

_____. *The Unbelievable Pre-Trib Origin.* Kansas City, Mo.: Heart of American Bible Society, 1973.

Marsden, George M. *Fundamentalism and American Culture-The Shaping of Twentieth-Century Evangelicalism: 1870-1925.* London: Oxford University Press, 1980.

Mauro, Philip. *Looking for the Savior.* New York: Fleming H. Revell, 1913.

_____. *The Seventy Weeks and the Great Tribulation.* Swengel, Pa.: Bible Truth Depot, 1944.

Miller, Edward. *The History and Doctrines of Irvingism.* 2 vols. London: C. Kegan Paul and Co., 1878.

Morris, Leon. *The Revelation of St. John.* Grand Rapids: Wm. B. Eerdmans Publishing Co., 1969.

Murry, George L. *Millennial Studies.* Grand Rapids: Baker Book House, 1948.

Payne, J. Barton. *Encyclopedia of Biblical Prophecy.* New York: Harper and Row, 1973.

_____. *The Imminent Appearing of Jesus Christ.* Grand Rapids: Wm. B. Eerdmans Publishing Co., 1962.

Pieters, Albertus. *A Candid Examination of the Scofield Bible.* Swengel, Pa.: Bible Truth Depot, 1938.

_____. *Studies in the Revelation of St. John.* Grand Rapids: Zondervan Publishing House, 1937.

_____. *The Seed of Abraham.* Grand Rapids: Wm. B. Eerdmans Publishing Co., 1950.

Reese, Alexander. *The Approaching Advent of Christ.* London: Marshall, Morgan, and Scott Co., 1937; reprint ed., Grand Rapids: Grand Rapids International Publications, 1975.

Robinson, J. A. T. *Jesus and His Coming: The Emergence of a Doctrine.* New York: Abingdon Press, 1957.

Sandeen, Ernest R. *The Origins of Fundamentalism.* Historical Series, no. 10. Philadelphia: Fortress Press, 1968.

_____. *The Roots of Fundamentalism.* Chicago: University of Chicago Press, 1970; reprint ed., Grand Rapids: Baker Book House, 1978.

Summers, Ray. *Worthy Is the Lamb.* Nashville: Broadman Press, 1951.

Travis, Stephen H. *The Jesus Hope.* Downers Grove, Ill.: InterVarsity Press, 1976.

_____. *Christian Hope and the Future.* Downers Grove, Ill.: InterVarsity Press, 1980.

Tregelles, S. P. *The Hope of Christ's Second Coming: How Is It Taught in Scripture? And Why?* Worthing: 1925.

Vos, Geerhardus. *The Kingdom of God and the Church.* New York: American Tract Society, 1903.

_____. *The Pauline Eschatology.* Grand Rapids: Wm. B. Eerdmans Publishing Co., 1952.

Warfield, B. B. *Biblical Doctrines.* New York: Oxford University Press, 1929.

West, Nathaniel. *Daniel's Great Prophecy.* New York: The Hope of Israel Movement, 1898.

_____. *Studies in Eschatology: The Thousand Years in Both Testaments.* New York: Fleming H. Revell, 1889.

Wyngaarden, Martin J. *The Future of the Kingdom in Prophecy and Fulfillment.* Grand Rapids: Baker Book House, 1955.

2. Periodicals

Allis, Oswald T. "Modern Dispensationalism and the Doctrine of the Unity of the Scriptures." *Evangelical Quarterly* 8 (January 1936):22-35.

Baxter, J. S. "Our Lord's Return." *Evangelical Christian* 52 (June 1956): 273-74

Berkouwer, G. C. "The Church in the Last Days." *Christianity Today* 2 (April 1958):3-5.

Bietenhard, Hans. "The Millennial Hope in the Early Church." *Scottish Journal of Theology* 6 (March 1953):12-30.

Boettner, Loraine. "Christian Hope and a Millennium." *Christianity Today* 29 (September 1958):13-14.

Bowman, John Wick. "The Bible and Modern Religions: II, Dispensationalism." *Interpretation* 10 (April 1956):170-87.

Briggs, C. A. "The Origin and History of Premillennialism." *Lutheran Quarterly* 9 (April 1879):207-45.

Brown, Ira V. "Watchers for the Second Coming: The Millenarian Tradition in America." *Mississippi Valley Historical Review* 39 (December 1952):441-58.

Ladd, George Eldon. "Eschatology and the Unity of New Testament Theology." *Expository Times* 68 (June 1957):268-73.

_____. "Israel and the Church." *Evangelical Quarterly* 36 (October 1964): 206-13.

_____. "The Kingdom of God in I Enoch." *Bibliotheca Sacra* 110 (January 1953):32-49.

SELECTED BIBLIOGRAPHY 231

_____. "The Kingdom of God in the Jewish Apocryphal Literature." *Bibliotheca Sacra* 109 (January 1952):55-62.

_____. "Kingdom of God--Reign or Realm?" *Journal of Biblical Literature* 81 (1962):230-38.

_____. "The Revelation of Christ's Glory." *Christianity Today* 1 (September 1958):13-14.

Pieters, Albertus. "Darbyism Vs. the Historic Christian Faith." *The Calvin Forum* 2 (May 1936):225-28.

GENERAL INDEX

About the Author

Larry V. Crutchfield was born and raised in Wichita, Kansas. In 1974 he earned his B.A. degree in Communications with honors at Biola University. He was again graduated with honors by Denver Seminary in 1977, receiving an M.A. degree in New Testament Studies. At Drew University he was awarded both the M.Phil. (1983) and Ph.D. (1985) degrees in Theological and Religious Studies.

Dr. Crutchfield has written articles on a wide variety of Biblical, theological, and social topics for some of America's leading evangelical magazines and journals. His scholarly work has appeared in *Bibliotheca Sacra* and the *Journal of the Evangelical Theological Society*, and he was a contributor to *Twentieth-Century Shapers of American Popular Religion* (Greenwood Press) named to *Choice* magazine's list of "Outstanding Academic Books" for 1989. In the area of patristic studies, Dr. Crutchfield's significant work, *The Early Church Fathers and Abortion*, was published by the American Life League. Dr. Crutchfield is currently senior adjunct professor of religion at Burlington County College, Pemberton, New Jersey.